Losing Ground

LOSING
GROUND

American Social Policy,
1950–1980

CHARLES MURRAY

BASIC
BOOKS

A Member of the Perseus Books Group

Designed by Vincent Torre

Library of Congress Cataloging-in-Publication Data
Murray, Charles A.
    Losing ground : American social policy, 1950–1980.

    Bibliography: pp. 301–16
    Includes index.
        1. United States—Social policy—Evaluation.
    2. Afro-Americans—Social conditions—Evaluation.
    I. Title.
    HN57.M84 1984
    305.8′96073—dc19   83–46092
        ISBN 0–465–04231–7 (cloth)
        ISBN 0–465–04232–5 (paper)
        ISBN 0–465–04233–3 (second edition paper)

For Paul Schwarz

CONTENTS

PART I

A Generous Revolution

PART II

Being Poor, Being Black: 1950–1980

PART III
Interpreting the Data

PART IV
Rethinking Social Policy

A NOTE ON PRESENTATION

THIS BOOK tries to do two things that are not quite mutually exclusive, but almost. It draws upon a varied and sometimes technical body of social science data; and it addresses a general audience. How does one be fair to the data (which often entail complications and ambiguities) and still present the material in a way that an intelligent but not obsessive reader can be asked to follow? This tension has shaped the presentation in important ways.

Part of the solution has been to write what amounts to a subtext in the notes for the chapters in parts II and III. The reader who so wishes may read the book from beginning to end without once referring to the notes and (I trust) come away with an accurate understanding of the argument and the evidence. But every so often the reader is also likely to stop short and want to take a closer look. The notes, some of which amount to small essays, have been written for such occasions.

Another part of the solution has been to rely heavily on basic trendline data—graphs of what happened, using widely understood and accepted measures, from 1950 to 1980. Often such data need to be supplemented with more specialized analyses; occasionally, the trendline by itself will be misleading. But the most straightforward data are generally also the best ones for beginning to understand what happened.

Finally, I have added an appendix that includes much of the raw data. It is intended for readers who want to examine the trends from other perspectives or who want to apply these fundamental indicators to other questions.

PREFACE

LOSING GROUND grew out of sixteen years of watching people who run social programs, and my first debt is to them. Whether they have been counseling inner-city students in Atlanta, trying to keep Chicago delinquents out of jail, or teaching prenatal care to Thai villagers, they have shared an uncommon energy and dedication. Over the years, however, I was struck by two things. First, the people who were doing the helping did not succeed nearly as often as they deserved to. Why, when their help was so obviously needed and competently provided, was it so often futile? In the instances when the help succeeded, what were the conditions that permitted success? Second, the relationship between the ways people were to be helped and the quality of their lives became increasingly confused. Clearly, certain minimums of physical well-being were critical. But once those had been met, it was just as clear that, among the many things that produce satisfaction, dignity, and happiness, few were purely economic. How did the goods that social programs dispense fit in with the noneconomic assets? Two and a half years ago, I set out to pursue these lines of inquiry more systematically.

Some months later, Joan Kennedy Taylor of the Manhattan Institute saw the potential for a book in a monograph I had written. She shepherded the work (and me) through to the end. William Hammett, president of the Manhattan Institute, took a chance and decided to use the foundation's resources to underwrite the effort. Without them, the book would not have been written.

I relied principally on the collections at the Library of Congress and the

Bureau of the Census. The people who helped at both places are too numerous to list individually. At the Bureau of the Census, special thanks go to Bruce Chapman, then director, who took a heartening interest throughout the work. My thanks also go to Gordon Green of the Population Division and Carol Fendler of the Poverty Statistics Section, whose expertise made my job much easier. At the Federal Bureau of Investigation, Ken Candell oversaw the special computer runs I needed. At the Office of Family Assistance, Ken Lee, Laurence Love, Michael deMaar, Howard Rolston, and Jo Anne Ross patiently led me through the complicated history of the Aid to Families with Dependent Children (AFDC) program. Many others whose names I do not know in the libraries of the Bureau of Labor Statistics, the National Institute of Education, the National Institute of Justice, and the National Center for Health Statistics took time to answer my questions and look up elusive documents. The custodians of the federal data bases are extraordinarily ready to go out of their way to help the anonymous researcher, and I am grateful to them all.

Donald A. Cook, who was involved in the earliest planning for the War on Poverty, provided an extremely helpful commentary on my account of that period. Robert Krug and Norman Gold, longtime colleagues and veterans of the Office of Economic Opportunity, brought their experience to bear on the discussions of the job training and educational innovations of the reform period and thereafter. Others who read parts or all of the manuscript and provided invaluable criticisms were Paul Schwarz, mentor and friend for many years at the American Institutes for Research; Irving Kristol, whose encouragement came at just the right moment; and Michael Horowitz, of the Office of Management and Budget, who sees a common purpose in his civil rights work in Mississippi in the 1960s and in his efforts to cut social programs in the 1980s.

In an earlier phase of the work that led to the book, Burton Pines of the Heritage Foundation first gave me the chance to concentrate my thinking on why it is that we could have spent so much money and have bought so little. Sheldon Danziger at the Institute for Research on Poverty was always ready to talk over my questions and provide me with materials from the Institute's ongoing work. At Basic Books, Martin Kessler understood exactly what I was trying to accomplish and reminded me of it when necessary, and Nina Gunzenhauser was a meticulous, occasionally inspiring, copy editor. Together, they have improved the book immeasurably.

Losing Ground contains some contentious interpretations of recent history. Few of the people I have named share all of them; some of them share virtually none. It should be clear that neither the interpretations nor any factual errors that may remain are their fault. This is especially true of my most thoughtful critic, and dearest one, Catherine Cox. We knew from the beginning that she was unlikely to agree with every conclusion. But it has been essential that she approve of their spirit.

CHARLES MURRAY
Washington, D.C.
15 February 1984

INTRODUCTION TO THE TENTH-ANNIVERSARY EDITION

TO THE PERSON who wrote it, a book is a time machine. A paragraph in *Losing Ground* about labor force participation might recall to me a particular afternoon in the reading room at the Library of Congress, or the autumn leaves on the drive down Suitland Parkway to the Bureau of the Census, or one of a thousand memories of a small apartment on Capitol Hill or an even smaller one off Central Park in New York. My memory is in other respects the despair of my family and friends, but I can recall exactly where I was and what I was doing when I wrote almost every page of *Losing Ground*.

A few memories in particular stand out. When I reread the thought experiment about how to get people to quit smoking in chapter 16, I think of an August morning on a lake in Minnesota where I dreamed it up and the succeeding days when I completed the first draft—on my honeymoon. And whenever someone tells me what a wonderful title "Losing Ground" is (which indeed it is), I invariably flash back to the day I was visiting friends at my former employer, the American Institutes for Research, and talking to the late Paul Schwarz, my boss and friend for many years and the man to whom *Losing Ground* is dedicated.

It was the beginning of 1984, the manuscript was in copyediting, and I still didn't have a title, despite having thought about it for the last year and a half. I was venting my anxiety to Paul, who had read most of the manuscript. As we talked, his face abruptly went blank, as it always did when he was on the verge of an idea. Then there was the barest trace of a smile:

"*Fucking Over the Poor*," he said, and paused.

"Colon."

Pause.

"The Missionary Position."

It was the perfect title, as those of you who are new to *Losing Ground* will soon realize. Paul Schwarz's title encapsulates the narrative and thesis of the entire book in seven words. But somehow I couldn't see myself proposing it to the folks at Basic Books.

By a few weeks later, the deadline for a title was fast approaching, and we were truly desperate. The book was going to be called *Slipping Backward*—a play on the title of a nineteenth-century political book called *Looking Backward*, which perhaps fifty people in the entire country might have understood. Nobody liked *Slipping Backward*, but nobody could come up with anything better.

My wife, Catherine, and I were watching the 1984 Super Bowl at Paul's home. I mentioned the continuing title problem when we arrived, but nothing more was said as we watched the Raiders demolish the Redskins. Paul was helping me on with my coat as we were leaving when he said without preface, "I think that 'losing ground' is more the concept you have in mind." And so *Losing Ground* finally got its name, the second most perfect name, in the nick of time.

Losing Ground's official publication date was in September 1984. By October, the book was beginning to be talked about in print. By December, it was being treated as a phenomenon. In early 1985, the *New York Times* felt compelled to denounce it in the lead editorial of a Sunday edition. Clearly, *Losing Ground* had arrived.

But just as clearly, a mythology about *Losing Ground* began to overshadow the book itself, and it was no longer necessary to read the book in order to talk about it. All you had to know, according to the mythology, was that Murray said that (1) the Great Society was a failure, (2) social programs only make problems worse, and (3) the welfare system ought to be scrapped. The other part of the mythology was that *Losing Ground* had become "the bible of the Reagan administration," as the *New York Times*'s Leonard Silk put it. Then a dark mythology began to be spread as well: Murray had written the book to order at the behest of right-wing interests. It had been promoted with a slick public relations campaign. Murray had fudged the numbers and ignored data he didn't like. I was a Social Darwinist, John Kenneth Galbraith said. A *New York Review of Books* cartoon had me in top hat and tails, grinning fiendishly, the silent movie villain who no doubt had just foreclosed on the widow and her children.

None of it—not even the good parts—was true. The great untold story about *Losing Ground* is that it was *not* popular within the Reagan administration, nor did it have any direct impact on policy. When a reporter for the

Wall Street Journal tried to write a story about *Losing Ground*'s influence on the White House and asked me for names of people she could interview, I had to tell her that, to my knowledge, no one in a senior position in the administration had even read it, let alone been influenced by it. She called back a few weeks later to tell me that she had spent a lot of time asking around, and that I was right.

What no one had noticed in all the furor was that *Losing Ground* was not congenial to the people who ran the Reagan White House in the second term. The book did not say that the problem with welfare was welfare cheats. It did not say that the problem of the underclass could be solved with minor reforms and a growing economy. If the Reagan administration had taken the message of *Losing Ground* seriously, it would have been obliged to confront messy, politically costly issues that the White House wanted to sidestep. The funniest example of this occurred when the administration came close to offering me a senior position in the Department of Health and Human Services. The secretary of the department, I am told, was given a copy of *Losing Ground*, dipped into it, and promptly scotched my appointment—I was far too radical.

In the end, *Losing Ground* did not have the hallmarks of a hot book. It got a lukewarm-to-critical reception from the mainstream press, was subjected to savage attack from the left, sold only about 30,000 copies in its hardcover version, and was largely ignored by the most conservative presidential administration in decades. And yet, observers from left and right agree that it has had an enormous impact on the social policy debate. Many have argued that it changed the terms of that debate. Why and how? I am probably the worst person to ask, for my observation of the reaction to *Losing Ground* is skewed in many ways. But here are my best guesses.

Part of *Losing Ground*'s effect came from its tone. I had been working for years with people who ran social programs at street level, and knew the overwhelming majority of them to be good people trying hard to help. I made my first acknowledgment in the preface to them. When I wrote in the prologue that the most troubling aspect of social policy was "not how much it costs, but what it has bought," I meant it, and most readers who came to the book as liberals accepted that. There is no glee in *Losing Ground*'s criticism of social programs, making it easier for many readers from the left of center to follow my argument.

Losing Ground also liberated people to the right of center. In my experience, principled conservatives tend to be compassionate and generous in their personal lives. The book gave them intellectual permission to acknowledge those qualities when talking about social policy. One can be saddened by the plight of poor children and yet be opposed to new government social programs intended to relieve their plight—a combination that would have surprised no one throughout most of American history, but had been impermissible since the 1960s.

I would like to think that another reason for *Losing Ground*'s influence is the power of its argument, but cause and effect are always ambiguous in such cases. Did it persuade people to change their minds, or did it articulate a view that many people had reached on their own? Some of both, presumably.

For whatever reasons, much of what was controversial when *Losing Ground* first appeared has since become conventional wisdom. It is now accepted that the social programs of the 1960s broadly failed; that government is clumsy and ineffectual when it intervenes in local life; and that the principles of personal responsibility, penalties for bad behavior, and rewards for good behavior have to be reintroduced into social policy.

Other aspects of the conventional wisdom have changed so radically that it is difficult to recall how different things were just a few years ago. In 1984, *Losing Ground* was attacked for the proposition that in the short term, a pregnant, low-income single woman is economically better off staying single and going on welfare than marrying a man with a typical low-income job. Now this idea is accepted by all sides in the debate over welfare reform. In 1984, at every college speaking engagement I had to defend the proposition that illegitimate births are a problem for children and for society. Now only the most militant feminists argue otherwise. In 1984, *Losing Ground*'s argument that a growing number of poor people were engaged in self-destructive personal behavior that would keep them at the bottom of society provoked angry retorts that I was blaming the victim. Today, no major figure in either academia or public life argues against the existence of such a group. It even has an accepted, uncontroversial name: the underclass.

Most astonishing is the evolution in attitude toward the policy proposal for which *Losing Ground* became perhaps best known: to end welfare altogether. In 1984, even I made the case tentatively, putting it forward as a thought experiment (chapter 17). As I write these words, ten years to the week since I held the first bound copy of *Losing Ground*, bills are before Congress that would do away with welfare for unmarried mothers. They will not pass this year, but abolishing welfare is now a live political issue—something that in 1984 I couldn't imagine ever happening.

These movements in the conventional wisdom toward the positions of *Losing Ground* have been driven partly by the findings of new research that has been published in the last ten years, but more fundamentally by the persistent intrusions of reality into the cloistered world of social science. Take, for example, the long-standing scholarly debate over whether there is such a thing as a "culture of poverty." In the 1960s, one of the main sources of data for arguing against a culture of poverty was opinion surveys showing that the poor held the same values as the middle class. If the poor were given a chance, it was concluded, they would get jobs, marry before having children, and be just as law-abiding as their more affluent counterparts. The same opinion surveys were cited against *Losing Ground* in the 1980s.

The man in the street might have wondered how much faith should be placed in a questionnaire asking people about their values, but commonsense doubts are not enough to discredit a study with scientific credentials. There must be countervailing data of some sort—no easy feat, since gathering directly countervailing data entails getting people to admit to a poll taker that they do *not* share the middle-class values of hard work, honesty, and personal responsibility. Academic attempts to refute the opinion surveys as evidence were bound to be ambiguous, and for a time after *Losing Ground* appeared, the survey results continued to be used in the public debate. But as the years went by, what had always been obvious to social workers and police officers who worked in underclass neighborhoods—that a lot of people in those neighborhoods were indeed living by a very different set of values from those of mainstream society—became incrementally more obvious in a wide variety of behavioral ways; the data from opinion surveys were used less and less. In a cumulative process, reality slowly forces social scientists to do a better job of asking questions.

Currently, the most active (and acrimonious) debate on such topics is over the question of whether welfare has an important causal role in producing illegitimate babies. I will go out on a limb and predict that this debate will have a similar trajectory to the one about whether an underclass exists. Ten years ago, the quantitative social science literature linking welfare and illegitimacy was thin. Today, it has expanded considerably. Ten years from now, it will be widely accepted among academicians that the existence of an extensive welfare system is a decisive enabling condition for illegitimacy. The prediction once again draws from the streets: Almost everyone I know who works in neighborhoods with high illegitimacy accepts as a matter of course that the welfare system has pervasive, complex influences on both men and women, encouraging behavior that, among other things, often ends up producing babies. Sooner or later, social science will catch up.

I am often asked when I will update *Losing Ground*. The answer is never. I confess to thinking about writing a book in another decade with the subtitle "American Social Policy, 1950–2000," but with a new main title and a new text. At the height of the controversy over *Losing Ground*, Milton Friedman gave me a piece of advice I have never forgotten. A book is like a child, he said. At the beginning, you can try to protect it. But sooner or later it has to go out and stand on its own. *Losing Ground* did that, and has carved out its own niche in the social policy literature of this half-century. It deserves to go undisturbed by an anxious author trying to improve it. But at least I can use this introduction to take a quick look at how things have been going in the decade since *Losing Ground* appeared.

Note two computational differences between the following figures and those in the main text. First, all figures here are expressed in 1990 dollars, whereas all the figures in the main text are in 1980 dollars (worth about $1.58 in 1990 dollars). Second, all racial comparisons are based on whites versus blacks, whereas the comparisons in the main text are based on whites versus "blacks and others" (because "blacks only" data did not extend back to 1950). All figures are taken from the same official compendia used to construct the tables in the appendix.

Chapter 4, "Poverty." Nothing much happened to rates of poverty in the 1980s. The great and simple truths about poverty are that (1) from World War II through the 1960s, the United States saw a decline in poverty that was roughly as steep in the 1940s, 1950s, and 1960s; and (2) from the early 1970s onward, the trend has been shallowly upward. The 1980s did not change this generalization. In 1990, the poverty rate was 13.5 percent, a bit higher than it had been in Lyndon Johnson's last year in office. The difference is that, as of 1968, even after four years of the Great Society had greatly increaséd spending, total social welfare expenditures were only $226 billion, compared with $614 billion in 1990. There were no conspicuous differences in the changes in poverty rates for blacks and for whites during the 1980s.

Chapter 5, "Employment." I began this chapter's discussion with unemployment among black males aged 16–24. During the 1980s, the picture shown in figure 5.2 improved. In 1990, the unemployment rate for black males aged 16–24 was 24.2 percent, down from 28.4 percent in 1980. White male unemployment had improved even more, however, so the gap in the black/white ratio (figure 5.3) continued to rise. Labor force participation (LFP) among black males aged 16–24 continued to drop during the 1980s, dipping below the 60 percent mark for the first time in 1990 (59.1 percent, compared with 62.0 percent in 1980).

Chapter 6, "Occupations and Wages." This is one of the few positive stories in part II, telling of black progress in entering white-collar professions and of strong gains in wages. The increase in blacks as white-collar professionals continued in the 1980s, though at a much slower pace than in the 1970s. The story for wages is "positive" in one sense: the racial gap between the median income for full-time, year-round male workers declined from 1980 to 1990, but only because the real median wage for whites declined more than the median for blacks. Despite the narrowing income gap for full-time, year-round male workers, the black-white gap in median family income increased, largely reflecting the continued decline in two-parent families among blacks.

Chapter 7, "Education." In terms of school enrollment through secondary school, blacks had already achieved parity with whites by 1980, and that parity persisted through the 1980s. In terms of college, the measure I used in chapter 7—the proportion of blacks aged 20–24 enrolled in school—increased markedly, from 17.7 percent in 1980 to 23.7 percent in 1990. The story on educational achievement is also positive. In 1980, average combined SAT scores of whites and blacks were separated by 234 points; by 1990, it was only 196 points. The magnitude of the remaining gap is large, however.

Chapter 8, "Crime." During the early part of the 1980s, the violent and property crime rates both fell. Then, in 1985, they began to increase again. Property crime increased slowly, but violent crime shot up as fast as it had during the 1970s. The chief racial comparison in chapter 8 is based on homicide committed by males. This is one of the few indicators on which blacks clearly continued to lose ground in the 1980s. While the rate for white males was dropping, the rate for black males was increasing from 66.6 to 69.2 per 100,000.

Chapter 9, "The Family." I used illegitimate births as the chief measure when I wrote chapter 9, and the news since then has been bad. In 1980, 55.2 percent of black births were to unmarried women. Even as I was writing *Losing Ground* in the early 1980s, I thought that the figure could not go much higher, and expected each new year's data to reveal that the increase in the proportion of illegitimate births had finally peaked. Each year I was wrong, and I have continued to be wrong every year since. By 1990, 65.2 percent of black births were to unmarried women. The illegitimacy ratio among whites rose even faster (proportionally) during those ten years, from 11.0 to 20.1 percent, augmenting the bad news.

How do these results add up? For the most part, the 1980s saw a continuation of existing trends, good and bad alike. The most persuasive interpretation to me is that the United States has settled into a long-term evolution in which the people who have something going for them—especially high cognitive ability—will do better and better, socially and economically, while those who do not will do worse and worse.

This represents an evolution in my views, which in turn brings me to the questions that I have been asked most often: How have I changed my mind since *Losing Ground* was published? What would I rewrite if I were to do it over?

I would mostly add material rather than amending—I can think of half a dozen extended footnotes and additional calculations that I would insert at various points, to forestall some of the unnecessary debates that occurred after *Losing Ground*'s publication. But, surprising though it may seem for such a controversial book, there are not any errors of numbers or facts in *Losing Ground* that need to be corrected. I have had a few changes of mind, however.

In the concluding chapter, I predicted large changes in test scores and other measures of academic achievement if a voucher system were introduced. I still favor returning control of education to parents, but I am more guarded now about how much can be done to improve education, and have become worried about whether a federal voucher system might lead to the destruction of the existing private school system. I also treated illegitimacy as one problem among many others. I have subsequently become convinced that illegitimacy must be at the center of all calculations about how the underclass will evolve. As illegitimacy reaches the proportions in white lower-class communities that it reached in black lower-class communities in the early 1960s, my fear is that the problems we now associate with the black inner city will metastasize into the much larger white population, with disastrous results for American society.

More generally, when I wrote *Losing Ground*, I saw an America that had taken a wrong turn in the 1960s but that presumably could be put back on course. While I could not have been described as optimistic, neither was I apocalyptic. Now I am inclined to believe that the United States is likely, within the lifetime of my children and perhaps even within my own lifetime, to evolve into a segregated class society in which the remaining remnants of the original American idea—limited government, free people running their own lives, communities solving their own problems—have been lost altogether.

And yet. . . . Congress *is* beginning to consider the possibility of doing away with large portions of the welfare system. The importance of community to everyday life *has* become a central theme in intellectual life. Skepticism about the efficacy of the federal government *is* at a record high. Perhaps my pessimism is overwrought.

With only a little stretching, I can even muster some optimism. Taking a longer view than this half-century, it may be argued that the last two centuries have been a sort of adolescence for Western societies. The Industrial Revolution, and then the Darwinian and Freudian and Einsteinian revolutions, filled our heads with new ideas. They left us absolutely sure, as only adolescents can be, that we had new insights into the nature of the human being and the ways in which society must be organized. Conceivably, we are emerging from that adolescence, about to come to terms with that profound

French adage *Plus ça change, plus c'est la même chose.* The ways in which Thomas Jefferson saw human beings pursuing happiness are not really so different from the ways in which people pursue happiness today, and the frameworks for that pursuit—family, work, friendship, community—are the same as those of Jefferson's day (different though the trappings may be). The constructive and destructive characteristics of government remain as the Founders understood them.

All that is needed to translate these old truths into twenty-first-century American life is a sweeping change in the elite wisdom—and such a change is not impossible. The story of the last third of the twentieth century may be one of lost ground, but the story of the first two-thirds was one of ground gained, in great leaps, in every domain of American life. In chapter 3, I describe how the elite wisdom changed with extraordinary speed between 1964 and 1967. There is no reason why it cannot do so again, if we can accept how well we were served once (and might be again) by some pre-1960s principles of American government and conceptions of the American idea.

CHARLES MURRAY
Washington, D.C.
August 1994

Losing Ground

Prologue

1950

LIFE's issue of 24 April 1950 was the usual potpourri—the wedding of Franco's daughter and a lavish pictorial on the art of El Greco, an analysis of foreign policy by John Foster Dulles ("Averell Harriman's new advisor"), and a story on Bob Hope's first television show.

The magazine looked up from its perusal of these matters long enough to editorialize on the state of the economy. *Life* liked what it saw. "Two years ago, four years ago," the editors wrote, "the U.S. was hip-deep in a postwar boom—and the news today is that it is still smack in the middle of the same boom. The darned thing goes on and on and on."[1] The writers expanded at some length on this theme, happily cataloging the achievements of American free enterprise.

The editorial closed with a cautionary note. Mindless materialism was a growing threat. The life of the spirit, through the arts, science, and religion, was the real point of it all, the editorial reminded; too many people were forgetting that. "Are the American people really coming to value prosperity as a means to the larger good?" *Life* asked.

The editorial did not mention poverty. It did not mention that an entire

3

race of Americans was still consigned to second-class status. It did not mention the possibility that "prosperity" and "the larger good" were equally unreal to millions.

Life was not alone. In that year of transition from the first half of the century to the second, the leading popular magazines—*Time, Newsweek, The Saturday Evening Post, Look, Colliers, The Reader's Digest*—contained very little about social or economic injustice.

The Negro problem? There was a Supreme Court decision in June of 1950, ruling that the University of Oklahoma could not require its one black student to sit alone in a separate part of the dining hall, and that the University of Texas could not claim that the law school it set up exclusively for a black student was really separate but equal, consisting as it did of a single room. But the Court did not repudiate the underlying "separate but equal" doctrine. Civil rights advocates were disappointed, but the *New York Times* counseled patience. "This republic cannot recognize degrees of citizenship," its editors wrote. "But as long as considerable numbers of people, including the majority or dominant elements of whole communities, think differently, we cannot expect the millenium." The editorial in the nation's most prestigious newspaper did not ask for a stronger stand by the Court or urge new civil rights legislation. Rather, the editors concluded, "the situation calls for a period of education—how long a period, no one can say."[2] At the end of the year, the American Civil Liberties Union released its survey of newspapers in sixteen major cities revealing that, although political and academic freedoms were imperiled, there were bright spots—labor rights, press freedoms, and race relations were in a "healthy" state.[3]

Poverty? Poverty was so far from being a topic of concern that the *lack* of poverty was said to be creating, if not exactly a problem, at least a challenge. Philanthropists would have to start being more creative in finding useful things to do with their money, wrote the head of one large foundation, "now that most of the crushing burden of relieving destitution has been removed from the shoulders of the individual giver to those of society, where it belongs."[4]

Two of the scarce references to poverty are instructive. The first was in a small journal which was at that time well to the left on the American political spectrum, *The New Republic*. In a fifteen-page "State of the Union" editorial with which it opened the new year, the magazine included a subsection entitled "The Lowest Third," referring to "the 10,000,000 American families who earn less than $2,000." But the writers could not muster much indignation. The subsection on the lowest third was buried in the middle of the editorial. The word "poverty" was not used. Aspirations for reform were modest. Acknowledging that "[s]ome of the causes for the condition of the lowest third are beyond the power of any Congress to solve," the magazine asserted only that many of the unskilled could do better if given the chance.[5] *The New Republic*'s prescription was for the president to create a Special Commission on Labor Training, a national scholarship program, and a Fair Employment Practices Commission.

A second exception to the general silence on the topic was a piece in the June issue of *Harper's*. Robert L. Heilbroner, a Harvard economist, had written a lengthy article entitled "Who Are the American Poor?" A little note at the bottom of the first page introduced him and then added a reassurance: "In calling attention to one of the imperfections of our economy, he assumes a basic condition of health which can withstand examination."[6]

Heilbroner's analysis should have been a shocker. He reminded his readers of the economic plight of the elderly, Negroes, and farmers; he discussed how the poverty level might be defined; and he eventually reached estimates of poverty that ranged from a quarter to a third of the entire U.S. population, depending on the definition and statistics one used.

His numbers were accurate. Retrospectively applying the official definition of poverty—the one now employed by the federal government, the news media, and scholars when they discuss poverty—there were in 1950 approximately 45 million American poor, or 30 percent of the population. By the standards of thirty years later, the United States was in the midst of a crisis of poverty. But hardly anyone noticed.

If by subsequent standards the poverty problem was appallingly large, the federal effort to deal with poverty was irresponsibly puny. In 1950, social welfare spending for the general public (excluding programs for veterans, and railroad and government personnel) cost a little over three billion dollars; about eleven billion in 1980 dollars. This figure includes Social Security, Aid to Families with Dependent Children (AFDC), Unemployment Insurance—the entire federal effort. In a country with 45 million living in poverty, it represented an annual expenditure of less than $250 (1980 dollars) per poor person.

1968

At the outset of 1968, the expansive confidence of 1950 would have been much more justifiable. Real Gross National Product had risen for nine straight years, and the increases added up to a boom. Inflation had been held to an average of only 1.6 percent during those same nine years. Real income, fringe benefits, job security—all had been improving.

For the poor who had been so ignored in 1950, unemployment was gone. That is, the unemployment rate was running at 3.6 percent, which economists considered to be tantamount to full employment. Their assessment could be validated at nearly any factory or union hiring hall or in the Help Wanted signs in the windows of restaurants and stores and gas stations and repair shops. If you wanted a job, presumably jobs could be had.

Not only the economy had boomed. The nation had moved dramatically to rid itself of discrimination and disadvantage. In the four years of the Johnson administration, Congress had passed into law landmark legislation in civil rights, medical care, housing, education, and job training. The Office of Economic Opportunity was a new and active force for urban renewal, community development, drug rehabilitation, alternatives for juvenile delinquents, and experimentation with solutions for just about every other known social problem. In the courts, the poor and uneducated were winning legal protections that previously had been enjoyed largely by people with the money to hire good lawyers. Constitutional precepts —separation of church and state, one man-one vote, protection against self-incrimination, to name a few—were being interpreted with unprecedented literalism and applied with unprecedented scope.

There was reason for satisfaction, but very little of it. The prevailing spirit ranged from determination to despair. Vietnam was part of the reason, of course, but hindsight can easily distort our memories of what happened when. As 1968 began, the Tet Offensive, generally accepted as the pivotal event in American public perceptions of the war, was still in the future. Cambodia and Kent State were more than two years away. Roxbury and Newark, in which riots broke out in the summer of 1967, and more recently Detroit, with forty-three dead in four days of violence, had been battlefields closer to home. In its lead editorial for the first issue of 1968, entitled forebodingly "Will We Make It?," *The New Republic*'s most strident rhetoric was reserved for the domestic situation. "We no longer ask whether there will be mass violence and racial war next summer, but whether it will break out sooner," the editors wrote.

To respond constructively would be to see what we are (and could be), and to admit that the United States, its immense wealth and managerial technology notwithstanding, has slipped out of rational control. Real reform could then begin.[7]

"Real reform"? What, if not "real reform," had been going on for the past four years? But the editors of *The New Republic* were not alone in dismissing the progress to date. Two months into the new year, the President's National Advisory Commission on Civil Disorders, comprising some of the most distinguished public servants, academicians, and businessmen in the nation, would release its report. It would recommend emergency legislation to create *two million* new jobs, lest the deep frustrations of the poor push them to more desperate measures to pry action from an unresponsive system—in an economy with an unemployment rate of 3.6 percent. From complacency in the face of want to hysteria in a time of plenty: in eighteen years, the public perception (or misperception) of what was happening had done an about-face.

1981

During the 1970s, the poor receded from public attention. Their plight was invoked when it had to be, as the justification for new and expanded social programs. But they were at the periphery of our national concerns, presumably taken care of, more or less.

Within three months of Ronald Reagan's inauguration on 20 January 1981 the poor were once more at center stage. A budget crisis was upon us, and something had to give. In the administration's view, the social welfare programs were prime targets for budget cuts. An intense debate began over what could be done without ripping the "social safety net." Conservatives wanted to save money without causing pain and argued that only "fat" was being excised from overgrown programs. Liberals insisted that this was wishful thinking. The editors of *Commonweal* described the basis of their fear:

> It is true that many of the targets of the budget cuts will be only marginally affected. Often enough, however, that may be the crucial margin that sustains the spirit if not even the body. . . . Some people will make do—by slipping into alcoholism, by taking out their rage on their neighbors and passers-by and then filling our prisons, by neglecting or abusing children and passing social costs onto another generation. Far more will "make do" by simply suffering quietly.[8]

Both sides proceeded from a tacit, common premise: that the important progress of recent years should be preserved. Few asked the questions it would seem natural to start with: How much progress in fact has been made? How have the poor been doing?

The unadorned statistic gives pause. In 1968, as Lyndon Johnson left office, 13 percent of Americans were poor, using the official definition. Over the next twelve years, our expenditures on social welfare quadrupled. And, in 1980, the percentage of poor Americans was—13 percent. Can it be that nothing had changed?

This book is about the answer to that and related questions. What *really* has been happening to the poor? To the disadvantaged? Not just since the Great Society, but since mid-century? What are the facts about poverty and the phenomena we have come to associate with being poor—crime and family disintegration and illiteracy and chronic unemployment? What are the facts about inequalities between blacks and whites? Are things better or worse or the same? What have been the trends?

The answers are complicated by the fact that our goals kept changing. Americans in 1950 were not simply blind to the existence of poverty and discrimination (although that was part of it). They also had very different perceptions from those of Americans in 1981 about the nature of "poverty" and "inequality," about their causes and cures. Indeed, our policy toward the poor and blacks was by 1981 almost the opposite of our policy in 1950. What happened to them is inextricably linked with what the larger society decided to do for them—or with them, or to them, depending on one's view. We begin with that story in part I.

Notwithstanding these changes in objectives, however, we shall be able to apply some stable measures. On the fundamentals of daily life—jobs, income, education, the family—we have the advantage of some broadly shared conceptions of what constitutes progress and some widely accepted official statistics for measuring them. We shall trace the status of the poor and disadvantaged on these criteria over the thirty-one-year period from 1950 to 1980. Part II presents those data.

To a certain extent, we also can address the more difficult question of causes. The coming of the Great Society triggered (and largely financed) intensive research into questions of poverty and discrimination. All of the social science disciplines participated. Some of the research was tendentious, some of poor quality. But there remains a large body of useful work. We know much more than we knew twenty years ago about the real-life consequences of alternative social policies. Part III examines this work.

The complex story we shall unravel comes down to this:

Basic indicators of well-being took a turn for the worse in the 1960s, most consistently and most drastically for the poor. In some cases, earlier progress slowed; in other cases mild deterioration accelerated; in a few instances advance turned into retreat. The trendlines on many of the indicators are—literally—unbelievable to people who do not make a profession of following them.

The question is why. Why at that moment in history did so many basic trends in the quality of life *for the poor* go sour? Why did progress slow, stop, reverse?

The easy hypotheses—the economy, changes in demographics, the effects of Vietnam or Watergate or racism—fail as explanations. As often as not, taking them into account only increases the mystery.

Nor does the explanation lie in idiosyncratic failures of craft. It is not just that we sometimes administered good programs improperly, or that sound concepts sometimes were converted to operations incorrectly. It is not that a specific program, or a specific court ruling or act of Congress, was especially destructive. The error was strategic.

A government's social policy helps set the rules of the game—the stakes, the risks, the payoffs, the tradeoffs, and the strategies for making a living, raising a family, having fun, defining what "winning" and "success" mean. The more vulnerable a population and the fewer its independent resources, the more decisive the effect of the rules imposed from above. The most compelling explanation for the marked shift in the fortunes of the poor is that they continued to respond, as they always had, to the world as they found it, but that we—meaning the not-poor and un-disadvantaged—had changed the rules of their world. Not of our world, just of theirs. The first effect of the new rules was to make it profitable for the poor to behave in the short term in ways that were destructive in the long term. Their second effect was to mask these long-term losses—to subsidize irretrievable mistakes. We tried to provide more for the poor and produced more poor instead. We tried to remove the barriers to escape from poverty, and inadvertently built a trap.

The final chapters, part IV, take up the extraordinarily difficult question of what to do. They urge that we think again about what our deepest ambitions for social policy ought to be, and what the constraints surrounding "helping" really are. A moral dilemma underlies the history of social policy from 1950 to 1980, an anciently recognized dilemma that in the enthusiasms of the 1960s we dismissed as fusty and confuted. It is indeed possible that steps to relieve misery can create misery. The most troubling aspect of social policy toward the poor in late twentieth-century America is not how much it costs, but what it has bought.

PART I

A Generous Revolution

O UR TOPIC is the poor and the discriminated-against as they have been affected by "social policy." We may narrow the focus: I shall be discussing the *working-aged* poor and discriminated-against, not the elderly, and *federal* social policy, not variations among states and localities.

I use the term "social policy" for want of a better one. "Welfare policy" is more concrete, but far too narrow. "Social welfare policy" is closer to what I have in mind, but it too connotes providing reified "things" to people; and "things" are only a small part of what government has given to the poor and disadvantaged. By "social policy," I mean a loosely defined conglomeration of government programs, laws, regulations, and court decisions touching on almost every dimension of life. Welfare programs are part of social policy toward the poor, obviously. Jobs programs are part of social policy. So also are federal efforts to foster better health and housing among the disadvantaged. So also are the Miranda decision and Affirmative Action and the Department of Education's regulations about bilingual education.

What each of these examples has in common is a worthy objective (less poverty, fairer courts) that, it has been decided, merits a transfer of resources from the haves to the have-nots. In the case of an AFDC program, the content of the transfer is straightforward (money from the richer to the poorer), but the rules governing who gets what are elaborate. In the case of a Miranda decision, the transfers are more subtle—of money in part (to support the greater demands on the public defense system), but also of other, intangible sorts.

The period we will cover, 1950 to 1980, saw extraordinary changes in the nature of those transfers. Consider just the money, on just the core programs—federal social welfare expenditures in 1950 alongside 1980, using a constant, official definition and constant dollars as the basis for the comparison:

- Health and medical costs in 1980 were six times their 1950 cost.
- Public assistance costs in 1980 were thirteen times their 1950 cost.
- Education costs in 1980 were twenty-four times their 1950 cost.
- Social insurance costs in 1980 were twenty-seven times their 1950 cost.
- Housing costs in 1980 were 129 times their 1950 cost.

Overall, civilian social welfare costs increased by twenty times from 1950 to 1980, in constant dollars.[1] During the same period, the United States population increased by half.

Clearly, something went on during those three decades that reflected a fundamental change in policy. The federal government did not simply augment its expenditures; it increased them by many orders of magnitude.

It amounted to a revolution, a generous revolution. We altered a long-standing national consensus about what it means to be poor, who the poor are, and what they are owed by the rest of society.

1

The Kennedy Transition

THE REVOLUTION began as so many revolutions begin, with reform. It sprang from the simplest, most benign of objectives. John Kennedy wanted the welfare program to be a force for social progress. In his welfare message to Congress in 1962, he wrote:

> The goals of our public welfare program must be positive and constructive. . . . [The welfare program] must stress the integrity and preservation of the family unit. It must contribute to the attack on dependency, juvenile delinquency, family breakdown, illegitimacy, ill health, and disability. It must reduce the incidence of these problems, prevent their occurrence and recurrence, and strengthen and protect the vulnerable in a highly competitive world.[1]

Unexceptional as his words sound today, Kennedy was engaged in a major departure from precedent. No president—not Eisenhower, nor Truman, nor Franklin Roosevelt, nor any of their predecessors—had seen the federal role in this light. Understanding how recently our assumptions about the function of welfare were transformed is essential to understanding the nature of the changes that took place in the mid-1960s and thereafter. We begin therefore with the 1950s.

1950–57: Last Years of the Traditional Consensus

The fifties saw the last years of a consensus about the purpose of welfare that had survived with remarkably little alteration since the Republic was founded and, for that matter, could trace its roots to the Poor Laws of Elizabethan England. Its premise was elemental: A civilized society does not let its people starve in the streets. It makes "a decent provision," as Samuel Johnson put it, for those who would otherwise be destitute.

This decent provision was hedged with qualifications. For more than three centuries, the mainstream of western social thought among intellectuals and the general public alike held that welfare was pernicious at bottom—"a bounty on indolence and vice."[2]

Why? Because whereas some people are the deserving poor—the involuntary unemployed and the helpless, as the first Poor Law categorized them—others are the undeserving poor—the "vagrant"—taking advantage of the community's generosity. Thus the dilemma: How is a civilized society to take care of the deserving without encouraging people to become undeserving? How does it do good without engendering vice?

The dilemma was taken for granted. The very existence of a welfare system was assumed to have the inherent, intrinsic, unavoidable effect of undermining the moral character of the people. Not working is easier than working; not saving is easier than saving; shirking responsibility for parents and spouses and children is easier than taking responsibility. It was seen as a truism that a welfare system was perpetually in danger of tilting the balance in favor of the easy way out.

The voices for expressing this age-old fear have varied. In 1950, a family court judge in New York City was colloquially indignant:

> Every day, sitting in court, I amass new evidence that the relief setup is sapping [the recipients'] will to work; that it is encouraging cynicism, petty chiseling and bare-faced immorality.[3]

But the message was really no different from the more fastidious language of those who were trying to prevent pauperism in the New York of a century and a half earlier:

> Is not the partial temporary good which [relief measures] accomplish . . . more than counterbalanced by the evils that flow from the expectations they necessarily excite; by the relaxation of industry, which such a display of benevolence tends to produce; by that reliance on charitable aid, in case of unfavorable times, which must unavoidably tend to diminish . . . that wholesome anxiety to provide

for the wants of a distant day, which alone can save them from a state of absolute dependence, and from becoming a burden on the community?[4]

The message was unchanged, and so was the shortage of solutions. No one could devise a system that satisfied both the urgings of compassion and the sterner demands of morality. During much of the nineteenth century, the most enlightened mode of care was thought to be the almshouse. Its principal advantage, or so its advocates argued, was that the recipients were under the constant tutelage of the almshouse's staff. They would be taught thrift and the virtues of hard work and, while engaged in this healthy labor, they could also work off some of the costs of their upkeep.

Almshouses were not universally the bleak Dickensian poorhouse. They varied. Some were as bad as the caricatures suggested; others were well-designed, well-staffed facilities that were the forebears of our great public hospitals—Bellevue in New York City, for example. But fashions change. By the early twentieth century, the alternative form of welfare—to provide a dole directly to recipients who lived in their own homes—had taken hold.

Franklin Roosevelt and the New Deal introduced four lasting changes to the welfare system: Social Security, Aid to Families with Dependent Children (AFDC), Workmen's Compensation, and Unemployment Insurance. Conservative mythology notwithstanding, none of these had much to do with the purposes of welfare. They changed the locus of the institutions that provided the welfare, in itself a major reform that deserves the importance (in praise or in blame) that has been attached to it. But the *purposes* remained intact. Social Security and Workmen's Compensation were to take care of those who could not or should not have to work. Unemployment Insurance was to take care of workers thrown out of jobs for reasons beyond their control. AFDC was to take care of widows with small children. In each instance, the population being assisted was made up of upstanding citizens who had gotten a tough break or were too old to be expected to support themselves. Nothing in the New Deal provided help just because a person was poor or hampered by social disadvantages.

So matters stood in the fifties. Virtually all welfare expenditures went for cash grants and, with the most trivial exceptions, were spent on people whose indispensable claim to government help was that they had no job and no alternative means of support.

The appropriate size of the dole was defined in the fifties as it had been in the past. It was to be adequate, if used frugally, to purchase life's necessities. Whether the recipient was wise enough or responsible enough to use it carefully was not the government's business. And with the Great Depression over, it was not the government's business to help the welfare recipient escape from dependency. They were supposed to do that themselves, if they weren't too old or too sick, by eventually finding a job.

1958–60: Strains in the Consensus

By the late fifties, widespread dissatisfaction had developed with this state of affairs. Two broad, very different perceptions of the welfare system had fed the dissatisfaction.

On the right and among large numbers of blue-collar Democrats, there was increasing resentment at the permanency of welfare. It was acceptable to provide for the aged and disabled, they agreed. It was acceptable that a worker get unemployment checks while looking for a new job. But it was quite another thing for society to be supporting a healthy adult year after year.

AFDC was the focal point for the resentment. The New Deal sponsors of AFDC had intended to help the widow with small children. The support she received would tide her over in the interim between the loss of her husband and the day when the children were old enough to take over her support. AFDC was at the outset the most broadly acceptable of the New Deal innovations in social welfare.

From this innocuous beginning AFDC evolved into the *bête noire* of the social welfare system. By the fifties it had become embarrassingly, outrageously clear that most of these women were not widows. Many of them had not even been married. Worst of all, they didn't stop having babies after the first lapse. They kept having more. This had not been part of the plan.

The most flagrantly unrepentant seemed to be mostly black, too. The statistics might show that whites have always been the largest single group of AFDC recipients, but the stereotype that enraged the critics was the family of four, five, six and more children reared at government expense, and somehow the stories about such families always seemed to talk about black families.

This was not entirely a function of racial discrimination. On the average, black AFDC families were substantially larger than white ones.[5] But apart from this, the odds were stacked. Reporters and critics did not sample randomly but searched for the most extreme examples, and these usually ended up being black. Thus the *Atlantic Monthly*, a sober-minded and liberally oriented magazine, ran a story in its April 1960 issue describing in muckracking detail the cases of "Charlotte" with fourteen children, "Maude" with nine (several of whom were fathered, it was reported, by an illiterate mental defective), and others who were portrayed as mindlessly accumulating children, neglecting them, and producing generations that would come back to haunt us in the decades to come. All the examples were black, lending a troubling overtone to the closing paragraph. "What is particularly disturbing to social workers, judges, and other public officials," the author concluded, "is not simply the failure of these people to support themselves but the complete breakdown of moral values. . . ."[6]

Resentment of "these people" was not limited to magazine articles. The late fifties saw a variety of efforts to rein in a program that, in the eyes of its critics, had run amok. In New York, historically one of the most progressive states on social welfare issues, the state legislature passed a bill requiring one year of residency before becoming eligible for AFDC (Nelson Rockefeller vetoed it). Other state legislatures passed or threatened to pass legislation banning AFDC payments for illegitimate children. Louisiana actually reached the point of dropping twenty-three thousand illegitimate children from its AFDC rolls, eventually rescinding the order only after the Eisenhower administration threatened to cut off federal funds. A judge in Maryland promulgated a plan to cut off the problem at its source by jailing unwed mothers after their third child. The Social Security Administration, alarmed at the budding revolt against AFDC, felt obliged to produce a study with the purpose of demonstrating that AFDC was not really responsible for the rising rate of illegitimacy.

The irony is that the illegitimacy rate for the population as a whole had barely moved. In 1955, births to single women constituted 4.5 percent of all live births. In 1960, when the furor reached its height, the rate had increased by only eight-tenths of one percentage point, to 5.3 percent.[7] Both figures were trivially low by later standards. But numbers were not the issue; rather, it was the notion of subsidizing a life style that grated so harshly on the values held by a consensus of white middle-class Americans.

The consensus was broad and deep. Kinsey might have revealed that more people were doing (in private) what his readers were doing (in private) than his readers had realized, but the imperative to have children exclusively within the sanctity of marriage remained intact. It was not part of a preferred value system, but of the *only* system that the white American middle class and working class accepted as valid. "Alternative life styles" was an idea whose time had yet to come.

At the same time that voices from mainstream America were inveighing against the welfare mother, leaders of the left and minorities of all political persuasions were beginning to express their outrage at what they saw as pervasive injustice in the American system. For Michael Harrington, who would later play a leading role in rediscovering poverty, 1958 was the year when it all started to come together. "That autumn," he writes in his memoirs, "the sixties were beginning to stir within the fifties":

> The McCarthyites were in retreat. . . . Martin Luther King, Jr., had appeared in Montgomery, Alabama, in 1955 and the first black mass movement in the South since the days of Booker T. Washington had coalesced around him. . . . And, thanks to the National Association of Manufacturers and other conservative business forces, 1958 was also a year of liberal-labor resurgence. "Right-to-Work" laws were on the ballot in a number of states, including Ohio, California, Colorado, and Washington. They had provoked the most militant trade union political mobilization in years, and the "Class of '58" in Congress was the most liberal since the New Deal.[8]

Of these developments, the civil rights movement was the most visible, the most explosive, and the hardest for conscientious whites to ignore. The statistics on unemployment and wages, on infant mortality and life expectancy, on education and voting registration, the open, sanctioned discrimination in everything from union membership to access to lunch counters to admission to universities all were counterpoint to the articles about the Charlottes and Maudes on the dole. Yes, the messengers of the movement agreed, welfare was too often permanent, but because of opportunity denied rather than opportunity spurned.

If it is hard in the 1980s to recapture the seamlessness of the middle-class consensus about illegitimate children, it is equally hard to recapture the uncomplicated moral monopoly held by the early civil rights workers. The ethical complexities of a Bakke case or *de facto* segregation were far in the future. The television screens were showing little children who needed military escorts to get into the school next door to their homes, college students sitting at drugstore counters for the right to be served a cup of coffee, and the burning buses of the Freedom Riders. Many whites remained vitriolically opposed to integration and to the civil rights movement. But almost nowhere outside a few white-supremacist sects did the opponents of civil rights portray themselves as occupying the moral high ground.

Modern Republicans and Lower-Case Liberals

White indignation at the morals of the welfare recipients and white guilt over who was responsible for putting them in that state collided, and at about the same time when a new political center was recognized.

It is not clear even now, nor is it especially important for our purposes to decide, which caused what. For whatever reasons, the late fifties saw the Republicans finally come to terms with the New Deal, belatedly acknowledging that it was not necessarily the undoing of the American way after all. One contemporary observer put it this way as he pondered the presidential election of 1960:

> The Eisenhower Administration, seen in retrospect, was the Indian Summer of the New Deal. It found the New Deal and its policies controversial—hotly defended, hotly attacked, and a fighting word for all. It leaves with the New Deal policies enshrined in comfortable respectability and anchored in the consensus of a broad moderate majority.[9]

Reading over the political arguments of the day, one is struck by how little was being argued about. Arthur Krock, a conservative columnist with the *New York Times,* complained that "when the national platforms and candidates of 1960 have been chosen, the American voters will find it difficult to detect a major ideological difference between the two major parties."[10] He was right. In the late fifties, the political spectrum unobtrusively bunched up. It happened from both ends. With the exception of the William Buckleys and Barry Goldwaters, few Republicans in the public eye wanted to label themselves as "conservative" anymore. "Conservatives" were cartoon characters, rotund and vested and smoking cigars. They were old-fashioned, unable to adapt to reality. They were out of touch. In parallel fashion, very few Democrats wanted to be thought of as ideological liberals. "A Liberal" was an Adlai Stevenson, an egghead, a bleeding heart—good for a sentimental ovation at the 1960 convention, but already a relic.

Politicians with national ambitions, Republicans and Democrats alike, all wanted "liberal" to be associated with them as an adjective rather than as a noun. Charles Frankel captured the spirit of the times in an article for the *New York Times Magazine.* "The word [liberal]," he wrote, "apparently designates an attitude of mind and an outlook on the world which relatively few Americans are willing to say unequivocally that they do not

21

share." He pointed to such unlikely figures as Herbert Hoover, Dwight Eisenhower, and Richard Nixon, each of whom "had kind words to say about 'liberalism' and . . . would bridle if he were called 'anti-liberal.' "[11]

It was not so much a matter of issues as of a frame of mind. In 1960, "liberal" connoted a forward-looking, problem-solving, pragmatic, sleeves-rolled-up stance toward the world. It stood for the conversion of liberal idealism to fair-minded, efficient policies. What would a truly liberal person expect of a good welfare system for example? It was obvious to Frankel:

> He will not be content with attitudes of *noblesse oblige* or with policies that merely "take care" of the poor . . . [H]is ultimate test of a welfare program will be the effect it will have on producing individuals who, like Eliza Doolittle at the conclusion of "Pygmalion," are prepared to walk out on those who have helped them and to open competitive enterprises of their own.[12]

It was a statement of an emerging consensus toward welfare that both Nixon and Kennedy would echo in the campaign to come, and that would resurface in 1962 as the common-sense starting point for straightening out the welfare mess.

"A Hand, Not a Handout"

Kennedy recognized the basis for convergence in the disparate sources of disgruntlement with the welfare system. The essence of the unifying appeal was expressed in the slogan that later became a rallying cry for the War on Poverty, "Give a hand, not a handout." It tapped one of the most deeply shared understandings about how the American system was supposed to work. And if it really did succeed in diminishing the welfare rolls, so much the better for those whose interest was less in social justice than in the size of the tax bite.

In substance, the program Kennedy proposed in his 1962 message to Congress was modest—by later standards, miniscule. It consisted of a few training programs and other rehabilitative efforts amounting to only $59 million in the 1963 budget. But if the program was small, the idea behind it represented a major departure nonetheless. By shifting the focus of welfare policy away from the dole and toward escape from the dole, Kennedy brought the federal government into a role that it had barely considered in the past: not mounting a WPA as an emergency measure to relieve unemployment, but instead taking a continuing responsibility for helping Americans to help themselves. The *New York Times* editorialized approvingly:

> President Kennedy's welfare message to Congress yesterday stems from a recognition that no lasting solution to the problem can be bought with a welfare check. The initial cost will actually be higher than the mere continuation of handouts. The dividends will come in the restoration of individual dignity and in the long-term reduction of the need for government help.[13]

The *Times*'s earnest warning that "[t]he initial cost will actually be higher than the mere continuation of handouts" turned out to be monumental understatement. Its confidence that the new policy would lead to a "long-term reduction in the need for government help" now sounds naive. But at that moment in history it seemed possible. The country was at peace, the economy was booming, and the cause was worthy. In the spirit of the since-maligned best and brightest, the members of the Kennedy administration and later of Johnson's War on Poverty saw themselves as hard-nosed idealists who would be able to get results where the social workers had failed. Their premise: Most of the ablebodied on welfare would work if given the opportunity. Their program: Train the chronically unemployed, train the youngsters growing up without skills or resources, help them get that first job. Their promise: The ablebodied will be on their way to permanent self-sufficiency.

Kennedy implemented fragments of his program—the Public Welfare Amendments of 1962 and the first Manpower Development and Training Act (MDTA), for example. But, taken as a whole, the social innovations he presided over were not costly. It is not widely claimed as one of Kennedy's achievements, but it is a fact nonetheless, that social welfare spending under his administration rose less rapidly than it had under Eisenhower's. Kennedy's legacy to Lyndon Johnson was not a new system, but a new tone and new expectations.

Johnson lost no time in implementing the Kennedy rhetoric. The initial antipoverty bill was written, debated, passed, and signed—in August 1964 —within Johnson's first nine months in office. The bill was a faithful attempt to follow the "hand, not a handout" script. It provided for job training, part-time jobs for teenagers and college students, community antipoverty projects, loans to low-income farmers and businessmen, and the establishment of VISTA, the domestic Peace Corps. There was not a handout in the lot. Johnson was careful to point this out at the signing ceremony, incorporating into his remarks the cheerful prediction that "the days of the dole in this country are numbered."[14]

2

"The System Is to Blame"

THE PASSAGE of the first antipoverty bill marked a transition. Through 1964, the rationale for new social action programs was the one set by Kennedy: The government should take a more active role in helping people get on their feet. Then new agenda, new assumptions, and a rush of events (not the least of them Vietnam) complicated the situation.

For one thing—and the importance of this must not be forgotten during the ensuing discussion—an accident of history brought a master legislator to the presidency at a moment when the other forces were converging. The antipoverty bills, Food Stamps, Medicare, Medicaid, public housing programs, manpower training, expansions of entitlements, all followed pell-mell. It was a legislative blitzkrieg, not the implementation of a master plan.

Apart from the idiosyncratic influences of Lyndon Johnson's ego and skills, a fundamental shift in the assumptions about social policy was occurring. Four forces pushed it: The economists seemed to have found the secret of lasting prosperity; policymakers and intellectuals discovered structural poverty; the civil rights movement moved north; and the original antipoverty programs failed to show the expected results. Together with other, less directly related tides in the American polity, they worked the revolution. In only three years, from 1964 to the end of 1967—what I shall refer to as the "reform period"—social policy went from the dream of ending the dole to the institution of permanent income transfers that embraced not only the recipients of the dole but large new segments of the American population. It went from the ideal of a color-blind society to the reinstallation of legalized discrimination. They were polar changes that were barely recognized as such while they were happening.

The Triumph of the Economy

One explanation for the reforms of the 1964–67 period, and why they came then rather than earlier, is so simple that it is sometimes overlooked: 1964–67 was the first time that we thought we could afford them. We were extremely rich and extremely secure about our ability to continue getting richer. The performance of the American economy had been spectacular.

In part, it was a phenomenon that stretched back to the onset of the Second World War. In 1940, just before the war years, GNP had been less than $100 billion. Twenty-five years later, it was $685 billion, a sevenfold increase. Even after discounting for inflation, real GNP had nearly tripled.[1]

But history alone was not the goad. During the 1964–67 period in which the shift in social welfare premises took place, Lyndon Johnson and the Congress were making decisions under the impression—based on persuasive evidence—that the boom was no longer part of an ungovernable cycle of economic expansion and contraction. The Eisenhower administration had been punctuated by two recessions, recessions that the new generation of Keynesian economists who came to Washington with Kennedy said they could avoid. Kennedy had cautiously implemented their advice. And it had worked, exactly as the economists had said it would: steady growth, no inflation. From 1961 to 1965, GNP went from $520 billion to $685 billion in increments of $40 billion, $30 billion, $42 billion, and $53 billion. The inflation rate was about 1 percent per year.

Hubris won out. "We can't prevent every little wiggle in the economic cycle," Johnson's budget director, Charles Schultze, acknowledged, but, he added confidently, "we now can prevent a major slide."[2] Keynes was on the cover of *Time*'s last issue of 1965. "Even the most optimistic forecasts for 1965 turned out to be too low," the magazine wrote. "If the nation has economic problems, they are the problems of high employment, high growth, and high hopes."[3]

The next two years brought more of the same—growth of $65 billion in the GNP in 1966 and $44 billion in 1967. Inflation was a bit higher, around

3 percent, but still manageable. There was no recession, no stumbling. "We are all Keynesians now," said Richard Nixon, and it seemed to be eminently reasonable to be so. It appeared that the economists were making good on translating theory into practice.

Thus we made our decisions about the poor and about social policy from what seemed at the time to be a position of impregnable economic strength. Not only were we enjoying an unprecedented boom, we now thought we had the tools to sustain it indefinitely. If there was poverty amidst plenty (a favorite phrase among writers of the time), and its solution did not come as easily as the initial optimism had projected, then there was still no good reason to back off. All the changes in policy during the 1964–67 period must be considered in light of this central fact: At the time, almost everyone thought the economic pie would grow ever larger.

The Discovery of Structural Poverty

Even as the War on Poverty was beginning, its premises of self-help and open opportunities were lagging behind a new intellectual consensus that would shape policy very shortly.

To understand its power, one first must understand that poverty did not simply climb upward on our national list of problems; it abruptly reappeared from nowhere. In the prologue to this book, 1950 was described as a year in which poverty was not part of the discourse about domestic policy—indeed, as a year in which the very word "poverty" was seldom used. The silence was not peculiar to 1950. From the outset of the Second World War until 1962, little in the popular press, in political rhetoric, or in the published work of American scholars focused on poverty in America.[4]

When poverty did get into the news before 1964, the treatment of it tended to reflect surprise that it existed at all. In November 1960, three weeks after the presidential election and the day after Thanksgiving (a deliberate juxtaposition), Edward R. Murrow broadcast a *CBS Reports* called "Harvest of Shame." It showed that tens of thousands of migrant workers were miserably paid, housed, educated, and nourished—problems that middle-class America apparently associated only with the 1930s and *The Grapes of Wrath.*

The viewing public and numerous editorial writers were shocked—a fact in itself illustrative of the obliviousness toward poverty. The more instructive reaction, however, was Murrow's own. A few months later, the day after he was sworn in as director of the United States Information Agency, one of his first acts was to try to persuade the BBC to cancel a scheduled broadcast of "Harvest of Shame." That Edward R. Murrow, the embodiment of journalistic independence, would try to stop a news show on grounds that it would be taken out of context suggests how aberrant the poverty in "Harvest of Shame" was taken to be.

In the intellectual community, phenomena such as poverty among migrant workers were seen as peripheral. Norman Podhoretz, recalling the leftist intellectual circles in which he moved during the 1950s, points out that the essential *economic* success of the American system was taken as a given even by those who were most bitterly critical of the social system. He continues:

> That there were still "pockets" of unemployment and poverty, and that there was still a great spread in the distribution of income and wealth, everyone realized. But the significance of such familiar conditions paled by comparison with a situation that now seemed to defy the rule that there could be nothing new under the sun: the apparent convergence of the entire population into a single class.[5]

Podhoretz's observation held true through the 1960 presidential campaign. Poverty was, in the terms of that campaign, something that happened mostly in Appalachia—not only in the Kennedy campaign rhetoric, but in the minds of those Democrats who considered themselves true liberals. When Arthur Schlesinger decided to proselytize among members of the liberal establishment on behalf of John Kennedy in 1960, he made his case on issues that he knew to be the ones that were exercising his friends and colleagues in the liberal wing of the party. He chose as his theme that Kennedy was the man for an era in which the struggle for material subsistence had essentially been solved.[6]

Against this backdrop, the emergence of the structural view of the poverty problem was unexpected and rapid. As of the beginning of 1962, no one was talking about poverty; by the end of 1963 it was the hottest domestic policy topic other than civil rights. But it was not just "poverty" that was being talked about. "Structural poverty" was now at issue.

"Structural poverty" refers to poverty that is embedded within the nature of the system (or demographics) and will not be eradicated by economic growth. Its elimination, according to the proponents of this view of poverty, requires radical surgery. "The most visible structuralists," writes James Patterson, "were not social workers or government bureaucrats looking for ways to improve the situation of individuals, but social scientists and left-wing writers who took a broad and reformist view of the functional relationship between inequality and the social system."[7]

One such writer was Michael Harrington, who in 1962 published a book that was the most visible single reason for the sudden popularity of poverty. The book was *The Other America*. Its thesis was that a huge population of poor people—fifty million by his count—was living in our midst, ignored. They consisted of the aged, the unskilled, the women heading households with small children, and others who were bound to be bypassed no matter how much economic growth occurred, because of the way that the system distributed income.[8]

The importance of Harrington's book was not in its details but in its central message: America was not the single-class, affluent society that a complacent intellectual establishment had assumed, but a deeply riven society in which the poor had been left to suffer unnoticed. Kennedy read *The Other America* and Dwight MacDonald's evangelizing review of it in *The New Yorker* and ordered the beginning of the staff work that Lyndon Johnson would later seize upon for his crusade.[9]

It was a time when books became banners for causes—*Silent Spring* was published at about the same time, and *Unsafe at Any Speed* followed a few years later—and it is always difficult in such cases to determine how much was cause and how much effect. Certainly others had been forwarding a structuralist view of poverty both within and without the Kennedy administration.[10] But even if the poor were bound to have been rediscovered in the early 1960s, Harrington was their pamphleteer, *The Other America* their *Common Sense*.

Once the argument had been made, it became very unfashionable for an intellectual in good standing to argue with it. A few, such as Irving Kristol, made note of Harrington's factual inaccuracies and his reliance on dubious evidence.[11] Later, even some of Harrington's sympathetic colleagues would dispute the centerpiece arguments about intergenerational poverty.[12] But much of what Harrington had to say seemed indisputable. The population did include large numbers of poor people, and they didn't seem to be moving up the way that they were supposed to do. To quibble was to sound like the Chamber of Commerce.

If poverty was not an aberration, not a matter of "pockets" but structurally built into the American system, then it was necessarily true that the initial antipoverty bills represented a half-hearted and wrong-headed approach to the problem. Poverty was not going to be eradicated by a Job Corps or a few loans to small businessmen. Sweeping changes in the income distribution system were needed—a cool analytic conclusion to some, but more often a conviction held with "a passionate sense of urgency," as Jeremy Larner and Irving Howe put it. "[I]n a nation as rich as the United States," they declaimed, "it is an utter moral scandal that even the sightest remnant of poverty should remain."[13]

In a technical sense, the structuralists made a case only for the proposition that much, not all, of American poverty derived from structural characteristics. Their message was an antidote to the folk wisdom that anyone with enough gumption could make a good living. But the "passionate sense of urgency" got in the way of balance. What emerged in the mid-1960s was an almost unbroken intellectual consensus that the individualist explanation of poverty was altogether outmoded and reactionary. Poverty was not a consequence of indolence or vice. It was not the just deserts of people who didn't try hard enough. It was produced by conditions that had nothing to do with individual virtue or effort. *Poverty was not the fault of the individual but of the system.*

For the Harringtons, it was a statement of political and economic dogma. For the politicians and policymakers and implementers of the programs, it was about to become the indispensable rationale for coping with two empirical developments that few were anticipating when the War on Poverty got under way.

The Civil Rights Movement Moves North

Speaking to an interviewer in 1967, Daniel Patrick Moynihan summed up in a few sentences the toils in which the social welfare experiment had wound itself when the civil rights movement moved north.

> In the South . . . there were a great many outcomes—situations, customs, rules —which were inimical to Negro rights, which violated Negro rights and which were *willed* outcomes. Intended, planned, desired outcomes. And it was, therefore, possible to seek out those individuals who were willing the outcomes and to coerce them to cease to do so.
>
> Now, you come to New York City, with its incomparable expenditures on education; and you find that, in the twelfth grade, Negro students are performing at the sixth grade level in mathematics. Find for me the man who wills *that* outcome. Find the legislator who has held back money, the teacher who's held back his skills, the school superintendent who's deliberately discriminating, the curriculum supervisor who puts the wrong books in, the architect who builds the bad schools. He isn't there![14]

By and large—not perfectly by any means, but by and large—the legal system outside the southern states had rid itself of designed-in racism. There were no voter "literacy" tests to get rid of, no Jim Crow laws to repeal. While northern racism might simply be more subtle, as many black leaders claimed, it provided few specific, reified targets to hit out against.

And yet equality of rights under the law had not been accompanied by equality of outcome. Blacks in the North as in the South lived in worse housing than whites, had less education, ate less nutritious food, and so on down the list of indicators that were used to measure well-being. On virtually every one, a large difference between black and white remained, and it was always to the disadvantage of the blacks. Whites were made aware of this by accounts such as Kenneth Clark's "Youth in the Ghetto," passed everywhere in mimeograph by poverty planners long before it was published.[15] Blacks who lived in the ghetto did not need to read about it. Their response followed a pattern that could be used as a textbook example of a revolution of rising expectations.

The first phase of the civil rights movement culminated in the passage of the Civil Rights Act of 1964 on 3 July. For all practical purposes, the national legislative struggle for equality was over. The Voting Rights Bill remained to be enacted a year later, but the generalized legal clout granted in the 1964 act was enormous: No one could with impunity deny someone *access* to the institutions of this country because of race without being liable to criminal penalties or inviting a nasty and probably losing lawsuit. The civil rights movement had triumphed—and thirteen days later came the first of the race riots, in Harlem.

The riots continued that summer in Rochester, Paterson, Philadelphia, and Dixmoor, a suburb of Chicago. They quieted during the winter, then erupted again in Watts, in August 1965, with a violence that dwarfed the disturbances of the preceding year. They would crescendo in 1967, with riots in more than thirty cities.

The riots changed, or coincided with a change in, what had until then been a movement of legal challenges, nonviolent demonstrations, and coalition-building. Writing from a Marxist perspective, some observers saw this as the trigger for the explosion in social spending that occurred during the same period: The white power structure needed to control the restiveness of blacks, and the shift from "a hand, not a handout" to income transfers was in the nature of a bribe.[16]

A careful review of what bills passed when, with what support, casts doubt on this argument, though it retains intuitive plausibility.[17] But the post-1964 militancy unquestionably had another and arguably more pernicious long-term effect. It tightly restricted the permissible terms of debate within academia and the government on issues involving blacks—which is to say, virtually every issue associated with social policy.

Specifically, the riots and the militancy adjoined the moral monopoly that the civil rights movement of 1964 still enjoyed. The year 1964 was not only the year when the Civil Rights Act passed and the first riots occurred. It was also the year when Martin Luther King, Jr., won the Nobel Peace Prize. It was the year when Chaney, Goodman, and Schwerner were tortured and killed in Mississippi. It was, in short, the year in which all that created the moral monopoly was most in evidence.

Black leaders blamed the riots on whites—or, coextensively, The System. Stokely Carmichael and Rap Brown said it with a rhetoric as bloody-minded and as unapologetic as the rioters. Martin Luther King said it with more elegance, thoughtfulness, and political astuteness, but said it nonetheless. "A profound judgment of today's riots," King told a convention of social scientists, "was expressed by Victor Hugo a century ago. He said, 'If a soul is left in darkness, sins will be committed. The guilty one is not he who commits the sin, but he who causes the darkness.' "[18]

As a statement about ultimate causes, the black interpretation was nearly unarguable. But history was not the issue. The exigent question was: What do we do now, today, in response to people rioting in the streets? Devising an answer put whites in a terrible moral bind—not one that blacks were likely to have much sympathy with, but a bind nonetheless. A white who had supported the simple, purely "good" civil rights movement against the nasty southerners and now said, "Wait a minute, that doesn't mean you can start burning northern cities" was exposed as a summer soldier. Manifestly, racial discrimination continued to exist; manifestly, it was a moral perversity. Therefore. . . . And that was the hard part. What came after the "therefore"?

Whites who saw themselves as friends of the civil rights movement had to agree that the riots were regrettable but not the fault of blacks. The inevitability of the riots, even their reasonableness, had to be accepted, not as a matter of historical causation but as the basis for the white policy reaction. Of course the civil rights legislation had not forestalled violence, *Newsweek* told us. After all, "The promises of the present could not undo in a day the ugly legacy of the Negro past," the magazine wrote in its lead paragraph on the Watts riot. "A summer ago, that past exploded in a bloody war of rioting across the urban North. And last week, on a steamy, smoggy night in Los Angeles, it exploded again."[19] A few pages later, a poll of whites' reactions to the riots divided the discussion into two paragraphs—the "intelligent" reactions, meaning those who understood that the riots were an understandable manifestation of past injustice, and those who were "less perceptive," meaning the people who said that the rioters were breaking the law and ought to be punished. The two stands were widely perceived as being mutually exclusive.

Not everybody agreed. "White backlash" was a phrase coined at about the same time as "black power." The year 1966 saw the the election of an ideologically adamant conservative governor in California, Ronald Reagan, and widely publicized campaigns by racial hardliners like Boston's Louise Day Hicks. But even on Main Street, well into the riot years, a majority remained in favor of taking new steps to remedy black grievances.[20]

Within the Establishment (for lack of a better term), a much narrower, circumscribing mindset took hold: The blame is embedded in the structure of the system, and the system must be made right.

The most vocal advocates for sweeping reform were from the left, but it would be mistaken to treat the sense of guilt as "liberal" versus "conservative." The *mea culpa* resounded everywhere, including the most unlikely places. For example:

> [W]e are creating a monster within our midst, a people being alienated from the mainstream of American life . . . [We must] cease thinking of racial relations as a nice and good thing, as one important national and local task—*among many others*—to do. American race relations today, like religion and basic ideologies historically, must have an absolute priority or we are as a nation lost! [Emphasis in the original][21]

Strong words—not from a political rostrum, but from the lead article in the January 1967 issue of *The American Journal of Economics and Sociology,* a sober academic journal. But they were no more unexpected than an angry editorial, entitled "Cry of the Ghetto," complaining bitterly of "white society's stubborn refusal to admit that the ghetto is a problem it must solve, that its promises, broken and inadequate, are no longer tolerable."[22] It appeared in *The Saturday Evening Post*—the staid, middle-American, Norman-Rockwell-covered *Saturday Evening Post*—during that bloody August of 1967.

The National Commission on Civil Disorders, headed by an ex-governor of Illinois and comprising a distinguished selection of Americans from the business and professional worlds as well as from public life, put the imprimatur of the federal government on the explanation for the riots, concluding that "[w]hite racism is essentially responsible for the explosive mixture which has been accumulating in our cities since the end of World War II."[23] The report presented no proof for this statement, but few objected. Its truth was self-evident.

Whether the Establishment view of the black condition in the last half of the 1960s was right or wrong is not the issue that concerns us. The fact that this view was so widely shared helped force the shift in assumptions about social welfare. White America owed black America; it had a conscience to clear.

The moral agonizing among whites was strikingly white-centered. *Whites* had created the problem, it was up to *whites* to fix it, and there was very little in the dialogue that treated blacks as responsible actors. Until July 1964 most whites (and most blacks) thought in terms of equal access to opportunity. Blacks who failed to take advantage were in the same boat with whites who failed to take advantage. By 1967 this was not an intellectually acceptable way to conceive of the issue. Blacks were exempted. Once more, in a new and curious fashion, whites had put up the "Whites Only" sign.

White confusion and guilt over the turn of events in the civil rights movement created what Moynihan has called "a near-obsessive concern to locate the 'blame' for poverty, especially Negro poverty, on forces and institutions outside the community concerned."[24] The structuralists, with their view of poverty as embedded in the American economic and social system, provided a ready-made complement to this impulse. If society were to blame for the riots, if it were to blame for the economic and social discrepancies between whites and blacks, if indeed it were to blame for poverty itself among all races, and *if society's responsibility were not put right by enforcing a formalistic legal equality,* then a social program could hardly be constructed on grounds that simply guaranteed equality of opportunity. It must work toward equality of *outcome.* A "hand" was not enough.

Hard Noses and Soft Data

The riots and black militancy constituted one of the two empirical developments that made the structural view of poverty attractive. The second was the early realization, within the ranks of the Johnson administration as well as among its critics, that the antipoverty programs were not working as expected.

For this part of the story, we return to the fall of 1964, when the first antipoverty bill had just been passed and the Office of Economic Opportunity (OEO) was being organized. Our focus shifts from the academicians, the journalists, the cabinet officers and congressional leaders to the people who did the work—the middle- and lower-echelon officials who designed and implemented the programs that constituted the War on Poverty.

They were an assortment of New Frontiersmen (Sargent Shriver at OEO being the most conspicuous example) and people who came into the bureaucracy especially to play a role in the great social reform that Johnson had launched. Few were bureaucrats, few were from the social-work tradition. They tended to see themselves as pragmatic idealists. "Hardnosed" was a favorite self-descriptor in the Kennedy years, and it carried over. The first poverty warriors did not intend to get bogged down in interminable debates about doctrine. They had a job to do and, from the accounts of people who participated in those early years of the Great Society, it was an exciting job. The recountings have the flavor of war stories—of all-night sessions preparing for crucial Senate hearings; of small, sweaty working groups designing new programs on impossibly short schedules; of meetings in Newark or Chicago or Biloxi where the people across the table were not mayors and city planners, but the heads of tenants' associations and ghetto churches and street gangs. Speaking of his staff, the director of one of the early programs wrote:

> All were the antithesis of the stereotyped bureaucrat cautiously protecting his career. Their approach right down the line was: "What needs to be done? How can we do it best, and faster?" When the answers were clear, they were all willing to risk their careers and their health and sacrifice their personal lives, to get the job done well and quickly. Something happened to us all . . . that created a rare combination of shared dedication, excitement, and satisfaction.[25]

Such people characterized the early years both in Washington and in the field offices. They had no serious doubts that they would have an impact on the poverty problem. It seemed obvious to them (as it did to many observers at the time) that the only reason we continued to have poverty at a time of such manifest national affluence was that nobody had really been trying to get rid of it. Once the effort was made, so their assumption went, progress would surely follow.

Their optimism had two bases. One was that the programs depended on human responses that seemed natural and indeed nearly automatic to them. The gloomy implications of the "culture of poverty" argument did not carry much weight at OEO in 1964 and 1965. A sensible, hard-working poor person would find much to work with in the opportunities offered by the initial antipoverty programs. Or to put it another way, if the people who ran the programs had suddenly found themselves poor, they probably would have been quite successful in using the antipoverty programs to rescue themselves. The early programs put chips on the table; as their advocates had promised, they did indeed give some of the poor a chance at a piece of the action, with the operative word being "chance." The staff at OEO and its companion agencies scattered around Washington did not think that the loan programs or the community development programs would transform the ghetto instantaneously, but they had no doubt that such programs would be individually successful—steps in the right direction.

In the case of the training programs such as the Job Corps, success seemed to be still more natural. The logistics of providing training were straightforward. The educational technology was adequate and in place. There were plenty of welfare recipients who said they wanted jobs and who acted as though they wanted jobs. During the 1960s, and especially after the Vietnam War heated up, jobs were available for people with the kinds of skills that could be acquired in the training programs. The training programs would work, without question. What was to stop them?

It would be important to document the successes that were about to emerge. In the spirit of cost-effectiveness that McNamara had taken to the Pentagon, the early poverty warriors were prepared to be judged on the hardest of hardnosed measures of success. The programs would be removing enough people from the welfare rolls, from drug addiction, and from crime to provide an economically attractive return on the investment.

But how was this information to be obtained? Social scientists who had been at the periphery of the policy process—sociologists, psychologists, political scientists—had the answer: scientific evaluation. The merits of doing good would no longer have to rest on faith. We would be able to *prove* that we had done good, as objectively as a scientist proves an hypothesis.

In the space of a few years, applied social science and especially program evaluation became big business. In Eisenhower's last year in office, 1960, the Department of Health, Education, and Welfare (HEW) spent $46 million on research and development other than health research.[26] It took three more years for the budget to reach $90 million, followed by sizable jumps in 1964 and 1965. Then, in a single year, 1966, the budget doubled from $154 million to $313 million. Similar patterns prevailed at the other departments, agencies, institutes, and bureaus engaged in the antipoverty struggle.

The product of all this activity and money was a literature describing what was being accomplished by the antipoverty programs. It is what scholars call a "fugitive" literature, with most reports being printed in editions of a few dozen photocopies submitted to the government sponsor. The release of a major evaluation might get a column or two on a back page of a few of the largest newspapers. But otherwise, the work of the evaluators went unread by the outside world.

Within those governmental circles where the reports *were* read, they led to a rapid loss of innocence about what could be expected from the efforts to help people escape from welfare dependency. Starting with the first evaluation reports in the mid-sixties and continuing to the present day, the results of these programs have been disappointing to their advocates and evidence of failure to their critics.

The War on Poverty had originally struck on two fronts: For depressed neighborhoods and entire communities, "community action" programs were funded in profusion, to further all sorts of objectives; for individuals, manpower programs provided training or job opportunities. We shall be discussing the substance of what the evaluators found, not only in 1964–67 but subsequently, when we examine explanations for the breakdown in progress. For now, a few examples will convey the tenor of the findings.

THE COMMUNITY ACTION PROGRAMS

The community action programs fared worst. A number of histories and case studies are available to the public at large, Moynihan's *Maximum Feasible Misunderstanding* being the best known.[27] With the advantage of hindsight, it is not surprising that the community development programs so seldom got off the ground. Faith in spontaneity and in *ad hoc* administrative arrangements were traits of the sixties that met disillusionment in many fields besides the antipoverty programs. Surprising or not, the record they compiled was dismal. For every evaluation report that could document a success, there was a stack that told of local groups that were propped up by federal money for the duration of the grant, then disappeared, with nothing left behind.

Each project had its own tale to tell about why it failed—an ambitious city councilman who tried to horn in, a balky banker who reneged on a tentative agreement, and so on. There were always villains and heroes, dragons and maidens. But failure was very nearly universal.

The course of the projects followed a pattern. To see how this worked in practice, we have the example of the Economic Development Administration's major employment and urban development program in Oakland, the subject of a scholarly case study.[28] This was the sequence:

The story broke with considerable fanfare. *The Wall Street Journal* of 25 April 1966 had it on page one, under the headline "URBAN AID KICK-OFF: ADMINISTRATION SELECTS OAKLAND AS FIRST CITY IN RE-BUILDING PROGRAM."[29] The governor of California and the assistant secretary of commerce for economic development held a press conference announcing a program of $23 million in federal grants and loans. The program was an assortment of community-run economic development projects bankrolled by the government. Various incentives were designed to prompt private business to invest in the ghetto. In the short term, 2,200 jobs were to be provided, and more were to follow from "spinoffs." These jobs would go to the unemployed residents of the inner city.[30]

As far as its national publicity told the story, the program was a great success. A book *(Oakland's Not for Burning)* was in the bookstores by 1968, claiming that the program "may have made the difference" in preventing a riot in Oakland.[31] *The New Yorker* told its readers that the program had "managed to break a longtime deadlock between the Oakland ghetto and the local business and government Establishment."[32] Oakland was a showcase of the War on Poverty.

It was not until a year after these stories had appeared that the *Los Angeles Times* printed a follow-up story revealing that the activities described in the book and in *The New Yorker* had in actuality never gotten beyond the planning stage. All told, only twenty jobs had been created. The program was bogged down in bureaucratic infighting.[33] The authors of the case study, writing from the perspective of four years later, concluded that the effect of the project on "despair and disillusionment" among blacks was probably to have made matters worse.[34]

The Oakland project was not chosen for study as an example of failure; the study began while hopes were still high. The Oakland experience was representative, not exceptional, and the gradual realization of this by those connected with the poverty programs was one source of their dampened hopes for the "hand, not a handout" approach. Few of them reacted by giving up; through the rest of the 1960s and well into the 1970s, it was argued that the community action programs were slowly learning from their failures and would do better next time. But if their proponents did not give up, neither did they speak so boldly about the imminent end of the dole.

THE TRAINING PROGRAMS

The failure of the training programs was a greater surprise still. These of all programs were expected to be a sure bet. They dealt with individuals, not institutions, and teaching a person who wants to learn is something we know how to do. But starting with the first evaluation reports in the mid-sixties and continuing to the present day, the results failed to show the hoped-for results, or anything close to them. The programs were seldom disasters; they simply failed to help many people get and hold jobs that they would not have gotten and held anyway.

As with the community development programs, the findings varied in detail but not in pattern. In one of the most recent and technically precise studies of the Manpower Development and Training Act (MDTA), the linchpin of Kennedy's original program and one that eventually grew to a multibillion dollar effort, the final conclusion is that male trainees increased their earnings between $150 and $500 *per year* immediately after training, "declining to perhaps half this figure after five years." For the females, the study found a continuing effect of $300 to $600 per year.[35] A panel study of the effects of vocational training found a wage increase of 1.5 percent that could be attributed to the training.[36] The early studies of Job Corps trainees found effects of under $200 per year, and these early findings have been repeated in subsequent work.[37] Effects of this magnitude were far from the results that had been anticipated when the programs began.[38]

Even as the program designers and evaluators debated what to do next and how to do it better, they could not avoid recognizing some discomfiting realities. It was quickly learned that people on welfare do not necessarily enroll in job training programs once they become available. Those who enroll do not necessarily stick it through to the end of the program. Those who stick it through do not necessarily get jobs. And, of those who find jobs, many quickly lose them. Sometimes they lose them because of their lack of seniority when layoffs occur. Sometimes they lose them because of discrimination. Sometimes they lose them because they fail to show up for work or don't work very hard when they do show up. And—more often than anyone wanted to admit—people just quit, disappearing from the evaluator's scorecard.[39]

Unable to point to large numbers of trainees who were escaping from welfare dependency, the sponsors of the training programs turned to other grounds for their justification. They found two. First, a cost-effectiveness case could be wrenched even from small increments in income. If the average trainee's earnings increase even by a few hundred dollars, sooner or later the increase will add up to more than the cost of the training, and it was this type of calculation to which the sponsors were reduced. "The average effect [on earnings] for all enrollees is quite large," we find in one evaluation of Job Corps, then read on to the next sentence, where it is revealed that the "quite large" effect amounted to $3.30 per week. It was a statistically significant gain.[40]

Second, the training programs lent themselves to upbeat anecdotes about individual success stories: John Jones, an ex-con who had never held a job in his life, became employed because of program X and is saving money to send his child to college. Such anecdotes, filmed for the evening news, were much more interesting than economic analyses. They also were useful in hearings before congressional appropriations committees. Tacit or explicit, a generalization went with the anecdote: John Jones's story is typical of what this project is accomplishing or will accomplish for a large number of people. That such success stories were extremely rare, and that depressingly often John Jones would be out of his job and back in jail a few months after his moment in the spotlight—these facts were not commonly publicized. The anecdotes made good copy. Thus the training programs continued to get a good press throughout the 1970s. They were the archetypal "hand, not a handout" programs, and they retained much of the intellectual and emotional appeal that had made them popular in the early 1960s. To some extent, whether they worked or not was irrelevant.

We have been scanning a record that has accumulated over the years since the first antipoverty projects in the early 1960s. But the loss of innocence came early. It soon became clear that large numbers of the American poor were not going to be moved off the welfare rolls by urban development schemes or by training programs.

At another time, that might have been the end of the attempt. Or, at another time, perhaps we would have done a better job of learning from our mistakes and have developed less ambitious, more effective programs. But the demands for urban renewal programs and jobs programs and training programs were growing, not diminishing, as the disappointing results began to come in. We were not in a position to back off, and, in fact, funding for such programs continued to grow for years. Neither, however, could we depend on such programs to solve the poverty problem.

The forces converged—not neatly, not at any one point that we can identify as the crucial shift. But the intellectual analysis of the nature of structural poverty had given a respectable rationale for accepting that it was not the fault of the poor that they were poor. It was a very small step from that premise to the conclusion that it is not the fault of the poor that they fail to pull themselves up when we offer them a helping hand. White moral confusion about the course of the civil rights movement in general and the riots in particular created powerful reasons to look for excuses. It was the system's fault. It was history's fault. Tom Wicker summed up the implications for policy toward the poor:

Really compassionate and effective reforms to do something about poverty in America would have to recognize, first, that large numbers of the poor are always going to have to be helped. Whether for physical or mental reasons, because of environmental factors, or whatever, they cannot keep pace. . . . Thus the aim of getting everyone off welfare and into "participation in our affluent society" is unreal and a pipe dream. . . . [A] decent standard of living ought to be made available not just to an eligible few but to everyone, and without degrading restrictions and policelike investigations.[41]

The column ran on the day before Christmas, 1967. It followed by only a few months an announcement from the White House. Joseph Califano, principal aide to Lyndon Johnson, had called reporters into his office to tell them that a government analysis had shown that only 50,000 persons, or *1 percent* of the 7,300,000 people on welfare, were capable of being given skills and training to make them self-sufficient.[42] The repudiation of the dream—to end the dole once and for all—was complete.

3

Implementing the Elite Wisdom

I N *The Structure of Scientific Revolutions,* Thomas Kuhn describes the history of science as a sequence of "paradigm shifts."[1] The universe is Aristotelian for centuries, then, abruptly, Newtonian; Newtonian for centuries, then, abruptly, Einsteinian. There is no in-between—no half-Newtonian, half Einsteinian physics. The new paradigm rules utterly. Kuhn likens it to a religious conversion experience. What was heresy yesterday becomes dogma today. Whether Kuhn was right about science is still being debated. But he could well have been describing the turnaround in the American intellectual consensus from 1964 to 1967. The change can be seen as analogous to Kuhn's "paradigm shifts" in two respects—how the shift occurred, and among whom.

An Elite Wisdom

In speaking of the paradigm shift of the reform period, it is important to specify who did the shifting. The mid- and late-1960s did not see a revolution in American opinion. The analogy to the reform period in the sixties is not the New Deal, which enjoyed broad, often enthusiastic public support. Rather, the 1964–67 reform period reminded Daniel Patrick Moynihan of the English suffrage reform of 1867, "most especially in the degree to which neither was the result of any great popular agitation on behalf of the measures that were eventually adopted."[2] For the blue-collar and white-collar electorate, not much changed. For them, the welfare cheats and loafers still loomed large, and sturdy self-reliance was still a chief virtue. For them, criminals ought to be locked up, students ought to shut up and do what the teacher says, demonstrators ought to go home and quit interrupting traffic.

The shift in assumptions occurred among a small group relative to the entire population, but one of enormous influence. The group is, with no pejorative connotations, best labeled the intelligentsia—a broad and diffuse group in late-twentieth-century America, but nonetheless identifiable in a rough fashion. It includes the upper echelons of (in no particular order of importance) academia, journalism, publishing, and the vast network of foundations, institutes, and research centers that has been woven into partnership with government during the last thirty years. An important and little-recognized part of the intelligentsia is also found in the civil service, in the key positions just below the presidential appointment level, where so much of the policy formation goes on. Politicians and members of the judiciary (Senator J. William Fulbright and Justice William O. Douglas are examples from the sixties) and bankers and businessmen and lawyers and doctors may be members of the intelligentsia as well, though not all are. I do not mean to provide a tightly constructed definition, but a sense of the population: people who deal professionally in ideas.

For purposes of understanding the nature of the shift in assumptions, the salient feature of the intelligentsia is not that it holds power—though many of its members occupy powerful positions—but that at any given moment it is the custodian of the received wisdom. It originates most of the ideas in the dialogue about policy, writes about them, publishes them, puts them on television and in the magazines and in memoranda for presidential assistants. Most of all, it confers respectability on ideas. I do not mean to trivialize the seriousness of the process, but it is akin to fashion. Ideas are "in" and ideas are "out," for reasons having something to do with their merit but also with being au courant. We may recall the fashionability of being thought "liberal" in the early sixties (and, for that matter, the unfashionability of being thought "a liberal" in the early eighties).

My thesis is that the last half of the 1960s saw remarkably broad agreement on the directions in which a just and effective social policy must move, and this agreement—this "elite wisdom"—represented an abrupt shift with the past.

The shift in assumptions first became apparent in 1964. By the end of 1967—probably earlier—the nature of the political dialogue had been altered unrecognizably. It was not just that by the end of 1967 certain types of legislation had more support than formerly, but the premises—the unconscious, "everybody-knows-that" premises—shifted in the minds of the people who were instrumental in making policy.

The New Premises

We may debate the list of new premises and their order of priority. Theodore White (among many others) describes the shift from "equality of opportunity" to "equality of outcome" as a fundamental change.[3] The sponsors of the Civil Rights Act of 1964, with Hubert Humphrey in the lead, had come down adamantly on the side of equality of opportunity—the nation was to be made color-blind. The wording of the legislation itself expressly dissociated its provisions from preferential treatment. Yet only a year later, speaking at Howard University commencement exercises, Lyndon Johnson was proclaiming the "next and most profound stage of the battle for civil rights," namely, the battle "not just [for] equality as a right and theory but equality as a fact and equality as a result."[4] A few months later, Executive Order 11246 required "affirmative action." By 1967, people who opposed preferential measures for minorities to overcome the legacy of discrimination were commonly seen as foot-draggers on civil rights if not closet racists.

A number of writers have pointed to a combination of two events: the ascendency of legal stipulations as the only guarantor of fair treatment and the contemporaneous Balkanization of the American population into discrete "minorities." Before 1964, blacks were unique. They constituted the only group suffering discrimination so pervasive and so persistent that laws *for that group* were broadly accepted as necessary. By 1967, blacks were just one of many minorities, each seeking equal protection as a group. Each assumed that express legislation and regulation spelling out its rights was —of course—the only way to secure fair treatment of the individual member of the group. For minorities such as juveniles and the mentally handicapped, the remedy was access to legal due process. Before 1964, it was assumed that their interests were best looked after by parents and relatives, with a limited role for the court. Even when the court did become involved, it was in a parental role. After 1967, it was assumed (by Supreme Court decision) that due process was the only adequate protection for anyone.[5] For populations such as the elderly, women, and the physically handicapped, the change meant regulatory intervention. Why should they be less protected from discrimination than blacks?

Too many things were going on too fast during the 1960s for us to identify the nuclear change in the elite wisdom with certainty. But the new stances just described, though important in themselves, were enabled by a deeper change in the perception of how American society works. There was a reason why they made sense when only a few years earlier they had not. I suggest that this more primitive change was the one described in the last chapter: from a view of the American system as benign and self-correcting to the pervasive assumption that if something was wrong, the system was to blame. *Why* was it necessary to use the government to promote equality of outcome? Because, left alone, the system would perpetuate unacceptable inequality. *Why* was it necessary to spell out the prohibitions against any form of discrimination against any group and to buttress them with enforcing agencies? Because, left alone, the system would tolerate discriminatory behavior. Ultimately, the rationale for the sweeping changes in practice that occurred in the last half of the 1960s had to fall back upon a belief that the system as it existed prior to 1964 was deeply flawed and tended to perpetuate evils.

The New Alms

The policy ramifications of the new wisdom were labyrinthine. The accepted ways of looking at poverty, race, education, crime, and the natural role of the federal government all acquired a new center from which political and intellectual discourse radiated. Of these, I shall argue that the most important, with the most profound influence on the lives of the poor and disadvantaged, was the change in the meaning of "a job." The change was vast, written into law, and accepted as the natural thing to do by both the Johnson and Nixon administrations.

In the fiscal 1964 federal budget, the last of the pre-Johnson budgets, public assistance funds for working people were effectively nil, as they always had been. The major programs for the working-aged population—AFDC and Unemployment Insurance—were for the jobless.

The exclusion of working people (no matter how small their incomes) was not accidental, but neither was it much talked about. A citizen in good standing was self-supporting. To have a job was ipso facto to be self-supporting. If the income from that job was less than one liked, it was up to the job-holder to do something about it. This was not only the opinion of middle America; it was the old elite wisdom as well. Politically, it did not visibly occur to leaders of either major party prior to 1964 that people who had jobs ought to get welfare assistance.

At bottom, however, the pre-1964 consensus about no welfare for working people rested on a fragile assumption: that adults are responsible for the state in which they find themselves. It was fragile because most people had recognized for years that the assumption, strictly speaking, was not true. One's inheritance mattered. Circumstances mattered. Luck mattered. Because it was not true, a second assumption was needed to buttress it: All things considered, the system was doing all that it properly could by trying to provide equal opportunity.

Once the consensus about the second assumption had been breached—once it was accepted that the system was to blame for people being poor—policy principles that had gone unargued were instantaneously outdated. Among these was the principle that the government should not support employed people. If the system was to blame that the person was trapped in a job that paid too little money for a decent existence, then the principle was palpably unfair—so unfair that, like the principle it replaced, it did not need to be debated.

This was the "conversion" aspect of the paradigm shift. Before 1964, we did not debate welfare for working people because the reasons against it were so self-evident; after 1967 we did not debate the issue because the reasons in favor of it were so self-evident. There was no great debate in the interim, no moment at which the nation could observe itself changing its national policy. The change happened unannounced. The thematic congressional debate after the mid-1960s was not whether to include the working poor in new programs, but the conditions under which they would be included.

Richard Nixon, always a pugnacious critic of welfare, exemplified the breadth of the new consensus. Nixon had lambasted the Great Society during the 1968 campaign. His administration promptly set about dismantling its appurtenances (for example, OEO). But it was Nixon who, only six years after the first antipoverty bill, introduced the Family Assistance

Plan (FAP), a form of negative income tax, so that "[t]he government would recognize that it has not less of an obligation to the working poor than to the non-working poor."[6]

Congress rejected the FAP for reasons that have been told in fascinating detail elsewhere.[7] But Supplemental Security Income (SSI) and expansions of Food Stamps, public housing, Social Security, and other forms of welfare for working people were passed by the same Congresses that debated the FAP. Hardly anyone except the most obdurate reactionaries opposed such programs in principle. Hardly anyone argued that it was fundamentally *wrong* to take tax dollars from one worker whose paycheck, the government had decided, was too large, and give them to another worker whose paycheck, the government had decided, was too small. Ten years earlier, hardly anyone would have argued that it was right.

The Reforms

The shift in policy toward poverty, welfare, and the working poor was paralleled by policy changes in education, law enforcement, and social services that we will be reviewing in subsequent chapters. Throughout the presentation of these specifics and the exploration of their consequences, I will be taking for granted some characteristics of the reforms that may not be familiar to some readers.

NEW RULEMAKERS

The reform period coincided with the Johnson administration in that almost all of the enabling *actions*—the legislation, the court decisions, and the changes in administrative policy within the executive branch (mainly HEW) with which we will be concerned—occurred during that period. The "changes in the rules," as I characterize the reforms, were announced to the players during those years.

Some of the changes were also implemented then. But almost none of these early changes had to do with the legislation that is usually associated with the Great Society. It took some years for the funding programs to get up to speed, and the effects of those programs are to be sought in the seventies. It was the changes caused by administrative fiat that could and often did have pervasive effects on people almost immediately.

Sometimes such reforms were promulgated unilaterally by government agencies. The legislation concerning consumer safety and environmental safety, for example, gave broad latitude to agencies to establish mandatory standards, and these often had lasting effects, good and bad, on the people and industries to whom they were applied. Even when the changes were legislatively authorized, the mechanisms that gave them their influence had less to do with the formal penalties of the law than with other factors. As Nathan Glazer puts it, referring specifically to Standard Form 100 of the Equal Employment Opportunity Commission: "Today crucial documents in American history are not necessarily to be found in legislation, executive action, or even the court orders of our powerful judiciary. The modest reporting forms issued by regulatory agencies may be as consequential as any of these."[8]

Sometimes the changes just "happened," more or less invisibly. Disability compensation is a case in point. The program was established in 1956 and liberalized in 1960. Thereafter, the Congress occasionally changed the law a bit—most conspicuously in 1965, when eligibility was changed from permanent or long-lasting disability to a disability lasting twelve consecutive months. But a disability lasting twelve consecutive months is very likely to be "long-lasting" anyway, so the change did not attract much attention. The definition of a qualifying disability remained quite strict.[9] Medical advances in rehabilitating the disabled during the period were striking. By all logic, the proportion of the population receiving disability insurance should have dropped over time. Or perhaps not dropped, given the liberalized rules, but increased modestly. Instead, this is what happened from 1960 through the time that the program was subsumed under Supplemental Security Income:[10]

Year	Number of Disability Beneficiaries	Change (Base: 1960)
1960	687,000	
1965	1,739,000	+153%
1970	2,665,000	+288%
1975	4,352,000	+533%

During the same period that the number of beneficiaries increased by 533 percent, the number of workers covered by the program increased by 30 percent.[11] Something odd was happening to the way Americans used the disability insurance program and the way the government administered it.[12] It amounted to an unnoticed extension of a welfare program that importantly affects the lives of millions of Americans.

Other instances are widely believed to exist, but we have only vague ideas about their real magnitude. Enforcement of eligibility rules for Unemployment Insurance, AFDC, and other welfare programs changed during the 1960s—occasionally by explicit federal policy directives, but often through a generally understood but hard-to-document change in the "way of doing business." The operation of the courts changed dramatically during the 1960s, only partly for reasons that can be pinned down in Supreme Court directives and legislative specifications.

Of all the procedural changes, the most important have been those mandated by the courts. Some decisions are famous: the busing decisions and those affecting the rights of criminal defendants, for example. Others such as *Gault* v. *Arizona* or *King* v. *Smith* are unfamiliar to the general public but were highly significant in transforming practice in the areas where they applied (juvenile justice and education in the case of *Gault,* AFDC in the case of *King*). Furthermore, and in sharp contrast to the slow pace with which legislation is translated into action, the court decisions can have (and often did have, under the Warren Court) effects on behavior within a matter of months—occasionally, days.

THE MONEY CAME LATER

In contrast, the great legislative victories that required money for implementation did not begin to affect large numbers of persons until about 1967–68 and did not reach full scope until the 1970s. The underlying principles changed earlier. The rhetoric began earlier. The implementing agencies began earlier. The legislation began earlier. But the income maintenance and social action programs that were authorized during Johnson's legislative hegemony in 1964–66 had relatively small budgets and scope during his term in office. Two examples, the Food Stamp program and the jobs programs, will illustrate the point.

The Food Stamp program under Lyndon Johnson began with 424,000 participants in 1965.[13] When Johnson left office, it served 2.2 million people. In the first two Nixon years, that number doubled. By the end of the next two, it had quintupled. By 1980, the number of participants had grown to 21.1 million—fifty times the coverage of the original Great Society legislation, ten times the coverage of the program at the end of the Johnson administration.

Under Lyndon Johnson, first-time enrollees in work and training programs reached a high of 833,300 in 1967. Under the Comprehensive Employment and Training Act (CETA), passed in 1973, annual first-time enrollments ranged between a low of 1.9 million (2.3 times the Johnson peak) and a high of 4.0 million (4.8 times the Johnson peak).[14]

In terms of real expenditures on social programs, the Johnson years were more like the Kennedy and Eisenhower years than they were like the Nixon, Ford, or Carter years. To illustrate this, consider the public aid category of the federal budget.[15] Using constant 1980 dollars as the basis of comparison, we find that during the five Johnson years (fiscal 1965–69), the federal government spent a total of $66.2 billion on public aid. This was $30 billion more than was spent during the five preceding years—a major increase. But in the five years immediately after Johnson, public aid spending rose by $80 billion. In other words, the increase in the five years after Johnson was 2.7 times larger (in constant dollars) than the increase from Eisenhower/Kennedy to Johnson.[16]

Figure 3.1 shows the size of the public aid component of the social welfare budget from 1950 to 1980. In addition to using constant dollars, the expenditures are shown on a per capita basis to take population increase into account. The broken lines are drawn to indicate where the 1980 social welfare budget would have been had the current rates of increase been sustained. The "take-off" effect of the Johnson years is evident. Note also that the rate of growth in expenditures did not slow during the Nixon years. It continued to accelerate.

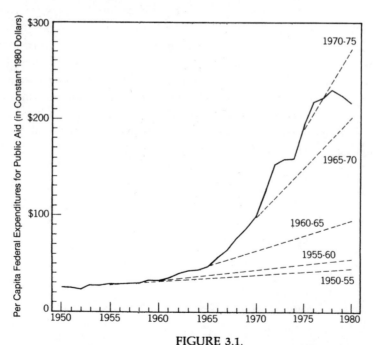

FIGURE 3.1.
Per Capita Public Aid Expenditures, in Constant Dollars, 1950–1980
DATA AND SOURCE INFORMATION: Appendix tables 1 and 2.

By the end of the 1970s, inflation was eating into budget increases to such an extent that real expenditures declined slightly. Despite this, overall growth of real expenditures over the 1975–80 period, an uneventful period for social policy, was about as great as during the Johnson years. The norm had changed. We will see the same pattern repeatedly with other elements of the budget: comparatively small budget increments during 1964–68, followed by a surging rise.

ON HORSES AND CARTS

In the next chapters, because I am focusing on federal social policy, the federal role looms too large. Even if Johnson had not issued Executive Order 11246, there would have been state and local attempts to implement something like Affirmative Action. Even if the Supreme Court had remained silent, many educators would have been urging a more sympathetic approach to the needs of troubled students. Even if Congress had not passed the Food Stamp program, many states would have been trying to increase public support for poor people. The federal reforms generally ratified an elite wisdom that would have had substantial influence on local and state practices regardless of action at the federal level. It is surely inaccurate to infer from the discussion that, without Lyndon Johnson and the Warren Court, none of this would have happened.

But federal legislation is generally harder to repeal than city council resolutions. Supreme Court decisions are harder to reverse than a ruling by a local judge. Federal actions apply nationwide, not to a few cities or states. Because of what happened at the federal level, the new elite wisdom did not have just a moment in the sun in scattered communities. It became national policy, embedded beyond the reach of easy reconsideration in laws, regulations, and judicial precedent.

PART II

Being Poor, Being Black: 1950–1980

DATA are not essential to certain arguments about social policy and indeed can get in the way. The terms of debate can be grounded wholly in preferences about how the world ought to be, not how it is. But in practice most of us are not entirely indifferent to what has happened. We are prepared to modify our prescriptions if not our preferences.

The problem is that almost no one knows "what happened." We know the current unemployment figure, and perhaps what it was a year ago. But few can draw a sketch of the unemployment rate over the last ten years, let alone the last three decades. Most of us know that divorces and crime and illegitimate births are "high," and we have a general idea that they have been getting higher. But since when? At what rates? For other important indicators such as labor force participation, few people other than specialists have an idea even of the direction in which the trendlines have been moving. The foggy impressions that do exist are often mistaken.

The purpose of the following chapters is to describe trendlines for some of the most basic social and economic indicators. We ask: How have the poor and the disadvantaged been doing?

For one indicator—the poverty line—answering the question is a matter of counting how many people are poor. For all the other indicators, we must first identify who "the poor and the disadvantaged" are and then obtain the statistics that describe their experience. And as soon as we try to do that, we encounter a barrier.

Even if we had available to us breakdowns by income level, they would not answer the question. It will do us no good to ask, for example, whether unemployment among the poor has been improving, because we bias the answer by insisting that the subjects be poor. What we really want to know is whether the poor are successful in getting steady, well-paid jobs (which then take them out of poverty), or whether their children are successful in getting jobs. What we would really like is a longitudinal sample of the disadvantaged—people who are poorly educated, downtrodden, disproportionately shut out of participation in American society. If social policy is successful, we should see improvement in their situation over time.

The customary—indeed, virtually the only practicable—way to deal with this problem is by using a racial breakdown, namely, by comparing the trendline among blacks with the trendline among whites. But let me be precise about what is being compared.

The use of racial breakdowns is common in the technical literature and in a variety of popular statistics—news reports of the unemployment rate, for example.[1] In the popular press, a discrepancy between the black figure and the white figure is usually interpreted as (or the audience is allowed to assume it to be) evidence of continuing racial discrimination. In the technical literature, the analyst ordinarily tries to find out how much of the racial discrepancy remains after other explanatory factors are taken into account.

The presentation here follows the assumption in the technical literature that race is confounded with other factors. Given the published material, however, we cannot control for the "other factors" over three decades of data; if we want to take a look at trends over the long run, we give up that capacity.[2] But we do know that blacks in the United States, besides being vulnerable to outright racial discrimination, are disproportionately poor and disproportionately disadvantaged in educational background, economic status, and social status. We may take advantage of this situation to use the statistics for blacks in the United States as the best-available proxy for the longitudinal sample of "disadvantaged Americans" that would be preferable.

The comparison is by no means pure. On the contrary, it is highly contaminated. In 1980, for example, there were 1.4 million black households with a money income in excess of $25,000, the members of which are surely exasperated at the impressions left by constant invidious statistical comparisons of blacks with whites.[3] By the same token, large numbers of whites are poor, ignorant, and vulnerable to exploitation. In 1980, 19.7 million whites were living beneath the poverty level (about 2.3 times the number of blacks), many of whom are surely exasperated at comparisons that make "white" interchangeable with "doing fine."[4]

The comparison is further contaminated because, although I often use the term "blacks" in the text, the data almost always will refer to "blacks and others," with the "others" consisting almost entirely of Asians and American Indians. (Note that "Hispanic" is not a racial category, and Hispanics are not included in the "others" category.)[5] I use "black and others" data instead of black-only because there is no choice; on all except a few indicators, the data were not broken down more finely until the mid-1960s. The problem is that, first, most of the "others" (two-thirds, by the end of the 1970s) have been Asian, a population group that often is conspicuously *above* the national norms on measures of income and educational achievement; and second, the proportion of the "others" category grew from 4.5 percent of the "black and others" category in 1950 to about 16 percent in 1980, softening somewhat the harshness of the trends we will be examining.[6]

But we are speaking of proportions. The comparison between black (or "black and others") and white is an imprecise but nonetheless useful comparison over time between "disadvantaged" Americans in general (blacks) and "advantaged" Americans in general (whites), blurred by the members of both groups who fail to fit their category.

This does not mean we must ignore the effects of discrimination against blacks, nor differences in black and white culture, nor the specific impact during the 1960s of the civil rights movement. To do so would be myopic. But I always approach the data with the preliminary hypothesis that a black-white difference murkily reflects a difference between poor and not-poor, not a racially grounded difference. This hypothesis is almost never completely right, and the discussion in following chapters will repeatedly make note of that fact. But social and economic phenomena that we have too readily considered to be "black" in recent history are often phenomena that have been occurring predominantly among poor and disadvantaged people, black and white alike, and have been occurring at much lesser levels among people who are not poor or disadvantaged, black and white alike. Our explanations of why they have been occurring must start from this observation.

4

Poverty

REDUCING POVERTY was the central objective of federal social programs during the reform period. Policymakers and legislators hoped for a variety of good things from the War on Poverty and OEO, the entitlements, and the widening population of eligible recipients. But, whatever else the programs were to accomplish, they were to put more money in the hands of poor people. They were to reduce poverty.

The story of what happened to poverty in the years after the reforms took effect, in comparison with what was happening earlier, epitomizes the history of the other indicators we will be examining. The figures do not "make sense" on their own—just as the figures on unemployment, labor force participation, education, crime, and the family will not make sense. The numbers go the wrong way at the wrong time.

The popular conception about poverty is that, at least on this one fundamental goal, the Great Society brought progress. The most widely shared view of history has it that the United States entered the 1960s with a large population of poor people—Harrington's "other America"—who had been bypassed by the prosperity of the Eisenhower years. The rich and the middle class had gained, but the poor had not. Then, after fits and starts during the Kennedy years, came the explosion of programs under Johnson. These programs were perhaps too ambitious, it is widely conceded, and perhaps the efforts were too helter-skelter. But most people seem to envision a plot in which dramatic improvement did not really get started until the programs of the Great Society took effect.[1]

The reality is that improvement was stopping, not starting, during that time. The nature of the puzzle to be explored for the next six chapters is shown for the case of poverty in figure 4.1. The definition of "poverty" is the official one, based on cash income. An extended discussion of the nature of the official poverty measure may be found in the notes.[2] The line labeled "dollars" refers to the amount of cash for the needy given out by the federal government.[3] Poverty did fall during the five Johnson years, from 18 percent of the population in 1964 to 13 percent in 1968, his last year in office, and the slope of the decrease was the steepest during this period. But the rest of the graph showing poverty before 1964 and after 1968 reveals the fallacy in the popular conception of historical cause and effect.

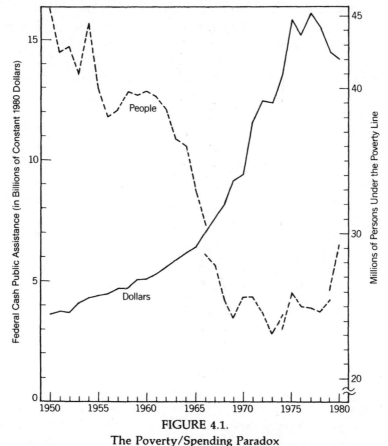

FIGURE 4.1.
The Poverty/Spending Paradox

DATA AND SOURCE INFORMATION: Appendix table 3 (cash public assistance) and appendix table 5 (people in poverty).
NOTE: Breaks in the poverty line indicate revisions in the method of calculation.

In the first place, as noted in chapter 3, the Great Society reforms had very limited budgets through the Johnson administration. The real annual expenditures of the 1970s were far larger—by many orders of magnitude, for some of the programs—than expenditures in the sixties. Yet progress against poverty stopped in the seventies. The steep declines in poverty from 1964 to 1968 cannot glibly be linked with government antipoverty dollar expenditures.

Secondly, the declines in poverty *prior* to 1964 were substantial. In 1950, the first year shown in figure 4.1, poverty had stood at approximately 30 percent of the population. From there it declined to the 18 percent of Johnson's first year. The size of the officially "impoverished" population dropped by about 17 percentage points in the years from 1950 to 1968, of which the Johnson years accounted for five: about their fair share.[4]

Then, after two decades of reasonably steady progress, improvement slowed in the late sixties and stopped altogether in the seventies. The proportion dipped to its low point, 11 percent, in 1973. A higher proportion of the American population was officially poor in 1980 than at any time since 1967. By then it stood at 13 percent and was heading up. The number of people living in poverty stopped declining just as the public-assistance program budgets and the rate of increase in those budgets were highest. The question is why this should be.

If we were asking about progress in reducing a problem like chronic unemployment, explanations would be easier. Fixing the last 10 percent of a problem is often more difficult than fixing the first 90 percent of it. But poverty as officially defined is a matter of cash in hand from whatever source. The recipient of the benefits does not have to "do" anything—does not have to change behavior or values, does not have to "qualify" in any way except to be a recipient. To eliminate such poverty, all we need do is mail enough checks with enough money to enough people. In the late sixties, still more in the seventies, the number of checks, the size of the checks, and the number of beneficiaries all increased. Yet, perversely, poverty chose those years to halt a decline that had been underway for two decades.

"Of Course Progress Stopped—The Economy Went Bad"

The explanation that comes first to mind is that the bright hopes of the sixties dimmed in the seventies as the economy slowed. According to this view, inflation and the dislocations brought on by the Vietnam War, along with the revolution in energy prices, hobbled the economy. As the expansionist environment of the sixties vanished, strategies and programs of the War on Poverty had to be put aside.

What, if anything, do the data suggest about the merits of this economic explanation? Let us take the simplest, most widely used measure of the state of the economy, growth in GNP, and examine its relation to changes in the number of people living in poverty. The answer, despite the ridicule heaped on "trickle-down" as a way to help the poor, is that changes in GNP have a very strong inverse relation to changes in poverty. As GNP increases, poverty decreases. But we cannot use this relationship to explain why we stopped making progress against poverty in the 1970s. Economic growth during the 1970s was actually *greater* than during the peacetime 1950s, memories of Eisenhower prosperity notwithstanding. The average annual growth rate from 1953 to 1959 was 2.7 percent, noticeably lower than the average annual growth of 3.2 percent from 1970 to 1979.[5] Moreover, the lower growth of the seventies took the form of a few very bad years. During those years that had growth rates as high as those of the palmy days of the 1960s, the trendlines on poverty "should" have behaved as they did during the comparable growth years of the fifties and sixties. But they did not.[6]

Upon consideration, it will also be apparent that in important ways the 1970s were even richer than the percentage increases in GNP indicate, because the base for calculating the percentage increase kept getting larger. The real dollar increase in GNP during the 1970s was half again as large as in the 1950s. This sizable increase holds up when we also control for population change. Figure 4.2 shows a second aspect of the poverty paradox, the way that poverty quit dropping while per capita GNP continued to grow. Even after holding both population change and inflation constant, per capita GNP increased only a little less rapidly in the seventies than it had in the booming sixties, and much faster than during the fifties. Growth did not stop. But, for some reason, the benefits of economic growth stopped trickling down to the poor.

"Of Course Progress Stopped—Because of the Old People"

This book is about social policy as it affects the working-aged and their children. Social policy for the elderly is a completely different topic, de-

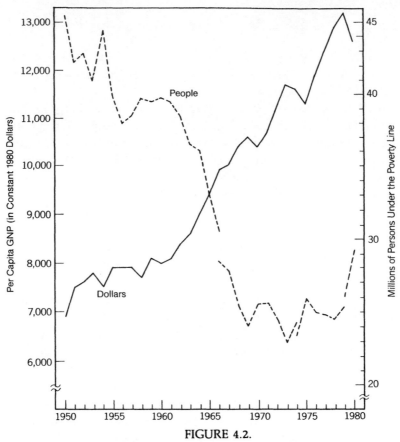

FIGURE 4.2.

Poverty and Economic Growth, 1950–1980

DATA AND SOURCE INFORMATION: Appendix tables 1 and 3 (for computation of GNP per capita) and appendix table 5 (people in poverty).
NOTE: Breaks in the poverty line indicate revisions in the method of calculation.

manding a full treatment of its own. But the population of retirement-aged persons provides a plausible explanation for the poverty paradoxes. The hypothesis is that, as the proportion of elderly in the population increased from 9.9 percent in 1970 to 11.3 percent in 1980, the number of people dependent on government help inevitably increased as well, and it is this which explains the flattening trendlines in the seventies. The income transfers worked as planned, according to this line of argument, but their effectiveness among the working-aged population was masked by the increasing amounts of money that were going to retired persons with no other income except government payments.

The validity of the hypothesis is easily checked. The poverty statistics for 1959 and for 1966–80 include separate figures for the elderly. I use these to calculate official poverty among the working-aged. The results are shown in figure 4.3. Eliminating the elderly only accentuates the trends we

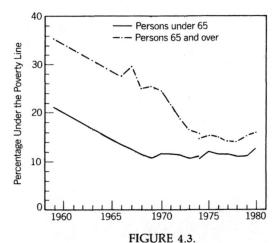

FIGURE 4.3.
Poverty Among the Working-Aged, 1959–1980
DATA AND SOURCE INFORMATION: Appendix table 5.

have examined. Progress against poverty stopped *sooner* and *more completely* for the working-aged than for the population as a whole. Progress among the under-65s did not just begin to slow in the late sixties (as for the population as a whole). It effectively hit bottom.

"Progress Didn't Really Stop—Blacks Kept Gaining"

Even if poverty had stopped decreasing among the population as a whole, there is reason, given the logic of the structuralist school of poverty, that poverty among blacks might have continued to drop nonetheless.[7] Suppose that racial discrimination had created a segmented labor market and otherwise kept poor blacks from sharing in the bounty of a growing economy. If so, then the black population as of the late 1960s would have included a large proportion of poor people who were trapped in poverty despite the economic boom. In that case, white reductions in poverty might track with economic growth, but black reductions would be contingent on the income transfers, jobs programs, and other special measures that moved into high gear in the seventies. Let us compare this possibility with what actually happened to working-aged blacks (persons under 65) in figure 4.4.

As the figure indicates, black progress did not continue into the seventies. It stopped very much as white progress stopped. But it does provide,

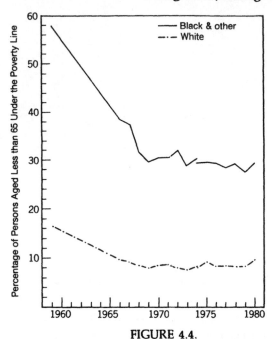

FIGURE 4.4.
Poverty and Working-Aged Blacks, 1959–1980
Data and Source Information: Appendix table 5.

vividly, the reason why many still remember the Great Society fondly.
Imagine that you were shown the graph a few months after Lyndon Johnson had left office in 1969. The impulse to credit the government programs
would have been almost irresistible. In 1959, 58 percent of working-aged
blacks were below the poverty line. A single decade later, the percentage
was 30 percent—a precipitous drop of 28 percentage points in ten years.
Blacks did indeed make economic progress in the sixties, huge progress for
such a short period of time.

But we are not examining the graph as it looked in 1969. We are seeing
it with the experience of the seventies tacked on, and our perspective on
the sixties has changed accordingly. We know that in 1969 funding of the
programs that were then being given credit for the progress was still
relatively low compared with later years (when progress did not continue).
We are more aware that greatest progress occurred in 1963, 1964, 1965, and
1966, when the reforms were little more than rhetoric. We are more aware
of the pump that the Vietnam War was giving to the economy from 1966
through the end of the decade.

Most important, we are aware that the graph for the 1970s did not
continue that steep downward sweep, but rather stopped short—that the
figure reached in 1969 for blacks was about 1 percentage point from its

bottom. During the period following 1959, black progress against poverty among the working-aged coincided with the civil rights movement and with the general economic boom that began in the early 1960s. Progress *stopped* coincidentally with the implementation of the Great Society's social welfare reforms. This need not be accepted as evidence of causality (though I will argue causality eventually). It must, however, be recognized as a statement of fact.

"Progress Didn't Really Stop—The Poverty Measure Is Misleading"

The official poverty statistic is based on gross cash income. What would happen if we were to include the dollar value of the "in-kind" assistance (Food Stamps, Medicaid, housing benefits) in income? What would happen if we were to take underreporting of income into account? What would happen if we were to take tax and social security liabilities into account? In other words, what would the poverty figure look like if we were to consider net income available for consumption spending? Timothy Smeeding, then at the Institute for Research on Poverty, developed such an estimate, which I shall refer to as "net poverty": the percentage of the population remaining beneath the poverty level after net income for consumption spending has been estimated.[8]

In the fifties, in-kind transfers were so small that we may assume the percentage of net poor was within a percentage point or two of the official figure (the underreporting factor was the source of any difference between the figures, offset to some extent by tax liabilities). As late as 1968, the gap between official poverty and net poverty was still quite small—only 2.9 percentage points.

The decreases in net poverty continued into the early 1970s. It was 1972 when progress on net poverty slowed, two years after the marked slowdown in the fall of official poverty. Thereafter, net poverty failed to sustain additional reductions. In 1979, net poverty stood at 6.1 percent of the population, compared with 6.2 percent in 1972, despite more than a doubling of real expenditures on in-kind assistance during the interim. Using net poverty as the measure changes the size of the baseline of persons living in poverty, but it does not change the nature of the puzzle: Huge increases in expenditures coincided with an end to progress.[9]

The Most Damning Statistic: Latent Poverty

Imagine that the United States has decided to eliminate poverty among, say, Native Americans, and to that end it has put them all on reservations where there are no jobs to be had and has given everyone an income just above the poverty level. Can we claim to have eliminated poverty? In one sense, yes—the sense measured by the poverty statistic we have been using. But there would also be widespread outcry about the plight of the Indians because everybody on the reservation would be poor without government help. The "latent poverty" level, as I shall term it, is 100 percent.

In 1964, when the War on Poverty began, almost all the emphasis was on eliminating poverty in this more fundamental sense of eliminating dependence on public assistance for a decent standard of living. Kennedy and Johnson alike wanted to eliminate the need for a dole. The official poverty statistic does not measure progress toward this goal—a fact that has not been brought to the fore in public debate of progress against poverty. The official measure has nothing to do with the ability of people to make a living for themselves.

I therefore ask: What is the number of poor *before* the governmental transfers are taken into account? This population constitutes the "latent poor." It has been determined by subtracting all government payments (AFDC, Social Security, Disability Payments, SSI) from total reported income in the March Current Population Survey of the Bureau of the Census, then comparing the remaining income with the poverty level.[10] Thus the "latent poor" include those who show up below the poverty level in the official measure, plus those who are above the poverty line in the official measure only by virtue of government support. The concept of latent poverty enables us to examine the dependent population in this country, those whom the Kennedy and Johnson initiatives started out to help in the first place. Figure 4.5 displays the trendline for latent poverty, with the "official" and "net" poverty figures drawn in for purposes of comparison.

Latent poverty decreased during the 1950s from approximately a third of the population to 21 percent by 1965.[11] Put another way, economic dependency decreased by about a third during the years 1950–65, up to the beginning of Johnson's War on Poverty. Increasing numbers of people had been able to make a living that put them above the poverty line.

The proportion of latent poor continued to drop through 1968, when the percentage was calculated at 18.2. This proved to be the limit of progress.

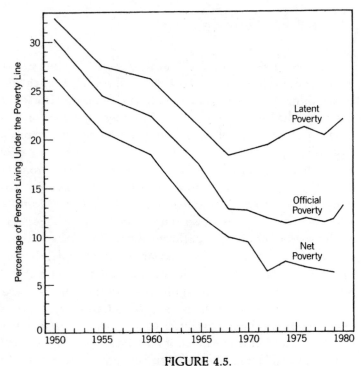

FIGURE 4.5.

Three Views of Poverty, 1950–1980

SOURCES: All figures are based on the March Current Population Survey conducted by the Bureau of the Census. "Official poverty" is the standard statistic published by the Bureau of the Census. See appendix table 5 for data and source information. "Latent poverty" figures for 1965–78 were taken from Sheldon Danziger and Robert Plotnick, "The War on Income Poverty," in *Welfare Reform in America,* edited by Paul M. Sommers (Boston: Kluwer-Nijhoff, 1982), table 3.1, 40. Latent poverty for 1980 was computed using the same procedures and a comparable data base, as reported in *Focus: Newsletter of the Institute for Research on Poverty* 7 (Winter 1984): 2. Figures for "Net poverty" are taken from Timothy M. Smeeding, "Recent Increase in Poverty in the U.S.: What the Official Estimates Fail to Show" (Testimony prepared for the Subcommittee on Oversight and Subcommittee on Public Assistance and Unemployment Compensation, Committee on Ways and Means, U.S. House of Representatives, 18 October 1983, table 4, 17). Figures for latent poverty and net poverty in 1950, 1955, and 1960 are estimated. See note 11, chapter 4.

At some point during 1968–70, the percentage began to grow, reaching 19 percent in 1972, 21 percent in 1976, and 22 percent by 1980.[12]

The reason for calling this the most damning of the statistics is that economic independence—standing on one's own abilities and accomplishments—is of paramount importance in determining the quality of a family's life. Hardly anyone, from whatever part of the political spectrum, will disagree. For this independence to have *decreased* would be an indictment of the American system whenever in our history it might have occurred. For it to begin decreasing in 1968–70 was odd but perhaps attributable to the slowing of the boom. For it to have continued to decrease throughout the seventies was extraordinary.

"It Would Have Been Worse Otherwise"

Once we have accepted that progress against poverty did in fact stop during the 1970s and, in the case of latent poverty, reversed, might there not be reason for thinking that things would have been much worse if the antipoverty transfers had not been enacted? We may consider, for example, the huge influx of women and baby-boom youths into the labor force during that period. From 1970 to 1980, the size of the total labor force increased by 24 percent, compared with a 13 percent increase from 1950 to 1960 and a 19 percent increase from 1960 to 1970.[13] Even a strong economy could not possibly absorb so many people, we hypothesize. The antipoverty budget made up for those who were left out. This logic is coordinate with a variety of other hypotheses about the effects of changes in the economy (a shift away from unskilled labor, for example) that made it more difficult for people at the bottom of the ladder to get a start.[14]

There is surely some truth to such arguments. On the other hand, employers for the millions of new jobs that were created during the 1970s did not hang out signs reading "Poor people need not apply." What happened, then, to the acquisition of jobs by the poor and disadvantaged? We begin with unemployment and labor force participation, and some events of the 1960s that confounded traditional expectations of the job market.

Summary of the Federal Effort

TO EACH of the chapters in part II, I append a brief account of the legislation, court decisions, and executive actions that constituted the federal effort during the reform period.

In the case of poverty, the scope of the federal effort to reduce poverty by means of income transfers dwarfs the rest of the programs we will consider. More accurately, it encompassed most of them and added other, very large programs as well. We will ignore for present purposes the jobs programs, equal employment efforts, and educational programs. On top of all these efforts was a huge expansion in the transfer of money and in-kind support. The principal components of the cash increases were expansions in public assistance (AFDC), Social Security and its associated programs, Unemployment Insurance, and general welfare assistance in the form of "Supplemental Security Income." The eligibility rules for AFDC were liberalized first through the 1962 Social Security Amendments, then through changes in HEW administrative guidelines in the mid-sixties, and finally by Supreme Court decisions (described in more detail in chapter 12). The size of the benefits kept increasing as well. Social Security was changed five times in the 1964–74 period. Eligibility rules were liberalized in a variety of ways—in the age limits for survivor benefits, in the amount of money that a person could earn without losing benefits, and the like. Congress passed across-the-board benefit increases of 7 percent (1965), 13 percent (1967), and 15 percent (1969), and then, in 1972, it hitched Social Security benefits to the Consumer Price Index. Unemployment insurance was broadened to cover more persons and to last longer.

The principal components of the in-kind transfers were Medicaid (for low-income persons), Medicare (for Social Security beneficiaries), Food Stamps, and housing programs. With the exception of Medicare, the in-kind transfers were "means-tested"; eligibility depended essentially on income level. All except the housing programs were creations of the 1964–67 reform period.

The trendline for total expenditures breaks naturally into halves: one slope for 1950–65, a distinctly steeper one for 1965–78. In 1979–80, extremely high inflation leveled off real expenditures, even though expenditures in current dollars continued to climb. The magnitude of the expenditures requires some thinking about before they become real: over $100 billion (in 1980 dollars) each year since the late-1960s; over $200 billion annually since the mid-1970s.

For an excellent summary of the expansions of the transfer programs, see Laurence E. Lynn, Jr., "A Decade of Policy Developments in the Income Maintenance System," in Robert H. Haveman, ed., *A Decade of Federal Antipoverty Programs: Achievements, Failures, and Lessons* (New York: Academic Press, 1977), pp. 55–117.

5

Employment

ONE REASON that economic growth in the 1970s lost its power to reduce poverty was that many of the poor were without jobs. If one has no job, it makes no difference how much the economy grows. Poverty remains.

The relationship between unemployment and poverty is not new. But a new element was added to the unemployment problem beginning in the mid-1960s. The job market behavior and experience of one critical group in the struggle against poverty—young black males—changed radically. These changes constitute perhaps the most curious of the phenomena of the post-reform period (the late 1960s and thereafter) and certainly one of the most significant.

Jobs as the Magic Bullet

In the early days of OEO, it was thought that enough jobs would win the war against poverty. Some poor people would have to be given other kinds of help as well—the disabled, some of the elderly, perhaps single-parent mothers of young children—but for most of the working-aged population, making a job available was believed to be the answer.

The apostles of structural poverty soon did away with that view in intellectual circles, but popular and political faith in the power of jobs to solve the problem survived through the 1970s. Among many in both political parties, "jobs programs" have been seen as the obvious solution to poverty if only the nation were willing to commit itself fully.

In reality, the United States mounted an immense and sustained effort to provide jobs and job training during the post-reform period. "A Summary of the Federal Effort" at the end of this chapter provides more detailed information, but a few summary statistics will convey a sense of the magnitude of the effort and how suddenly it came upon the American scene.

Between 1950 and 1960, the Department of Labor did virtually nothing to help poor people train for or find jobs. During the first half of the 1960s (1960–64), it spent a comparatively trivial half-billion dollars (in 1980 dollars) on jobs programs. From 1965 to 1969, as the Johnson initiatives got under way, a more substantial $8.8 billion was spent. In the 1970s through fiscal 1980, expenditures totaled $76.7 billion.[1]

The numbers of persons involved are even more impressive than the dollars. Figure 5.1 shows the history of first-time enrollees in job training and employment programs administered by the Department of Labor. From the time that the first MDTA trainees were cycled through the program in 1962–63 through fiscal 1980, 32.6 *million* persons were reported to have enrolled in one of the Department of Labor's programs. The number cannot be taken at face value—many of the program interventions were short or weak, many participants dropped out before they finished, and many in that figure of 32.6 million were repeaters. But the training and employment programs constituted an enormous national effort nonetheless. From 1965 to 1980, the federal government spent about the same amount on jobs programs, in constant dollars, as it spent on space exploration from 1958 through the first moon landing—an effort usually held up as the classic example of what the nation can accomplish if only it commits the necessary resources.[2]

Furthermore, the effort was concentrated on a relatively small portion of the population. From the beginning, the government jobs programs spent most of their money on disadvantaged youths in their late teens and early twenties. They were at the most critical time of their job development, they were supposed to be the most trainable, and they had the longest time to reap the benefits of help. In 1980, not an atypical year, 61 percent of the

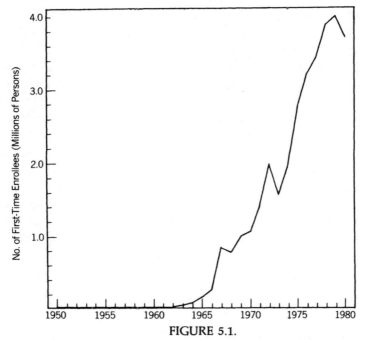

FIGURE 5.1.

First-time Enrollments for Work and Training Programs Administered by the
Department of Labor, 1950–1980

DATA AND SOURCE INFORMATION: Appendix table 4.

participants under CETA were 21 or younger, with a large but indeterminable additional proportion in their early twenties, and 36 percent were black.[3] To give a sense of the concentration of effort among blacks, there were two black CETA participants (of any age) for every five blacks aged 16–24 in the labor force. In the same year (1980), there was one white CETA participant for each fourteen whites in the same age range.

The contrast between the government's hands-off policy in the 1950s and intervention in the 1970s is so great that it seems inconceivable that we should not be able to observe positive changes in the macroeconomic statistics. And yet in fact the macroeconomic statistics went in exactly the wrong direction for the group that was at the top of the priority list.

Black Unemployment Rates: A Peculiarly Localized Problem

Let us first examine unemployment as officially defined[4] among those who were the primary beneficiaries of the jobs-program effort, black youth at the entry point to the labor market. Figure 5.2 shows the employment history for three age groups within this population from 1951 (the first year for which we have an age breakdown by race) to 1980, using a five-year moving average plot to highlight long-term trends.[5]

The picture is a discouraging one. In the early 1950s, black youths had an unemployment rate almost identical to that of whites. In the last half of the 1950s, the rate of unemployment among young blacks increased. John Cogan has recently demonstrated that the increase may be largely blamed on the loss of agricultural jobs for black teenagers, especially in the South.[6] As this dislocating transitional period came to an end, so did the increases in the unemployment rate for black youths. The rate stabilized during the early 1960s. It stabilized, however, at the unacceptably high rate of roughly a quarter of the black labor force in this age group. It appeared to observers during the Kennedy administration that a large segment of black youth was being frozen out of the job market, and this concern was at the heart of the congressional support for the early job programs.

Black unemployment among the older of the job entrants improved

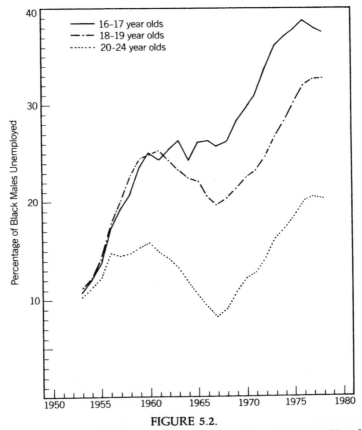

FIGURE 5.2.
Unemployment Among Black Job Entrants, 16–24 Years Old: Five-Year Moving Average, 1951–1980

DATA AND SOURCE INFORMATION: Appendix table 7.

somewhat during the Vietnam War years, although the figures remained higher than one would have predicted from the Korean War experience. But in the late 1960s—at the very moment when the jobs programs began their massive expansion (see figure 5.1)—the black youth unemployment rate began to rise again, steeply, and continued to do so throughout the 1970s.

If the 1950s were not good years for young blacks (and they were not), the 1970s were much worse. When the years from 1951 to 1980 are split into two parts, 1951–65 and 1966–80, and the mean unemployment rate is computed for each, one finds that black 20–24-year-olds experienced a 19 percent increase in unemployment. For 18–19-year-olds, the increase was 40 percent. For 16–17-year-olds, the increase was a remarkable 72 percent. If the war years are deleted, the increases in unemployment are higher still. Focusing on the age groups on which the federal jobs programs were focused not only fails to reveal improvement; it points to major losses. Something was happening to depress employment among young blacks.

The "something" becomes more mysterious when we consider that it was not having the same effect on older blacks. Even within the 16–24-year-old age groups, we may note that the relationship between age and deterioration seems to have been the opposite of the one expected. The older the age group, the less the deterioration. What happens if we consider all black age groups, including the ones that were largely ignored by the jobs and training programs? The year-by-year data are shown in the appendix, table 7. The summary statement is that, for whatever reasons, older black males (35 years old and above) did well. Not only did they seem to be immune from the mysterious ailment that affected younger black males, they made significant gains. We may compare the black male unemployment trends by age through the following figures:

Age Group	Change in Mean Unemployment, 1951–65 to 1966–80
55–64	−38.0 %
45–54	−32.9 %
35–44	−31.5 %
25–34	−15.9 %
20–24	+18.6 %
18–19	+39.7 %
16–17	+72.4 %

During the same fifteen-year period in which every black male age group at or above the age of 25 experienced *decreased* unemployment compared with the preceding fifteen years, every group under the age of 25 showed a major *increase* in unemployment. If it were not for the young, the overall black unemployment profile over 1950–80 would give cause for some satisfaction.

Black Youth versus White Youth: Losing Ground

If young whites had been doing as badly, we could ascribe the trends to macro phenomena that affected everybody, educated or not, rich or poor, discriminated-against or not. But young blacks lost ground to young whites. This is apparent when we examine the ratio of black unemployment to white unemployment—the measure of the racial differential—for the job entrants, as shown in figure 5.3:

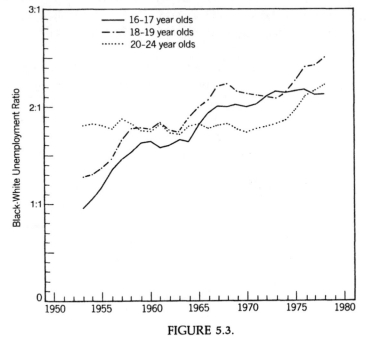

FIGURE 5.3.

Black-White Unemployment Ratio Among Male Job Entrants: Five-Year Moving Average, 1951–1980

DATA AND SOURCE INFORMATION: Appendix table 7.

The position of black youths *vis-à-vis* white youths worsened for all three groups. For teenagers, the timing was especially odd. From 1961 to 1965, for example, when there were virtually no jobs programs, the black to white ratio for 18–19 year-olds averaged 1.8 to 1. From 1966 to 1969, with a much stronger economy *plus* the many new jobs programs, the ratio jumped to an average of 2.2 to 1.[7] Without trying at this point to impose an explanation of why black youth unemployment rose so drastically from the late sixties onward, I note in passing that satisfactory explanations do not come easily. The job situation of young blacks deteriorated as the federal efforts to improve their position were most expensive and extensive—efforts not just in employment *per se*, but in education, health, welfare, and civil rights as well. Nor does it help to appeal to competition with women, to automation, to the decay of the position of American heavy industry, or any other change in the job market. These explanations (which may well explain a worsening job situation for unskilled workers) still leave unexplained why blacks lost ground at the height of the boom, and why young blacks lost ground while older black workers (who were hardly in a better position to cope with a changing job market) did *not* lose, and in fact gained, ground. The facile explanation—jobs for young blacks just disappeared, no matter how hard they searched—runs into trouble when it tries to explain the statistics on labor force participation.

The Anomalous Plunge in Black Labor Force Participation

"Labor force participation" is the poor cousin of unemployment in the news media. Each month, the latest unemployment figures are sure to have a spot on the network news broadcasts; if times are hard, the lead. Labor force participation is less glamorous. It has no immediate impact on our daily lives, and its rise and fall does not decide elections.

Yet the statistics on labor force participation—"LFP" for convenience— are as informative in their own way as the statistics on unemployment. In the long run, they may be more important. The unemployment rate measures current economic conditions. Participation in the labor force measures a fundamental economic stance: an active intention of working, given the opportunity.

The Great Society reforms were not framed in terms of their effect on LFP, but in reality this was at the center of the planners' concerns. What was commonly called the "unemployment" problem among the disadvantaged was largely a problem of LFP. The hardcore unemployed were not people who were being rebuffed by job interviewers, but people who had given up hope or ambition of becoming part of the labor force. For them, the intended effect of the manpower programs was to be not merely a job, but stable, long-term membership in the labor force.

As in the case of unemployment, my analyses of LFP are based on males. The role of women in the labor market changed drastically during the three decades under consideration, especially during the 1972–80 period (see the appendix, table 10, for data on women in the labor force). Interpretations of the relationship between LFP and social welfare policy are confounded by this separate revolution. But society's norm for men remained essentially unchanged. In 1950, able-bodied adult men were expected to hold or seek a full-time job, and the same was true in 1980.

Unlike unemployment, LFP historically has been predictable, changing slowly and in accordance with identifiable rules. Therefore the Bureau of Labor Statistics had in the 1950s been able to project LFP into the future with considerable accuracy, and starting in 1957 such projections became part of the basic LFP statistics reported annually in the *Statistical Abstract of the United States*. In the 1967 volume, the *Abstract* for the first time broke down these projections by race, showing anticipated labor force participation to 1980 based on the experience from 1947 to 1964. The trend during those years plus the coming, known demographic shifts in the labor force of the 1970s led to projections of a modest increase in LFP for both black and white males.[8] What actually happened was quite different.

In 1954, 85 percent of black males 16 years and older were participating in the labor force, a rate essentially equal to that of white males; only four-tenths of a percentage point separated the two populations. Nor was this a new phenomenon. Black males had been participating in the labor force at rates as high as or higher than white males back to the turn of the twentieth century.[9]

This equivalence—one of the very few social or economic measures on which black males equaled whites in the 1950s—continued throughout the decade and into the early 1960s. Among members of both groups, LFP began to decline slowly in the mid-1950s, but the difference in rates was extremely small—as late as 1965, barely more than a single percentage point.

Beginning in 1966, black male LFP started to fall substantially faster than white LFP. By 1972, a gap of 5.9 percentage points had opened up between black males and white males. By 1976, the year the slide finally halted, the gap was 7.7 percentage points. To put it another way: from 1954 to 1965, the black reduction in LFP was 17 percent larger than for whites. From 1965 to 1976, it was 271 percent larger.

In the metrics of labor force statistics, a divergence of this size is huge. The change that occurred was not a minor statistical departure from the trendline, but an unanticipated and unprecedented change. America had encountered large-scale *entry* into the labor market before, most recently by women, and had legislated withdrawal from the labor market—of children, in the early part of the century. But we had never witnessed large-scale voluntary withdrawal from (or failure to enlist in) the labor market by able-bodied males.

That the decline was most rapid during the exceedingly tight labor market of the last half of the 1960s made the phenomenon especially striking. A contemporary (1967) analysis of LFP published in *The American Economic Review* used data from 1961 to 1965 to reach the confident conclusion that, if unemployment dropped (as in fact was happening), we could expect major reductions in urban poverty among blacks as a tight labor

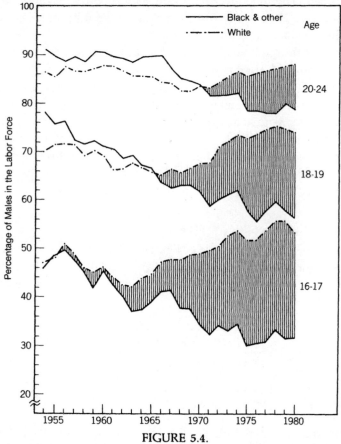

FIGURE 5.4.

Labor Force Participation Among Young Males by Race, 1954–1980

DATA AND SOURCE INFORMATION: Appendix table 8.

market drew wives into the labor force. It was assumed that black male LFP would behave as it had in the past.[10] It was a technically exact extrapolation from recent experience, but it was contradicted by events even as the author was waiting for his manuscript to be published.

Let us take a closer look at who was causing the divergence in black and white male LFP.

As in the case of unemployment, age is at the center of the explanation: As before, the young account for most of the divergence with whites. We begin with the three youngest age groups, the "job entrants," aged 16–17, 18–19, and 20–24, as shown in figure 5.4.

It is the unemployment story replayed. The younger the age group, the greater the decline in black LFP, the greater the divergence with whites, and the sooner it began. The parallelism with the unemployment age trends is so complete that it is important to note that the two measures are not confounded. The unemployment rate is based only on those who are in the labor force. The people who were causing the drop in LFP were not affecting the calculation of unemployment.

On the face of things, it would appear that large numbers of young black males stopped engaging in the fundamental process of seeking and holding jobs—at least, visible jobs in the above-ground economy. There are at least two explanations, however, which would render the LFP statistic misleading: (1) that fewer young blacks participated in the labor force because they were going to school instead—a positive development; (2) that fewer young blacks participated in the labor force because the high unemployment rates made "discouraged workers" of them—why bother to look for a job if none are available?[11] Both require examination.

"THEY WERE GOING TO SCHOOL INSTEAD"

First, let us consider the merits of the education hypothesis. From 1965 to 1970, LFP among black males dropped by the following amounts (expressed as the percentage of the population in 1970 minus the percentage of the population in 1965).

Age Group	Reduction in LFP
16–17	−4.5
18–19	−4.9
20–24	−6.3

At the same time, school enrollment increased by these amounts, using the same metric:[12]

Age Group	Increase in School Enrollment
16–17	+1.8
18–19	+.5
20–24	+5.2

Even if we make the extreme assumption that *all* of the increased enrollment represented students who would have been in the labor force if they had not gone to school and that *none* of the people who were added to the school population also participated in the labor force, the increases in school enrollment would not cover the decreases in LFP. In fact, of course, those assumptions are incorrect, further shrinking the proportion of the reduction in LFP that could be explained by school enrollment. More than a third of students in those age groups participate in the labor force, and many who are not students do not participate.[13] The white experience indicates that school enrollment may be altogether irrelevant in explaining the change in black LFP. White male LFP in two of the three job-entry age groups increased along with school enrollment:

Age Group	Change in	
	LFP	School Enrollment
16–17	+4.3	+2.8
18–19	+1.6	+1.6
20–24	−2.0	+2.3

The "school enrollment" hypothesis explains at best a small fraction of the reduction in black LFP; judging from the white experience, we may not be justified in using it to explain any of the reduction.

"THEY GAVE UP LOOKING FOR JOBS THAT WEREN'T THERE"

The "discouraged worker" hypothesis is probably an explanation for part of the reduction in certain age groups in certain years. For rural populations, the disappearance of agricultural jobs meant picking up roots, establishing a new home and a new style of life, and accommodating to the demands of a strange job market. The adjustment was a difficult one, and the reductions in black teenage LFP in the last half of the 1950s can plausibly be read, at least in part, as a reflection of this. Economic bad times also produce discouragement. During recessions—1957–58, for example, or

1974–75—the reductions in LFP among the most vulnerable workers (young black males) are easily seen as discouragement.

But it is not possible to use discouragement as an explanation for the long-term trend. Why should young black males have become "discouraged workers" in greater numbers in the 1960s than they did during the less prosperous 1950s and 1970s? Even within the decade of the 1960s, the "discouraged worker" hypothesis fails. In 1960, young black males (ages 16–24) had an LFP rate of 74.0 percent, 2.7 percentage points higher than the LFP rate of white males of the same age range. By 1970, the gap was 3.6 percentage points in the other direction (whites higher than blacks). Here is how the gap developed in each half of that key decade:

Years	Ground Lost in LFP Percentage by Young Black Males in Comparison with Young White Males (Aged 16–24)	Mean Male Unemployment
1960–65	2.3 percentage points	5.1 %
1965–70	6.1 percentage points	3.4 %

In the half of the decade when the economy was not only strong but operating at full capacity, the difference between young whites and blacks grew fastest—more than two and a half times as fast as during the first half of the decade, with its considerably higher overall unemployment rate.

LFP among older age groups of black males during the same period is given in the appendix. In general, white and black LFP rates changed in tandem. Divergences were perceptible in each of the age groups: The participation rates of blacks and whites in the 1950s were uniformly closer than in 1980. In each case, the major portion of the divergence occurred during the 1970s. But among older workers the absolute changes were quite small.

A Question of Generations

The age breakdowns show an oddly regular pattern, as if contagion were spreading slowly upward from young to old. What was really happening, of course, is that the same people were getting older. The 16-year-olds of 1963, when the black-white gap widened, were 19 in 1966—when blacks of *that* age fell noticeably behind whites—and 24 in 1971, when the crossover point was reached for the 20–24 year-old age group. We are watching a generational phenomenon. For whatever reasons, black males born in the early 1950s and thereafter had a different posture toward the labor market from their fathers and older brothers.

What was different about being born after 1950? The difference lay in the environments in which different groups came of age in the labor market. Those born in 1950 turned 18 in 1968, when the rules governing the labor market had been changed radically. The intended changes were all for the better, surely—more training programs for poor and minority youth, better regulations on equal opportunity and widespread social support for their enforcement, higher minimum wages, a red-hot economy. Yet, the 1950 black youngsters behaved conspicuously differently from their older brothers and from their white counterparts. And, to put it another way, a population of disproportionately poor youngsters behaved conspicuously differently from the way poor people in previous generations had behaved.

Escaping Stereotypes

The data I have just described are too often sidestepped by appealing to either of two stereotypes. One stereotype is the welfare loafer, living contentedly off the dole and making no effort to work. The other is the steadfast job-seeker, fruitlessly going from door to door looking for any kind of work. Neither fits very many of the people who account for the changes in the unemployment and LFP statistics. More often, these people share some of the characteristics of both stereotypes, at different times. Martin Feldstein describes the situation in a year typical of the seventies, 1979:

> In 1979, more than half of those who became unemployed were no longer unemployed at the end of four weeks. More than half of the unemployed were less than 25 years old and half of these were teenagers, many of whom were looking for part-time jobs while still attending schools. More than half of those who were officially classified as unemployed did not become unemployed by losing their previous job, but were youngsters looking for their first job or those who were returning to the labor force after a period in which they were neither working nor looking for work. . . . In short, the unemployed typically are young, have generally not lost their previous job, and have very short periods of unem-

ployment. . . . It is a picture that stands in sharp contrast to the image of a stagnant pool of job losers who must remain out of work until there is a general increase in the demand for goods and services.[14]

The problem with this new form of unemployment was not that young black males—or young poor males—stopped working altogether, but that they moved in and out of the labor force at precisely that point in their lives when it was most important that they acquire skills, work habits, and a work record. By behaving so differently from previous generations, many also forfeited their futures as economically independent adults.

Summary of the Federal Effort

THE JOHNSON job-training programs started from near zero. From the onset of the Second World War until Kennedy came to office, the federal government effectively stayed out of the jobs business. When it came to finding work, the poor and the unemployed mostly fended for themselves; private agencies and scattered state-level programs were the only sources of help.

In the 1960s, John Kennedy reopened federal involvement in employment with the Area Redevelopment Act (ARA) in 1961 and the Manpower Development and Training Act (MDTA), passed in 1962. ARA was restricted to narrowly defined "depressed areas," and MDTA was to retrain displaced employees, not help the chronically unemployed. It remained for the first antipoverty bill to introduce broadly based efforts to help the disadvantaged in the employment market.

From 1964 to 1970, the programs focused on skills training. Job Corps was perhaps best-known, but it was dwarfed in size by other programs which proliferated throughout the rest of the decade— Operation Mainstream, New Careers, and Job Opportunities in the Business Sector, to name a few. Some programs did not offer skills training *per se* but were intended to serve a general antidelinquency and socialization function for youths. The Neighborhood Youth Corps was the largest such effort—an "aging vat," as Sar Levitan has put it, in which youngsters at a critical transition point could be kept from dropping out. By 1969, at least seventeen programs were generating more than 10,000 specific manpower "projects" of varying size and scope.

In 1971, the emphasis changed. The Emergency Employment Act moved away from skills-training and toward counter-cyclical employment. Training programs continued, but alongside new and expanded programs whose main purpose was the simpler one of providing work for the disadvantaged, with emphasis on the young. The multiple agencies and departments involved in the overall jobs/training effort were brought under a single administrative umbrella through the Comprehensive Employment and Training Act (CETA) of 1973. At its height, CETA had an annual budget of $10.6 billion.

For an overview of the training programs, see Henry M. Levin, "A Decade of Policy Developments in Improving Education and Training for Low-Income Populations," in Robert H. Haveman, ed., *A Decade of Federal Antipoverty Programs: Achievements, Failures, and Lessons* (New York: Academic Press, 1977), pp. 123–188.

6

Wages and Occupations

AT THE SAME TIME that more and more black youth were out of the labor market or unemployed, the economic penalties of being black were lifting. A profound irony of the trends of the sixties was that growing numbers of blacks seemed to give up on getting ahead in the world just as other blacks were demonstrating that it was finally possible to do so. The period from 1950 to 1980 saw major advances in black occupations relative to white occupations and in black wages relative to white wages. The part of the story we are about to examine is not an unqualified triumph, but it is decidedly positive.

Occupational Gains

One of the indispensable elements of the American dream is movement up the occupational ladder from common laborer to skilled worker, from blue collar to white collar, from white collar to executive—if not in one's own life, then in the life of one's children. Much of the purpose of the Affirmative Action and Equal Employment regulations was to foster such mobility. It was observed that many blacks and other minorities were being shut out of opportunities to which their abilities and training entitled them, and it was hoped that the right policy could open some of those doors.

To obtain an overview of progress, let us first examine the general category of "white-collar" occupations.[1] Figure 6.1 shows the racial breakdown for 1959 to 1980. During the years between 1959 and 1980, blacks made extraordinary progress in entering white-collar jobs: from only 14 percent of employed blacks in 1959 to 39 percent in 1980. Furthermore, the overall gap with whites narrowed substantially. In 1959, the ratio of whites to blacks in white-collar jobs was 3.2 to 1. In 1980, the ratio had fallen to 1.4 to 1. If in 1980 five out of ten whites wore white collars to work, so did four out of ten blacks—many times the almost nonexistent black white-collar class of the 1950s.

Most of these gains came in two categories: "professional and technical" and clerical. The gain in managerial positions was proportionately large, but the absolute number of employed blacks in managerial positions remained small (5.2 percent in 1980), and the gap between white and black remained very large—5.2 percent of employed blacks compared with 12.0 percent of employed whites.

We know from more detailed analyses that much of the progress in the 1970s was concentrated in the less-prestigious jobs within each occupational category. Among professional and technical occupations, the bulk

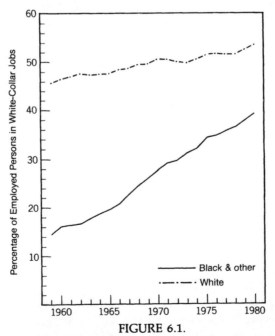

FIGURE 6.1.

White-Collar Employment by Race, 1959–1980

Data and Source Information: Appendix table 11.

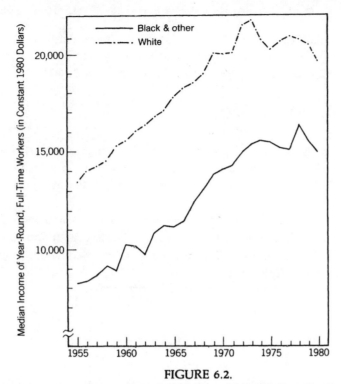

FIGURE 6.2.

Median Income of Year-Round, Full-Time Male Workers (in Constant 1980 Dollars) by Race, 1955–1980

DATA AND SOURCE INFORMATION: Appendix table 11.

of increases occurred among jobs such as nursing, technical trades, and counseling, not among physicians and engineers and accountants. The new black members of the managerial class were much more likely to be found managing small businesses and service establishments than divisions of major corporations.[2]

Another factor that complicates simple conclusions is that much of the increase in white-collar jobs was owed to government jobs. Michael Brown and Stephen Erie concluded from their analysis that about 55 percent of the increase in black professional, managerial, and technical employment between 1960 and 1976 occurred in the public sector, and employment in social welfare programs accounted for approximately half of that increase.[3] Since most of the spending that created such jobs was concentrated at the end of that period, a graph of black professional employment in the private sector shows nearly the same upward slope in the 1950s and early 1960s that we observed in figure 6.1, but much slower progress after the mid-1960s—in fact, very little progress at all. Blacks have not been integrated into the woof and warp of the American economy to the degree that the trendlines may suggest.

But these are qualifications to a history that is otherwise highly positive. Blacks who sought entrance to the jobs that formerly had been the pre-serve of whites found increasing success, especially after 1960.[4]

Income of Full-Time Workers

Employed blacks also made important gains in the struggle against wage discrimination. The overall picture for males is shown in figure 6.2. The trendline shows the median income of year-round, full-time workers, converted to constant 1980 dollars.

Income of black workers rose at roughly the same slope as income for white workers. The dollar gap fluctuated around $5,000 (1980) dollars for the entire period. But the ratio of black income to white income improved, as shown for males in figure 6.3:

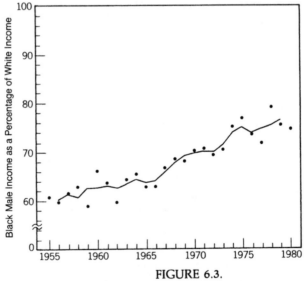

FIGURE 6.3.

Black-White Male Income Ratio, 1950–1980

DATA AND SOURCE INFORMATION: Appendix table 11.
NOTE: Line is three-year moving average.
SAMPLE: Civilian male full-time, year-round workers, 18 years and older.

In 1955, the wage gap between black and white workers was $5,271; the typical black male worker was earning only 61 percent of the white worker's wage. In 1980, the gap was $4,993 but computed from a much higher real base, so that the black worker was earning 75 percent of the white worker's wage. It was a major improvement, practically as well as statistically.

These data do not tell us much about racial disparities. Blacks gained, yes, but we also know that black occupational patterns improved as well. Black income could have gone up relative to white income and still reflected a situation in which they received lower pay for the same work. To draw conclusions about wage differentials between whites and blacks, simple trendlines will not take us much further. We must examine the more detailed analyses, using special data bases or disaggregations of the published data, to reach judgments about the state of affairs in black income and occupational gains.

We may begin with a generalization. There is now a broad scholarly consensus that the gains in income parity are real and large among that subpopulation of blacks who obtained an education and stayed in the labor force. At the top of the ladder, the black-white discrepancy has shrunk to a few percentage points. By 1980, black males in professional and technical occupations were making 86 percent of the salary of their white counterparts. Black females made 98 percent.[5]

When additional factors are taken into account—differences in quality of education, years of experience, and so on—it may be that, for all practical purposes, the racial difference has disappeared for this one subgroup. Richard Freeman, a Harvard economist, argues that "[d]etailed investigation of the National Longitudinal Survey shows that the occupational position of young black men entering the market after 1964 is essentially the same as that of young whites with similar backgrounds," a conclusion that finds additional support in the 1973 Occupational Change in a Generation (OCG) survey.[6] Members of the "black elite" entering the job market have achieved something very close to parity.

This constitutes a major change. Historically, highly educated blacks were, relatively speaking, more discriminated against than blacks with less education. Statistically, this took the form of a gap between black and white incomes that increased as the educational level increased. Discrimination against the black intellectual elite also surfaced in such curiosities as Dunbar High School in Washington D.C., whose faculty in the 1930s and 1940s was said to have had the highest proportion of Ph.D.s of any high school in the nation—black Ph.D.s who were shut out of positions in white universities.[7]

This peculiar form of reverse discrimination—"the more highly qualified you are, the more we will discriminate against you"—was believed to exist into the late 1960s. Analysts continued to find that, statistically, socioeconomically successful black parents were unable to transmit their success to their children to the same degree that white parents could.[8] They also continued to find that, in the economists' phrase, black "returns to education" were lower. Thus as late as 1972, when Christopher Jencks and his colleagues published *Inequality,* they cited 1961 data showing that "employers paid relatively uneducated blacks in unskilled and semiskilled jobs about 25 percent less income than comparable whites [while paying] blacks with average amounts of education in middle-level jobs about 35 percent less than similar whites. Blacks in professional and managerial jobs may have been even more discriminated against."[9] The authors went on to hypothesize (as have many others) that "one reason blacks remained at the bottom of the ladder was that the economic rewards of climbing were so slight."[10]

What changed this gloomy assessment? Largely, our understanding of what the data really meant. While it might be true that *all* blacks with an "average amount of education" in Jencks's 1961 data earned 35 percent less than *all* whites with an average amount of education, that did not mean that blacks who were just entering the job market were earning 35 percent less. Taking this factor (the "vintage effect") into account changed the picture. In 1973, Finis Welch published a pioneering article revealing that returns to education for blacks had achieved parity with whites in the 1950s and surged ahead in the early 1960s.[11] The data he compiled (from the 28,552-person sample of males 14–70 years old for the Survey of Economic Opportunity) revealed the following pattern:

Year of Entry into the Labor Force	Percentage Increase in Wages per Extra Year of Schooling	
	Blacks	Whites
1934–46	4.9	6.9
1947–54	6.2	9.0
1955–58	7.9	8.2
1959–62	14.2	10.6
1963–65	23.0	14.6

At some point between 1959 and 1962, blacks entering the labor force found a market in which their percentage increase in wages per unit of education was greater than that of whites. By 1965, the increase for blacks was more than half again as large the increase for whites. It was an indispensable step in closing wage gaps arising out of past discrimination.[12]

The second group that made the most progress was black women—not just a highly educated elite, but women in a broad spectrum of occupations. Black women in all nonagricultural occupations had by 1980 effectively wiped out the racial discrepancy—which is to say, they were by then no more underpaid relative to white males than were white women. From managerial positions (106 percent of the white wage) to household workers (141 percent of the white wage), black women as of 1980 were earning as much as their white female counterparts. Of all nonfarm categories, the lowest ratio of black:white women's wages (100 means equality) was a high 94.3, for blue-collar operatives. In agriculture, the ratio was 81.4.[13]

Problems with wages and careers remain. Edward Lazear, among others, has argued that blacks unknowingly trade off higher initial wage levels for a flatter earnings profile in later career. Affirmative Action programs have made it more difficult for employers to discriminate in wages, he suggests, and therefore employers decrease the more-difficult-to-observe on-the-job training that is an important component of earnings.[14] Lazear does not explore the rationales whereby employers are led to behave in this fashion. Recent studies indicate that simple racial discrimination seems to account for very little.[15] But there are ample alternative explanations for why highly educated blacks start at excellent salaries, perhaps higher than those of their white peers, then find themselves with a truncated career path. Sometimes blacks are tokens, put in visible positions and then left there. Sometimes the phenomenon is more complex. In the occupation with which I am most familiar, for example, it is exceedingly difficult (unless one is indifferent to money) for a young black social scientist to follow a normal career path. He (in this example) is hired as one of the senior staff for a research grant that must have a black in a senior position, because of the grantor's preferences or the topic of the research. A brand-new sociology Ph.D. from a top school, he is hired for much more than the salary he could make as an assistant professor—there are not enough well-trained black sociologists to go around. Given his role on the project, he is not expected to prepare questionnaire items or wrestle with computer printouts or even write the first drafts of the analysis. He is given people to do all that *for* him. He is not forced to serve his apprenticeship, and, unless he has exceptional determination, he forever remains a black with a degree in sociology instead of developing into a sociologist. Black engineers, lawyers, and professionals of all sorts can recount similar tales of hidden cul de sacs. As Lazear found, the black in such a position is shortchanged in on-the-job training and eventually falls behind white peers on the slower but more open-ended professional ladder.

Whether because of tokenism or for more complicated reasons, the effect is the same—a ceiling on wages over the course of a career. The problem does not, however, negate the importance of the overall gains that blacks have made in the job market. Few would dispute that it is better to be in the position of the black sociologist I have just described than that of his or her counterpart of thirty years ago, forced to look for a job teaching high school for lack of opportunities in the white world. A job offer for the wrong reasons is incomparably better than no job offer at all.

Taken together, the jobs indicators point to a bifurcation within the black community that we will see again on other, noneconomic indicators. If we wear blinders that limit our view to employed persons, blacks made certain types of progress, occasionally quite remarkable progress, from 1960 to 1980. But we know also that the same period saw large-scale reductions in labor force participation and, especially in the 1970s, increases in black unemployment. The result is what Martin Kilson has called a "pulling-away" process in which a large segment of the black population (Kilson estimates roughly 60 percent) is effectively tapping white middle-class resources for upward mobility and another large segment is becoming mired in intergenerational poverty.[16]

The data also provide an antidote to a needlessly pessimistic view of black economic progress. For many years prior to the period we are examining, blacks who tried to take the middle-class route to prosperity—education—found themselves penalized for their efforts with greater discrimination. The 1950s saw a crucial shift in that relationship as black "returns to education" surpassed those of whites. The basis for eliminating income inequality for blacks and whites of similar credentials had been established.

But rewards for possessing credentials are the mirror image of penalties for failing to possess them. The persons driving the rising unemployment rates and the falling labor participation rates were not black electrical engineers, or skilled black craftsmen, or even unskilled youngsters with a solid high school education. They were, for the most part, the labor market's analog to the Displaced Person, without education, without skills that the job market could use. To reap the higher returns to education, it is necessary to become educated, and during the 1960s and 1970s fewer and fewer seemed to do so. We turn now to that story.

Summary of the Federal Effort

THE CORE LEGISLATION was Title VII of the 1964 Civil Rights Act, which forbade discrimination in hiring, promotion, firing, transfer, training, and pay, among all employers, employment agencies, and labor unions engaged in industry affecting commerce. In 1972, an amendment to the act extended its provisions to include any business employing more than fifteen workers and to employees of state and local governments and educational institutions.

The initial objective was to give everyone an equal shot at a job. "Affirmative Action," destined to be one of the most highly charged legacies of the Great Society, took that objective one step further. The disadvantaged were to be given something more than just an equal chance; they were also to be given a leg up. It was a sensible and just response to a history of exploitation, in the view of its advocates; race discrimination in reverse, according to the critics. It began in September 1965 with the signing of Executive Order 11246, which enjoined government contractors and others receiving government funds to take concrete measures to promote hiring of blacks and other minorities.

These steps to assist the discriminated-against individual looking for a job were supplemented by other programs, less well known, to assist the minority businessman. Section 8A of the Small Business Act, for example, provided that a portion of all government contracts be reserved for minority-owned firms. Such contracts, known as "minority set-asides," were to encourage the formation and survival of enterprises owned by disadvantaged persons.

The influence of these efforts was slower in coming than a literal reading of the laws might suggest. For example, the federal government did not revoke a contract for noncompliance with Executive Order 11246 until 1971, six years after the order was signed. The Equal Employment Opportunity Commission (EEOC) established by the 1964 Act had no enforcement powers until 1972.

Teeth began to be put into the Equal Opportunity and Affirmative Action provisions in the late 1960s as the EEOC, acting as *amicus curiae* in civil suits, achieved a number of successes in getting its view of the laws accepted by the courts. In 1968 and 1969, the courts ruled against seniority systems that had the effect of perpetuating racial discrimination in advancement and job security. (*Quarles* v. *Phillip Morris*, 1968; *United States* v. *Local 189, United Papermakers and Paperworkers*, 1969.) In 1970, a federal court ruled that "specific [hiring] goals and timetables"—quotas of a sort, though the word "quota" was avoided—were "no more or less than a means for implementation of the Affirmative Action obligations of Executive Order 11246." *(Contractors of Eastern Pennsylvania* v. *Schultz*, 13 March 1970.)

The pivotal case, however, came in 1971 in the form of *Griggs* v. *Duke Power*. Could an employer impose minimum credentials (such as a high-school diploma) as a prerequisite for employment? A unanimous Supreme Court said no—not unless the credential can be demonstrated to be significantly related to successful job performance. Even if a hiring practice were "fair in form," and even if there were no discriminatory intent, it was proscribed if, in the Court's words, it acted as a "built-in headwind" for minority groups. "Congress has placed on the employer," the Court held, "the burden of showing that any given requirement must have a manifest relationship to the employment in question." *(Griggs* v. *Duke Power*, 1971.)

Griggs was followed by other major cases, but between 1968 and 1972 the basic guidelines had been established. Thereafter, the EEOC could take enforcement action on its own, and the breadth of the requirements for Affirmative Action and nondiscrimination in job practices was considerable.

The influence was more pervasive than a count of court convictions indicates. A business that relied on the federal government for its income, or a substantial portion of its income, could find itself in big trouble even if noncompliance was only being investigated. A market developed for persons who were good at writing Affirmative Action plans and certifications of compliance. In some of the most basic ways that were intended by the regulations, behavior did change. Job notices were more widely and carefully advertised in places where blacks were more likely to see them, such as placement offices of black universities. Records were kept on the race (and sex and age) of persons interviewed for a job. Personnel directors fretted when too few of the underrepresented minority were interviewed, and they fretted even more when many were interviewed but few were hired. Whatever the numbers might say about the effects on actual jobs, employers in the 1970s were conscious of racial hiring practices to a degree that was unheard of in the 1950s. For more details on the chronology, see Phyllis A. Wallace, "A Decade of Policy Developments in Equal Opportunities in Employment and Housing," in Robert H. Haveman, ed., *A Decade of Federal Antipoverty Programs: Achievements, Failures, and Lessons* (New York: Academic Press, 1977), pp. 329–59. See also Nathan Glazer, *Affirmative Discrimination: Ethnic Inequality and Public Policy* (New York: Basic Books, 1975) on the general issue of Affirmative Action.

7

Education

I N 1983, a "National Commission on Excellence in Education," appointed by the secretary of the Department of Education, released its final report with the foreboding title *A Nation at Risk*. The report told us that American education had been going downhill for nearly twenty years and had arrived at a terrible state. "We have, in effect," wrote the Commission, "been committing an act of unthinking, unilateral educational disarmament."[1]

A Nation at Risk put the imprimatur of official Washington on a conclusion that nearly everyone was prepared to accept anyway. But the story of what happened, and when, is more interesting than a tale of unbroken disaster. The schools deteriorated after 1964, yes; but what is less publicized is that there were signs in the 1950s and early 1960s that the schools were doing quite well in many respects and were improving. Nor were the improvements for only a favored few. On the contrary, the data suggest that education was improving for the poor and the disadvantaged as well as for the affluent.

The Federal Dollars

As in the case of the jobs programs, the federal investment during the reform period and after was huge. Between 1965 and 1980, more than $60 billion (1980 dollars as always) was earmarked for the improvement of elementary and secondary education of the disadvantaged, and more than $25 billion was spent on grants and loans to students engaged in post-secondary education.[2] And as in the case of the jobs programs, very little had been spent for these purposes by the federal government prior to 1965. What was the return on the investment? We will inquire into the education of the poor and disadvantaged, using black children as the basis for our assessment. We will examine first the quantity of education they received, then consider the quality of that education.

Quantity I: Enrollment in High School

In 1950, nearly one out of four black youths of high school age was not officially enrolled in school. By 1980, only one out of eighteen was not officially enrolled in school.[3] By any standard, the progress was enormous. Virtually all of it occurred before the reform period. Figure 7.1 shows the pertinent trendline:

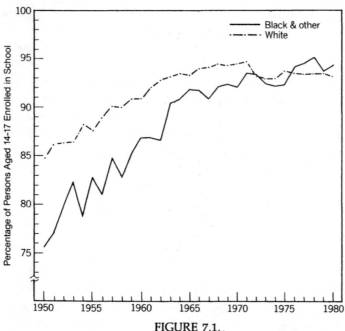

FIGURE 7.1.
School Enrollment of Persons 14–17 Years Old by Race, 1950–1980
DATA AND SOURCE INFORMATION: Appendix table 12.

From 1950 to 1963, the black enrollment percentage increased from 76 percent to over 90 percent. By 1965, 92 percent of minority children of high school age were enrolled in school, compared with about 93 percent of white children. Essential parity had been achieved. In subsequent years, enrollment rates rose more slowly—a natural result of nearing the saturation point—and stood in 1980 at 94 percent for blacks and 93 percent for whites. For both whites and blacks, enrollment was effectively universal.

In one respect the gains made by black children are not adequately reflected in these data. Prior to the 1950s, black children in segregated systems (segregation was compulsory in seventeen states and permitted in four others when the *Brown* decision was handed down) not only had inferior facilities but often had a shorter school year than did white students. Even before the *Brown* decision took effect (which did not happen widely until the late 1960s and early 1970s), the 1950s saw major improvements in such dimensions. By 1954, the length of the school year in black southern schools had come within two days of the national average, and average days attended per pupil had closed to a nine-day difference from a twenty-six-day difference in 1940 and a forty-six day difference in 1930.[4]

In another sense, the quantity of education has probably been diminishing for blacks of high school age. Reported enrollment figures in inner-city schools exaggerate actual enrollees, and reported days of attendance exaggerate actual hours of class time. Based on a reconstruction of real versus reported attendance at five inner-city high schools in New York City, Atlanta, and Indianapolis, the statistics grossly underestimate actual classes missed. Underestimates of dropout rates are also very high.[5]

Two reasons account for the discrepancy in the school systems from which I have data. One is a policy of "enrolled until proved otherwise." In some school systems, unless a student formally declares to the school that he or she has dropped out, the student is carried on the rolls to the end of the current year—in some cases (although not by official policy), indefinitely. These practices are not necessarily a product of loose standards. State and federal aid is typically linked to the number of students enrolled. School systems strapped for resources have a clear and present incentive to show as many students on the books as possible.

The second reason relates to overload. In a school where 99 percent of the students are in class, the 1 percent roaming the halls is conspicuous and easily dealt with. When large numbers of students are in the halls and the stairwells, congregated in groups, they are not easily dealt with. Thus it happens that students in some schools could with impunity use the school as a sort of social center, going to home room in the morning and cutting most or all of the rest of their classes. The student is nonetheless shown on the books as having attended school that day and counted in the computation of attendance figures.

I am not aware of data that permit generalizations about the magnitude of the problem or the relative problem in inner-city and suburban schools even for a single year, let alone for a time series stretching back to the 1960s and 1950s. But a significant problem is generally if unsystematically conceded to exist and, completely apart from the issue of quality of education, must lead us to wonder what an accurate plot of "hours spent in class" would look like for black students from 1950 to 1980.

Quantity II: College and Beyond

The 1960s saw an unprecedented increase in college attendance by black students. In 1960, only 7 percent of blacks aged 20–24 were enrolled in college; in 1970, this figure had more than doubled, to 16 percent. The period of most rapid increase came with the onset of the federal programs to provide financial assistance. Figure 7.2 shows the enrollment figures for persons aged 20–24. In 1967, the first school year in which significant

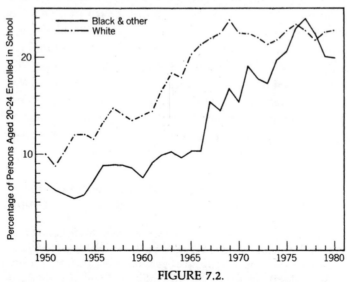

FIGURE 7.2.
School Enrollment of Persons 20–24 Years Old by Race, 1950–1980
DATA AND SOURCE INFORMATION: Appendix table 12.

funding from the education acts of 1965 became available, black enrollment jumped by half, from 10 to 15 percent of that age group. Progress
continued through 1977, as black enrollment in colleges continued to increase during a period when white enrollment was dropping slightly. In
1977, blacks caught up—24 percent of blacks aged 20–24 were enrolled in
school, compared with 23 percent of whites in the same age group. Only
eleven years earlier, the proportions of whites enrolled was twice that of
blacks. After 1977, the proportion of black students 20–24 years of age
enrolled in school fell each year through 1980, despite continuing increases
in loans and grants during those years.

Quality: What Has Been Learned?

We have no single measure for documenting the quality of education.
There is no equivalent to the unemployment rate for assessing educational
achievement. Until 1983, the deterioration of American public education
had been documented mostly through horror stories in newspaper feature
articles about rampant illiteracy among high school graduates and about
chaotic high schools in the inner city where the teachers worked in fear
of their students. In 1981, the Department of Education, concerned by
what it called "the widespread public perception that something is seriously remiss in our educational system," appointed the national commission. Over a period of eighteen months, the commission ordered special
papers; heard voluminous testimony from educators, parents, scholars, and
public officials; and reanalyzed the existing data bases. In the end, their
much-publicized report documented most of the horror stories. The commission found them to be true, to a greater extent and in more dismaying
dimensions than most had imagined. A few examples:

- Nearly 40 percent of 17-year-olds could not draw inferences from written
  materials; two-thirds could not solve a mathematics problem requiring a sequence of steps.[6]
- "Secondary school curricula have been homogenized, diluted, and diffused to
  the point that they no longer have a central purpose." Whereas in 1964 only 12
  percent of high school students were on a "general" track (neither vocational nor
  preparatory to college), by 1979 that proportion had grown to 42 percent.
- By 1980, remedial mathematics courses constituted a quarter of all mathematics
  courses taught in public universities.

- Traditional performance standards had become meaningless; as homework decreased and real student achievement declined, grades *rose*.
- "Minimum competency" examinations were tending to lower educational standards for all.

The commission used a quote from Paul Copperman to summarize the state of decay it had found:

Each generation of Americans has outstripped its parents in education, in literacy, in economic attainment. For the first time in the history of our country, the educational skills of one generation will not surpass, will not equal, not even approach, those of their parents.[7]

Only scattered, limited criticisms of the report were voiced, despite the harsh language that the commission used. Few were prepared to defend the state of American education.

But when did all this happen? Whose education was most harmed? Was anyone's helped? The commission focused on the 1970s; we want to know about the 1950s and 1960s as well. The commission generalized about American education as a whole; we want to track the quality of education provided to the poor and disadvantaged.

Events have conspired to make this task extremely difficult. Educational measures are the ones on which we have the most trouble documenting precisely how the children of the poor, and especially poor black students, have fared. The lacuna is no accident. Until the mid-1960s, breakdowns of standardized test scores and other achievement measures by race were meager because educational policy frowned upon—often forbade—racial identification on test sheets or transcripts. It was one of the ways in which institutions in the 1950s were inching toward the ideal of a color-blind society. After the mid-1960s, the situation was reversed. The student's race became a crucial piece of information to be used on behalf of minority students in such things as admissions. But data about black test scores remained sparse because of fears that too much would be made of poor scores.

Drawing from the scattered data that do exist, I will venture two conclusions: (1) Education for the disadvantaged was probably improving, perhaps dramatically, during the 1950s and early 1960s; and (2) the federal investment of $60 billion in elementary and secondary education for the disadvantaged bought nothing discernible. After the mid 1960s, public education for the disadvantaged suffered as much as, and probably even more than, education for youth in general.

Looking Up: Progress Until the Mid-1960s

In the discussion of jobs and earnings, I pointed to the dramatic increase in black "returns to education" during the 1940s, 1950s, and 1960s. To recapitulate, an extra year of education in the 1940s and earlier brought a much smaller proportional increase in income for a black than it did for a white. As time went on, this gap narrowed. Then blacks gained ground rapidly in the late 1940s and 1950s and reached a crossover point sometime between 1959 and 1962. By 1963–65, the proportional increase in wages per extra year of schooling was 58 percent *larger* for blacks than for whites —a remarkable turnaround. But what caused it? The answer could not be national policy: The large increases in returns to education occurred before any of the significant civil rights legislation or court decisions had affected school practices.

Finis Welch, who first identified the change in black returns to education, advanced the hypothesis that schooling had improved for blacks. First, he pointed to the black-white differences in statistics on schools. "There," he writes, "the data are clear: Through time the relative quality of black schooling has risen rapidly."[8] By the time of the *Brown* decision, disparities in black and white enrollment, attendance, and expenditures had fallen dramatically from those of the 1920s and 1930s. Acknowledging that some of the increased returns to education might be traced to a downward drift in market discrimination, Welch pointed out that such explanations had great difficulty in explaining the data:

> In behalf of the quality of schooling hypothesis let me summarize the trends revealed here with which [alternative hypotheses] must contend. First, not only have relative black incomes increased but the gain has been greatest for higher school completion levels. Second, the phenomenon of rising returns to schooling is not only true in comparing black relative to white incomes but holds within the races as well: Young blacks fare better in comparison to young whites than do older blacks in comparison to older whites *and* schooling contains more of an income boost for young blacks and young whites than for older generations of their own races [emphasis in the original].[9]

Simple reductions in racial discrimination would not produce these results. Improving education would.

These are some of the indirect reasons for thinking that education for blacks was improving meaningfully during the 1950s. When we turn to the fragmentary test data that are available, we find some confirmation. New York City reading score data compiled by Welch are strikingly consistent with his argument. These were the "grade equivalent" scores from schools with at least 90 percent black enrollment:

	Grade Equivalent Scores for	
Year	Third Graders	Sixth Graders
1957	2.67	4.88
1960	2.87	5.22
1965	3.19	5.67

Put roughly, whereas the average sixth-grader in 1957 was functioning at a level more than one year behind the norm, a sixth-grader in 1965 was only a few months behind. Third-graders caught up completely. According to these data, black education was improving significantly through 1965.[10]

We find further support from the results of tests administered to two large, nationally representative samples of students in 1960 and 1965. In 1960, the American Institutes for Research, under the sponsorship of the U.S. Office of Education, began an unprecedented attempt to capture a slice of the American population for lifelong study. It was called "Project TALENT," and it assembled extensive academic and personal data on all students in a nationally representative stratified sample of 987 high schools. As part of the Project TALENT instruments, a battery of seven cognitive tests was administered to each student, and a weighted composite called "General Academic Aptitude" was computed.[11] These were the mean scores for ninth graders in 1960:

	Males	Females	Total
White	444	469	456
Black	300	319	309

The black mean score in 1960 was approximately a third lower than the white score.

In the fall of 1965, we have another fix on the racial difference from a national, stratified sample plan covering 900,000 pupils in the first and twelfth grades. The study, commissioned by the Office of Education, became known as the "Coleman Report."[12] The battery consisted of five tests (nonverbal, verbal, reading, mathematics, and general information). The results were:

Test	White	Black
Nonverbal	52.0	40.9
Verbal	52.1	40.9
Reading	51.9	42.2
Mathematics	51.8	41.8
General Information	52.2	40.6
Average of the Five Tests	52.0	41.1

The results still showed a major black-white difference, and the study as a whole was used as evidence for the need for massive federal assistance to help black students catch up. But insofar as we can determine from a comparison with the 1960 test, black students were already in the process of catching up. The intuitive way to see this is by putting the black-white scores in terms of proportions—in 1960, the black score was only 68 percent of the white score; in 1965, the black score was a noticeably higher 79 percent of the white score. For a variety of reasons, comparisons of proportions can be meaningless across different tests. But in this case, the intuitive sense that the 1965 black-white gap was smaller than the 1960 gap is corroborated by a comparison of standard deviations, the technical basis for comparing inter-group differences across tests.[13] The black-white difference on the 1960 test was equal to 1.28 standard deviations; in the 1965 test, the difference had narrowed to 1.09 standard deviations.

Comparing results on different test batteries is always tricky. But the general aptitude batteries in the Project TALENT and Coleman studies were testing for similar qualities and used very large and representative samples; there is reason to pay some attention to the narrower difference in the 1965 results. Added to the other bits of evidence, and given no countervailing data that black education was getting worse during the pre-1965 period, the evidence available to us points to the conclusion that public elementary and secondary education for blacks was getting better —in terms of test scores, and in terms of the economic benefits that better education seems to have been yielding.

The State of Black Education by 1980

The rest of the story is grim, so grim that it is reasonable to question whether the data I am about to present can be taken at face value. For that reason, an extended discussion of the "cultural bias" issue and test scores is presented in the notes.[14] Put briefly, as of 1980 the gap in educational achievement between black and white students leaving high school was so great that it threatened to defeat any other attempts to narrow the economic differences separating blacks from whites. We will consider first the overall profile of youth, then concentrate on those who are college-bound.

Educational Achievement: The Average High School Graduate

Since the Second World War, the Department of Defense has administered a basic test of vocational aptitude to its recruits and draftees. The results of these tests could not be used to interpret trends in the population at large, because the nature of the population of recruits entering the armed forces varies so widely over time. In 1980, the Department of Defense decided to investigate how the scores of its recruits compared with the general population of youth. It therefore coordinated the administration of its Armed Service Vocational Aptitude Battery with the National Longitudinal Survey (NLS) of Youth Labor Force Behavior to provide a nationally representative, large-sample assessment of persons aged 18–23.

The results for the basic test of verbal and numeric skills (the Armed Forces Qualification Test, or AFQT) were as follows:

	Males	Females	Total
White	56.6	55.3	56.0
Black	23.9	24.7	24.3

Overall, the white mean score was 2.3 times the black mean score. The ratio was roughly the same for all age categories within the 18–23 year-old population.[15] More detailed breakdowns by educational level and other variables are shown in table 15 of the appendix.

It is difficult to specify exactly what such a difference means, except that it is obviously extremely large. A better idea of the substantive meaning of the difference is conveyed by the results of a test of reading skills included in the survey: The average white was reading at nearly a tenth-grade level (9.9), while the average black tested was reading at a seventh-grade level (7.0).[16] But a still clearer sense of the seriousness of the gap may be seen from a test with which most readers have personal experience: the Scholastic Aptitude Test (SAT).

Educational Achievement: The College-Bound

The College Board, which administers the SAT, did not begin to collect background information on its testing population until 1971–72, and not until 1981 did the College Board finally decide to make public the racial breakdown of scores. It took until then for the Board to resolve a controversy between, as the Board put it, "those who fear that publication of these data will serve to convey a misperception of minority students' ability, and those who believe that exposure of the data to public scrutiny will better serve minority interests by demonstrating the need for (and thus lead to) more affirmative action with respect to access to higher education."[17]

As of 1980, the mean SAT score of blacks was 330 for the verbal test and 360 for the math test, more than 100 points lower in each test than the mean for whites. The gap was concentrated in the extremely poor scores. The lower bound for the SATs is 200. Whereas only 3.5 percent of white test-takers scored less than 300, fully a quarter—25.0 percent—of black test-takers scored in that category. The extent of the difference is shown graphically in figure 7.3, using the scores from the mathematics component of the SAT.

There are no hard-and-fast rules about the college performance of people who score at various levels on the SAT. Hard work, motivation, and a variety of other factors are all important. Nonetheless, an SAT score in the region of 400 or less indicates a deficiency of skills that makes it extremely difficult for a student to cope with a demanding college curriculum. Applying the rule, rough as it is, to the distribution of scores on the SAT tests, the implication for classroom performance of a cross-section of black test-takers is that a large majority would fail a true college-level course: 71 percent of black students taking the SAT in 1980 scored less than 400 in the mathematics component of the SAT, and 77 percent scored less than 400 in the verbal component.[18]

When this state of affairs is combined with pressure (indeed, legal demands) not to show racial patterns in grading and placement in honors

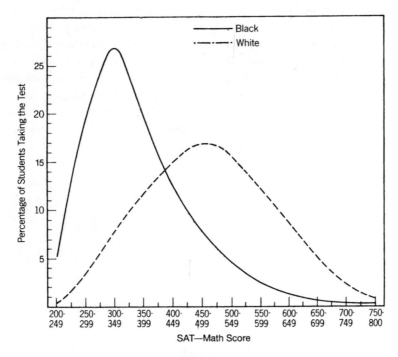

FIGURE 7.3.
Distribution of SAT-Math Scores by Race, 1980
DATA AND SOURCE INFORMATION: Appendix table 16.

courses, at least one reason for the widely publicized deterioration in educational standards is obvious. The only way to avoid racial patterns in grading or placement in honors courses, or any other decisions based on achievement measures, is to employ a double standard of some sort if in fact one racial group has a markedly different pattern of achievement.[19]

In drawing an overall assessment from these data, the echoes of the results on wages and occupations and the "pulling away" process are unmistakable. At the top of the ladder, there was surely progress. The mere fact that so many more blacks were going to college in the 1970s than in the 1950s and early 1960s suggests that improvement occurred. (Even if college education has been getting worse and preparation has been inadequate, we will assume that a bad college education is better than none at all.) We cannot make the same statement about the large majority of black students who do not get that far. At the high-school level, the basic job of keeping kids in school had already come within a fraction of saturation by 1965. The large historical gap in school enrollment between blacks and whites had been closed to within 2 percentage points. While the quality of secondary education was sliding downhill, it could not cling to the excuse that at least it was providing some education to disadvantaged students who previously had gotten none. It was providing worse education, period. Everything we know about inner-city schools suggests that the deterioration in these schools, which served the most disadvantaged of all students, was greater than anywhere else.

Summary of the Federal Effort

IN THE BEGINNING of the period 1950–80, there was no federal effort to speak of. The reasons for federal standoffishness were "race, religion, and fear of federal control," as Diane Ravitch has put it. Northerners were unwilling to fund segregated southern schools, and southerners would not vote for a bill that excluded them. An analogous standoff prevented funding that would include or exclude non-public (largely Catholic) schools. And everyone was determined that the federal government not intrude into decisions about local education—in America, one of the most fiercely protected preserves of local government.

The harbinger of the expanded role was *Brown* v. *Board of Education* in 1954, which struck down the "separate but equal" doctrine. But for several years its importance was more symbolic than real. *Brown I* (the actual decision) spoke eloquently against segregated schools as a violation of constitutional protections. *Brown II* (the guidelines for implementing *Brown I,* issued a year later) left the working-out of desegregation in the hands of local authorities. The result was that, despite a few dramatic pitched battles—the desegregation of Central High School in Little Rock, George Wallace and his stand in the schoolhouse door, the admission of James Meredith to the University of Mississippi—relatively little changed in southern school attendance patterns until late in the 1960s. It was not until 1968, in *Green* v. *County School Board,* that the Court said that "freedom of choice" solutions were inadequate unless they actually resulted in mixed classrooms, and that desegregation must be ended "root and branch" by whatever means worked. See Frank T. Read, "Judicial Evolution of the Law of School Integration Since *Brown* v. *Board of Education,*" *Law and Contemporary Problems* 39 (Winter 1975), pp. 7–49. Meanwhile, in the North, *de jure* segregation was not the problem.

When the federal government finally did become involved in financing education, it was out of fear for the nation's standing vis-à-vis the Soviet Union. The shock of Sputnik in the fall of 1957 jarred loose the first major federal funding of public education so that we might catch up with the Russians. The name of the legislation, "The National Defense Education Act of 1958" (NDEA), reflected its narrowly construed justification.The Congress continued to thwart efforts to pass more general bills to assist the schools.

The huge legislative majority that President Johnson brought away from the 1964 election—68 to 32 in the Senate, 295 to 140 in the House—overwhelmed the special interests that had stymied past efforts to involve the federal government in education. As in so many other initiatives, poverty provided a new rationale: in this instance, for sidestepping the public school–private school controversy. The basis for aid would be the poverty of the students. Whether they attended private or public schools, they would be eligible to receive the services dispensed by public agencies. The result was the Elementary and Secondary Education Act (ESEA) of 1965.

Even as that bill passed, however, other considerations were leading to an expansion of federal involvement in the schools and its hopes for them:

- The federal government wanted to eliminate racial segregation of the schools—not only the *de jure* segregation struck down in the *Brown* decision, but the *de facto* segregation that was nearly universal in urban America.
- It wanted to provide compensatory education for students who were at a special disadvantage—physically, mentally, economically, or sociologically.
- It wanted to protect students' rights.
- It wanted to keep all students in school through the twelfth grade.
- It wanted to remove race bias, sex bias, and a variety of other biases from the curriculum and from the pedagogy of the nation's schools.
- It wanted different, better methods of teaching those who were not doing well under traditional methods—with several schools of thought contending about how this might be done.
- It wanted to provide bilingual education for students, mainly Hispanic, whose first language was not English.

Some of these goals came attached to legislation, some to Supreme Court decisions, some to policies promulgated by the Office of Education (later the Department of Education). To further complicate matters, each of these goals had its own constituency in the public at large and within the educational establishment in particular. Moreover, the transformation of the federal role in education during the period we are examining—and transformation is not an extravagant word for it—was an overlay on an existing system, and the interaction between what the government found itself doing, what educators were intending to do on their own, and what was going on in society outside the school is exceedingly complex. In the subsequent interpretation (chapter 13) of what went wrong, I shall pick out certain elements that seem to me to stand out as especially important —namely, those that affected the ability of a teacher to engage in the act of teaching. But for the moment let us consider the dollars. At least, our educational deficiencies in the period since 1965 cannot be blamed on federal neglect.

Title I of ESEA opened the door to direct federal support of elementary and secondary education, allocating funds to the states according to the number of children from families that fell below specified income levels. The purpose of the funds was "compensatory education" for low-income students. Even from the beginning, funding was high. ESEA and the other programs for disadvantaged students are an important exception to the generalization that the Great Society programs were not implemented in a big way until after the reform period. Funding for disadvantaged elementary and secondary students went from nowhere in 1964 to over $3 billion (in 1980 dollars) by 1966. By 1968, funding had reached the real spending level it would maintain through the first half of the 1970s. See W. Vance Grant and Leo J. Eiden, *Digest of Educational Statistics 1981* (Washington, D.C.: Government Printing Office, 1982), table 161. This source, prepared by the National Center for Educational Statistics, is hereafter designated *DES-81*.

In higher education, the first problem facing disadvantaged students was getting the money to go to school. To that end, the NDEA loan program begun in 1958 was augmented by the Higher Education Act of 1965, which for the first time provided federal scholarships (not just loans) for undergraduates. Total funding of grants and loans combined ran just under a billion dollars (1980 dollars) through 1970, and slightly more than a billion through 1973. Then the budgets took off, doubling in another two years and reaching more than $4 billion annually by 1980. (The figures for student loans include both NDEA and insured loans. The figures for grants are predominantly Basic and Supplemental Educational Opportunity Grants, plus a scattering of other programs (*DES-81*, table 163, note 6).

To get a sense of how large the effort became, consider that grants and loans totalling $4.4 billion—the figure for 1980—are equivalent to a million annual awards of $4,400 in support. Even in 1972, when the size of the grant and loan programs was comparatively small, 32 percent of all college freshmen were receiving federal assistance. Among freshmen in the lowest socioeconomic quartile, 47 percent were receiving federal assistance. Fifty-three percent of all black students were receiving federal support in a year when the size of the program, in constant dollars, was only a fifth of the size it would reach by 1980 (*DES-81*, table 135).

Diane Ravitch's *The Troubled Crusade: American Education 1945–1980* (New York: Basic Books, 1983) is the best single account of the course of American education during the period we are examining. For a review of the provisions of federal education programs, see Ravitch, *Troubled Crusade*, and Henry M. Levin, "A Decade of Policy Developments in Improving Education and Training for Low-Income Populations," in Robert H. Haveman, ed., *A Decade of Federal Antipoverty Programs: Achievements, Failures, and Lessons* (New York: Academic Press, 1977), 123–96.

8

Crime

PEOPLE SURVIVE. Large and increasing numbers of young persons in the 1960s were no longer in the job market, or were in the job market only intermittently, or were unsuccessful at finding a job when they tried. Large numbers of them were functionally illiterate and without skills that the larger society values. Yet they were surviving. One of the ways in which they were surviving was through crime. In the mid-1960s, in a marked departure from the trends of recent American history, the number of people engaging in criminal activity—and the number of their victims—increased explosively. The people who suffered most from this change were urban blacks.

The primary source of data we shall use is the Uniform Crime Report (UCR) program conducted by the FBI. For data on victims we shall also draw on the victimization surveys that have been conducted periodically since the mid-1960s. These data, like all crime data, are subject to numerous caveats. Readers are referred to the notes that accompany specific points. Because of the inherent complexity of interpreting crime data, which deal with an especially hard-to-observe phenomenon, I shall limit the discussion to a few of the most basic trends. In all cases, we shall focus on the "index" offenses—murder, rape, robbery, and aggravated assault (summed to make the "Violent Crime" index) and burglary, larceny, and auto theft (summed to make the "Property Crime" index).[1] The trendlines for the two crime indexes are shown in figure 8.1.

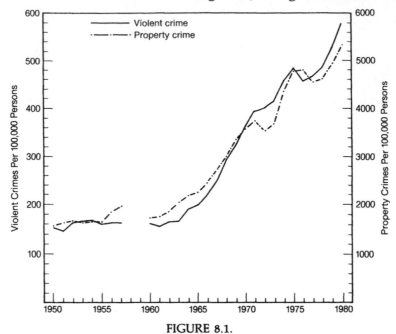

FIGURE 8.1.

Crimes Reported to the Police: Indexes for 1950–1980

DATA AND SOURCE INFORMATION: Appendix table 18 and note 2, chapter 8.
NOTE: Data for 1950–57 are based on 353 cities of 25,000 population or greater. Data for 1960–80 include all reporting jurisdictions.

Crime from 1950 to 1980: An Overview

It may come as a surprise to those who remember J. Edgar Hoover's annual warnings during the 1950s that crime was dangerously on the rise or the 1950s movies about the breakdown of law and order (*Blackboard Jungle, The Wild Ones*), but the crime rate in those days was almost tediously constant and low. Violent crime remained nearly unchanged during the 1950s, while property crime probably increased slightly in the last half of the 1950s. Rates for both types of crime were stable in the first few years of the 1960s.[2]

Some kinds of crime actually decreased during the 1950s and into the early 1960s. Homicide, the crime for which historical data are most complete and most accurate, went from 5.3 per 100,000 in 1950 to about 4.5 throughout the last half of the 1950s, and as late as 1964 it stood at only 5.1.[3]

Then, in about 1964—the take-off year varies by type of crime—the crime rate started to climb steeply for both property and violent crime. The rates for the individual elements of the indexes are as follows:

	Percentage Change, 1963–80
Violent Crime	
Murder	+122
Forcible Rape	+287
Robbery	+294
Aggravated Assault	+215
Property Crime	
Burglary	+189
Larceny	+159
Auto Theft	+128

All sorts of crime got worse—not only according to the UCR data, but also according to other, independent measures. The general topic of the UCR data and the "real" crime rate has been a subject of intense research and debate over the years. After a period of controversy about whether crime was really increasing at all (for a time, the increase was argued to be an artifact), a degree of consensus has been established.[4] During the late 1960s and early 1970s, crime of all types did, in fact, soar.[5] For trends after 1973, there is still argument. The UCR data show substantial increases in both indexes, while the National Crime Survey shows slight changes both up and down.[6] The jury is still out on where the true increase lies.

The Criminals

The focus of our interest is the 1960s, and not the crime but the criminal and the victim. Who was behind the sudden rise? Who was hurt?

We begin with the criminals. We know first that they were male; that has been true for as long as statistics have been kept. In 1954, males accounted for 89 percent of arrests for violent crimes; in 1974, they accounted for 90 percent. In this regard, little changed.

Second, they were young. In 1954, persons under twenty-five years of age accounted for 40 percent of arrests for violent crimes. In 1974, that proportion had increased to 60 percent.

Third, they were more often black than white, but no more so than they had been in the past. In 1954, blacks accounted for 57 percent of arrests for violent crimes. In 1974, that proportion had dropped—not increased, as the folk wisdom usually has it—to 52 percent.

But proportionate changes do not address the issue that concerns us. Our purpose is not to fix the "blame" for the crime problem, but to identify the difference between the behavior of the poor and disadvantaged before the surge in crime and during it. We are using blacks as our proxy for that group. And in this sense, black behavior toward crime changed in a way that is qualitatively different from the way that white behavior changed.[7]

THE SPECIAL CASE OF HOMICIDE

The crime for which we have the best historical data is homicide. Homicide is almost always reported; almost always solved; and has been the subject of careful record-keeping. Figure 8.2 shows the trendline for victims from 1950 to 1980, and for arrests from 1960 to 1980.

Before considering the steep, abrupt rise in the 1960s, let us consider the experience of 1950–60, when homicide victimization dropped—22 percent for black males.[8] It was a large reduction for a single decade. It was all the more remarkable when one considers that it coincided with a period of rapid black migration into urban centers—a 24 percent increase from just

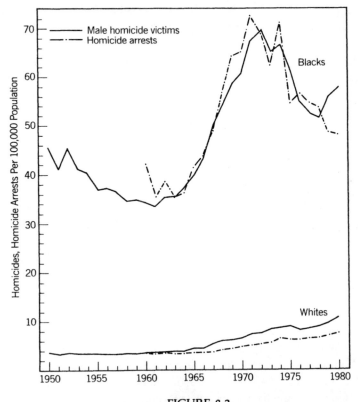

FIGURE 8.2.

Male Homicides and Homicide Arrests by Race, 1950–1980

DATA AND SOURCE INFORMATION: Appendix table 18.

1950 to 1960 in the proportion of blacks living in central cities, a much faster increase than in subsequent years.[9] The black homicide rate "should" have been rising in the statistics, if only because so many more blacks were moving to places where the homicide rate tends to be high. But it fell instead.

If this reduction in the black homicide rate had occurred following the institution of a program that was supposed to reduce crime, it would have been cause for dozens of analyses. Perhaps because it happened on its own, it has attracted little attention, and we know little about it except for the fact that it did occur, was substantial, and was highly positive.

Then came the rise. Put simply, it was much more dangerous to be black in 1972 than it was in 1965, whereas it was not much more dangerous to be white. Lest this be thought an abstraction, consider the odds. Arnold Barnett and his colleagues at the Massachusetts Institute of Technology have calculated that, at 1970 levels of homicide, a person who lived his life in a large American city ran a greater risk of being murdered than an American soldier in the Second World War ran of being killed in combat.[10] If this analysis were restricted to the ghettoes of large American cities, the risk would be some orders of magnitude larger yet, and larger than it had been ten years before.

VIOLENT CRIMINALS IN GENERAL

Blacks historically have been arrested at much higher rates than whites for all violent crimes, not just homicide. The pattern in the homicide arrest data has parallels in the UCR data on arrests for the other predatory crimes that are the crux of "the crime problem."

We may make use of these data to draw inferences despite knowing that arrest does not always mean guilt. The notes discuss some of the technical issues at length, including the contaminating factor of racism. The conclusion (as suggested by the close match between homicide arrest and victimization trends in figure 8.2) is that the trendlines are indeed interpretable as evidence of the incidence of criminal behavior. There is reason to believe that, if anything, the increase in black criminal activity is considerably understated by the official data.[11]

In 1960, when our detailed examination of the racial breakdown for crime other than homicide begins, blacks were being arrested for violent crimes (homicide, robbery, rape, aggravated assault) at a rate 10 times the rate for whites (arrests relative to the size of the male population aged 13–39).[12] As in the case of homicide, however, the arrest rates as of the early 1960s seemed to be holding steady or dropping.

Then, as in the case of homicide, the rates went up for both blacks and whites—but in different magnitudes and different patterns. Among blacks, the increase per 100,000 was much larger, and it was much more concentrated in the late 1960s and early 1970s. Consider the period from 1965 to 1970, which "should" (if the trend had been linear) have accounted for about 25 percent of the overall change in violent crime from 1960 to 1980. The year-by-year rates are presented in table 20 of the appendix, along with additional breakdowns for property crimes and for juveniles versus adults (appendix table 21). These numbers summarize the situation for arrests for violent crimes per 100,000 males aged 13–39:

	Blacks and Others	Whites
Rate of arrests in 1960	2,529	250
Change in the rate, 1965–70	+866	+118
Rate of arrests as of 1980	3,485	661
Percent of the 1960–80 increase that occurred during 1965–70	91%	29%

Source: Computed from UCR arrest data and CPS population data. See note 12 for discussion.

The increase in arrests for violent crimes among blacks during the 1965–70 period was seven times that of whites. The proportion of the 1960–80 increase that occurred in 1965–70 was 91 percent—compared with a barely-higher-than-expected 29 percent of the white increase. In reality, the bunching in the black increase is even more concentrated than the 1965–70 period suggests. From just 1966 to 1969, black arrests for violent crime increased by 958 per 100,000—slighter more in that brief time than the net increase of 956 per 100,000 during the entire period 1960–80. It is fundamentally misleading to see the black crime problem as one that has been getting worse indefinitely. It got worse very suddenly, over a very concentrated period of time.

Interpretations of why crime increased must accommodate this unusual profile. I will suggest one interpretation in chapter 13. Another, however, presents itself so intuitively that it deserves brief comment here: The late 1960s were the riot years. The nation went through a time of intense racial strife during which blacks widely rejected the legitimacy of white norms and white laws. Crime went up as one symptom of that rejection.

As a statement about how inner-city blacks who were committing crimes during those years felt about what they were doing, the explanation may have merit; I will not argue the point. The problem with using it as a statement about *why* crime increased is that the increase outlasted the riots. Black arrest rates during the 1970s generally peaked in mid-decade and subsided to some extent for some crimes thereafter (as shown in appendix table 20), but as of 1980 the rates were still roughly where they were after they shot upward in the late 1960s. Broadly construed, the reason presumably lies in a socialization process that took root in the sixties. But whatever part political socializing forces of the sixties contributed to the initial surge, they cannot easily be used to account for the continuing vitality of the black crime rate throughout the 1970s. Nor is it intellectually satisfying to hypothesize that blacks "got used to" sustaining the higher crime rate out of some sort of inertia. The jump in black arrests for violent crimes (and, for that matter, for property crimes) was too sudden, too large, and lasted too long to be dismissed as just an anomaly of a turbulent decade.

The Victims

Meanwhile, what of the victims? It has become a truism in discussions of what is wrong with the American system of justice that the victim is forgotten. It is more accurate to say that black victims, and especially low-income black victims in the inner-city, have been forgotten. Judging from the available data, they have paid a far heavier price for the rise in crime than have whites.

The first good data are from 1965–66, when the President's Commission on Law Enforcement and the Administration of Justice conducted a large-scale survey of criminal victimization. The survey, which occurred near the beginning of the rise in crime, revealed the dramatic effect of both race and economics on the probability of becoming a victim. To take just one example: Among middle-income whites (income of roughly $15,700–26,000 in 1980 dollars), only 42 per 100,000 were victims of robbery. Among poor whites (income of less than $7,800), the rate was 116. Among poor blacks, the rate was 278.[13]

As crime rose in last half of the 1960s, the augmented risks of daily life were vastly greater for the poor, and especially for poor blacks, than they were for the affluent and the white. To see this, let us think in terms of the numbers of persons "penalized" by being poor or black in 1979 compared with 1965. I use victimizations per 100,000 for middle-income whites as the baseline number—a sort of "standard number of victims" at any given point in history—and ask, how many more people (for each 100,000 persons) are victimized among poor whites? Among poor blacks? These are the results for 1965 versus 1979:

	1965	1979
Excess victimizations among poor whites (per 100,000)		
Raped	48	169
Robbed	74	382
Assaulted (aggravated)	−1	768
Excess victimizations among poor blacks (per 100,000)		
Raped	101	211
Robbed	236	1,143
Assaulted (aggravated)	242	660

Sources: Philip H. Ennis, "Criminal Victimization in the United States. Field Surveys II. A Report of a National Survey," President's Commission on Law Enforcement and the Administration of Justice (Washington, D.C.: Government Printing Office, 1967), 31. Timothy J. Flanagan, David J. van Alystyne, and Michael R. Gottfredson, eds., *Sourcebook of Criminal Justice Statistics—1981* (Washington, D.C.: Government Printing Office, 1982), table 3.12.

I put the numbers in these terms ("excess" victimizations) to emphasize a point. It is true that rising crime has been a problem for everyone. The white middle-income victimization rates in 1979 were far higher than they were in the 1965 survey—seven times higher for rape, almost ten times higher for robbery, six times higher for aggravated assault.[14] But more than enough attention has gravitated to such numbers, and to the image of the black urban street mugger preying on the innocent white middle class. The purpose of the comparison I have drawn is to highlight the great human price paid for this increase in crime by poor people and blacks.[15]

Summary of the Federal Effort

PRIOR TO 1968, the federal role in crime-stopping had been limited essentially to the work of the Federal Bureau of Investigation, with a few other bits and pieces in the Department of the Treasury. It was a highly visible role; under the direction of J. Edgar Hoover, the FBI sustained for many years the image of an elite, nearly infallible instrument for catching criminals. But the FBI's charter was limited to certain categories of crime (for the most part, interstate cases) and to a modest training function for local law-enforcement agencies. In the late 1960s, as the federal government was launching ambitious initiatives in every other area of social policy, it was only natural that some way would be found to apply federal muscle to the crime problem. But which way to go? Get tough (the conservative prescription)? Or attack the problem at its roots (the liberal prescription)?

The conservatives (and apparently much of the electorate) got what they wanted, a program that would try to strengthen the hand of the law enforcers in catching criminals. A national police force was out of the question. But the federal government could *assist* local law enforcement, whence the rationale for the Law Enforcement Assistance Administration (LEAA), created as part of the omnibus crime bill passed in the election year of 1968.

LEAA provided help of all kinds. It gave grants directly to police departments, courts, and correctional facilities; it also dispensed large "block grants" to the states for apportioning to localities. LEAA's research arm, the National Institute of Law Enforcement and Criminal Justice, sponsored research to augment our knowledge about crime and its causes. It developed uniform criminal justice "standards" against which to assess and, it was hoped, reduce the enormous diversity in practices. It tried to introduce rationality and method into a system that, from a national perspective, was a tangle of local idiosyncracies and suspect traditions.

Side by side with LEAA, the federal government undertook much more extensive programs that, in the liberal view, were likely to do more to reduce crime than anything LEAA could come up with. They did not bear the label of "anticrime" programs, but their sponsors openly saw crime as the understandable response of people who lacked alternatives and saw the social programs of the late 1960s as the best hope for providing those alternatives.

The social programs were accompanied by an unlegislated but widespread alteration in the norms of operation for the criminal justice system. Sometimes these changes were mandated by court decisions, sometimes they were ordered by administrators, sometimes they just happened as a result of a collective agreement about the right way to do things. From whatever source, practices such as release on recognizance, use of probation, plea bargaining, alternative sentences, and suspended sentences expanded.

The competing demands of the two approaches were most clearly evident in the federal effort to combat juvenile delinquency. The image of the delinquent had been radically altered by the experience of the 1960s. Among members of the general public, the decade saw a transformation of the image of the delinquent from truant and hubcap thief to urban mugger. But the persons manning the antipoverty programs saw the urban delinquent as a leading emblem of society's failure to deal with the problems of youth, especially urban black youth. "Youth-serving" programs grew rapidly. By 1972, a federal inventory of such programs counted 166 of them, scattered among the Departments of Labor, Housing and Urban Development, Agriculture, Justice, and HEW. In 1974, the Congress acted to consolidate and coordinate the programs by creating the Office of Juvenile Justice and Delinquency Prevention. The language of the act (PL 93–415) explicitly instructed the new agency to minimize institutionalization, to focus on prevention rather than crime-suppression activities, and in general to implement the doctrine of the "least drastic alternative" (that is, choose the least punitive, disrupting option in dealing with an apprehended delinquent).

The dollar commitment to these efforts followed the familiar curve. In 1950, the combined budget of the Department of Justice and the FBI was $455 million in 1980 dollars. The combined figure climbed steadily but slowly through the 1960s (as in other instances, the increase in expenditures lagged behind the increase in rhetoric), standing at $1.2 billion in 1969, the first year that LEAA's budget was added in. Within only three years, that total had nearly doubled to $2.3 billion. Annual funding for the Department of Justice, FBI, and LEAA eventually reached more than $3.4 billion before disillusionment with LEAA set in during the late 1970s and its allocations were cut. By 1980, annual funding was at $2.6 billion.

These figures understate the funding for programs to prevent crime by omitting the substantial sums expended under the initial antipoverty bills and by agencies other than those included in the Department of Justice. But determining how much money to assign to the anticrime effort (as opposed to general efforts to help disadvantaged populations) is highly subjective. The figures for the Department of Justice capture the bulk of the money spent directly on the criminal and the delinquent and the justice system, and as such they may be read as a minimum representation of the total effort.

9

The Family

IT WAS NO ACCIDENT that John Kennedy's message calling for welfare reform put "the integrity and preservation of the family unit" first on the list of his goals for public welfare.[1] Even in 1961, the welfare system as exemplified by AFDC was widely thought to be undermining the families of the poor. Little in the tone of public debate has changed since. No topic has been more controversial in the discussion of social policy than the effects of such policy on the family.

The following discussion will reinforce some popular conceptions about what has happened to the family in recent years and will moderate some others. We will find that the trendlines for impoverished black families have been about as ominous as most people think they have been. But in the case of the family, unlike crime or education, the data permit us to compare trends among the poor versus the not-poor as well as the trends among blacks versus whites. What we will observe—as I suggest we have been observing throughout this book—is largely explained as a concomitant of poverty, one which in the 1960s for some reason became suddenly more common.

Choosing Measures

When we assess what has happened to the family during 1950–80, choosing measures is a problem: On many dimensions, it is not clear which direction is up. Take, for example, the case of the working mother. How does one decide who is gaining and who is losing? Some women are entering the work force because they want to; others because they have to. Some women with children lead richer lives if they hold a job outside the home; others do not. Some children are better off when the mother stays at home; others are not. Deciding whether net changes in an indicator such as "percent of children in families with a working mother" represent a plus or a minus is possible only for the most dogmatic. Similarly, how does one interpret data on the living arrangements of the elderly? Is it good or is it bad when larger numbers live apart from their children? Sometimes it's good, sometimes it's bad. The aggregate numbers do not tell us which. We will concentrate on two indicators that almost everybody agrees are important evidence of problems with the family: illegitimate births, and families headed by a single female.[2]

Illegitimate Births

In the publicity surrounding the rising problem of illegitimate births, one of the least-mentioned statistics regarding this emotional topic is that the *proportion* of unmarried women having babies has increased hardly at all in the last twenty years. In 1960, 22 out of every 1,000 single women gave birth to a live baby. In 1980, 29 of every 1,000 single women gave birth to a live baby. It is an increase, even a noteworthy increase. But it is not an epidemic.

If the mildness of the increase is not sufficiently surprising, consider that unmarried black women were having babies at a considerably *lower* rate in 1980 than they were in 1960. Further, the birth rate among black single women had fallen almost without a break since its high in 1961. The birth rate among single black women was 98 live births per 1,000 women in 1960, 90 in 1970, and 77 in 1980.

So where is the crisis in illegitimacy? It consists first of all in the mathematics of a growing population. It is true that the rate per 1,000 has changed relatively little, but the numbers have grown substantially. In 1960, approximately 224,000 children were born to single mothers. In 1980, the number had grown to 665,747. The crisis consists secondly in the relationship of this number to the overall number of births. Birth rates for women aged 15–44 fell from 118 per 1,000 in 1960 to 68 in 1980, and the result was that an increasing proportion of newborns were illegitimate. This problem was most acute for blacks. Figure 9.1 shows illegitimate births not as a rate per 1,000 women, but as a percentage of all births:

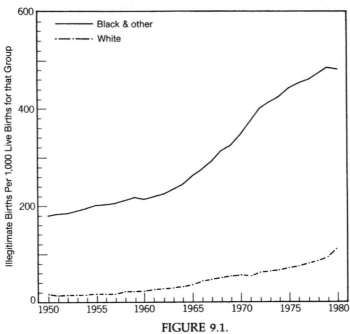

FIGURE 9.1.
Illegitimate Births Per 1,000 Live Births by Race, 1950–1980
DATA AND SOURCE INFORMATION: Appendix table 24.

From 1950 through 1963, black illegitimate births rose slowly and linearly, from about 17 percent of all black births to 23 percent. This was the source of the growing anger with AFDC in the late 1950s—the black rate was much higher than the white rate to begin with, and was growing much faster. Yet as it turned out, the increase that caused the uproar was trivial compared with what followed. If the trendline from 1950 to 1963 had remained unchanged, the black illegitimacy rate would have increased another 6.8 percentage points by 1980. Instead, the slope of the trendline suddenly steepened. The increase was not 6.8 percentage points, but nearly four times that. In 1980, 48 percent of live births among blacks were to single women, compared with 17 percent in 1950.

126

During the same period, white illegitimate births were increasing as well, from less than 2 percent in 1950 to 11 percent in 1980. The proportional increase was high, but the number of births per hundred remained relatively low—still much lower, by way of comparison, than the black rate of thirty years earlier.[3]

The problem lay not just in the number of illegitimate births, but in who was having them: teenagers. In 1955, teenaged girls gave birth to nearly half a million babies (490,000). But of these half million, only about 70,000 of the mothers were unmarried. In 1980, the number of children born to teenagers was not markedly greater than in 1955—about 562,000. But the number of single young mothers—teenagers—had grown to 272,000.

Among black teenagers, the predominance of illegitimate births was approaching unity: In 1980, among black young women aged 15–19, 82 percent of all births were illegitimate. The birth rates among American black teenagers in general and single black teenagers in particular were anomalous not only from the perspective of the American historical experience, but from that of worldwide experience. In a study of fertility among thirty-two populations in developed nations, Charles Westoff and his associates at Princeton University concluded:

> To put it in a dramatic perspective, the 1980 teenage fertility rate for U.S. blacks is the highest of all 32 populations examined here, and it is 37 percent higher than the next highest rate, for Arab Israelis. Even more vivid is a comparison of fertility rates for women under 18 years of age in 1979/80: Among blacks in the United States this rate is 237 per 1,000, whereas the highest rate in the remaining populations is 103 births per 1,000 (in Hungary).[4]

The Westoff study added two other points that need emphasis. The fertility rate among black teenagers that was so high relative to the rest of the developed world in 1980 had *gone down* by 28 percent since 1971. And the second-place population in 1980 (Arab-Israeli) consisted of a traditional population of young women who marry at a very young age. If the study had been limited to illegitimate births, the fertility rate of U.S. black teenagers would have been much further out of proportion to the international range than it already was.

In the United States, the aspect of teenage behavior that stands out is its inconsistency with the prevailing trends among other women. To illustrate how differently teenagers in general behaved from married women and older single women, let us consider the crucial period from 1965 to 1970, when the greatest divergence occurred:

	Change in Birth Rate, 1965–70 (In Live Births/1,000)
Married Women, White	
25–29 Years	−12
20–24 Years	−27
15–19 Years	−11
Married Women, Black and other	
25–29 Years	−29
20–24 Years	−26
15–19 Years	−80
Single Women, White	
25–29 Years	−3
20–24 Years	+0.5
15–19 Years	+3
Single Women, Black and other	
25–29 Years	−67
20–24 Years	−27
15–19 Years	+14

SOURCE: National Center for Health Statistics, *Vital Statistics of the United States, 1978*, Vol. I. DHHS Pub. No. (PHS)82–1100 (Washington, D.C.: Government Printing Office, 1982), tables 1–32 and 1–33, pp. 1–54 to 1–57

This is a variation on a theme that we have considered previously under headings of unemployment, labor force participation, and crime: the very young behaved differently from everyone else, even from their own older siblings. We are faced again with a complex problem of causation. Without question, broad forces of one sort or another were at work to decrease the birth rate. To the extent that they were affected by changing sexual mores and sexual roles, unmarried women seemed to be exercising a new freedom *not* to have children. The only exceptions to this generalization were single 15–19-year-olds, black and white alike, and, by a fractional amount, single 20–24-year-old white women. For this narrow population of women, something overrode the broad social (and medical) trends that produced falling birth rates among everyone else.

The long-range effects of the change in birth patterns are not fully captured by quantitative measures. When we speak of single teenagers with babies, we are speaking of young women who are experiencing all of the problems that go with adolescence in late twentieth-century America. In addition, they most commonly have little money, little education, no job, and no permanent partner to help make up for the financial and psychological deficits. The lives of such young women are irretrievably changed by the fact of their single motherhood—education, access to a job ladder, and simple freedom to mature without the pressures of raising a child are made extraordinarily more difficult. The lives of their children are affected as decisively—not just because of the stigma that continues to attach to illegitimacy, but because poor, uneducated, single teenaged mothers are in a bad position to raise children, however much they may love them.[5]

Although quantifiable measures are not the most important measures of the problem, one of them suggests its seriousness. Low birth weight (less than 2,500 grams) is a predictor of a wide variety of health problems in infants, including many permanent physical and mental handicaps. Low birth weight is also associated with the age of the mother, with teenagers tending to have a higher proportion of such infants than mothers in their twenties. The radical change in the composition of the child-bearing population among blacks may have contributed to an increase from 10.4 to 11.5 percent in the proportion of low-birth-weight newborns from 1950 to 1980, despite great progress in the technology of prenatal and infant care during the intervening years. During the same period, the white percentage of low-birth-weight newborns (already lower to begin with) dropped from 7.2 to 5.7.

"Female Householder, No Husband Present"

In 1965, a report written by an obscure assistant secretary of labor in the Johnson administration named Moynihan reaped widespread publicity and no little invective for its author because it discussed the breakup of black families.[6] At the time Moynihan wrote his report, the rate of decline in two-parent families that had caused the uproar was about to triple.[7]

A racial difference in family composition has existed since statistics have been kept, but by the middle of this century the proportions for whites and blacks, while different, were stable. As of 1950, decenniel census figures, show that 88 percent of white families consisted of husband-wife households, compared with 78 percent of black families. Both figures had remained essentially unchanged since before the Second World War (the figures for the 1940 census were 86 and 77 percent, respectively). From the beginning of annual CPS data (which should not be compared directly with the census estimate) through 1967, the black figure moved in a range between 72 and 75 percent, tending to decline. The figures for white families were nearly unvarying throughout the same period.

Then, in a single year (1968), the percentage for black families fell from 72 to 69, the beginning of a steep slide. In the next five years, the proportion of black husband-wife families dropped another six percentage points, to 63 percent. By the end of 1980, the proportion was 59 percent —a drop of 13 percentage points in twelve years. (During the same twelve years, the figure for whites dropped by three percentage points.) Like the drop in black male LFP, a change of this magnitude is a demographic wonder, without precedent in the American experience.

Black Americans have had to put up with much disapprobation, not to mention racist rhetoric, because of statistics of the kind I have just presented. But how much of family breakdown is really a phenomenon of black culture and how much is a matter of economic class?

Official figures breaking down illegitimate births as such by income group are not available. We can, however, use official data on poverty to compare the family structures (one- or two-parent households) of different economic groups. The published poverty statistics show the number of people living below the poverty level, and below 125 percent of the poverty level, in families headed by a "female householder, no husband present," as the Census Bureau puts it. This category includes persons in families of divorced mothers, widows, and never-married women.[8] "Un-

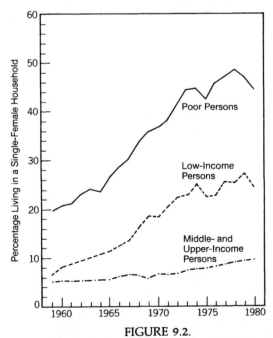

FIGURE 9.2.

Persons in Single-Female Households by Income Group, as Percentage of Persons Living in Families, 1959–1980

DATA AND SOURCE INFORMATION: Appendix table 25.

related individuals"—including single females living alone—are excluded from this calculation. We may use these data, available back to 1959, to examine trendlines by income group and by race.

In figure 9.2, race is not shown. Instead, the population of persons who live in families has been broken into three income groups: those whose income is below the poverty level ("poor"), those whose income falls between the poverty level and 125 percent of the poverty level ("low-income"), and those whose income is greater than 125 percent of the poverty level ("middle- and upper-income"). The graph plots the percentage of persons in each income group who lived in families headed by a single female.

The association of income with trends in family composition is clear from the plot. The percentage of middle- and upper-income persons who live in single-female families scarcely changed during the sixties and seventies. Among low-income persons, the percentage increased noticeably,

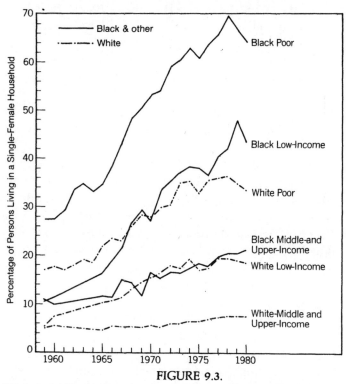

FIGURE 9.3.

Persons in Single-Female Households by Race and Income Group, as Percentage of Persons Living in Families, 1959–1980

DATA AND SOURCE INFORMATION: Appendix table 25.

from nearly the same as the middle- and upper-income group to 25 percent by 1980. Among the poor, the increase was precipitous, from about 20 percent in 1960 to almost half (45 percent) in 1980. A major portion of what has been treated as a racial difference may be treated as an economic one.

Not all, however. The published data on poverty permit a breakdown by both race and income group, revealing important remaining racial differences even after income is taken into account, as shown in figure 9.3.

In percentage points, the most conspicuous difference was between whites and blacks below the poverty line. As of 1980, 65 percent of all poor blacks who were living in families were living in families headed by a single female. The parallel statistic for whites was 34 percent.

But if the situation among blacks below the poverty line is most dramatic, the trend among low-income blacks—those with an income of 100–125 percent of the poverty level—is the most puzzling. In 1959, low-income blacks lived in families very much like those of low-income whites and, for that matter, like those of middle- and upper-income persons of all races. Barely one in ten of the low-income blacks in families was living in a single-female family. By 1980, the 10 percent figure had become 44 percent. The prevalence of the one-parent family among low-income blacks in 1980 had not only risen far above the level of their more affluent counterparts, both white and black, but had risen above the level of poor whites.

What are causes and what are effects? Did reductions in poverty create a new profile of the poor (in effect, weeding out the two-parent families), or did poor people start to behave differently with regard to marriage and divorce? Two different issues are involved. If the question is, "Are families headed by a single female disproportionately poor?" the answer is yes, and it has led to what is known as the "feminization of poverty." But if the question is, "Did poor people start to behave differently?" the answer is also yes. The number of poor families headed by a single female increased dramatically, not just as a proportion of people living in poverty but in absolute numbers as well, and these numbers were out of proportion to increases in the overall population. If one compares extremes—the white not-poor with the black poor—the contrast is stark. Much is made of the changes in family structure that swept America during the 1960s and 1970s. Statistically, however, the changes in family composition among the white not-poor were negligible. If these families broke up more often, new two-parent families regrouped. Meanwhile, the structure of the poor black family was transformed.

Family Composition and Poverty

When I began in chapter 4 to present the data on being poor and being black from 1950 to 1980, I posed the poverty/spending paradox. How could it be that, despite the combination of economic growth and huge increases in expenditures on the poor, the number of poor stopped shrinking in the early 1970s and then began growing? We have encountered a variety of explanations. Some of the poverty was accounted for by working-aged males who formerly would have been in the labor force but no longer were. Some of it was accounted for by males who were in the labor force but were experiencing growing levels of unemployment. Now we have an additional explanation: the increasing prevalence of a certain type of family—a young mother with children and no husband present. Such families have historically shown high rates of poverty, whether because the single-female head of household is untrained to work at a well-paying job, because of her need to stay home to care for the children, or because of chronic unemployment for other reasons. Gordon Green and Edward Welniak, analysts at the Bureau of the Census, examined the effects of this trend on the poverty statistics. They asked what would have happened if the proportions of different types of families had remained at their 1970 levels. The answer they found was that "[o]verall, changes in family composition have accounted for 2,017,000 additional poor families" in the 1980 statistics—32 percent of the number of poor families actually reported.[9]

In reality, the Gordon and Welniak analysis captures only a part of the story. By 1970, when their data begin, a large proportion of the increase in single-female households had already occurred. If the baseline had been 1965 instead of 1970, the effects would have been that much greater; exactly how much cannot be determined with the data at hand.

Summary of the Federal Effort

Virtually every new social program during the reform period included among its justifications that it would stabilize the family. Jobs programs, education programs, health programs, the income-maintenance programs—all were hoped to have indirectly beneficial effects on the formation and sustenance of families. Arriving at an estimate of federal expenditures on the family is accordingly unrealistic. The growth pattern follows the general increase in social spending. The events in federal policy affecting the family are detailed in chapter 12.

10

The View from 1966

THE PROPOSITION underlying the last six chapters is that things not only got worse for the poor and disadvantaged beginning (in most cases) in the last half of the 1960s, they got much worse than they "should have gotten" under the economic and social conditions that prevailed in the society at large. This is of course a hazardous assertion. It is not susceptible to proof, and, *ex post facto,* we can concoct some sort of benign explanation for almost any catastrophe—benign in that it tells us we were helpless to prevent it.

But the explanations must indeed be after the fact. For no one prior to the reform period could have predicted the trendlines in the years to follow *even if one had been given prescient knowledge of the state of the economy* and other salient factors. To illustrate, a little role-playing may help.

Let us set our role-play in December 1959. The civil rights movement is gaining momentum, but the economy is still suffering the after-effects of a major recession, the Congress is divided, and the president is passive. Let us say that I am a policy analyst appearing at a colloquium on Negro progress during the 1950s. (No one will ask me about the progress of the poor during the 1950s; the poor had yet to be rediscovered.) In my comments I acknowledge a generally upward trend in the progress of Negroes, but I express my concern about the wide gap still separating whites and

Negroes on almost every dimension of economic and social well-being. Then the moderator puts a hypothetical question to me:

> Suppose that in the next decade we pass sweeping civil rights legislation forbidding all discrimination on the basis of race—in hiring practices, public accommodations, and voting. Suppose that we further require businesses and schools to take special measures to recruit Negroes. Suppose further that the civil rights movement leads to an upsurge of racial pride and assertiveness among Negroes. Suppose further that we pass legislation that will pay for college for just about everybody who qualifies and provides free job training to just about anyone who wants it. Suppose, finally, that during this same period we enjoy continuous economic growth. What then would you predict for Negro progress in closing these gaps you speak of?

From my vantage point of 1959, I reject the suppositions as preposterously optimistic. But if they all did come true? Of course, the gaps would narrow. It would be inconceivable to predict anything else.

Then, let us imagine, the panelist sitting beside me says: "No, what will happen is that the younger generation of Negroes will leave the labor force, form huge numbers of single-parent families, and experience soaring rates of crime and illegitimacy and unemployment."

My reaction is that I am listening to nonsense. Even if my prescient colleague could foresee the riots and the Vietnam War, it would be extremely difficult to explain to me or any other observer in 1959 how such events could possibly override the progress that would be sure to accompany the hypothetical changes. I respond that *something else,* of extraordinary influence, would have to be added to the scenario to produce the outcomes predicted by my colleague.

The purpose of the role-playing is to point up that our *ex post facto* explanations cannot easily pass off what happened in the 1960s and 1970s as "part of the times." Any explanations must take into account the many respects in which the trends went *against* the grain of the times.

Now, let us be more specific about the numbers. I have referred periodically throughout the last six chapters to the "steepening trendline" or the "unexpected change" in the late 1960s. To convey a sense of how the disparate indicators and trends hang together, let us again do some pretending.

This time, let us imagine that it is June 1966. I am a policy analyst in the Johnson White House. My task is to help design the next phase of the War on Poverty. To this end I have been asked to project the progress of the disadvantaged some years out—to, say, 1980. I am told to use as my test population for this purpose the most disadvantaged group of all, black

Americans. The analytic question is this: Based on what we know now—through 1965—what can we expect the future to hold? The purpose of the analysis is to separate the problems that will more or less solve themselves in the natural course of events from those that will continue to plague the disadvantaged unless special remedial steps are taken.

As analysts often do in such cases, I begin by defining an "optimistic" scenario and a "pessimistic" scenario. If I project on this basis for each of the scenarios independently, an envelope is formed within which the true future is likely to fall.

As the basis for the optimistic scenario, I am inclined to take the years since John Kennedy came to office to the present—that is, 1961 to 1965. The year 1961 is a natural breakpoint, dividing the Eisenhower from the post-Eisenhower period. Also, I reason, 1961–65 has been a period of steady economic growth, reductions in poverty, stabilization of black unemployment among the young, and reductions of black unemployment among older workers. As the basis for the pessimistic scenario, I take the years 1954–61—the post-Korea Eisenhower years. I choose 1954 in part out of necessity—it is the first year for which detailed annual information about the black population is available—but it also has a symbolic appropriateness as well, marking the *Brown* v. *Board of Education* decision, the first of the great civil rights victories in the courts.

I call the scenarios "optimistic" and "pessimistic," but in reality I consider both of them to be biased toward the pessimistic side. Even the optimistic one says, "This is what 1980 will look like if the rate of progress is no better and no worse than it was from 1961 to 1965," and, from my perspective in 1966, that is not an ambitious objective. I do not consider that the period 1961–65 has been an exceptionally good one for blacks. Black voices have been raised, but black economic and social progress has been slow. The civil rights movement has not yet brought about the necessary rates of improvement. It has finally produced the instruments—legislation, court rulings, regulations—that are indispensable to adequate improvement, but the effects of these steps have barely begun to be felt. The economic and social action programs of the Great Society are just getting off the ground. It must be presumed that the implementation of these laws and programs will accelerate the bootstrap progress that blacks have made to date. And there is no telling what additional social legislation will be passed in future, especially given Johnson's continuing legislative hegemony. On all these counts, a straight-line projection of black progress in either 1954–61 *or* 1961–65 should tend to underestimate the real rate of improvement from 1965 to 1980.[1]

As I proceed with my analysis, I choose indicators of two types. First I choose five indicators to assess the progress of the poorest blacks who have survived on the fringes of American society. Two of the indicators represent the problems that have been much worse for these blacks than for other groups:

- black victims of homicide, and
- black illegitimate births.

I want to see both of them go down. The other three of the indicators represent paths for getting off the bottom and up the socioeconomic ladder:

- labor force participation of black males aged 20–24 (it should go up);
- jobs for young black males (I use the unemployment ratio of black males aged 20–24 to white males of the same age, and hope to see it diminish); and
- two-parent families (which, aside from their noneconomic merits, are a mechanism whereby poor people accumulate resources, and are hoped to increase).

The second set of indicators that I choose for my analysis for the White House is primarily for assessing the progress of blacks who are already within the economic mainstream—seldom rich, but regularly employed, making a decent living. They have been held down by discrimination. How will they fare by 1980? I select four measures:

- income ratio of full-time, year-round black workers to comparable white workers (it should rise);
- unemployment ratio of black males aged 45–54 (an age group representing the mature male, with a family to support, who is almost always in the labor force unless physically incapacitated) to comparable white workers (it should come down);
- percentage of black workers employed in white-collar jobs (it should go up); and
- percentage of black persons of college and graduate school age (20–24) enrolled in school (it should go up).

Upon calculating my upper and lower bounds for each indicator, I soon discover that my "optimistic" and "pessimistic" scenarios do not altogether square with what has happened as of 1966. On six out of my nine indicators (unemployment ratio among young males, two-parent families, illegitimate births, arrests for violent crimes, income ratio of full-time workers, and persons of college age enrolled in school), a linear projection from the period 1954–61 yields a more positive projection for 1980 than the one based on 1961–65.

I attribute this to extremely low baselines for some of the indicators (see note 1). For the others, it seems plausible (*ex post facto* thinking at work) that the ferment of change in the black community might have short-term dislocating effects, causing such things as a higher illegitimacy rate and lower proportion of two-parent families. These are presumably only temporary phenomena. But I do re-label my trendlines, putting the "optimistic" label on whichever line is more positive, regardless of whether it came from the 1954–61 period or the 1961–65 period. I prepare my graphs, give them to my supervisor, and they show up in someone's briefing book a few weeks later. By 1980, I have forgotten that I ever made such foolish guesses.

Had anyone in 1966 actually been given the task of projecting these indicators to 1980 (analogous exercises were actually conducted[2]), the projections would have been of the same order as the ones in the graphs we are about to examine—not because people were naive then, not because the techniques are inherently inappropriate, but because, in the absence of some strange and powerful intervening factor, they are roughly the ranges within which reasonable people would have expected these indicators to fall.[3] With that in mind, let us examine the mocked-up 1966 projections, adding to them the true value of each indicator as of 1980. I begin with a sample of the general format, a projection of real per capita GNP (see fig. 10.1):

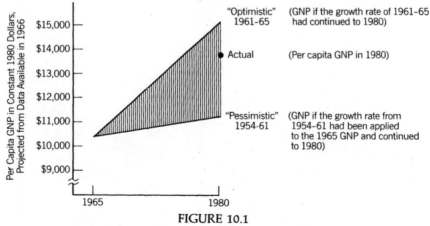

FIGURE 10.1
A Projection of Per Capita GNP from 1965 to 1980
DATA AND SOURCE INFORMATION: Appendix tables 1 and 3.

The other graphs follow this model, with abbreviated notation. Before leaving the sample, take note that real per capita GNP was just about where it was supposed to be by 1980, a bit toward the optimistic side of the envelope.

Figure 10.2 shows the indicators pertaining especially to the black poor.

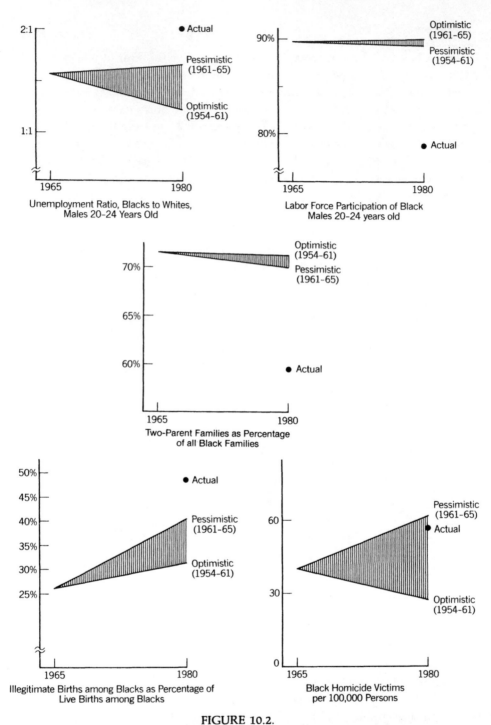

FIGURE 10.2.

The View from 1966, Part I: Black Prospects on Indicators Especially Pertinent to the Poor

DATA AND SOURCE INFORMATION: Appendix tables 7 (unemployment), 8 (labor force participation); 18 (homicides), and 24 (illegitimate births and two-parent families).

The graphs convey in summary form, and perhaps more vividly than any of the individual discussions could, one of the themes of the last six chapters: how far outside the "normal course of events" the black poor have moved. Nor are these indicators unrepresentative. One may choose virtually any measure concerning the black poor for which data are available and come up with the same finding.[4] In 1966, we were very far off the mark when we tried to imagine what "pessimistic" might mean when it came to projecting the future of the most disadvantaged of black Americans.

Figure 10.3 shows the other theme of these chapters—that some have done quite well, even extraordinarily well. Consider the indicators of progress especially pertinent to working- or middle-class blacks:

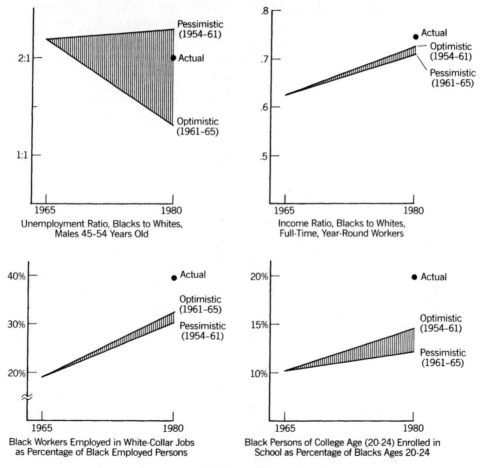

FIGURE 10.3.

The View from 1966, Part II: Black Prospects on Indicators Especially Pertinent to the Not-Poor.

DATA AND SOURCE INFORMATION: Appendix tables 7 (unemployment), 8 (labor force participation), 11 (white collar jobs), and 12 (school enrollment).

The optimistic projection from 1966 was that white-collar employment of black workers would increase by 65 percent. The real increase turned out to be 101 percent. The optimistic projection from 1966 was that the proportion of young black adults (20–24 years old) in school would increase by 41 percent. The real increase was 95 percent. The income ratio of black full-time workers to white full-time workers reached 75 percent in raw form, slightly above the top of the projection envelope. Only the unemployment ratio of middle-aged workers fell short of the optimistic projection—and it was at least within the projected range. In short, for middle-aged blacks, middle-class blacks, and blacks who obtained middle-class credentials, the years 1965–80 were generally as good as or better than either the 1954–61 or 1961–65 periods would have led us to expect.

The profiles of the two populations are at odds with each other—one much worse than we would have anticipated, the other doing quite well. Such was the burden of the more detailed analyses of these issues in part two. Such is the puzzle of causation that, finally, we begin to examine.

PART III

Interpreting the Data

AS the *Sturm und Drang* of the 1960s faded and we settled into the 1970s, the realization gradually spread that things were getting worse, not better, for blacks and poor people in this country. It was seldom put in just that way. The lower poverty percentages were insistently credited to the reforms. Each court decision affirming the constitutionality of steps to equalize outcome was seen as a victory for civil rights. But few could avoid recognizing that the inner cities were more violent and ravaged than ever before. It was difficult to take much satisfaction in the poverty statistics —which by the early 1970s had stopped looking better anyway—when pictures of the devastated South Bronx kept getting into the newspapers. It was difficult to take much satisfaction in the legal edifice of black rights when black teenage unemployment was approaching 40 percent.

For most of the 1970s, mainstream politicians, academicians, journalists, and bureaucrats remained stuck in a mindset. The War on Poverty had become a domestic Vietnam in which they were committed to a way of thinking about poor people and race and social policy that did not seem to be working as it was supposed to. But, not unlike Lyndon Johnson with the Vietnam War, they saw no choice but to sweat it out. The budgets for the CETAs and entitlements and social-action programs continued to grow by inertia.

There had been an alternative set of ideas all along, of course. If during the 1960s and 1970s there was an elite wisdom that shaped the direction of social policy, there was also a popular wisdom about why things were falling apart.

This popular wisdom, which is as prevalent today as it was then, is just that—the views to be heard in most discussions in most blue-collar bars or country-club lounges in most parts of the United States. It is the inarticulate constellation of worries and suspicions that helped account for Ronald Reagan's victory in 1980. It is perhaps more precisely called a white popular wisdom, but some of its major themes are also voiced quietly by a conservative black working class.

The popular wisdom is characterized by hostility toward welfare (it makes people lazy), toward lenient judges (they encourage crime), and toward socially conscious schools (too busy busing kids to teach them how to read). The popular wisdom disapproves of favoritism for blacks and of too many written-in rights for minorities of all sorts. It says that the government is meddling far too much in things that are none of its business.

The hostility one hears in the *vox populi* may account for the reluctance of many intellectuals to consider whether this view might not be right. To listen carefully to the popular wisdom is also to hear a good deal of mean-spirited (often racist) invective. Acknowledging the merits of its insights is seen as approving of the invective as well. And one might add that to the minds of many professional social analysts, the explanations of the popular wisdom are too *simple*, too unsubtle, to be true.

By the end of the 1970s, however, a synthesis of wisdoms was underway. Too much of what we saw going on around us confirmed too many of the popular view's premises to be ignored. Stripped of the prejudices and the bombast, these, as I see them, are three core premises of the popular wisdom that need to be taken into account:

- Premise #1: People respond to incentives and disincentives. Sticks and carrots work.
- Premise #2: People are not inherently hard working or moral. In the absence of countervailing influences, people will avoid work and be amoral.
- Premise #3: People must be held responsible for their actions. Whether they *are* responsible in some ultimate philosophical or biochemical sense cannot be the issue if society is to function.

The thesis of the chapters that follow is that social policy since 1964 has ignored these premises and that it has thereby created much of the mess we are in.

11

The Social Scientists and the Great Experiment

THE BARE FACT that a cause-effect relationship links certain social policies to some of the trends we examined in part II has been established. It was most clearly established, oddly, in an ambitious attempt to discredit the notion that such links exist. Most of our inquiry in the following chapters will wrestle with the dynamics of the causes and effects at work, but it is worth our while to document first the persuasive evidence that causes, not just coincidences of timing, are at work. For that, we turn to the story of the Negative Income Tax experiment.

The Social Scientists Go to Washington

In the account in chapter 2 of the disillusionment about the first War on Poverty programs, I mentioned the role of the program evaluators who reluctantly brought the bad news. The evaluators constituted only one small part of the story, however. When OEO was setting up shop in 1965, social scientists of all sorts were reaching out from the campus to become part of the excitement in Washington, bringing with them a tool kit of new methods with which they hoped to help build the Great Society.

The theory behind their techniques was not new. But in the absence of computers, applications had been limited. Quantitative social science had been for the most part restricted to research questions involving only a few variables and small samples; the computational burden otherwise was too great.

By the mid-1960s, the technological lid had been lifted. The social scientist could answer real-life questions that intuition and simpler methods could not. What is the effect of Policy X on, for example, monthly income when one holds sex, race, age, prior education, and ten other variables constant? With the computer to do the work, the social scientists knew how to reach an answer.

It turned out to be harder than it looked, of course—the theoretical power of the leading techniques (mainly forms of regression analysis and factor analysis, at the time) was greater than their practical utility when put to work. A few colossal blunders were made and, in some instances, discovered only after the government had acted on the basis of the erroneous analyses.[1] But theory and practice continued to improve as the quantitative researchers learned from their mistakes. By the mid-1960s, any social scientist who was not at least conversant with sophisticated statistics was unable to follow much of the professional literature that, only a few years earlier, had seldom included anything more complicated than a cross-tabulation. Graduate students were routinely performing analyses that had been beyond the reach of any scholar only a few years earlier. And it was all happening at just the moment when the hardnosed idealists of the OEO were gearing up for their assault on poverty. A partnership between the policymakers and the newly equipped social scientists was sought by both sides. When die-hard southern congressmen ranted that these social programs were leading the country to perdition, the social scientists would have the evidence—cool, impartial, conclusive evidence—that no such thing was happening. Whence the origins of the great experiment that followed.

The Negative Income Tax Experiment

The foundation of the scientific method is the controlled experiment. The investigator takes two identical sets of subjects, exposes one but not the other to a specified stimulus or condition, and observes the subsequent differences between the two. No other procedure is as elegant in its assumptions, and no other evidence of causation carries as much weight.

By 1966–67, the planners at OEO thought they needed this demanding level of proof. Power at OEO had passed from the apostles of opportunity to the structuralists. It was increasingly taken for granted that some form of guaranteed annual income was the only way that the War on Poverty was going to be won. But the president was refusing to introduce such legislation. Even if he could be won over, passing the legislation was going to be exceedingly difficult. There was opposition, of course, from the remaining congressional conservatives, and moderates were on the fence. They were sympathetic to the goals of a guaranteed annual income, but they were worried about its negative effects on the "work ethic" and about how they could justify their support of such a program to working-class constituencies who would see it as a welfare giveaway. Somehow, *proof* must be established that a guaranteed income would not cause people to reduce their work effort, get married less often, divorce more quickly, or do any of the other things that the popular wisdom said it would cause them to do.

The OEO's vehicle for providing the proof took the form of the most ambitious social-science experiment in history. No other even comes close to its combination of size, expense, length, and detail of analysis. It went under the unprepossessing name of the Negative Income Tax (NIT) experiment.[2] It began in 1968, ultimately used 8,700 people as subjects, and lasted for ten years. (A planned twenty-year subsample was cancelled in 1980.) It resulted in a body of literature that, as of 1980, included more than one hundred published titles and countless unpublished reports.[3] Its cost ran far into the millions; accountings vary.

Very briefly, a negative income tax provides payments to persons whose income falls below a certain floor. As implemented in the NIT experiment, it strayed far from its intellectual origins. Conservative economists, not liberal social reformers, had first advocated a negative income tax as a replacement for the existing welfare system.[4] They took for granted that any form of welfare payments produced work disincentives. The point of an NIT was not to get people off welfare, but to fill the welfare system's functions with somewhat fewer unwanted side-effects. The negative income tax was not felt to be especially "good"; it was just considered better than the alternatives.[5]

By the time that the NIT experiment was ready for implementation, such thoughts had been lost as the NIT concept was embraced by new proponents for whom it had nothing to do with efficiency, but instead had become "a pervasive way of thinking about poverty as an economic phenomenon [and] a device for trying to solve the problem of welfare dependency . . .," as Heclo and Rein put it.[6] More colloquially, the proponents of the NIT in the Johnson administration were out to slay the folk beliefs that welfare makes people shiftless. The NIT, properly redesigned, would provide work incentives and get people off the welfare rolls.

A disquieting element about the experiment was that it would be, as one close observer put it, "sponsored, designed, and even administered by 'believers.' "[7] Critics watched the work suspiciously for signs that the data were being cooked. But OEO had no such fears for its own integrity. "[I]t was the faith in the method of investigation, not the disinterestedness of the initial impulse, which would rescue their partisanship and lend credibility to the final results."[8] In the end, this faith in the method was justified.

The procedure followed the classic experimental paradigm. In each site, a sample of low-income persons was selected and randomly split into two groups: the "experimental" group and the "control" group. The members of the experimental group were told that for a specified number of years (usually three) they would have a floor put under their incomes.[9] The benefits varied among participants, to test the sensitivity of the results to the generosity of the guaranteed income. The most common benefit level put the floor at approximately the official poverty line. The members of the control group received no benefits.

For the next ten years, results dribbled in. The New Jersey and Pennsylvania sites opened the experiment between 1968 and 1972. Then came tests with rural populations in Iowa and North Carolina, from 1970 to 1972. A predominantly AFDC population was tested in Gary, Indiana, between 1971 and 1974. The largest, longest, and best-evaluated experiments were in Seattle and Denver from 1971 to 1978, the "SIME/DIME" of so many research reports (Seattle Income Maintenance Experiment/Denver Income Maintenance Experiment). As the results appeared, they were subjected to methodological critiques. Experimental and analytic procedures were tightened for the next round, results were compared across sites, data were reanalyzed, and finally, by the end of the 1970s, a body of results was established that was broadly accepted as valid.[10] With rigor and in enormous detail, the scientists validated not the sponsors' hopes but their fears. The results were more or less what the popular wisdom said they would be.

EFFECTS ON WORK

The key question was whether a negative income tax reduced work effort. The answer was yes. The reduction was not the trivial one that NIT sponsors had been prepared to accept, but substantial. In the SIME/DIME sites (which produced neither the largest nor the smallest changes, but probably the most accurately measured ones), the NIT was found to reduce "desired hours of work" by 9 percent for husbands and by 20 percent for wives.[11] "Desired hours of work" was measured by actual employment after factoring involuntary work reductions out of the calculation.

The 9-percent reduction for husbands was not in itself a fearsome number. If the reduction had consisted of husbands who were working a few hours less—giving up overtime opportunities, for example—to increase the time they could devote to other worthy pursuits, these results would have been defensible, even agreeable to the sponsors of the experiment. But the reduction in SIME/DIME and the other experiments appeared to have consisted primarily of men who had opted out of the labor market altogether.[12] In the most detailed examinations, it was found that "reductions in the probability of employment are due primarily to reduced rates of entry into employment."[13]

The results among husbands were disappointing but not the most troubling. As the analysts dug deeper into who was being affected and how, they found that the groups who showed the largest negative effects were precisely the ones who were in a position to cause the most long-term damage to the goal of reducing poverty.

The first of these groups was wives. At least from the Second World War (and much earlier for some groups) through the early 1960s, wives represented for poor families a source of marginal income that could push a family out of the poverty trap and into a more secure long-term future—either by continuing to work indefinitely, or by providing income that permitted the husband to upgrade his skills, move to another labor market, or make some other investment in long-term gains that requires a short-term expense.[14] Thus the 20-percent reduction in work hours compared with the control group not only was quite large but implied that substantial numbers of families were, whether they knew it or not, climbing off one of their most promising ladders to prosperity.

The second group of special interest was young males who were not yet heads of families ("nonheads," in the jargon). They were at a critical age in their lives: about to enter into the responsibilities of marriage and just establishing themselves in the labor force. If they were to escape from poverty, this was the moment to start. The NIT had a disastrous impact on their hours of work per week: down 43 percent for those who remained nonheads throughout the experiment, down 33 percent for nonheads who married.[15]

Perhaps they were going to school to better themselves? No, the possibility was investigated and rejected. Perhaps it was only a temporary effect? No, on the contrary, the response seemed to be stronger in the five-year experiment than in the three-year experiment. The investigators summed it up with perhaps excessive restraint:

> The reduction in work effort by male nonheads who become husbands is clearly important. These males are reducing their work effort at the time when they are undertaking family responsibilities. Not only is their response important in the current period, but the reduction in work effort may also have long-term effects on their labor supply behavior.[16]

The effects on work effort were associated with collateral effects among all the subpopulations. Perhaps the most striking was the increase that NIT produced in periods of unemployment when a member of the experiment lost his or her job. Such periods lengthened by nine weeks (27 percent) for husbands, fifty weeks (42 percent) for wives, and fifty-six weeks (60 percent) for single female heads of families, in comparison with the control group.[17]

EFFECTS ON THE FAMILY

Does welfare undermine the family? As far as we know from the NIT experiment, it does, and the effect is large. In the SIME/DIME sites, the dissolution of marriages was 36 percent higher for whites receiving the NIT payments than for those who did not; for blacks the figure was 42 percent. In the New Jersey site, there was no difference among the white families in the experiment, but black family breakup was 66 percent higher in the experimental group than in the control group, and in the Spanish-speaking sample it was 84 percent higher.[18] In one experiment, Gary, no effect was observed. When researchers looked into the possible reasons why, they found that, in Gary, couples were under the impression that if they split up, they would lose their NIT payments.[19]

The results were exhaustively analyzed, as researchers checked out the alternative explanations. None worked. The only salient difference that seemed to explain the substantially higher rates of marital instability in the two groups was the "treatment" itself, the NIT.[20]

IT'S EVEN WORSE THAN IT LOOKS

The results I have just reviewed are noteworthy as they stand. But the true negative effects of the NIT were considerably larger than the data indicate. A variety of biases tended to suppress the negative effects.[21] We cannot be sure how large the understatement was; it was surely substantial. The notes refer the reader to some of the analyses of this issue, Martin Anderson's being the most exhaustive.[22] Two of the most important of the reasons for the bias are these:

First, the observed effects were not obtained through a comparison with a "pure" control group (one experiencing no work disincentives), but in comparison with a population that was receiving all the normal welfare benefits of the 1970s, which were extensive and growing during the same period that the NIT experiment was conducted. The reductions in hours worked, the lengthened periods of unemployment, and every other effect are reductions *over and above* the effect of the work disincentives in the existing system.

Second, the great majority of the participants in the NIT experiment knew from the outset that they could count on the payments for only three years. Presumably people are less likely to burn bridges behind them if they know that the guaranteed income ends in three years than if it is legislated for life. Insofar as the subsamples given five-year and (in a very few cases) 20-year guarantees permit estimates, common sense is borne out —the longer the guarantee, the greater the negative effects of the NIT.[23]

The NIT experiment made a shambles of the expectations of its sponsors. But at the same time it was being conducted, the disincentives it would later demonstrate were being woven into the fabric of the welfare system.[24] For our purposes, the NIT experiment directly answers the question we posed about causation, at least for the outcomes relating to welfare, work, and marriage: The only time we have been able to put the question to a controlled test, the causal effect was unambiguous and strong.

1 2

Incentives to Fail I: Maximizing Short-Term Gains

WHEN LARGE NUMBERS of people begin to behave differently from ways they behaved before, my first assumption is that they do so for good reason. In this chapter and the one that follows, I will apply this assumption to the trends of the 1960s and 1970s and suggest that it fits the facts.

Specifically, I will suggest that changes in incentives that occurred between 1960 and 1970 may be used to explain many of the trends we have been discussing. It is not necessary to invoke the *Zeitgeist* of the 1960s, or changes in the work ethic, or racial differences, or the complexities of postindustrial economies, in order to explain increasing unemployment among the young, increased dropout from the labor force, or higher rates of illegitimacy and welfare dependency. All were results that could have been predicted (indeed, in some instances were predicted) from the changes that social policy made in the rewards and penalties, carrots and sticks, that govern human behavior. All were rational responses to changes in the rules of the game of surviving and getting ahead. I will not argue that the responses were the right ones, only that they were rational. Even of our mistakes, we say: It seemed like a good idea at the time.

I begin with the proposition that all, poor and not-poor alike, use the same general calculus in arriving at decisions; only the exigencies are different. Poor people play with fewer chips and cannot wait as long for results.[1] Therefore they tend to reach decisions that a more affluent person would not reach. The reformers of the 1960s were especially myopic about this, tending not only to assume that the poor and not-poor were alike in trying to maximize the goods in their lives (with which I agree), but also that, given the same package of benefits, the decision that seems reasonable to one would seem reasonable to the other. They failed to recognize that the behaviors that are "rational" are different at different economic levels.

In the American setting, a racial overlay obscures this obvious point. The rational (albeit wrong) decisions we will be talking about are the ones that poor people (mostly black, it seems) made. The not-poor people (mostly white, it seems) made other, better decisions. The result of the overlay has often been embarrassed silence. Let us drop the racial baggage that goes with the American context and make the point first in a less emotional setting.

Imagine for a moment that you have been asked to explain the seemingly irrational behavior of a farmer in a developing country. This farmer, you are told, cultivates rice on land that is badly suited for rice but ideally suited for jute. An agriculture officer has explained this to the farmer and explained also that by growing jute he will have enough money to buy all the rice he needs and a large surplus as well. A benign government has offered to train the farmer in the art of jute cultivation, yet the farmer refuses to switch. Why is he so stubborn?

After some reflection, you arrive at a few reasonable hypotheses for explaining the farmer's behavior. For example, he knows he can eat the rice if he cannot sell it, whereas he cannot eat the jute. Also, he has no personal knowledge that the government is correct about next year's price for jute. He has no personal knowledge that jute will grow as well as promised under local conditions. He does know, however, with absolute certainty, that he cannot tolerate even a small chance that the new crop will fail. The penalty for being wrong can be starvation. Therefore, quite rationally, he refuses to take an unacceptable risk. Such might be your reasoning, and it would come down to this: *If I were in the farmer's position, I would make the same decision.*

Experts may disagree with your explanation. They may point out that you have not read the literature on this particular agrarian culture, that the farmer's behavior in fact reflects a complicated and ancient heritage.[2] You listen and are impressed by the scholarship and the intricate tracings of causes and effects. But your earlier analysis is valid. On strictly economic grounds, it still makes sense not to switch to jute. The subtle anthropological explanation is interesting. It may even be true. But it is *not necessary* to explain the farmer's behavior.

Much the same applies to many of the commentaries about the intractability of American poverty and its associated problems despite the many programs that are supposed to help. Fascinating explanations are offered. Many of these explanations surely have an element of truth—they "explain some of the variance," as the statisticians put it. But surprisingly little has been made of the distinction between the behaviors that make sense when one is poor and the behaviors that make sense when one is not poor.

In the exercise we are about to conduct, it is important to suspend thoughts about how the world ought to work, about what the incentives should be. The objective is to establish what the incentives *are* (or were), and how they are likely to affect the calculations of a person who has few chips and little time. It is also important to put aside the distant view of long-term rewards that we, surveying the scene from above, know to be part of the ultimate truth of self-interest, and instead to examine the truth as it appears at ground level at the time decisions must be made.

Dramatis Personae

Our guides are a young couple—call them Harold and Phyllis. I deliberately make them unremarkable except for the bare fact of being poor. They are not of a special lower-class culture. They have no socialized propensities for "serial monogamy." They are not people we think of as "the type who are on welfare." They have just graduated from an average public school in an average American city. Neither of them is particularly industrious or indolent, intelligent or dull. They are the children of low-income parents, are not motivated to go to college, and have no special vocational skills. Harold and Phyllis went together during their last year in high school and find themselves in a familiar predicament. She is pregnant.

They will have a child together. They will face the kinds of painful decisions that many young people have had to face. What will they decide? What will seem to them to be "rational" behavior?

We shall examine the options twice—first, as they were in 1960, then as they were only ten years later, in 1970. We shall ignore the turbulent social history of the intervening decade. We shall ignore our couple's whiteness or blackness. We simply shall ask: Given the extant system of rewards and punishments, what course of action makes sense?

Options in 1960

HAROLD'S CALCULATIONS, PRE-REFORM

Harold's parents have no money. Phyllis has no money. If Harold remains within the law, he has two choices: He can get a job, or he can try to get Phyllis to help support him.

Getting Phyllis to support him is intrinsically more attractive, but the possibilities are not promising. If Phyllis has the baby, she will qualify for $23 a week in AFDC ($63 in 1980 purchasing power).[3] This is not enough to support the three of them. And, under the rules of AFDC, Phyllis will not be able to contribute more to the budget. If she gets a job, she will lose benefits on a dollar-for-dollar basis. There is in 1960 no way to make the AFDC payment part of a larger package.

Also, Harold and Phyllis will not be able to live together. AFDC regulations in 1960 prohibit benefits if there is "a man in the house." Apart from its psychic and sexual disadvantages, this regulation also means that Harold cannot benefit from Phyllis's weekly check. The amount cannot possibly be stretched across two households.

It follows that, completely apart from the moral stance of Harold, his parents, or society, it is not possible to use Phyllis for support. Whether or not he decides to stay with her, he will have to find a job.

The only job he can find is working the presses in a dry cleaning shop. It pays the rock-bottom minimum wage—$40 for a forty-hour week, or about $111 in the purchasing power of the 1980 dollar. It is not much of a living, not much of a job. There is no future in it, no career path. But it pays for food and shelter. And Harold has no choice.

The job turns out to be as tedious as he expected. It is hot in the laundry, and Harold is on his feet all day; he would much rather not stay there. But the consequences of leaving the job are intolerable. Unemployment Insurance will pay him only $20 ($56 in 1980 purchasing power). He stays at the laundry and vaguely hopes that something better will come along.

PHYLLIS'S CALCULATIONS, PRE-REFORM

Phyllis has three (legal) options: to support herself (either keeping the baby or giving it up for adoption); to go on AFDC (which means keeping the baby); or to marry Harold.

Other things being equal, supporting herself is the least attractive of these options. Like Harold, she can expect to find only menial minimum-wage employment. There is no intrinsic reason to take such a job.

The AFDC option is worth considering. The advantage is that it will enable her to keep the baby without having to work. The disadvantages are the ones that Harold perceives. The money is too little, and she is not permitted to supplement it. And Harold would not be permitted to be a live-in husband or father. If she tries to circumvent the rules and gets caught, she faces being cut off from any benefits for the foreseeable future.

If Phyllis thinks ahead, the economic attraction of AFDC might appear more enticing. The total benefits she will receive if she has several children may seem fairly large. If she were already on AFDC it might make sense to have more children. But, right now, setting up a household with Harold is by far the most sensible choice, even given the miserable wage he is making at the laundry.

Being married (as opposed to just living together) has no short-term economic implications. This is shown in the following table:

		Living Together	
		Unmarried	Married
Harold employed?	Yes	$111	$111
	No	0	0

The choice of whether to get married is dependent primarily on noneconomic motivations, plus the economic advantages to Phyllis of having Harold legally responsible for the support of her and the baby.

Once the decision not to go on AFDC is made, a new option opens up.

As long as Phyllis is not on AFDC, no penalty is attached to getting a part-time or full-time job.

Options in 1970

Harold's and Phyllis's namesakes just ten years later find themselves in the identical situation. Their parents have no money; he doesn't want to go to school any longer; she is pregnant; the only job he can get is in the back room of a dry cleaners. That much is unchanged from 1960.

HAROLD'S CALCULATIONS, POST-REFORM

Harold's options have changed considerably. If he were more clever or less honest (or, perhaps, just more aggressive), he would have even more new options. But since he is none of those things, the major changes in his calculations are limited to these:

First, the AFDC option. In 1960, he had three objections to letting Phyllis go on welfare: too little money, no way to supplement it, and having to live separately from his family. By 1970, all three objections have been removed.

Economically, the total package of AFDC and other welfare benefits has become comparable to working. Phyllis will get about $50 a week in cash ($106 in 1980 dollars) and another $11 in Food Stamps ($23 in 1980 dollars). She is eligible for substantial rent subsidies under the many federal housing programs, but only a minority of AFDC recipients use them, so we will omit housing from the package. She will get Medicaid. We assume that a year's worth of doctor's bills and medication for a mother and infant is likely to be more than $250 (many times that if there is even one major illness), and we therefore add $5 a week (1980 dollars) onto the package.[4] Without bending or even being imaginative about the new regulations, without tapping nearly all the possible sources of public support, and using conservative estimates in reaching a dollar total, the package of benefits available to Phyllis in a typical northern state has a purchasing power of about $134. This minimal package adds up to $23 more than the purchasing power of forty hours of work at a minimum-wage job ten years earlier, in 1960.

Also, the money can be supplemented. If Phyllis works, she can keep the first thirty dollars she makes. After that, her benefits are reduced by two dollars for every three additional dollars of income.

Harold has even greater flexibility. *As long as he is not legally responsible for the care of the child*—a crucial proviso—his income will not count against her eligibility for benefits. He is free to work when they need a little extra money to supplement their basic (welfare) income.

The third objection, being separated from Phyllis, has become irrelevant. By Supreme Court ruling, the presence of a man in the house of a single woman cannot be used as a reason to deny her benefits.

The old-fashioned solution of getting married and living off their earned income has become markedly inferior. Working a full forty-hour week in the dry-cleaning shop will pay Harold $64 ($136 in 1980 dollars) *before* Social Security and taxes are taken out.[5] The bottom line is this: Harold can get married and work forty hours a week in a hot, tiresome job; or he can live with Phyllis and their baby without getting married, not work, and have more disposable income. From an economic point of view, getting married is dumb. From a noneconomic point of view, it involves him in a legal relationship that has no payoff for him. If he thinks he may sometime tire of Phyllis and fatherhood, the 1970 rules thus provide a further incentive for keeping the relationship off the books.

PHYLLIS'S CALCULATIONS, POST-REFORM

To keep the baby or give it up? To get married or not? What are the pros and cons?

Phyllis comes from a poor family. They want her out of the house, just as she wants to get out of the house. If she gives up the baby for adoption (or, in some states by 1970, has a legal abortion), she will be expected to support herself; and, as in 1960, the only job she will be able to find is likely to be unattractive, with no security and a paycheck no larger than her baby would provide. *The only circumstance under which giving up the baby is rational is if she prefers any sort of job to having and caring for a baby.* It is commonly written that poor teenaged girls have babies so they will have someone to love them. This may be true for some. But one *need* not look for psychological explanations. Under the rules of 1970, it was rational on grounds of dollars and cents for a poor, unmarried woman who found herself to be pregnant to have and keep the baby even if she did not particularly want a child.

In Phyllis's case, the balance favors having the baby. What about getting married?

If Phyllis and Harold marry and he is employed, she will lose her AFDC benefits. His minimum wage job at the laundry will produce no more income than she can make, and, not insignificantly, he, not she, will have control of the check. In exchange for giving up this degree of independence, she gains no real security. Harold's job is not nearly as stable as the welfare system. And, should her marriage break up, she will not be able to count on residual benefits. Enforcement of payment of child support has fallen to near-zero in poor communities. In sum, marriage buys Phyllis nothing—not companionship she couldn't have otherwise, not financial security, not even increased income. In 1970, her child provides her with the economic insurance that a husband used to represent.

Against these penalties for getting married is the powerful positive inducement to remain single: Any money that Harold makes is added to their income without affecting her benefits as long as they remain unmarried. It is difficult to think of a good economic reason from Phyllis's viewpoint why marriage might be attractive.

Let us pause and update the table of economic choices, plugging in the values for 1970. Again, we assume that the two want to live together. Their maximum weekly incomes (ignoring payroll deductions and Harold's means-tested benefits—see note 5) are:

		Living Together	
		Unmarried	Married
Harold Employed?	Yes	$270	$136
	No	$134	$134

The dominant cell for maximizing income is clearly "living together unmarried, Harold employed." If they for some reason do decide to get married and they live in a state that permits AFDC for families with unemployed fathers (as most of the industrial states do), they are about equally well off whether or not Harold is employed. Or, more precisely, they are about equally well off, in the short run, if Harold moves in and out of the labor market to conform to whatever local rules apply to maintaining eligibility. This is a distinction worth emphasizing, and it is discussed at more length in the notes: the changed rules do not encourage permanent unemployment so much as they encourage periodic unemployment.[6]

Harold and Phyllis take the economically logical step—she has the baby, they live together without getting married, and Harold looks for a job to make some extra money. He finds the job at the laundry. It is just as unpleasant a job as it was in 1960, but the implications of persevering are different. In 1970, unlike 1960, Harold's job is *not* his basic source of income. Thus, when the back room of the laundry has been too hot for too long, it becomes economically feasible and indeed reasonable to move in and out of the labor market. In 1980 dollars, Unemployment Insurance pays him $68 per week. As the sole means of support it is not an attractive sum. But added to Phyllis's package, the total is $202, which beats the heat of the presses. And, if it comes to it, Harold can survive even without the Unemployment payment. In 1970, Phyllis's welfare package is bringing in more real income than did a minimum-wage job in 1960.

Such is the story of Harold and Phyllis. They were put in a characteristically working-class situation. In 1960, the logic of their world led them to behave in traditional working-class ways. Ten years later, the logic of their world had changed and, lo and behold, they behaved indistinguishably from "welfare types." What if we had hypothesized a more typical example—or at least one that fits the stereotype? What if we had posited the lower-class and black cultural influences that are said to foster high illegitimacy rates and welfare dependency? The answer is that the same general logic would apply, but with even more power. When economic incentives are buttressed by social norms, the effects on behavior are multiplied. But the main point is that the social factors are not necessary to explain behavior. There is no "breakdown of the work ethic" in this account of rational choices among alternatives. There is no shiftless irresponsibility. It makes no difference whether Harold is white or black. There is no need to invoke the spectres of cultural pathologies or inferior upbringing. The choices may be seen much more simply, much more naturally, as the behavior of people responding to the reality of the world around them and making the decisions—the legal, approved, and even encouraged decisions—that maximize their quality of life.[7]

What About Work Incentives?

The stories of Harold and Phyllis were constructed to reflect four major changes in the administration of AFDC that took place in the 1960s. In 1961, federal law was changed to permit AFDC payments to families with an unemployed father. Eventually, twenty-five states adopted this option. In 1966, the Department of Health, Education and Welfare issued guidelines forbidding unannounced visits to the home to check eligibility. At about the same time, lawyers from the federal Legal Services program began filing cases challenging eligibility restrictions. The challenges had immediate effects on the practices of individual states. In 1968 these effects were generalized to the nation as a whole by the Supreme Court's decision in *King* v. *Smith,* which struck down the man-in-the-house eligibility restriction.[8]

The other and most highly touted improvement (at the time, all of these changes were seen by a variety of sponsors as long-needed improvements) in the administration of AFDC occurred in 1967. The work disincentives associated with AFDC had been widely recognized for many years. To diminish these barriers to work, Congress passed what came to be known as the "thirty-and-a-third" rule, which permitted women on AFDC to keep the first $30 of earnings without losing their AFDC benefit and thereafter took only two of each three dollars of earnings. The intent was to provide a positive incentive for women on AFDC to get a job and eventually become self-sufficient. The political refrain at the time was that AFDC participants remained on welfare because they had no reason to get a job. Earnings were taxed at 100 percent until they amounted to more than the welfare check, and at exorbitantly high effective rates beyond that point. It was true that the thirty-and-a-third rule taxed income after $30 at a 67 percent rate. But, clearly, this was better than the 100 percent exacted by the earlier rules.

In the story of Harold and Phyllis, however, the thirty-and-a-third rule played a negative role in their calculations: It improved the total package available to them, and served as an added reason to choose the welfare option. This was not an idiosyncracy of the situation in which we placed Harold and Phyllis. The legislation accomplished its purpose in a limited, technical sense. It provided an incentive to work for those women who were already on welfare. The problem is that the same rule provided a much stronger incentive for women who were not on welfare to get on it and then become trapped in it. The net effect was to raise the value of being eligible for AFDC and thereby, via a classic market response, increase the supply of eligible women.[9]

This inherent quality of the thirty-and-a-third rule was first explicated by economist Frank Levy in an article in the *Journal of Human Resources.* His conclusions follow from an unembellished layout of the labor/leisure choice, translated from the way the reform was written. As Levy summarizes it:

> [A]ny AFDC parameter change which increases the program's break-even income will reduce expected labor supply in the population . . . *But greater work incentives, including lower tax rates, greater disregards, and a more liberal deductions policy, will likewise lower expected hours of work.* While these incentives may encourage increased work among women who previously worked very little, the increase will be more than offset by other women who are induced to cut back on work, including some women who were former nonrecipients. [Emphasis in the original][10]

The important point about the thirty-and-a-third rule (and the story of Harold and Phyllis) is that rules designed to have a certain narrow effect can in fact have a broad spectrum of unintended effects. They affect men as well as women, calculations about marriage and children as well as calculations about jobs and welfare. They interact with changes in divorce and abandonment law. They interact with changes in the Unemployment Insurance rules, minimum wage rates, the eligibility requirements for Food Stamps and subsidized housing and Disability Insurance. It is the total effect of well-intentioned changes in the incentive structure, not any one specific change, that is the key to comprehending what happened.

Timing of the Changes in Incentives

I chose 1960 and 1970 as the comparison years because the changes in incentives were concentrated within the narrow time span of the 1960s. The timing of the specific changes, including one in the 1970s, is instructive. To recapitulate:

- *1950s:* Little change in regulations or benefits.
- *1961:* Federal law is changed to permit AFDC payments to families with an unemployed father. Eventually, twenty-five states adopt this option.
- *1966:* HEW issues guidelines forbidding at-home eligibility checks. Legal Services lawyers begin filing cases challenging eligibility restrictions.
- *1967:* Enactment of the thirty-and-a-third rule.
- *1968:* Supreme Court strikes down man-in-the-house eligibility restrictions.
- *1969:* Supreme Court strikes down one-year state residency requirements for welfare eligibility.
- *1974:* Enactment of stricter child support enforcement provisions (the IV–D provision).

The money incentives changed in tandem with the regulatory incentives: The real dollar value of AFDC benefits increased slowly from 1950 to 1960 (up 11 percent for the decade), then more rapidly during the early 1960s (up 9 percent from 1960 to 1965). From 1965 to 1970 the real value of benefits rose very rapidly—24 percent in the average AFDC payment, plus new accessibility to Food Stamps, Medicaid, and public housing or rent subsidies. In all, real benefits during 1965–70 probably rose on the order of 50 percent—more in some states, less in others. After 1970, the increase slowed again. After the mid-1970s, the net value of payments after inflation is taken into account increased little if at all in most states.[11]

A Predictable Trendline

Our analysis of incentives leads us to make some predictions about the AFDC caseload based on this sequence of events. In the 1950s, the caseload should have remained stable. In the early 1960s, it should have risen slowly. In the late 1960s, it should have risen rapidly. In the 1970s, it should have stabilized. Each prediction follows naturally from the analysis (little change in incentives during the 1950s, major changes during the 1960s, no changes during the early 1970s, and a new disincentive in 1974). Figure 12.1 shows the shape of the actual trendline in AFDC caseload. It could be coincidence. But as a case for the incentives explanation, the

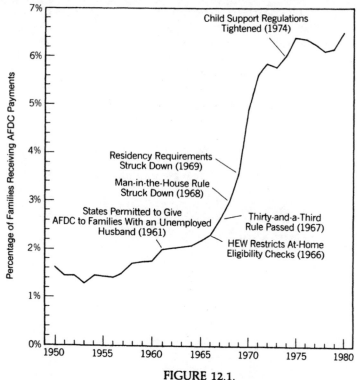

FIGURE 12.1.
AFDC Families as a Percentage of All Families, 1950–1980
DATA AND SOURCE INFORMATION: Appendix table 4.

trendline offers strong circumstantial evidence. During the 1950s, the overall increase in the AFDC caseload was 7 percent. From 1960 to 1965, it was 24 percent; *from 1965 to 1970, 125 percent;* from 1970 to 1975, 29 percent; from 1975 to 1980, 3 percent.

Rational decision-making is not, of course, the only possible explanation.[12] For example, the historian James Patterson, in his history of the period, reviews a variety of possibilities, including revisions in "hoary practices" such as the man-in-the-house rule and rude investigations of eligibility. But these were secondary, he concluded. The "most important of all" the changes in those years were clearly the increases in the proportion of the potentially eligible who actually sought assistance, and increases in the percentage who were in fact assisted. "What prompted this dramatic, historic development?" he asks. He provides an answer:

The source of it most obvious to contemporaries was changing attitudes of poor people themselves. Despite the hostility of the middle classes to increases in welfare, poor Americans refused at last to be cowed from applying for aid. Despite the continuing stigma attached to living on welfare, they stood firm in their determination to stay on the rolls as long as they were in need. Welfare was not a privilege; it was a right . . . Compared to the past, when poor people —harassed and stigmatized by public authorities—were slow to claim their rights, this was a fundamental change.[13]

But why did the attitudes change? And to what good end?

13

Incentives to Fail II: Crime and Education

I OPENED the discussion of incentives with choices affecting work, marriage, and raising a family because the changes of the 1960s were so concrete in these areas and because the presumptive role of economics is so great. Throughout history and among people in every social and economic stratum, choices of when and whether to seek work, when to marry, when and how often to have children, have been intimately bound up with economic considerations. It was not until recently (in historical perspective) that other considerations were nearly as important.

But comparable changes in incentives surrounded other behaviors as well. The most important of these had to do with getting an education and resisting the lure of crime. The rules did not change in the specific, discrete ways that the rules of welfare and employment changed. Nonetheless, incentives changed. My proposition is that the environment in which a young poor person grew up changed in several mutually consistent and interacting ways during the 1960s. The changes in welfare *and* changes in the risks attached to crime *and* changes in the educational environment reinforced each other. Together, they radically altered the incentive structure. I characterize these changes, taken together, as encouraging short cuts in some instances (get rich quick or not at all) and "no cuts" in others— meaning that the link between present behavior and future outcomes was obscured altogether.

Crime

Let us assume an economic view of crime: Crime occurs when the prospective benefits sufficiently outweigh the prospective costs. When the risks associated with committing a crime go down, we expect crime to increase, other things being equal. Now, consider two elements of the "risk" equation as they changed from the perspective of the potential offender during the 1960s: the risk of being caught and the risk of going to prison if caught.

Figure 13.1 uses UCR data to plot the odds of getting away with

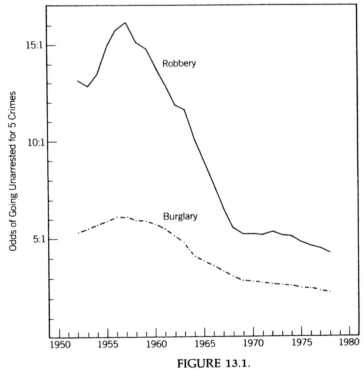

FIGURE 13.1.

The Declining Risk of Apprehension, 1954–1980

DATA AND SOURCE INFORMATION: Appendix table 18.

NOTE: Five-year moving average was computed from clearance data in appendix table 18. Note that estimate is based on reported crimes. Risk of apprehension is overestimated by exclusion of unreported crimes.

(not being arrested for) five robberies or burglaries as they changed during the period from 1954 to 1980.[1] The decline, which was concentrated during the 1960s, was substantial for burglary, precipitous for robberies.

The question of causation does not arise. It makes no difference for our purposes whether the increasing number of crimes overburdened the police, causing the reduction in clearance rates, or whether the declining risk of apprehension encouraged more crime. I simply observe that a thoughtful person watching the world around him during the 1960s was accurately perceiving a considerably reduced risk of getting caught. A youth hanging out on a tough urban street corner in 1960 was unlikely to know many (if any) people who could credibly claim to have gotten away with a string of robberies; in 1970, a youth hanging out on the same street corner might easily know several. When he considered his own chances, it would be only human nature for him to identify with the "successes."

The data on risk of imprisonment tell much the same story, as figure 13.2 shows:

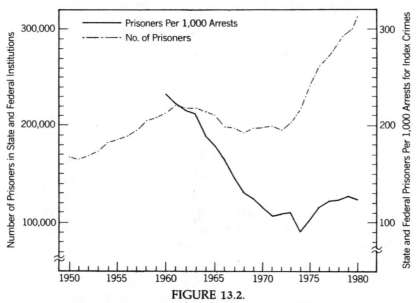

FIGURE 13.2.
Decline in Risk of Imprisonment if Caught, 1950–1980

DATA AND SOURCE INFORMATION: Appendix table 23.
NOTE: Local jails are not included. Plot represents a trend over time, not the specific probability of being incarcerated as a result of an arrest.

In this case, causes and effects are not quite so entangled. It was not just that we had more people to put in jails than we had jails to hold them (the overburdening problem); we also deliberately stopped putting people in jail as often. From 1961 through 1969, the number of prisoners in federal and state facilities—the absolute number, not just a proportion of arrestees —dropped every year, despite a doubling of crime during the same period.[2]

The two types of risk are not confounded. The "risk of arrest" and "risk of punishment" each dropped independently. Combined, the change in incentives was considerable.

Accompanying these changes in the numbers were changes in the rules of the game that once again disproportionately affected the poor. The affluent person caught by the police faced effectively the same situation in 1960 and in 1970. The poor person did not. In 1960, he could be picked up more or less on the police officer's intuition. He was likely to be taken into an interrogation room and questioned without benefit of counsel. He was likely to confess in instances when, if a lawyer had been sitting at his side, he would not have confessed. He was likely to be held in jail until his court date or to have to post bail, a considerable economic punishment in itself. If convicted, he was likely to be given a prison term. By 1970, the poor person had acquired an array of protections and stratagems that were formerly denied him—in effect, the same protections and stratagems that the rich had always possessed.

These changes extended the practice of equal treatment under the law (good). They also made crime less risky for poor people who were inclined to commit crimes if they thought they could get away with them (bad). One may recognize the latter without opposing the former.

For juveniles, the changes in incentives were especially dramatic. They were concentrated not in the smaller towns and cities, where juveniles generally continued to be treated as before, but in the large cities, where an upsurge in juvenile crime coincided with a movement toward a less punitive approach to delinquents. Consider the punishment of juveniles in Cook County, which includes the city of Chicago. In 1966, when the juvenile crime rate was entering its highest rate of increase, approximately 1,200 juveniles from Cook County were committed to the Illinois state system of training schools. For the next ten years, while the rate of juvenile crime in Cook County increased, the number of commitments dropped steadily. In 1976, fewer than 400 youths were committed—a reduction of two-thirds at a time when arrests were soaring.[3] A single statistic conveys how far the risk of penalty had dropped: By the mid-1970s, the average number of arrests of a Cook County youth before he was committed to a reform school *for the first time* was 13.6.[4] In such cities—and as far as we know, Chicago is typical—the risk of significant punishment for first arrests fell close to zero.[5] In discussions of why some juveniles become chronic delinquents, it should first of all be noted that, during the 1970s, a youngster who found criminal acts fun or rewarding and had been arrested only once or twice could have chosen to continue committing crimes through the simplest of logics: There was no reason not to.

The reduction in present punishment was accompanied by what may have been the single most significant change (well known to juveniles) in the rules of the game: In many states, including most of the northern urban states, laws were passed that provided for sealing the juvenile court record, tightening existing restrictions to the juvenile record, or, in sixteen states by 1974, purging or "expunging" it—destroying the physical evidence that the youth had ever been in trouble with the courts. The purpose of such acts was to ensure that, no matter what a vindictive prosecutor or judge might want to do, a youth who acquired a record as a juvenile could grow up without the opprobrium of a police record following him through life.

The increased inaccessibility of the juvenile record did little to change the incentives for the minor delinquent who had been arrested a few times for youthful transgressions. Such a record was not going to prevent him from getting many jobs nor would it make much difference if he were arrested as an adult. But the increased restrictions on accessibility had quite important implications for the delinquent with a long record of major offenses. By promising to make the record secret or, even more dramatically, by actually destroying the physical record, the juvenile justice system led the youth to believe that no matter what he did as a juvenile, or how often, it would be as if it had never happened once he reached his eighteenth birthday. Tight restrictions on access to the juvenile arrest and court records radically limited liability for exactly that behavior—chronic, violent delinquency—that the population at large was bemoaning. A teenager engaged in such behavior (or contemplating doing so) could quite reasonably ignore his parents' lectures about the costs of getting a police record. His parents were in fact wrong.

There is growing empirical evidence that raising the costs of criminal behavior—deterrence—reduces its frequency; it is summarized in the notes.[6] But to some extent the evidence, hard-won against technical problems and ideological resistance, is superfluous. James Q. Wilson has made the point very well:

> People are governed in their daily lives by rewards and penalties of every sort. We shop for bargain prices, praise our children for good behavior and scold them for bad, expect lower interest rates to stimulate home building and fear that higher ones will depress it, and conduct ourselves in public in ways that lead our friends and neighbors to form good opinions of us. To assert that "deterrence doesn't work" is tantamount to either denying the plainest facts of everyday life or claiming that would-be criminals are utterly different from the rest of us.[7]

For years, the latter assumption has been buried within other explanations—"Crime is a response to exploitation and poverty, therefore deterrence will not work" (a non sequitur), or, "People are not thinking that far ahead when they commit crimes, therefore deterrence will not work," and so on. If such explanations are to be truly plausible (that is, believable even to the people who assert them), the inescapable but unspoken conclusion has been, as Wilson suggests, that such persons are utterly different from the rest of us. The assumption is unwarranted, unnecessary, and objectionable.

Education

The basic problem in education has not changed. Persuading youngsters to work hard against the promise of intangible and long-deferred rewards was as tough in 1960 as in 1970. The challenge of creating adequate incentives was no different. But as in the case of crime, the disincentives for a certain type of student changed.

We are not considering children whose parents check their homework every night, or children who from earliest childhood expect to go to college, or children with high IQs and a creative flair. Rather, we are considering children with average or below-average abilities, with parents who ignore their progress or lack of it, with parents who are themselves incompetent to help with homework. We are not considering the small-town school with a few students, but the large urban school. Such children and such schools existed in 1960 as in 1970. Yet among those who stayed in school, more students seemed to learn to read and write and calculate in 1960 than in 1970. How might we employ an incentives approach to account for this?

While learning is hard work, it should be exciting and fun as well. But most large urban schools, though they may try to achieve that ideal, have other concerns that must take priority. They must first of all maintain order in the classroom and secondly make students try to do the work even if they do not want to. With students who come from supportive home environments, these tasks are relatively easy for the school; a bad grade or a comment on a report card is likely to trigger the needed corrective action. But with students who have no backup at home, these tasks are always difficult. Sanctions are required. In 1960, such sanctions consisted of holding a student back, in-school disciplinary measures, suspension, and expulsion. By the 1970s, use of all these sanctions had been sharply circumscribed.

During the same period, the incidence of student disorders went from nowhere to a national problem. Robert Rubel, who has compiled the most extensive data on this topic, divides the history of school disorders into three periods. From 1950 to 1964, disorders were of such low levels of frequency and seriousness that they were hardly worth mentioning. From 1964 to about 1971, disorders exploded, especially those that Rubel calls "teacher-testing." After 1971, the disorders were less patterned, but they continued to exist at the high levels they had reached during the late 1960s.[8] Why should disorders have increased at that time? Rubel points to the generally chaotic nature of the times. Another answer is that we began to permit them.

In part, the intellectual climate altered behavior. Books such as *Death at an Early Age* led the way for educational reforms that de-emphasized the traditional classroom norms in favor of a more open, less disciplined (or less repressive and ethnocentric, depending on one's ideology) treatment of the learning process.[9] The black pride movement added voices claiming that traditional education was one more example of white middle-class values arbitrarily forced on blacks.[10] But there were more concrete reasons for students and teachers alike to change their behavior.

In part, the federal offices that dispensed government help had a hand. They could establish projects implementing preferred strategies, which in the 1960s invariably favored a less traditional, less white-middle-class attitude toward education. They could support efforts to limit the use of suspension and expulsion. They could make imaginative use of the provisions of Title VI of the 1964 Civil Rights Act (enabling them to withdraw federal funds if a school system was found to be discriminating on grounds of race) to bring reluctant school systems around to their point of view.

In part, the judiciary had a hand. The key event was the Supreme Court's *Gault* v. *Arizona* decision in 1967. The case involved a juvenile court, but the principle enunciated by the Court applied to the schools as well, as the American Civil Liberties Union was quick to point out to school systems nationwide.[11] Due process was required for suspension, and the circumstances under which students could be suspended or otherwise disciplined were restricted. Teachers and administrators became vulnerable to lawsuits or professional setbacks for using the discretion that had been taken for granted in 1960.[12] Urban schools gave up the practice of making a student repeat a grade. "Social promotions" were given regardless of academic progress.

For all these reasons and many more, a student who did not want to learn was much freer not to learn in 1970 than in 1960, and freer to disrupt the learning process for others. Facing no credible sanctions for not learning and possessing no tangible incentives to learn, large numbers of students did things they considered more fun and did not learn. What could have been more natural?

A concomitant to these changes in incentives was that teachers had new reasons *not* to demand high performance (or any performance at all). In the typical inner-city school, a demanding teaching style would be sure to displease some of the students—as indeed demanding teachers have done everywhere, from time immemorial. But now there was this difference: The rebellious students could make life considerably more miserable for the teacher than the teacher could for the students—through their disruptive behavior in class, through physical threats, or even through official channels, complaining to the administration that the teacher was unreasonable, harsh, or otherwise failing to observe their rights. In the 1960s and into the 1970s, teachers who demanded performance in an inner-city school were asking for trouble.

The dramatic problems of confrontation were combined with the less dramatic ones of absenteeism, tardiness, and failure to do homework. Jackson Toby describes the results:

> When only a handful of students attempt to complete homework, teachers stop assigning it; and of course, it is difficult to teach a lesson that depends on material taught yesterday or last week when only a few students can be counted on to be regularly in class. Eventually, in these circumstances, teachers stop putting forth the considerable effort required to educate.[13]

Toby traces the rest of the chain: Teachers take the maximum number of days off to which they are entitled. Substitute teachers are hard to recruit for the same reasons that the teachers are taking days off. The best students, both black and white, transfer to private or parochial schools, making it that much more difficult to control the remainder. Absent teachers and loss of control lead to more class-cutting. More class-cutting increases the noise in the halls. "In the classrooms, teachers struggle for the attention of the students. Students talk to one another; they engage in playful and not-so-playful fights; they leave repeatedly to visit the toilet or to get drinks of water."[14] Learning does not, cannot, occur.

School administrators in the last half of the 1960s had to finesse the problem of the gap between white and black achievement (see chapter 7). Pushing hard for academic achievement in schools with a mix of blacks and whites led to embarrassment and protests when the white children always seemed to end up winning the academic awards and getting the best grades and scoring highest on the tests. Pushing hard for academic achievement in predominantly black urban schools led to intense resentment by the students and occasionally by parents and the community. It was not the students' fault they were ill-prepared—racism was to blame, the system was to blame—and solutions that depended on the students' working doubly hard to make up their deficits were accordingly inappropriate, tantamount to getting the students to cover for the system's mistakes.

As in the case of work effort, marital behavior, and crime, the empirical evidence is accumulating that the changes in incentives in the classroom are causally linked to the trends in educational outcomes.[15] But, as in the the case of Phyllis and Harold, or the case of the villager refusing to grow jute, perhaps the most persuasive evidence is one's own answer to the question, "What would *I* do given the same situation?" Given the changes in risks and rewards: If you were a student in the inner-city school of 1970, would you have behaved the same as you would have in 1960? If you were a teacher, would you have enforced the same standards? If you really loved teaching, would you have remained a teacher in the public schools?

Misdirected Synergism

The discrete empirical links between changes in sanctions for crime and criminal behavior, between changes in school rules and learning, or between changes in welfare policy and work effort are essential bits of the puzzle, but they are also too tightly focused. None of the individual links is nearly as important as the aggregate change between the world in which a poor youngster grew up in the 1950s and the one in which he or she grew up in the 1970s. All the changes in the incentives pointed in the same direction. It was easier to get along without a job. It was easier for a man to have a baby without being responsible for it, for a woman to have a baby without having a husband. It was easier to get away with crime. Because it was easier for others to get away with crime, it was easier to obtain drugs. Because it was easier to get away with crime, it was easier to support a drug habit. Because it was easier to get along without a job, it was easier to ignore education. Because it was easier to get along without a job, it was easier to walk away from a job and thereby accumulate a record as an unreliable employee.

In the end, all these changes in behavior were traps. Anyone who gets caught often enough begins going to jail. Anyone who reaches his mid-twenties without a record as a good worker is probably stuck for the rest of his life with the self-fulfilling prophecy he has set up—it is already too late for him to change the way he thinks about himself or to get others to think differently of him. Any teenager who has children and must rely on public assistance to support them has struck a Faustian bargain with the system that nearly ensures that she will live in poverty the rest of her days. The interconnections among the changes in incentives I have described and the behaviors that have grown among the poor and disadvantaged are endless. So also are their consequences for the people who have been seduced into long-term disaster by that most human of impulses, the pursuit of one's short-term best interest.

Present Sticks, and a Distant Carrot

The alternative future for a Harold and Phyllis is not the executive suite and an estate in the country. It is probably no more than getting by. If I were to concoct an imaginary ending, neither too optimistic nor too pessimistic, to the story of the 1960 Harold and Phyllis it would go something like this.

When we left Harold, he had taken the job in the laundry. He was stuck with the steam press he hated. Sometimes, however, he got a chance to do a little part-time work driving a delivery truck for the laundry. After three years of this, the regular driver left and Harold replaced him. Driving the truck paid a little more money than the presses, but not much. After six years of driving the delivery truck, a truck-driver friend of Harold's helped him get a similar job for a large company. It was a unionized job, and Harold was still working for the company in 1970, with occasional layoffs —fewer, as his seniority piled up. Phyllis had two more babies, and Harold's wage, even though he now made $5 an hour, was barely enough to go around. But it did go around.

It is not much of a Horatio Alger story. The 1960 Harold had a little luck, no more and maybe a little less than one can reasonably expect. His experience typifies the job path of millions of American workers: starting on an unskilled job near the minimum wage, picking up a few skills along with a record as a reliable worker, eventually happening across an opportunity to move into a job with a little more money and security.

The rationale for holding onto a bad job is thus very tentative, long-term, and without guarantees: "Work hard, stick to the job no matter how bad it is, and you will probably climb out of poverty but not very far out." For blacks, the uncertainty and distance of the incentive have been compounded by discrimination that makes it harder to get and hold jobs. The rewards for studying in school and keeping out of trouble with the law are uncertain and not enticing.

Against this meager incentive on the plus side, we have examined an array of negative incentives. The imbalance is not a function of a particular social policy. It is not a function even of a particular social system. Rather, there is this truth: The tangible incentives that any society can realistically hold out to the poor youth of average abilities and average industriousness are mostly penalties, mostly disincentives. "Do not study, and we will throw you out; commit crimes, and we will put you in jail; do not work, and we will make sure that your existence is so uncomfortable that any job will be preferable to it." To promise much more is a fraud.

Given this Hobbesian state of affairs, why have I presented the story of Harold's and Phyllis's changed incentives as a negative one? In 1960 the couple was condemned to an income at a bare survival level. In 1970, the same miserable job plus the supplements from government support gave the two of them a combined real income more than twice as large. Why is this not progress? One answer is that what we did for the mediocre hurt many others who were *not* of average abilities and (originally) average industriousness. Another answer is that, even for many of the Harolds and the Phyllises, we demeaned their quality of life in ways that the added dollars could not compensate. The changes in incentives not only interacted to produce a different short-term rationality; they interacted to change the very nature of the satisfactions and rewards. Let us leave behind the economic incentives and turn to another set: the incentives associated with status.

14

The Destruction of Status Rewards

STATUS AND MONEY are the most influential rewards that society uses to manage behavior.[1] Indeed, for many people, the dominant motive for making money is to buy status. We will be discussing status in terms of two quite distinct functions it serves.

One is familiar: the lures of status as a goad for ambition. We could hardly get along without them—official Washington, for example, which induces senior executives to work for a fraction of the salaries they could command in the private sector, would break down altogether if we withdrew status rewards, and so would much of the academic competitiveness that generally serves us so well. As a way of getting our ablest people to work sixteen-hour days and do things that eventually benefit the rest of us, status rewards are the best bargain in town.

The second function of status is to reward the virtuous (however the culture defines them) at all levels. Not everybody is going to get rich. Not everybody is going to be brilliant or beautiful. Societies concoct ways in which people can live satisfactory lives anyway. Of these ways, status distinctions are perhaps the most important. In rigidly hierarchical societies, they take the form of elaborate caste systems that not only define one's present status but also confine one to that status perpetually. Part of the genius of the system in the United States is that status is not immutable. Those on the bottom at any given time can see themselves as just passing through on the way up; parents stuck at their level can vicariously enjoy their children's progress. Another part of the genius of our system in earlier years was that, even at the moment of being economically at the bottom of the heap, there were status rewards to be enjoyed by those who earned them.

Both functions of status, as goad and solace, are crucial, and both permeate every aspect of our lives. Whether one is describing Beverly Hills or the South Bronx, the means whereby status is conferred, enjoyed, recognized, and lost are central to the life of the people who live there. In this chapter, I will explore the ways in which the revolution in social policy altered status relationships within poor communities. I will argue two propositions: (1) Status was withdrawn from the low-income, independent working family, with disastrous consequences to the quality of life of such families; (2) Status was withdrawn from the behaviors that engender escape from poverty.

The discussion will be directed at the situation affecting blacks, and especially young blacks living in all-black, poor communities. I introduce the racial element, after avoiding it so assiduously in the presentation of Harold and Phyllis, because in the 1960s blacks were in a unique position: They were the objects of white ambivalences and white guilt that shaped status rewards among black poor while affecting white poor persons less directly. The larger society cannot necessarily impose values on smaller communities, but it can invalidate them—and that is what white society did to poor black communities in the 1960s. (See chapter 2 for a discussion of the white response to the civil rights movement and the riots.)

In part, the changes in status relationships and their consequences were accidental, one more of the "unintended outcomes" that plagued the policies of the Great Society. But this is one instance in which there was an element of deliberate, aggressively sought change. We begin with that aspect.

The Homogenization of the Poor

Historically, the United States has been a nation of people who were either poor or the children of poor parents. Only in the last half of the twentieth century has a large proportion of the middle class become so far removed from poverty that the lack of money became horrifying in itself.[2]

Few of the American poor defined their lives in terms of their poverty. Neither did society. The "poor" were a varied lot with complex status distinctions to be drawn. There were the genteel poor who had lost their money but not their manners. There were the poor people who were called "trash"—not just without money, but also uncouth and generally unpleasant company. There were the immigrant poor who, at the same time they were climbing out of poverty, maintained elaborate status structures even in the most crowded tenements. And there were the farmers. Forty-two percent of the population lived on farms in 1900, and most of them were cash-poor. But, from the time of Jefferson down through the years, the farmers were widely seen as (or saw themselves to be) the backbone of the nation and on a considerably higher moral plane than the effete rich.

Status distinctions among the poor began with the assumption that people are responsible for their actions and, specifically, responsible for taking care of themselves and their families as best they could. Missouri farmers and New York immigrants might have had wildly different status distinctions in other respects, but in both communities, and everywhere that poor people lived together, the first distinction was made on this basis. A person might work hard and be poor; that was the way of the world. Poverty had nothing to do with dignity. A person might be out of a job once in while because of hard times. That too was the way of the world, and a temporary situation. But a person who was chronically unable to hold onto a job, who neglected children and spouse, was a bum and a no-good, consigned to the lowest circle of status.

Once it was assumed that the system is to blame when a person is chronically out of work and that the system is even to blame when a person neglects spouse and family, then the moral distinctions were eroded. The first casualty inevitably was the moral approbation associated with self-sufficiency. In the 1950s, the reason for "getting people off welfare" was to keep them from being a drag on the good people—meaning the self-sufficient people—and to rescue them from a degrading status. It was not necessary to explain *why* it was better to be self-sufficient; it was a precondition for being a member of society in good standing. In the late 1960s, with the attack on middle-class norms and the rise of the welfare rights movement, this was no longer good enough. Self-sufficiency was no longer taken to be an intrinsic *obligation* of healthy adults.

Among the people who held this view, the next casualty of the assumption that "the system is to blame" was the distinction between the deserving poor and the undeserving poor. Blame is the flip side of praise. To praise the poor who are self-sufficient is to assign to them responsibility for their upstandingness. But if one family is responsible for its success, the next family bears at least a measure of responsibility for its failure. It was much less complicated simply to treat "the poor" as a homogeneous group of victims.

It must be remembered that the shift in opinion was localized. A survey in 1967 showed that 42 percent of Americans still thought poverty reflected "lack of effort," another 39 percent thought that lack of effort had at least something to do with it, and only 19 percent blamed poverty on "circumstances beyond control."[3] But what the mass of Americans thought did not shape the reform period. In academic and policy-making circles, the conversion was nearly unanimous. The very term "deserving poor" was laughed out of use—witness the reaction of political columnists and cartoonists to the use of "truly needy" by the Reagan administration.

Only the poor were homogenized. In the day-to-day life of the rest of society, the elite, like the broad middle class, continued as always to differentiate the clever from the dull, the upright from the outlaw, the industrious from the indolent. But when it came to the poor, all must be victims. They were not permitted to be superior to one another.

The Policy Implications of Homogenization

If the poor were all victims, then policy had to be changed. First of all, welfare had to be cleansed of its stigma. Welfare historically had been a blot on the recipient's reputation; to be on welfare was to be inferior to one's neighbors who were not on welfare. But if it was not the welfare recipient's fault that welfare was needed, the stigma was wrong and unfair.

The portrayal and administration of the welfare system changed dramatically to fit the new wisdom. The key administrative changes for AFDC were reviewed in chapter 12: directives against investigations of eligibility and court decisions easing restrictions on eligibility. In addition, OEO took a more direct stand against stigma. As early as 1965, it was sending emissaries to spread the word that it was morally permissible to be on welfare. Community Action grants provided the wherewithal for booklets, speeches, and one-on-one evangelizing by staff workers. Welfare was to be considered a right, not charity.

The government's efforts were reinforced by the National Welfare Rights Organization, founded in 1966 and led by George Wiley. By 1967, the NWRO was large enough to hold its first annual convention in Washington. The innovative aspect of the welfare rights movement was not that poor people were organizing. Poor people had been marching on Washington since the town was built. But the age-old slogan was missing. No longer, as always before, did the protesters proclaim that "We don't want charity, we want jobs." In the last half of the 1960s the NWRO demonstrators were not demonstrating so much for jobs as for the right to long-term, unfettered, generous charity.[4]

Piven and Cloward cite evidence that the efforts of the community organizers were successful in reducing the stigma.[5] Such results are plausible. One of the major sources of the stigma attached to welfare was the middle class. For poor people who aspired to be like them in respectability, the appearance of in-the-flesh representatives of the middle class saying that welfare was their due must have had a telling effect. One may visualize, for example, the situation of parents in a slum who have taught their offspring to believe it is shameful to accept welfare. Then the children come home reporting that the supervisors on the Summer Job program, or the organizers of the Community Development project, or the lawyers down at the Legal Services storefront office are saying that such notions are all wrong. Welfare is a right. The parents are dupes. The irony is that parents who have taught their children that welfare is shameful tend to be the kind of people who also teach their children to treat lawyers and supervisors and organizers as role models. How do the parents now convincingly reply, "I don't care what those people [the very people you are supposed to admire] said, it's still wrong. . . ."?

Getting rid of the stigma of welfare was a deliberate goal. But another effect was not; it just happened as a logical consequence of denying that people are responsible for their condition: Because the system is to blame, all people on welfare are equally deserving of being given a hand. No one could disqualify himself on moral grounds from eligibility for public assistance—whether or not he was ready to help himself. There was no longer a mechanism for stamping someone unworthy. On the contrary, many of the social-service programs required as a condition of eligibility that the participants be failures. It could not be otherwise. Programs to rehabilitate drug addicts have to be restricted to drug addicts; programs to employ the hard-core unemployed must be restricted to the hard-core unemployed; and so on.

Theoretically, the social service and educational programs could have gotten around this selectivity by providing other programs aimed at those who were especially "worthy"—those who were giving their all and needed just a little more help to escape from poverty for good. But the mindset was too strong. "Elite" was fast becoming a dirty word in the mid-1960s among whites; "elitism" would soon be a form of bigotry to rank with racism and, later, sexism and ageism. Blacks were especially sensitized. Long ago, W.E.B. Du Bois had urged special emphasis on "the talented tenth" among blacks, and the approach had since become identified with a compliance with middle-class values (at best), Tom-ism (more likely), and general lack of militance at a time when power to the people was in vogue.

The unwillingness to acknowledge moral inequality was a hallmark of Great Society social programs and persisted throughout the 1970s. It was not just that the squeaky hinges (the failures) got the oil. Administrators of programs made Kafkaesque rules to avoid revealing that some poor people are brighter or of better character or more industrious than others.

One case in point, the "magnet schools," may be used to illustrate the general phenomenon. The purpose of the magnet schools was to lure white middle-class students back into urban school systems by setting up inner-city schools that were open to enrollment from throughout the city and were provided with special resources in a specific area—science, or the arts, or simply a strenuous college-prep program. The theory was that the magnet schools would not only reduce white flight among those who saw an opportunity in the magnet school; they would also break the back of the stereotypes that contributed to white flight from urban schools in general. It was one of the more plausible of the educational innovations of the time.

Some of the vocational schools and elementary schools achieved positive results.[6] But administrators of the high schools with an academic program soon ran up against a dilemma. Inner-city public education was so bad that only a few black students had adequate preparation to enter and successfully complete the curriculum in the magnet school. What should be done? One solution would have been to proceed as planned. The gifted black students who were in the program, even if they were fewer than had been hoped, would have a high-quality education they would not have gotten otherwise, and the white students (and their parents) would see what black students could do, given the opportunity. But few of the magnet schools took this course.

The common solution was rather to impose a racial quota to ensure that "enough" black students got into the magnet school. The results were as one would predict: To fill the quota, black students with inadequate skills were admitted. Then the school had either to flunk the students who could not keep up (unthinkable) or to soften the standards. But softening the standards destroyed the attractions of the magnet school for the white parents it was supposed to entice. And the stereotypes that the magnet schools were to dispel were reinforced. The white students went away with incontrovertible evidence from personal experience that even the brightest black students (for that is what they were *supposed* to be) were not competitive with white students.

The magnet schools story has numerous analogs among other programs of the time. Social programs were initiated with the professed purpose of creating successes from failures. But to create a success, an indispensable element is praise for accomplishment. And if praise for the ones who succeed is to be detailed, emphatic, and credible, it soon becomes necessary to distribute blame as well. Praise is meaningless without the assumption that the people who succeeded are in some practical way *better* than the people who failed, and this the administrators of the programs and the ideologues of the new wisdom were unwilling to confront head-on. To see some as better was perceived as denying that the failures were victims.

The Role of the Means-Tested Programs

Arguably the most insidious single change affecting status relationships within the poor community had nothing to do with the Great Society's social-action programs but with the introduction of "means-tested" welfare benefits.

One of the insights of game theory is the psychological importance of natural boundaries—those things that make it easier to quit smoking than to cut down and that lead bargainers to compromise on a round number or to "split the difference." With poor people, the boundary was accepting *no charity at all* from anyone outside the family. Many readers will be able to verify the power of this demarcation line from their earliest lessons about the family tradition: "We may not have had much money, but we never took a penny of charity," was one common formula; or "We have always paid our own way" or "We have always pulled our own weight." The idioms and the tradition were pervasive.

Means-tested programs effectively ended such useful boasts. One may approve or disapprove of Food Stamps and Medicaid and housing assistance, but one result was unavoidable. Virtually all low-income persons became welfare recipients (remember that by 1980 Food Stamps alone counted more than 21,000,000 recipients). Pride in independence was compromised, and with it a certain degree of pressure on the younger generation to make good on the family tradition.

More importantly, the working people who made little money lost the one thing that enabled them to claim social status. For the first time in American history, it became socially acceptable within poor communities to be unemployed, because working families too were receiving welfare. Over a period of years, such changes in the rules of the economic game caused status conventions to flip completely in some communities. Why, at bottom, should working confer social status? Originally, there were two reasons. One was that nonworking people were a threat to the wealth and well-being of the rest of the community. The second was that nonworking people were visibly outcasts; they lived worse than anyone else. Once these highly functional sources of the status are removed, the vaunted "work ethic" becomes highly vulnerable. The notion that there is an intrinsic good in working even if one does not have to may have impressive philosophical credentials, but, on its face, it is not very plausible—at least not to a young person whose values are still being formed. To someone who is not yet persuaded of the satisfactions of making one's own way, there is something laughable about a person who doggedly keeps working at a lousy job for no tangible reason at all. And when working no longer provides either income or status, the last reason for working has truly vanished. The man who keeps working is, in fact, a chump.[7]

Reconsider the data on labor force participation from this point of view. We know that values once acquired do not easily change. Older workers are likely to continue to work even if the economic incentives suggest they do not. (And rationally so: Insofar as *their* peers, in their generation, continue to value self-sufficiency, the status associated with remaining a "member of the club" is unaffected.) Further, we know that only those people who work near the minimum wage find the welfare alternative attractive. On both counts, we are drawn to an hypothesis about the labor force participation of younger workers: Because their values are more plastic and because their wages are more likely to be near the vulnerable minimum-wage level, they are likely to respond more quickly than the old to the changes in status and income rewards. The hypothesis certainly makes sense, and it certainly fits the data. The gap between black and white male LFP was far larger for the younger age groups than for the older ones. The younger the age group, the sooner the gap broadened (see chapter 5). As in the case of the AFDC rolls, the timing of the changes was striking.

Status and Upward Mobility

I have argued that the philosophical denial of personal responsibility for one's behavior prevents praise for worthy performance, and that the denial has had a pernicious homogenizing effect on the status of poor people. I have concentrated on status as something that makes life more pleasant: A poor family with pride is "happier" in every meaningful sense of the word than an equally poor family without pride, and that pride depends on the self-respect that status within the community can bring.

Now, let us consider the role of status in fostering the escape from poverty. We are no longer discussing a Harold, the average man of average ambition whose realistic hope is for no more than a secure job at a decent wage. We are envisioning a potential Horatio Alger. By taking away responsibility—by saying, "Because the system is to blame, it's not your fault that. . . ."—society also takes away the credit that is an essential part of the reward structure that has fostered social and economic mobility in the United States.

Socioeconomic mobility has been America's stock in trade. Immigrants arrive penniless and work their way up. The sharecropper's son becomes an assembly-line worker and his granddaughter goes to college. The immigrant who speaks no English has a son who goes to night school for nine years and finally gets a law degree. These are the personal triumphs that constitute the American epic.

To sustain this mobility, the United States has depended on the willingness of the poor to make investments—of time, energy, psychic commitment, and money. Because these investments are being made by people with very little to spare in the first place, investing means that an already difficult existence must be made even more difficult. The investments inevitably mean that something else has to be given up, whether free time or money.

The investments are made in hopes of long-term gains. But the ultimate payoff is remote. To sustain the effort over what may be a protracted period, the system must also offer incentives and rewards before the prize is attained.

The principal ongoing incentive has been *faith that investments do pay off,* based on what has happened to other people. This belief has to be assimilated during childhood and adolescence, and it must be based on an underlying reality. Role models have to exist of whom the youth can credibly say, "If he (she) could do it, it is possible that I can do it, too." This is one reason that a relatively few black basketball stars inspire endless hours of practice on inner-city basketball courts despite the astronomical odds against success. The stimulus is not just the glamour and the money of professional basketball. It is also crucially important that many of those stars started on the same kind of courts, under the same handicaps.

The principal ongoing reward has been *praise for trying*. This reward has been especially important for the largest single class of poor "investors," students who make present sacrifices to get an advanced education. Under the traditional model, the night school student may be skipping lunch to study. He may not have had a free evening in months. But his parents are proud of him, he is used as a model by other parents in the neighborhood, his classmates vote him most likely to succeed, and—an important plus— he knows that society itself applauds. He has read books and seen movies that have people like him as heroes. In the context of these incentives and rewards, the homogenization of the poor was a central error for heterogeneously poor communities. The incentive ("It is possible to succeed") and the reward ("People admire me for trying") were both gutted.

The black ghetto again forms the archetypal example of characteristics found (not only in America, but world-wide) wherever some members of society have been segregated and told they are inferior.[8] Virtually every commentator on what it is like to grow up black in America, whether novelist or sociologist or memoirist, has reflected on the devastating effects of racism on self-confidence.[9] Inside the ghetto, the rules and rule-setters are known. Moving outside, competing on white terms for what have traditionally been white perquisites, is objectively difficult. When the real difficulties are compounded by the fears engendered by centuries of white propagandizing that white is smarter (and by elements of self-denigration by blacks), the result can be immobilization of even the most able and ambitious.

This debilitating aspect of black socialization is not a recent creation. The problem is that post-1964 social policy fed it. Every assumption that a young black in the ghetto might make about his inability to compete with whites was nourished by a social policy telling him, through the way it treated him day to day, that he was an un-responsible victim. Society's actions were at odds with society's rhetoric telling him to be proud and to believe in himself.

Day to day, going to a typical inner-city high school, such a young person saw that most of the special programs were directed at the most conspicuous failures.[10] There were likely to be special programs for the mentally retarded, for the learning-disabled, and for the emotionally disturbed. The rules of school conduct placated the trouble-makers. Special tracks for the gifted were attacked as elitist. Where programs for the gifted (or just the hardest-working) did exist, they fell into the magnet-schools trap—to avoid trouble, the course materials were watered down and the demands (and sense of reward) were low. The ambitious and hard-working students were passed along with A's and with the teachers' gratitude for not contributing to the discipline problem, but without an education that enabled them to compete in a good university.

Outside of school, the rules of the game argued against the proposition that hard work pays off. The network of social service agencies—the most visible (legitimate) resource bank—existed to help the least provident and least able. The most conspicuous local success stories were drug dealers, pimps, and fences.[11] Friends who were arrested by the police went free or were assigned to educational or counseling programs for which the youth who went straight was not eligible. And when the hard-working student did get into a government-sponsored job program, his first lesson was that the ones who did no work were treated exactly the same as he was, except that he was likely to come under attack from his coworkers for threatening to get the others in trouble.[12]

This experience contained only one kind of lesson: In the day-to-day experience of a youth growing up in a black ghetto, there was no evidence whatsoever that working within the system paid off. The way to get something from the system was to be sufficiently a failure to qualify for help, or to con the system. What a racially segregated society once taught the young black about living with his inferiority was now taught by a benevolent social welfare system. The difference was that in an earlier age, a black parent could fight the competing influences. The parent could drum into the child's head the belief that he could make it—that the people who said otherwise were racists who obviously *wanted* him to fail. How did a parent in the aftermath of the reform period compete with a system that proclaimed its devotion to equality, but whose purpose was to minister to a black population that it tacitly assumed had proved its inability to compete in the straight, white system?

Let us once again do some role-playing. Let us say that I am an adolescent who has grown up surrounded by longstanding influences that make me doubt my ability to compete in the larger society. I look around and find evidence that others like me are unable to compete. I am told by spokesmen—white and black alike—that it is not my fault, that I am the victim of forces beyond my control. *If I expect to fail, it is extremely useful to believe what I am told.* In fact, it is essential. If I observe a peer who is studying hard, I am threatened. Such a peer is asserting one of two things, either of which is unacceptable. One assertion is that he is better than I (and is therefore free of the forces that excuse me for failing). The other assertion is even more threatening: that he is *not* better than I, but rather that I am wrong in excusing myself for failing. Either way, I have a motive to discourage such behavior by my fellow students.

Such dynamics are likely to have played a role in a phenomenon of recent vintage in black inner-city high schools: extraordinary pressure by students on other students not to compete in mainstream society. The situation varies from city to city and from school to school, but the norm in inner-city schools during the 1970s was that the hard-working student was said to be "acting white" and was subjected to severe criticism, isolation, even physical assaults. There was no "praise for trying"; instead there was social ostracism, which, for the typical adolescent, is perhaps the worst of punishments.

The attitudes I describe should not be confused with the normal teasing that the school "brain" has to put up with in high schools everywhere. Nor is it necessarily a traditional phenomenon in black schools. In a not-for-attribution discussion, a black journalist reflecting on the problem recalled a recent visit to his Newark high school to present the Honor Society awards—an occasion which in the early 1960s had been a major event for the school. He found that the ceremony was now held in the evening, with only the honorees attending—because a school-wide assembly could not be held without the student body jeering the proceedings to a halt. The Reverend Jesse Jackson's "Push for Excellence" campaign in the mid 1970s was inspired by a similar observation, that in too many inner-city schools excellence in any field except sports was mocked and denigrated. I am not aware of any systematic studies of this phenomenon, but it is of crucial importance in explaining the negative learning environment in many black urban schools.

I am suggesting that three conditions promote this state of affairs in a community of poor people: (1) insularity, the isolation of a community from intercourse with mainstream society; (2) expectation of failure, conditioning that leads to fragile self-confidence (independently of real abilities); (3) official sanction to reject personal responsibility for one's actions.

It happens that blacks in the ghetto live in the most isolated communities, experience the most severe negative conditioning, and have been granted (by policy) the most explicit dispensation from responsibility. My hypothesis is that white poor communities characterized by the same three conditions will exhibit the same attitudes among their youth and the same immobility, but I cannot point to examples. The closest analog is probably

Appalachian or southern tenant farmers, but the data are sparse, and the white elite never could rouse the same passion for excusing the white disadvantaged as it did for excusing the black disadvantaged.

We do know that some blacks did well, as noted in the discussion of the "pulling away" phenomenon we saw in chapter 6: the odd juxtaposition whereby major improvements in occupational status and wages among employed blacks existed side-by-side with the catastrophic declines in employment and labor force participation among young blacks.

The trends we witnessed in these data are consistent with an explanation based on the withdrawal of status reinforcements for upward mobility. Objectively (seen from our privileged position above the battle), the two critical conditions for a young black person to escape from the ghetto have been met: White society is rewarding those who have a good education, speak standard (white) English, behave with middle-class social graces, and otherwise play within traditional white rules. And social policy is, in a purely technical sense, providing the wherewithal for even the poorest youngster to acquire these assets: The best universities actively seek to enroll capable inner-city students and government programs for poor students provide generous help from college through graduate school. Objectively, the way up has been opened, and many blacks have taken advantage of it. Their successes show up in the data. But they do not seem to be the ones from the ghetto.[13] Why?

One answer is that taking the route remains very costly in the short term, as it always has been; in effect, it demands that the youngster reject a known culture for an alien one. Douglas Glasgow discusses why the efforts of the Los Angeles school system to inculcate the white rules and the white culture failed. In addition to the humiliation associated with the imputation that black ghetto culture is inferior, the timing couldn't have been worse:

> Compounding [the students'] antagonistic feelings was the fact that the schools were trying to engage them in an almost impossible adaptation at the same time they were undergoing the intense identity search of adolescence. At this age the socializing function of the streets, of peer culture, supersedes all other efforts to mold social skills, including even those of the family. The pressure to identify with Black life, not to reject it, was never greater.[14]

This and analogous accounts of the wrenching cultural transition involved in leaving the ghetto provide a plausible explanation for why large numbers of each generation do not escape. They do not provide an explanation for why the experience has become more, not less, wrenching over time. Leaving a Polish culture, or Japanese culture, or any of the other ethnic enclaves in American society has always been frightening. At any given point in the history of ethnic communities in the United States, most of the younger generation was staying in the enclave, wary of leaving the familiar and the comfortable. What set the black ghetto in the 1970s apart from historical precedents, including black ghettos in earlier years, was that the barrier separating the ghetto youth from the larger society had become nearly an airtight seal at a time when it should have become increasingly permeable. In addition to the effects of the changes in the tangible incentives discussed in the preceding chapters, I suggest that an important part of the explanation lies in the withdrawal of local, visible praise for trying to escape. The young ghetto black on his way up was not cheered on his way, as the young Jewish or Chinese or, for that matter, white Anglo-Saxon protestant youth has been. I further suggest that this withdrawal of support can be traced in some significant degree to the excuse that, starting in the mid-1960s, social policy actively pressed on the ghetto: "It's not your fault."

PART IV

Rethinking
Social Policy

BUT what should we *do?*" If the question is asked about what politically feasible bills should be introduced tomorrow or what politically feasible changes the Department of Health and Human Services should make in the AFDC regulations, I do not know the answer, nor, to my knowledge, does anyone.

We know from recent experience, however, that the political system's tolerance for reform is extremely limited. In the early years of the Reagan administration, we witnessed exceedingly bitter disputes about the passage of what were, at bottom, reductions in the rate of increase in social spending and parings from a nearly unchanged array of social programs. That proponents and opponents alike treated these as a major shift in federal policy toward the poor says much about the narrow range of reforms that are considered within the bounds of respectability. The number of "politically feasible" changes that would also make much difference is approximately zero.

In any event, thousands of people are paid well to do nothing but devise practical solutions. Let us leave that job to them and instead explore as a matter of intense intellectual and social interest some questions of "Why?" and "What if?"

15

What Do We Want to Accomplish?

THE LEGITIMACY of altering social institutions to achieve greater equality of material condition is, though often assumed, rarely *argued* for," Robert Nozick observes, and so it has been in debate on social policy.[1] Why pay for welfare? Why pay for Food Stamps? Why pay for scholarships for poor students? Most answers are not so much reasons as affirmations of faith. By and large, we have not for some years asked primitive questions about social policy. The debate over the size of the Food Stamps budget is vigorous. The debate over whether it is *right* that there be a Food Stamps budget has been limited to a few libertarians who are adequately answered, it is assumed, by the self-evident goodness of providing food to needy people.

I do not propose to argue the "why" questions in all their philosophical ramifications. Nor is this the place to try to construct a theory through which all competing answers may be reconciled. Rather, let us establish only that the answers to the "why" questions are not usually so abstract as "because it is the humane thing to do" or "because I am my brother's keeper." We are occasionally forced to fall back on these final and not very enlightening justifications, but usually we have something quite different in mind.

"Why Give Anything at All?"

If social policy may be construed, as I suggested at the beginning of the book, as transfers from the haves to the have-nots, the proper first question is, "What is the justification for any transfers at all?" Why should one person give *anything* to a stranger whose only claim to his help is a common citizenship?

Suppose that I am not opposed to the notion of government transfers, but neither do I think that equality of outcome is always a good in itself. I attach considerable value to the principle that people get what they deserve. In other words, "I" am a fairly typical citizen with a middle-of-the-road, pragmatic political philosophy.

I am asked to consider the case of a man who has worked steadily for many years and, in his fifties, is thrown out of his job because the factory closes. Why should I transfer money to him—provide him with unemployment checks and, perhaps, permanent welfare support? The answer is not difficult. I may rationalize it any number of ways, but at bottom I consent to transfer money to him because I want to. The worker has plugged along as best he could, contributed his bit to the community, and now faces personal disaster. He is one of my fellows in a very meaningful way— "There but for the grace of God. . . ."—and I am happy to see a portion of my income used to help him out. (I would not be happy to see so much of my income transferred that I am unable to meet my obligations to myself and my family, however.)

A second man, healthy and in the prime of life, refuses to work. I offer him a job, and he still refuses to work. I am called upon to answer the question again: Why should I transfer money to him? Why should I not let him starve, considering it a form of suicide?

It is a question to ponder without escape hatches. I may not assume that the man can be made to change his ways with the right therapeutic intervention. I may not assume that he has some mental or environmental handicap that relieves him of responsibility. He is a man of ordinary capacities who wishes to live off my work rather than work for himself. Why should I consent?

Suppose that I decide not to let him starve in the streets, for reasons having to do with the sanctity of life (I would prevent a suicide as well). The decision does not take me very far in setting up an ideal policy. At once, I run into choices when I compare his situation (we will call him the drone) with that of the laid-off worker.

Suppose that I have only enough resources either (a) to keep both alive at a bare subsistence level or (b) to support the laid-off worker at a decent standard of living and the drone at a near-starvation level. What would be the just policy? Would it be right, would it be fair, to make the worker live more miserably so that I might be more generous to the drone?

We may put the question more provocatively: Suppose that scarce resources were not a problem—that we could afford to support both at a decent standard of living. Should we do so? Is it morally appropriate to give the same level of support to the two men? Would it be right to offer the same respect to the two men? The same discretionary choice in how to use the help that was provided?

These are not rhetorical questions nor are they questions about expedient policy. They ask about the justice and humanity of the alternatives. I submit that it is not humane to the laid-off worker to treat him the same as the drone. It is not just to accord the drone the respect that the laid-off worker has earned.

The point is that, in principle, most of us provide some kinds of assistance gladly, for intuitively obvious reasons. We provide other kinds of assistance for reasons that, when it comes down to it, are extremely hard to defend on either moral or practical grounds. An ethically ideal social policy—an *intuitively* satisfying one—would discriminate among recipients. It would attach a pat on the back to some transfers and give others begrudgingly.

We have yet to tackle the question of whether the point has anything to do with recipients in the workaday world. Who is to say that the drone has no justification for refusing to work (he was trained as a cook and we offer him a job sweeping floors)? Who is to say whether the laid-off worker is blameless for the loss of his job (his sloppy workmanship contributed to the factory's loss of business to the Japanese)? Who is to say that the income of the taxpaying donor is commensurate with his value to society —that he "deserves" his income any more than the drone deserves the gift of a part of it? But such questions define the operational barriers to establishing a social policy that discriminates among recipients according to their deserts. They do not touch on the legitimacy of the principle.

Robbing Peter to Pay Paul: Transfers from Poor to Poor

When we think of transfers, we usually think in terms of economic transfers from richer to poorer. In reality, social policy can obligate one citizen to turn over a variety of "goods" as a donation on behalf of some other person; access to parking spaces reserved for the handicapped is a simple example.

Sometimes these noneconomic transfers, like the economic ones, are arranged so that the better-off give up something to the worse-off, and the argument about whether the transfer is appropriate follows the lines of the issues I have just raised. But in a surprising number of instances the transfers are mandated by the better-off, while the price must be paid by donors who are just as poor as the recipient.

Now suppose that the same hypothetical "I" considers the case of two students in an inner-city high school. Both come from poor families. Both have suffered equal deprivations and social injustices. They have the same intelligence and human potential. For whatever reasons—let us assume pure accident—the two students behave differently in school. One student (the good student) studies hard and pays attention in class. The other student (the mischievous student) does not study and instead creates disturbances, albeit good-natured disturbances, in the classroom.

I observe a situation in which the teacher expels the mischievous student from the classroom more or less at will. The result is that he becomes further alienated from school, drops out, and eventually ends up on welfare or worse. I know that the cause of this sequence of events (his behavior in class) was no worse than the behavior of millions of middle-class students who suffer nothing like the same penalty. They too are kicked out of class when they act up, but for a variety of reasons they stay in school and eventually do well. Further yet, I know that the behavior of the teacher toward the student is biased and unfairly harsh because the student is an inner-city black and the teacher is a suburban white who neither understands nor sympathizes with such students.

On all counts, then, I observe that the mischievous student expelled from the classroom is a victim who deserves a system that does not unfairly penalize him. I therefore protect him against the bias and arbitrariness of the teacher. The teacher cannot expel the student from class unless the student's behavior meets certain criteria far beyond the ordinary talking and laughing out of turn that used to get him in trouble.

The result, let us say, is that the student continues to act as before, but remains in the classroom. Other students also respond to the reality of the greater latitude they now have. The amount of teaching is reduced, and so is the ability of students to concentrate on their work even if they want to.

I know, however, that some benefits are obtained. The mischievous student who formerly dropped out of school does not. He obtains his diploma, and with it some advantages in the form of greater education (he learned something, although not much, while he stayed in school) and a credential to use when applying for a job.

This benefit has been obtained at a price. The price is not money—let us say it costs no more to run the school under the new policy than under the old. No transfers have been exacted from the white middle class. The transfer instead is wholly from the good student to the mischievous one. For I find that the quality of education obtained by the good student deteriorated badly, both because the teacher had less time and energy for teaching and because the classroom environment was no longer suitable for studying. One poor and disadvantaged student has been compelled (he had no choice in the matter) to give up part of his education so that the other student could stay in the classroom.

What is my rationale for enforcing this transfer? In what sense did the good student have an excess of educational opportunity that he could legitimately be asked to sacrifice?

The example has deliberately been constructed so that neither student was intrinsically more deserving than the other. The only difference between the two was behavioral, with one student behaving in a more desirable way than the other student. Even under these unrealistically neutral conditions, it is hard to avoid the conclusion that the transfer was unjustifiable. Now, let us make the example more realistic.

A student who reaches adolescence in an inner-city school with high motivation to study and learn does not do so by accident. The motivation is likely to reflect merit—on the student's part, on the parents' part, or on a combination of the two. In the good student's behavior I am observing not just a "desirable" response but a praiseworthy one.

Further, if we make the example realistic, the good student does not transfer simply an abstract deterioration in the quality of education, from a potentially fine education to a merely adequate one. The more likely loss is a much greater one, from an adequate education that might have prepared the good student to take advantage of opportunities for higher education to an inadequate education that leaves the good student, no matter how well motivated, without essential tools to pursue basic routes to advancement.

Once again, let me consider my rationale without giving myself an easy out. I may not assume that classroom instruction is not really affected by disruption; it is. I may not assume that counselors will be able shortly to change the behavior of the mischievous student. I may not assume that the school will provide separate tracks for the attentive student; the same philosophy that led to greater student rights also led to restrictions and even prohibitions on separate tracks for the better students. Most of all, I may not assume that the good student is superhuman. He may be admirable, but he is not necessarily able to get himself a good education no matter what obstacles I put in his way.

Such transfers from poor to poor are at the heart of the inequities of social policy. Saying that we meant well does not quite cover our transgressions. Even during the period of the most active reform we could not help being aware, if only at the back of our minds, of certain moral problems. When poor delinquents arrested for felonies were left on probation, as the elite wisdom prescribed they should be, the persons put most at risk were poor people who lived in their neighborhoods. They, not the elite, gave up the greater part of the good called "safety" so that the disadvantaged delinquent youth should not experience the injustice of punishment. When job-training programs were set up to function at the level of the least competent, it was the most competent trainees who had to sacrifice their opportunities to reach their potentials. When social policy reinforced the ethic that certain jobs are too demeaning to ask people to do, it was those who preferred such jobs to welfare whose basis for self-respect was stripped from them.

More generally, social policy after the mid-1960s demanded an extraordinary range of transfers from the most capable poor to the least capable, from the most law-abiding to the least law-abiding, and from the most responsible to the least responsible. In return, we gave little to these most deserving persons except easier access to welfare for themselves—the one thing they found hardest to put to "good use."

We blinked at these realities at the time. The homogenizing process which was discussed in chapter 14 helped us to blink; the poor were all poor, all more or less in the same situation, we said. All *would* be deserving, we preferred to assume, if they had not been so exploited by society, by the system. But at bottom it is difficult to imagine under what logic we thought these transfers appropriate.

The Net Happiness Challenge

The peculiarity of a transfer, as opposed to the other uses of tax monies, is that the direct benefit goes only to the recipient. If I pay for garbage collection, I, the payer, get a benefit. My garbage disappears. I may argue about whether the garbage collection service is efficiently operated and whether I am getting value for money, but I do not argue about whether, somehow, my garbage must be made to disappear, and so must my neighbor's garbage. If I pay for Food Stamps with my tax dollars, the government is making quite a different request of me and undertaking a much different responsibility. The government judges that my income is large enough that a portion of it should be given to someone whose income, the government has decided, is too small. And when, for example, the Food Stamps are buying milk for a malnourished child, I am pleased that they should do so. But I may legitimately ask two things of the government that exercises such authority. First, I may ask that the government be *right*— right in deciding that, in some cosmic scheme of things, my resources are "large enough" and the recipient's are "too small." Second, I may ask that the transfer be successful, and therein lies a problem.

If the transfer is successful, I, the donor, can be satisfied on either of two grounds: general humanitarianism ("I am doing good") or more self-interested calculations that make transfers not so very different from police service or garbage collection. For the sake of my own quality of life, I do not want to live in a Calcutta with people sleeping in the streets in front of my house. If it is true that putting delinquents in jail only makes them into worse criminals later on, then putting the neighbors at just a little more risk by leaving delinquents at large is worth it *to them*, because eventually it will reduce their risk. The short-term injustices are rescued by a long-term greater good for everyone.

Whether I choose humanitarianism or long-term self-interest as the basis for approving the transfer, I must confront the "net happiness" challenge. If the first questions of social policy ask why we approve of transfers at all, the next questions ask how we know whether our expectations are being justified. How, in an ideal world, would we measure "success" in assessing a transfer?

The social scientists who measure the effects of transfers look for success at two levels and of necessity ignore a third. The first level is, "Did the transfer reach the people it was intended to reach in the intended form?" (Do Food Stamps reach people who need extra food money?) The second level is, "Did the transfer have the intended direct effect on the behavior or condition of the recipients?" (Do Food Stamps improve nutrition?) The third, unattainable level is, "Did the transfer, in the long run, add to net happiness in the world?"

We may presume that better housing, nutrition, and medical care contribute to less misery and more happiness; so also do good parents, a loving spouse, safe streets, personal freedom, and the respect of one's neighbors. We know how to measure some of these aspects of the quality of life; others we cannot measure at all; and, most certainly, we are unable to compare their relative worth or to add up a net total. We have no "misery" or "happiness" indexes worthy of the name. But the concept of reducing misery and increasing happiness is indispensable to deciding whether a social policy is working or failing.

With that in mind, let us consider yet another hypothetical example. In this case, I am deciding upon my stance in support or opposition of a policy that automatically provides an adequate living allowance for all single women with children. I am informed that one consequence of this policy is that large numbers of the children get better nutrition and medical care than they would otherwise obtain. Using this known fact and no others, I support the program.

Now, let us assume two more known facts, that the program induces births by women who otherwise would have had fewer children (or had them under different circumstances), and that child abuse and neglect among these children runs at twice the national average. Does this alter my judgment about whether the allowance is a net good—that it is better to have it than not have it? I must now balance the better health of some children against the pain suffered by others who would not have suffered the pain if the program had not existed. I decide—although I wish I could avoid the question altogether—that, all in all, I still support the program.

What if the incidence of abuse and neglect is three times as high? Five times? Ten times? A hundred times?

The crossover point will be different for different people. But a crossover will occur. At some point, I will say that the benefits of better nutrition and medical care are outweighed by the suffering of the abused and neglected children. What then is the humane policy? Once more I must avoid false escape hatches. I may continue to search for a strategy that does not have the overbalancing side-effects. But what is my position toward the existing program in the meantime?

All of these examples—the worker versus the drone, the good student versus the bad student, the children helped versus the children hurt—are intended to emphasize a reality we tend to skirt. Devising a system of transfers that is just, fair, and compassionate involves extraordinarily difficult moral choices in which the issue is not how much good we can afford to do (as the choice is usually put), but how to do good at all. In the debate over social policy, the angels are not arrayed against the accountants.

The examples do not force one set of principles over all others. A socialist may use them in support of an internally consistent rationale for sweeping redistributive measures. At the other end of the spectrum, a libertarian may use them to support the eradication of transfers altogether. For those who fall somewhere in the middle, two more modest conclusions about what constitutes a just and humane social policy are warranted.

The first conclusion is that transfers are inherently treacherous. They can be useful; they can be needed; they can be justified. But we should approach them as a good physician uses a dangerous drug—not at all if possible, and no more than absolutely necessary otherwise.

The second conclusion is that, as a general rule, compulsory transfers from one poor person to another are uncomfortably like robbery. When we require money transfers from the obviously rich to the obviously poor, we at least have some room for error. Mistaken policies may offend our sense of right and wrong, but no great harm has been done to the donor. The same is not true of the noneconomic transfers from poor to poor. We have no margin for error at all. If we are even a little bit wrong about the consequences of the transfer, we are likely to do great injustices to people who least deserve to bear the burden.

And that, finally, is what makes the question of social policy not one of polite philosophical dispute but one of urgent importance. For the examples in this chapter are not really hypothetical. They are drawn directly from the data we reviewed. It is impossible to examine the statistics on a topic such as single teenaged mothers without admitting that we are witnessing a tragedy. *If* it had been inevitable, *if* there had been nothing we could have done to avoid it, then we could retain the same policies, trying to do more of the same and hoping for improvement. But once we must entertain the possibility that we are bringing it on ourselves, as I am arguing that both logic and evidence compel us to do, then it is time to reconsider a social policy that salves our consciences ("Look how compassionate I am") at the expense of those whom we wished to help.

16

The Constraints on Helping

IN THE LAST CHAPTER, I proposed some reasons for regarding transfers with suspicion. Any compulsory transfer from one person to another person unavoidably puts a terrific burden on the rule-maker to be "right" in decisions that call for very subjective, difficult judgments about who has a greater need of what, and about long-term versus short-term outcomes. But there are needs that do call out for assistance, for certain kinds of transfer from some members of society to others. In this chapter, the question is: Under what conditions may we reasonably expect transfers to accomplish more good than harm?

A Thought Experiment

To illustrate the general problem we are about to approach, let me pose a problem in the form that Einstein used to call a "thought experiment." Whereas Einstein used the device to imagine such things as the view from the head of a column of light, we will use it for the more pedestrian purpose of imagining the view from the office of a middle-echelon bureaucrat. Our task: to think through how to structure a specific government social-action program so that it might reasonably be expected to accomplish net good.

The experiment calls for us to put ourselves in the role of a government planner who must implement a new piece of legislation, The Comprehensive Anti-Smoking Act. The Act has several provisions common to the genre. It establishes a federal agency to coordinate the federal government's activities related to the goal of less smoking. A large anti-smoking advertising campaign is planned. Federal matching funds are provided for school systems that teach courses on the perils of smoking.

In addition to these initiatives, the legislation provides for direct, concrete incentives for people to quit smoking. A billion dollars will be appropriated annually for the indefinite future, to be used for cash rewards to persons who quit. We are in charge of designing this effort, with complete freedom to specify whatever rules we wish, provided they are consistent with constitutional rights. After five years an evaluation will be conducted to determine whether the number of cigarettes consumed and the number of smokers have been reduced by the program.

The challenge in this experiment is to use the $1 billion in a way that (in our own best estimate) will meet this test. My proposition is that we cannot do so: that any program we design will either (1) have no effect on smoking or (2) actually *increase* smoking. I maintain that we are helpless to use the billion dollars to achieve our goal.

DESIGNING THE PROGRAM

The heart of the problem is designing a reward that will induce smokers to quit—and will not induce others to begin smoking, continue smoking, or increase their smoking to become eligible to receive the reward. Let us work through one scenario to illustrate the nature of the conundrum.

Three sets of choices will decisively affect the success or failure of the program: choices about

- the size of the reward,
- conditions for receiving the reward, and
- eligibility to participate in the program.

What is a first approximation of a program that has a good chance of working?

Choosing the size of the reward. We know from the outset that the reward cannot be small. No one will quit smoking for pocket change, other than those who were going to quit anyway. On the other hand, the theoretical power of a cash reward is plausible—almost anyone would become and remain a nonsmoker in return for a million dollars. We settle on the sum of $10,000 as a reward that is an extremely powerful inducement to large numbers of persons.[1]

Conditions for receiving the reward. We seek a middle ground between conditions that maximize the likelihood that a person has permanently quit smoking and conditions that make the reward so difficult to win that few will bother. Thus, for example, we reject plans that would spread the reward over several years. Eventually we decide to require that a person must remain smoke-free for one year. We make the award a one-time prize, so that people have no incentive to recommence smoking to qualify for another $10,000. A repayment scheme is added: People who begin smoking again will have to give up their award.

Eligibility to Participate. The intent of the program is to appeal to the heavy smoker whose health is most at risk. On the other hand, it would defeat our purpose to limit eligibility too severely—to persons, for example, who have smoked three packs a day for twenty years—because in so doing we would disqualify many people in the vulnerable group of moderate smokers who are likely to become heavy, lifelong smokers unless something is done. The compromise solution we reach is to require that a person have smoked at least one pack a day for five years.

Now let us consider the results.

AFTER ONE YEAR

We think ahead a year, and are pleased. The $10,000 reward has substantial effects on the people who are eligible for the program on day one —that is, persons who have smoked at least a pack a day for five years at the time the experiment begins. The effect is not unfailing; not everyone quits smoking to get the reward; and we must assume that not everyone who stops for a year is able to avoid a relapse. Some cheating occurs despite our precautions. But some people quit smoking permanently as a direct result of the program.

We recognize, of course, that we achieve the effect inefficiently. Thousands of persons in the target population quit smoking every year even in the absence of a monetary reward. Under the program, they collect money for doing what they would have done anyway. But the problem posed in our thought experiment says nothing about being efficient; the problem is only to create a program that reduces net smoking.

AFTER TWO YEARS

We think ahead two years, and are disturbed. For now comes time to examine the effects of the program on people who have been smoking a pack a day but for a period of less than five years when the program begins.

Everyone who would have quit after four years and eleven months continues to smoke for another month. These cigarettes represent an increase in smoking that must be subtracted from the gross reduction in smoking created by the program. *Almost* everyone who would otherwise have quit during any point in the fifth year continues to smoke until the five-year requirement has been met. Or, to put it more generally: We find that for all persons who have been smoking less than the required period of time, the program provides a payment to continue. For the person who has been smoking for exactly four years, the payment is $10,000 in return for smoking for one more year. Given that the smoking habit has its own attractions, the payment is exceedingly effective. In fact, we notice an unfortunate imbalance: For the person who has already smoked for five years (our target population), the inducement of $10,000 to quit must fight against the attractions of smoking and is not always adequate to achieve the desired result. For the smoker who has not reached this limit, the inducement to continue smoking is reinforced by those very attractions. Thus the effective power of $10,000 to induce continued smoking for one year in the one population is much greater than its power to induce cessation of smoking for one year in the other.

To this point, we have been concerned only with those who were already smoking at the pack-a-day level. Now we consider the effects of the program on smokers who had been smoking less than that amount. We find that a significant number of smokers increase their consumption to a pack a day, for the same reason. (Everyone who smokes nineteen cigarettes a day increases to twenty, almost everyone who smokes eighteen cigarettes a day increases to twenty, and so on.) This effect is strongest among those persons who think they "should" quit but who doubt their ability to quit without help. For them—through a process of plausible but destructive logic—it seems that the best way to do what they think they want to do (to quit smoking) is to smoke more.

Among those who are nonsmokers, the effects are entirely negative. A considerable number of teenagers who were wavering between starting or not starting to smoke decide in favor of smoking—they can enjoy smoking now, and then give it up when they qualify for the reward.

AFTER FIVE YEARS

When we think ahead five years, we note a final logical by-product of the program. Quitting the habit after five years of smoking a pack a day is generally more difficult than quitting sooner and after lesser levels of smoking. Many people who try to stop when the fifth year is ended find that the $10,000 is no longer a sufficient inducement, though it may have seemed to them a few years earlier that it would be. The rules of the program have made heavy smokers out of people who would have remained light smokers and thereby have induced a certain number of people not only to smoke more and longer until they became eligible for the $10,000 but to become impervious to the effects of the reward once they do become eligible.

What is the net outcome? If 90 percent of the population had been smoking for five years when the program began, we might still argue that the program would show a net reduction in smoking. But only about 15 percent of the adult population smokes a pack a day or more.[2] Let us estimate that a third of this number have been smoking at that rate for more than five years. If so, our plan has the potential for reducing smoking among five percent of the adult population and the potential for increasing smoking among 95 percent of the adult population. It is exceedingly difficult to attach numbers to the considerations we have just reviewed without coming to the conclusion that the program as specified would have the net effect of increasing both the number of cigarettes consumed and the number of smokers.

BACK TO SQUARE ONE

When we reconsider the three parameters and try to select a combination that meets the challenge, the nature of their interdependence becomes clear. Suppose, for example, that we require a smoking history of at least ten years, and thereby, as intended, reduce the number of persons who are drawn into smoking just because of the reward. But such a step makes no difference in the calculations of those who have already been smoking more than five years (they are, in effect, operating under the logic of a five-year eligibility rule). Among those who have smoked less than five years, the change in the eligibility requirement has two counterproductive effects. First, persons who have smoked less than five years constitute a large proportion of smokers that the program should be reaching— younger, with more to gain from quitting. By extending the requirement to ten years, the program has been made irrelevant to many of them. For those who do think that far ahead, the effects will tend to be harmful, inducing a sense that there will be time to quit—and profit to be made— at a later point in their lives. Thus lengthening the eligibility period to ten years does not help; it makes matters worse.

As we ponder ways out of this bind, it becomes clear that the most dramatic reductions in smoking occur among persons who quit the soonest —a person who quits smoking at age sixty-five saves only a few years' worth of smoking, whereas a person who quits at twenty saves decades.

Why not focus our efforts among the very young? Even granting the tendency of the award to encourage smoking so as to qualify, perhaps this will be more than counterbalanced by the very long periods of "savings" that will result from each success. So we target the program at youth (perhaps by installing an age-eligibility criterion—the specific method makes no difference). But the results are even more disastrous. The qualification criteria must be loose, because only a tiny fraction of the teenaged smokers we want to reach have had time to smoke very long. The result, when combined with a significant reward for quitting, is that the inducement effect is overpowering. Even teenagers who have no desire to smoke at all find it worth inculcating the habit for a year (or whatever our time limit is reduced to). Once started, only a proportion of those who smoked *only* because the program existed and who fully intended to quit are actually able to quit. The age effect backfires: While it is true that inducing a youngster to quit (who otherwise would not have quit) saves decades of smoking, it is equally true that inducing a youngster to start costs decades of smoking, and we produce far more of the latter than the former.

TWO WAYS OUT

We give up on a continuing program. Instead, we propose that the program be made a one-time, never-to-be-repeated offer: Announce the program, give everyone who is *already* eligible a chance to enroll, but give no one a reason to starting smoking or to increase their smoking in order to become eligible. State loudly and unequivocally that the program will never be repeated. We will at least achieve the success of the first year.

Theoretically, this scheme might (but only might) reduce net smoking.[3] In practice, it is guaranteed that the program will be continued. A successful one-time effort will be refunded immediately and on a larger scale. Congress rarely cancels even a failed social program, let alone a successful one. (We may contemplate the prospect of Congress canceling a successful version of a thirty-and-a-third rule to help women get off AFDC, on grounds that its success could not be repeated.)

Ultimately, the logic of the situation drives us to the one configuration of awards that surely will reduce net smoking: we offer a dollar amount to everyone who does not smoke, but make them pay it back if they ever start. Since this will cost far more than a billion dollars a year, we seek permission to increase the budget, pointing out that, while it may be expensive, our way out will in fact reduce smoking, whereas the alternatives will not. But some unfriendly critic points out that all we need do is levy a fine on everyone who begins smoking (or who continues to smoke) that is equal to the reward we propose to offer for not starting. The effects on smoking will be essentially the same (a $10,000 penalty ought to have about as much effect as a $10,000 reward for persons at most income levels), and the government will get a lot of revenue to boot. This proposal is of course also rejected, on grounds that it is unfair to the poor.

As one experiments with different combinations of rules, it becomes apparent that the traps we encounter in the first approximations are generalizable. Any change in the parameters intended to reduce one problem raises a new one. Why should this be? Is it intrinsic to the process? Or is it a peculiarity of an example I carefully chose?

Laws of Social Programs

At first glance, the smoking example seems most apt for a certain type of social program, the one that seeks to change behavior from X to Y—what might be called "remedial" social programs. It seems less analogous, if not altogether irrelevant, to programs such as AFDC that simply provide an allowance without (through the allowance itself) trying to stimulate change. But in fact it applies to transfer programs of all types. In all cases, the transfer is legitimized by the recipient's being in a certain condition (whether smoking or poverty) that the government would prefer the recipient not be in. The burden of the smoking example is not that we failed to reduce smoking—to achieve the desired behavioral change—but that we increased the number of people who end up in the undesired condition. This charge applies to transfers in general.

The reasons why are not idiosyncratic. Let me suggest some characteristics we observed in the thought experiment that occur so widely and for such embedded reasons that they suggest laws. That is, no matter how ingenious the design of a social transfer program may be, we cannot—in a free society—design programs that escape their influence. Together, they account for much of the impasse we observe in the anti-smoking example and point to some important principles for designing social programs that work.

#1. **The Law of Imperfect Selection.** Any objective rule that defines eligibility for a social transfer program will irrationally exclude some persons.

It can always be demonstrated that some persons who are excluded from the Food Stamps program are in greater need than some persons who receive Food Stamps. It can always be demonstrated that someone who is technically ineligible for Medicaid really "ought" to be receiving it, given the intent of the legislation.

These inequities, which are observed everywhere, are not the fault of inept writers of eligibility rules, but an inescapable outcome of the task of rule-writing. Eligibility rules must convert the concept of "true need" into objectified elements. The rules constructed from these bits and pieces are necessarily subject to what Herbert Costner has called "epistemic error" —the inevitable gap between quantified measures and the concept they are intended to capture.[4] We have no way of defining "truly needy" precisely —not those who truly need to stop smoking, nor those truly in need of college scholarships or subsidized loans or disability insurance. Any criterion we specify will inevitably include a range of people, some of whom are unequivocally the people we intended to help, others of whom are less so, and still others of whom meet the letter of the eligibility requirement but are much less needy than some persons who do not.

Social welfare policy in earlier times tended to deal with this problem by erring in the direction of exclusion—better to deny help to some truly needy persons than to let a few slackers slip through. Such attitudes depended, however, on the assumption that the greater good was being served. Moral precepts had to be upheld. Whenever a person was inappropriately given help, it was bad for the recipient (undermining his character) and a bad example to the community at large.

When that assumption is weakened or dispensed with altogether, it follows naturally that the Law of Imperfect Selection leads to programs with constantly broadening target populations. If persons are not to blame for their plight, no real harm is done by giving them help they do not fully "need." No moral cost is incurred by permitting some undeserving into the program. A moral cost *is* incurred by excluding a deserving person. No one has a scalpel sharp enough to excise only the undeserving. Therefore it is not just a matter of political expedience to add a new layer to the eligible population rather than to subtract one (though that is often a factor in the actual decision-making process). It is also the morally correct thing to do, given the premises of the argument.

#2. The Law of Unintended Rewards. Any social transfer increases the net value of being in the condition that prompted the transfer.

A deficiency is observed—too little money, too little food, too little academic achievement—and a social transfer program tries to fill the gap —with a welfare payment, Food Stamps, a compensatory education program. An unwanted behavior is observed—drug addiction, crime, unemployability—and the program tries to change that behavior to some other, better behavior—through a drug rehabilitation program, psychotherapy, vocational training. In each case, the program, however unintentionally, *must* be constructed in such a way that it increases the net value of being in the condition that it seeks to change—either by increasing the rewards or by reducing the penalties.

For some people in some circumstances, it is absurd to think in terms of "net value," because they so clearly have no choice at all about the fix they are in or because the net value is still less desirable than virtually any alternative. Paraplegics receiving Medicaid cannot easily be seen as "rewarded" for becoming paraplegics by the existence of free medical care. Poor children in Head Start cannot be seen as rewarded for being poor. Persons who are in the unwanted condition *completely involuntarily* are not affected by the existence of the reward.

But the number of such pure examples is very small. Let us return to the case of the middle-aged worker who loses his job, wants desperately to work, but can find nothing. He receives Unemployment Insurance, hating every penny of it. He would seem to be "completely involuntarily" in his situation and his search for a job unaffected by the existence of Unemployment Insurance. In fact, however, his behavior (unless he is peculiarly irrational) *is* affected by the existence of the Unemployment Insurance. For example, the cushion provided by Unemployment Insurance may lead him to refuse to take a job that requires him to move to another town, whereas he would take the job and uproot his home if he were more desperate. Most people (including me) are glad that his behavior is so affected, that he does not have to leave the home and friends of a lifetime, that he can wait for a job opening nearby. But he is not "completely involuntarily" unemployed in such a case, and the reason he is not is that the Unemployment Insurance has made the condition of unemployment more tolerable.

Our paraplegic anchors one end of the continuum labeled "Degree of Voluntarism in the Conditions that Social Policy Seeks to Change or Make Less Painful," and our unemployed worker is only slightly to one side of him—but he is to one side, not in the same place. The apparent unattractiveness of most of the conditions that social policy seeks to change must not obscure the continuum involved. No one chooses to be a paraplegic, and perhaps no one chooses to be a heroin addict. But the distinction remains: very few heroin addicts developed their addiction by being tied down and forcibly injected with heroin. They may not have chosen to become addicts, but they *did* choose initially to take heroin.

Let us consider the implications in terms of the archetypical social program for helping the chronic unemployed escape their condition, the job-training program.

Imagine that a program is begun that has the most basic and benign inducement of all, the chance to learn a marketable skill. It is open to everybody. By opening it to all, we have circumvented (for the time being) the Law of Unintended Rewards. All may obtain the training, no matter what their job history, so no unintended reward is being given for the condition of chronic unemployment.

On assessing the results, we observe that the ones who enter the program, stick with it, and learn a skill include very few of the hardcore unemployed whom we most wanted to help. The typical "success" stories from our training program are persons with a history of steady employment who wanted to upgrade their earning power. This is admirable. But what about the hardcore unemployed? A considerable number entered the program, but almost all of them dropped out or failed to get jobs once they left. Only a small proportion used the training opportunity as we had hoped. The problem of the hardcore unemployed remains essentially unchanged.

We may continue to circumvent the Law of Unintended Rewards. All we need do is continue the job-training program unchanged. It will still be there, still available to all who want to enroll, but we will do nothing to entice participation. Our theory (should we adopt this stance) is that, as time goes on, we will continue to help at least a few of the hardcore unemployed who are in effect skimmed from the top of the pool. We may even hope that the number skimmed from the top will be larger than the number who enter the pool, so that, given enough time, the population of hardcore unemployed will diminish. But this strategy is a gradualist one and relies on the assumption that other conditions in society are not creating more hardcore unemployed than the program is skimming off.

The alternative is to do something to get more of the hardcore unemployed into the program, and to improve the content so that more of them profit from the training. And once this alternative is taken, the program planner is caught in the trap of unintended rewards. Because we cannot "draft" people into the program or otherwise coerce their participation, our only alternative is to make it more attractive by changing the rules a bit.

Suppose, for example, we find that the reason many did not profit from the earlier program was that they got fired from (or quit) their new jobs within a few days of getting them, and that the reason they did so had to do with the job-readiness problem. The ex-trainee was late getting to work, the boss complained, the ex-trainee reacted angrily and was fired.

We observe this to be a common pattern. We know the problem is not that the ex-trainee is lazy or unmotivated, but that he has never been socialized into the discipline of the workplace. He needs more time, more help, more patience than other workers until he develops the needed work habits. Suppose that we try to compensate—for example, by placing our trainees with employers who are being subsidized to hire such persons. The employer accepts lower productivity and other problems in return for a payment to do so (such plans have been tried frequently, with mixed results). Given identical work at identical pay, the ex-trainee is being rewarded for his "credential" of hardcore unemployment. He can get away with behavior that an ordinary worker cannot get away with.

May we still assume that the program is making progress in preparing its trainees for the real-world marketplace? Will the hardcore unemployed modify their unreliable behavior? What will be the effect on morale and self-esteem among those trainees who were succeeding in the program before the change of rules? It is tempting to conclude that the program has already ceased to function effectively for anyone anymore, that the change in rules has done more harm than good. But my proposition is for the moment a more restricted one: The reward for unproductive behavior (both past and present) now exists.

What of the case of a drug addict who is chronically unemployed because (let us assume) of the addiction? It might seem that the unintended reward in such a case is innocuous; it consists of measures to relieve the addict of his addiction, measures for which the nonaddict will have no need or use. If we were dealing with an involuntary disability—our paraplegic again—the argument would be valid. But in the case of drug addiction (or any other behavior that has its rewards), a painless cure generally increases the attractiveness of the behavior. Imagine, for example, a pill that instantly and painlessly relieved dependence on heroin, and the subsequent effects on heroin use.

Thus we are faced with the problem we observed in the thought experiment. The program that seeks to change behavior must offer an inducement that unavoidably either adds to the attraction of, or reduces the penalties of engaging in, the behavior in question. The best-known example in real life is the thirty-and-a-third rule for AFDC recipients. It becomes more advantageous financially to hold a job than not to hold a job (the intended inducement for AFDC recipients to work), but it also becomes more advantageous to be on AFDC (the unintended reward to nonrecipients).

We are now ready to tackle the question of when a social program can reasonably be expected to accomplish net good and when it can reasonably be expected to produce net harm. Again let us think in terms of a continuum. All social programs, I have argued, provide an unintended reward for being in the condition that the program is trying to change or make more tolerable. But some of these unintended rewards are so small that they are of little practical importance. Why then can we not simply bring a bit of care to the design of such programs, making sure that the unintended reward is *always* small? The reason we are not free to do so lies in the third law of social programs:

> #3. The Law of Net Harm. The less likely it is that the unwanted behavior will change voluntarily, the more likely it is that a program to induce change will cause net harm.

A social program that seeks to change behavior must do two things. It must induce participation by the persons who are to benefit, as described under the Law of Unintended Rewards. Then it must actually produce the desired change in behavior. It must succeed, and success depends crucially on one factor above all others: the price that the participant is willing to pay.

The more that the individual is willing to accept whatever needs to be done in order to achieve the desired state of affairs, the broader the discretion of the program designers. Thus, expensive health resorts can withhold food from their guests, hospitals can demand that their interns work inhuman schedules, and elite volunteer units in the armed forces can ask their trainees to take risks in training exercises that seem (to the rest of us) suicidal. Such programs need offer no inducement at all except the "thing in itself" that is the *raison d'être* of the program—a shapelier body, a career as a physician, membership in the elite military unit. Similarly, the drug addict who is prepared to sign over to a program a great of deal of control over his own behavior may very well be successful—witness the sometimes impressive success rates of private treatment clinics.

The smaller the price that the participant is willing to pay, the greater the constraints on program design. It makes no difference to an official running a training program for the hardcore unemployed that (for example) the Marine Corps can instill exemplary work habits in recruits who come to the Corps no more "job-ready" than the recruits to the job-training program. If the training program tried for one day to use the techniques that the Marine Corps uses, it would lose its participants. Boot camp was not part of the bargain the job trainees struck with the government when they signed on. Instead, the training program must not only induce persons to join the program (which may be fairly easy). It must also induce them to stay in the program, induce them to cooperate with its curriculum, and induce them, finally, to adopt major changes in outlook, habits, and assumptions. The program content must be almost entirely carrot.

There is nothing morally reprehensible in approaches that are constrained to use only positive inducements. The objections are practical.

First, it is guaranteed that success rates will be very low. The technology of changing human behavior depends heavily on the use of negative reinforcement in conjunction with positive reinforcement. The more deeply engrained the behavior to be changed and the more attractions it holds for the person whose behavior is involved, the more important it is that the program have both a full tool kit available to it *and* the participant's willingness to go along with whatever is required. The Marine Corps has both these assets. Social programs to deal with the hardcore unemployed, teenaged mothers, delinquents, and addicts seldom do.

Second, as inducements become large—as they must, if the program is dealing with the most intractable problems—the more attractive they become to people who were not in need of help in the first place. We do not yet know how large they must finally become. We do know from experience, however, that quite generous experimental programs have provided extensive counseling, training, guaranteed jobs, and other supports—and failed.[5] We can only guess at what would be enough—perhaps a matter of years of full-time residential training, followed by guaranteed jobs at double or triple the minimum wage; we do not know. Whatever they are, however, consider their effects on the people not in the program. At this point, it appears that any program that would succeed in helping large numbers of the hardcore unemployed will make hardcore unemployment a highly desirable state to be in.

The conditions that combine to produce net harm are somewhat different in the theoretical and the practical cases, but they come to the same thing. Theoretically, any program that mounts an intervention with sufficient rewards to sustain participation and an effective result will generate so much of the unwanted behavior (in order to become eligible for the program's rewards) that the net effect will be to increase the incidence of the unwanted behavior. In practice, the programs that deal with the most intractable behavior problems have included a package of rewards large enough to induce participation, but not large enough to produce the desired result.

My conclusion is that social programs in a democratic society tend to produce net harm in dealing with the most difficult problems. They will inherently tend to have enough of an inducement to produce bad behavior and not enough of a solution to stimulate good behavior; and the more difficult the problem, the more likely it is that this relationship will prevail. The lesson is not that we can do no good at all, but that we must pick our shots.

17

Choosing a Future

IN the last two chapters I suggested that the kinds of help we want to provide are more limited than we commonly suppose and that, even when we want to help, the conditions under which a national program can do so without causing more harm than good are more tightly constrained than we suppose. My arguments might seem tailor-made to relieve us of responsibility for persons in need. But I believe just the contrary: that the moral imperative to do something to correct the situation of poor people and especially the minority poor is at least as powerful now as when Lyndon Johnson took office. I have for the most part used the data to make a case that the reforms flowing from the new wisdom of the 1960s were a blunder on purely pragmatic grounds. But another theme of the discussion has been that what we did was wrong on moral grounds, however admirable our intentions may have been.

It was wrong to take from the most industrious, most responsible poor —take safety, education, justice, status—so that we could cater to the least industrious, least responsible poor. It was wrong to impose rules that made it rational for adolescents to behave in ways that destroyed their futures. The changes we made were not just policy errors, not just inexpedient, but unjust. The injustice of the policies was compounded by the almost complete immunity of the elite from the price they demanded of the poor.

Before responding with a new wave of federally engineered solutions, however, we would do well to remember that, historically, such mistakes tend to correct themselves, given time. One may predict with some confidence, for example, that education in the United States is going to improve for middle-class children in the years ahead. It is apparent that a national consensus now holds that we burdened the schools with too many social responsibilities and neglected basic educational tasks, and that the time has come to focus again on academic achievement. Congress will tack some new programs onto this national agenda. The Supreme Court may countenance forms of meritocratic discrimination in the schools that it would have forbidden in the sixties. But such federal activity will be following rather than creating a momentum that is rooted in a broad public perception of what needs to be done. The real work will take place in the local schools. Our resources are sufficient to make improvements; implementing the new consensus depends on choices about priorities for those resources. We are now making choices that we could have made ten years ago but did not, because the winds were different then.

Conceivably such corrective forces will reverse trends among the poor as well. It is now intellectually respectable, as until recently it was not, to argue that welfare children should be indoctrinated with middle-class values. One may, without being considered an ethnocentric Anglo, urge that poor Hispanic children be denied bilingual education. One may more freely argue that certain family living arrangements and ways of treating children are not only "different" from middle-class norms, but inferior. In short, some improvements may devolve from nothing more complicated than yet another change, already well under way, in the elite wisdom.

But if the behaviors of members of the underclass are founded on a rational appreciation of the rules of the game, and as long as the rules encourage dysfunctional values and behaviors, the future cannot look bright. Behaviors that work will tend to persist until they stop working. The rules will have to be changed.

How might they be changed? I present three proposals: one for education, one for public welfare, and one for civil rights. The proposals of greatest theoretical interest involve education and public welfare. I will approach them as I did the "thought experiment," using the discussion as a device for thinking about policy, not as a blueprint for policy. I begin, however, with the proposal for civil rights. It is simple, would cost no money to implement, and is urgently needed.

A Proposal for Social Policy and Race

Real reform of American social policy is out of the question until we settle the race issue. We have been dancing around it since 1964, wishing it would go away and at the same time letting it dominate, *sub rosa,* the formation of social policy.

The source of our difficulties has been the collision, with enormous attendant national anxiety and indecision, of two principles so much a part of the American ethos that hardly anyone, whatever his political position, can wholly embrace one and reject the other. The principles are equal treatment and a fair shake.

The principle of equal treatment demands that we all play by the same rules—which would seem to rule out any policy that gives preferential treatment to anyone. A fair shake demands that everyone have a reasonably equal chance at the brass ring—or at least a reasonably equal chance to get on the merry-go-round.

Thus hardly anyone, no matter how strictly noninterventionist, can watch with complete equanimity when a black child is deprived of a chance to develop his full potential for reasons that may be directly traced to a heritage of exploitation by whites. Neither can anyone, no matter how devoted to Affirmative Action, watch with complete equanimity when a white job applicant is turned down for a job in favor of a black who is less qualified. Something about it is fundamentally unfair—un-American—no matter how admirable the ultimate goal.

Until 1965, the principles of equal treatment and a fair shake did not compete. They created no tension. Their application to racial policy was simple: Make the nation color-blind. People were to be judged on their merits. But then the elite wisdom changed. Blacks were to be helped to catch up.

I spent many chapters tracing the results. In summarizing these results as they pertain to the poorest blacks, this harsh judgment is warranted: If an impartial observer from another country were shown the data on the black lower class from 1950 to 1980 but given no information about con-temporaneous changes in society or public policy, that observer would infer that racial discrimination against the black poor increased drastically during the late 1960s and 1970s. No explanation except a surge in outright, virulent discrimination would as easily explain to a "blind" observer why things went so wrong.

Such an explanation is for practical purposes correct. Beginning in the last half of the 1960s, the black poor were subjected to new forms of racism with effects that outweighed the waning of the old forms of racism. Before the 1960s, we had a black underclass that was held down because blacks were systematically treated differently from whites, by whites. Now, we have a black underclass that is held down for the same generic reason—because blacks are systematically treated differently from whites, by whites.

The problem consists of a change in the nature of white condescension toward blacks. Historically, virtually all whites condescended toward virtually all blacks; there is nothing new in that. The condescension could be vicious in intent, in the form of "keeping niggers in their place." It could be benign, as in the excessive solicitousness with which whites who considered themselves enlightened tended to treat blacks.

These forms of condescension came under withering attack during the civil rights movement, to such an extent that certain manifestations of the condescension disappeared altogether in some circles. A variety of factors —among them, simply greater representation of blacks in the white professional world of work—made it easier for whites to develop relationships of authentic equality and respect with black colleagues. But from a policy standpoint, it became clear only shortly after the War on Poverty began that henceforth the black lower class was to be the object of a new condescension that would become intertwined with every aspect of social policy. Race is central to the problem of reforming social policy, not because it is intrinsically so but because the debate about what to do has been perverted by the underlying consciousness among whites that "they"—the people to be helped by social policy—are predominantly black, and blacks are owed a debt.

The result was that the intelligentsia and the policymakers, coincident with the revolution in social policy, began treating the black poor in ways that they would never consider treating people they respected. Is the black crime rate skyrocketing? Look at the black criminal's many grievances against society. Are black illegitimate birth rates five times those of whites? We must remember that blacks have a much broader view of the family than we do—aunts and grandmothers fill in. Did black labor force participation among the young plummet? We can hardly blame someone for having too much pride to work at a job sweeping floors. Are black high-school graduates illiterate? The educational system is insensitive. Are their test scores a hundred points lower than others? The tests are biased. Do black youngsters lose jobs to white youngsters because their mannerisms and language make them incomprehensible to their prospective employers? The culture of the ghetto has its own validity.

That the condescension should be so deep and pervasive is monumentally ironic, for the injunction to respect the poor (after all, they are not to blame) was hammered home in the tracts of OEO and radical intellectuals. But condescension is the correct descriptor. Whites began to tolerate and make excuses for behavior among blacks that whites would disdain in themselves or their children.

The expression of this attitude in policy has been a few obvious steps —Affirmative Action, minority set-asides in government contracts, and the like—but the real effect was the one that I discussed in the history of the period. The white elite could not at one time cope with two reactions. They could not simultaneously feel compelled to make restitution for past wrongs to blacks and blame blacks for not taking advantage of their new opportunities. The system *had* to be blamed, and any deficiencies demonstrated by blacks had to be overlooked or covered up—by whites.

A central theme of this book has been that the consequences were disastrous for poor people of all races, but for poor blacks especially, and most emphatically for poor blacks in all-black communities—precisely that population that was the object of the most unremitting sympathy.

My proposal for dealing with the racial issue in social welfare is to repeal every bit of legislation and reverse every court decision that in any way requires, recommends, or awards differential treatment according to race, and thereby put us back onto the track that we left in 1965. We may argue about the appropriate limits of government intervention in trying to enforce the ideal, but at least it should be possible to identify the ideal: Race is not a morally admissible reason for treating one person differently from another. Period.

A Proposal for Education

There is no such thing as an undeserving five-year-old. Society, in the form of government intervention, is quite limited in what it can do to make up for many of the deficiencies of life that an unlucky five-year-old experiences; it can, however, provide a good education and thereby give the child a chance at a different future.

The objective is a system that provides more effective education of the poor and disadvantaged without running afoul of the three laws of social programs. The objective is also to construct what is, in my view, a just system—one that does not sacrifice one student's interests to another's, and one that removes barriers in the way of those who want most badly to succeed and are prepared to make the greatest effort to do so. So once again let us put ourselves in the position of bureaucrats of sweeping authority and large budgets. How shall we make things better?

We begin by installing a completely free educational system that goes from preschool to the loftiest graduate degrees, removing economic barriers entirely. Having done so, however, we find little change from the system that prevailed in 1980. Even then, kindergarten through high school were free to the student, and federal grants and loans worth $4.4 billion *plus* a very extensive system of private scholarships and loans were available for needy students who wanted to continue their education. By making the system entirely free, we are not making more education newly accessible to large numbers of people, nor have we done anything about the quality of education.

We then make a second and much more powerful change. For many years, the notion of a voucher system for education has enjoyed a periodic vogue. In its pure form, it would give each parent of a child of school age a voucher that the parent could use to pay for schooling at any institution to which the child could gain admittance. The school would redeem the voucher for cash from the government. The proposals for voucher systems have generally foundered on accusations that they are a tool for the middle class and would leave the disadvantaged in the lurch. My proposition is rather different: A voucher system is the single most powerful method available to us to improve the education of the poor and disadvantaged. Vouchers thus become the second component of our educational reforms.

For one large segment of the population of poor and disadvantaged, the results are immediate, unequivocal, and dramatic. I refer to children whose parents take an active role in overseeing and encouraging their children's education. Such parents have been fighting one of the saddest of the battles of the poor—doing everything they can within the home environment, only to see their influence systematically undermined as soon as their children get out the door. When we give such parents vouchers, we find that they behave very much as their affluent counterparts behave when they are deciding upon a private school. They visit prospective schools, interview teachers, and place their children in schools that are demanding of the students and accountable to the parents for results. I suggest that when we give such parents vouchers, we will observe substantial convergence of black and white test scores in a single generation. All that such parents have ever needed is an educational system that operates on the same principles they do.

This is a sufficient improvement to justify the system, for we are in a no-lose situation with regard to the children whose parents do not play their part effectively. These children are sent to bad schools or no schools at all—just as they were in the past. How much worse can it be under the new system?

This defect in the voucher system leaves us, however, with a substantial number of students who are still getting no education through no fault of their own. Nor can we count on getting results if we round them up and dispatch them willy-nilly to the nearest accredited school. A school that can motivate and teach a child when there is backup from home cannot necessarily teach the children we are now discussing. Many of them are poor not only in money. Many have been developmentally impoverished as well, receiving very little of the early verbal and conceptual stimulation that happens as a matter of course when parents expect their children to be smart. Some arrive at the school door already believing themselves to be stupid, expecting to fail. We can be as angry as we wish at their parents, but we are still left with the job of devising a school that works for these children. What do we do—not in terms of a particular pedagogical program or curriculum, but in broad strokes?

First, whatever else, we decide to create a world that makes sense in the context of the society we want them to succeed in. The school is not an extension of the neighborhood. Within the confines of the school building and school day, we create a world that may seem as strange and irrelevant as Oz.

We do not do so with uniforms or elaborate rules or inspirational readings—the embellishments are left up to the school. Rather, we install one simple, inflexible procedure. Each course has an entrance test. Tenth-grade geometry has an entrance test; so does first-grade reading. Entrance tests for simple courses are simple; entrance tests for hard courses are hard. Their purpose is not to identify the best students, but to make sure that any student who gets in can, with an honest effort, complete the course work.

Our system does not carry with it any special teaching technique. It does, however, give the teacher full discretion over enforcing an orderly working environment. The teacher's only obligation is to teach those who want to learn.

The system is also infinitely forgiving. A student who has just flunked algebra three times running can enroll in that or any other math class for which he can pass the entrance test. He can enroll even if he has just been kicked out of three other classes for misbehavior. The question is never "What have you been in the past?" but always "What are you being as of now?"

The evolving outcomes of the system are complex. Some students begin by picking the easiest, least taxing courses, and approach them with as little motivation as their counterparts under the current system. Perhaps among this set of students are some who cannot or will not complete even the simplest courses. They drop by the wayside, failures of the system.

Among those who do complete courses, *any* courses, five things happen, all of them positive. First, the system is so constructed that to get into a course is in itself a small success ("I passed!"). Second, the students go into the course with a legitimate reason for believing that they can do the work; they passed a valid test that says they can. Third, they experience a success when they complete the course. Fourth, they experience—directly—a cause-effect relationship between their success in one course and their ability to get into the next course, no matter how small a step upward that next course may be. Fifth, all the while this is going on, they are likely to be observing other students *no different from them*—no richer, no smarter—who are moving upward faster than they are but using the same mechanism.

What of those who are disappointed, who try to get into a class and fail? Some will withdraw into themselves and be forever fearful of taking a chance on failure—as almost all do under the current system anyway. But there is a gradation to risk, and a peculiar sort of guarantee of success in our zero-transfer system. Whatever class a student finally takes, the student will have succeeded in gaining entrance to it. He will go into the classroom with official certification—based on reality—that he will be able to learn the material if he gives it an honest effort. The success-failure, cause-effect features of the system are indispensable for teaching some critical lessons:

- Effort is often rewarded with success.
- Effort is not *always* rewarded with success.
- Failure in one instance does not mean inability to succeed in anything else.
- Failure in one try does not mean perpetual failure.
- The better the preparation, the more likely the success.

None of these lessons is taught as well or as directly under the system prevailing in our current education of the disadvantaged. The central failing of the educational system for the poor and disadvantaged, and most especially poor and disadvantaged blacks, is not that it fails to provide meaningful ways for a student to succeed, though that is part of it. The central failing is not that ersatz success—fake curricula, fake grades, fake diplomas—sets the students up for failure when they leave the school, though that too is part of it. The central failing is that the system does not teach disadvantaged students, who see permanent failure all around them, *how to fail.* For students who are growing up expecting (whatever their dreams may be) ultimately to be a failure, with failure writ large, the first essential contravening lesson is that failure can come in small, digestible packages. Failure can be dealt with. It can be absorbed, analyzed, and converted to an asset.

We are now discussing a population of students—the children of what has become known as "the underclass"—that comes to the classroom with an array of disadvantages beyond simple economic poverty. I am not suggesting that, under our hypothetical system, all children of the underclass will become motivated students forthwith. Rather, some will. Perhaps it will be a small proportion; perhaps a large one. Certainly the effect interacts with the inherent abilities of the children involved. But some effect will be observed. Some children who are at the very bottom of the pile in the disadvantages they bear will act on the change in the reality of their environment. It will be an improvement over the situation in the system we have replaced, in which virtually none of them gets an education in anything except the futility of hoping.

A Proposal for Public Welfare

I begin with the proposition that it is within our resources to do enormous good for some people quickly. We have available to us a program that would convert a large proportion of the younger generation of hardcore unemployed into steady workers making a living wage. The same program would drastically reduce births to single teenage girls. It would reverse the trendline in the breakup of poor families. It would measurably increase the upward socioeconomic mobility of poor families. These improvements would affect some millions of persons.

All these are results that have eluded the efforts of the social programs installed since 1965, yet, from everything we know, there is no real question about whether they would occur under the program I propose. A wide variety of persuasive evidence from our own culture and around the world, from experimental data and longitudinal studies, from theory and practice, suggests that the program would achieve such results.

The proposed program, our final and most ambitious thought experiment, consists of scrapping the entire federal welfare and income-support structure for working-aged persons, including AFDC, Medicaid, Food

Stamps, Unemployment Insurance, Worker's Compensation, subsidized housing, disability insurance, and the rest. It would leave the working-aged person with no recourse whatsoever except the job market, family members, friends, and public or private locally funded services. It is the Alexandrian solution: cut the knot, for there is no way to untie it.

It is difficult to examine such a proposal dispassionately. Those who dislike paying for welfare are for it without thinking. Others reflexively imagine bread lines and people starving in the streets. But as a means of gaining fresh perspective on the problem of effective reform, let us consider what this hypothetical society might look like.

A large majority of the population is unaffected. A surprising number of the huge American middle and working classes go from birth to grave without using any social welfare benefits until they receive their first Social Security check. Another portion of the population is technically affected, but the change in income is so small or so sporadic that it makes no difference in quality of life. A third group comprises persons who have to make new arrangements and behave in different ways. Sons and daughters who fail to find work continue to live with their parents or relatives or friends. Teenaged mothers have to rely on support from their parents or the father of the child and perhaps work as well. People laid off from work have to use their own savings or borrow from others to make do until the next job is found. All these changes involve great disruption in expectations and accustomed roles.

Along with the disruptions go other changes in behavior. Some parents do not want their young adult children continuing to live off their income, and become quite insistent about their children learning skills and getting jobs. This attitude is most prevalent among single mothers who have to depend most critically on the earning power of their offspring.

Parents tend to become upset at the prospect of a daughter's bringing home a baby that must be entirely supported on an already inadequate income. Some become so upset that they spend considerable parental energy avoiding such an eventuality. Potential fathers of such babies find themselves under more pressure not to cause such a problem, or to help with its solution if it occurs.

Adolescents who were not job-ready find they are job-ready after all. It turns out that they can work for low wages and accept the discipline of the workplace if the alternative is grim enough. After a few years, many —not all, but many—find that they have acquired salable skills, or that they are at the right place at the right time, or otherwise find that the original entry-level job has gradually been transformed into a secure job paying a decent wage. A few—not a lot, but a few—find that the process leads to affluence.

Perhaps the most rightful, deserved benefit goes to the much larger population of low-income families who have been doing things right all along and have been punished for it: the young man who has taken responsibility for his wife and child even though his friends with the same choice have called him a fool; the single mother who has worked full time and forfeited her right to welfare for very little extra money; the parents who have set an example for their children even as the rules of the game have taught their children that the example is outmoded. For these millions of people, the instantaneous result is that no one makes fun of them any longer. The longer-term result will be that they regain the status that is properly theirs. They will not only be the bedrock upon which the community is founded (which they always have been), they will be recognized as such. The process whereby they regain their position is not magical, but a matter of logic. When it becomes highly dysfunctional for a person to be dependent, status will accrue to being independent, and in fairly short order. Noneconomic rewards will once again reinforce the economic rewards of being a good parent and provider.

The prospective advantages are real and extremely plausible. In fact, if a government program of the traditional sort (one that would "do" something rather than simply get out of the way) could *as plausibly* promise these advantages, its passage would be a foregone conclusion. Congress, yearning for programs that are not retreads of failures, would be prepared to spend billions. Negative side-effects (as long as they were the traditionally acceptable negative side-effects) would be brushed aside as trivial in return for the benefits. For let me be quite clear: I am not suggesting that we dismantle income support for the working-aged to balance the budget or punish welfare cheats. I am hypothesizing, with the advantage of powerful collateral evidence, that the lives of large numbers of poor people would be radically changed for the better.

There is, however, a fourth segment of the population yet to be considered, those who are pauperized by the withdrawal of government supports and unable to make alternate arrangements: the teenaged mother who has no one to turn to; the incapacitated or the inept who are thrown out of the house; those to whom economic conditions have brought long periods in which there is no work to be had; those with illnesses not covered by insurance. What of these situations?

The first resort is the network of local services. Poor communities in our hypothetical society are still dotted with storefront health clinics, emergency relief agencies, employment services, legal services. They depend for support on local taxes or local philanthropy, and the local taxpayers and philanthropists tend to scrutinize them rather closely. But, by the same token, they also receive considerably more resources than they formerly did. The dismantling of the federal services has poured tens of billions of dollars back into the private economy. Some of that money no doubt has been spent on Mercedes and summer homes on the Cape. But some has been spent on capital investments that generate new jobs. And some has been spent on increased local services to the poor, voluntarily or as decreed by the municipality. In many cities, the coverage provided by this network of agencies is more generous, more humane, more wisely distributed, and more effective in its results than the services formerly subsidized by the federal government.

But we must expect that a large number of people will fall between the cracks. How might we go about trying to retain the advantages of a zero-level welfare system and still address the residual needs?

As we think about the nature of the population still in need, it becomes apparent that their basic problem in the vast majority of the cases is the lack of a job, and this problem is temporary. What they need is something to tide them over while finding a new place in the economy. So our first step is to re-install the Unemployment Insurance program in more or less its previous form. Properly administered, unemployment insurance makes sense. Even if it is restored with all the defects of current practice, the negative effects of Unemployment Insurance *alone* are relatively minor. Our objective is not to wipe out chicanery or to construct a theoretically unblemished system, but to meet legitimate human needs without doing more harm than good. Unemployment Insurance is one of the least harmful ways of contributing to such ends. Thus the system has been amended to take care of the victims of short-term swings in the economy.

Who is left? We are now down to the hardest of the hard core of the welfare-dependent. They have no jobs. They have been unable to find jobs (or have not tried to find jobs) for a longer period of time than the unemployment benefits cover. They have no families who will help. They have no friends who will help. For some reason, they cannot get help from local services or private charities except for the soup kitchen and a bed in the Salvation Army hall.

What will be the size of this population? We have never tried a zero-level federal welfare system under conditions of late-twentieth-century national wealth, so we cannot do more than speculate. But we may speculate. Let us ask of whom the population might consist and how they might fare.

For any category of "needy" we may name, we find ourselves driven to one of two lines of thought. Either the person is in a category that is going to be at the top of the list of services that localities vote for themselves, and at the top of the list of private services, or the person is in a category where help really is not all that essential or desirable. The burden of the conclusion is not that every single person will be taken care of, but that the extent of resources to deal with needs is likely to be very great—not based on wishful thinking, but on extrapolations from reality.

To illustrate, let us consider the plight of the stereotypical welfare mother—never married, no skills, small children, no steady help from a man. It is safe to say that, now as in the 1950s, there is no one who has less sympathy from the white middle class, which is to be the source of most of the money for the private and local services we envision. Yet this same white middle class is a soft touch for people trying to make it on their own, and a soft touch for "deserving" needy mothers—AFDC was one of the most widely popular of the New Deal welfare measures, intended as it was for widows with small children. Thus we may envision two quite different scenarios.

In one scenario, the woman is presenting the local or private service with this proposition: "Help me find a job and day-care for my children, and I will take care of the rest." In effect, she puts herself into the same category as the widow and the deserted wife—identifies herself as one of the most obviously deserving of the deserving poor. Welfare mothers who want to get into the labor force are likely to find a wide range of help. In the other scenario, she asks for an outright and indefinite cash grant—in effect, a private or local version of AFDC—so that she can stay with the children and not hold a job. In the latter case, it is very easy to imagine situations in which she will not be able to find a local service or a private philanthropy to provide the help she seeks. The question we must now ask is: What's so bad about that? If children were always better off being with their mother all day and if, by the act of giving birth, a mother acquired the inalienable right to be with the child, then her situation would be unjust to her and injurious to her children. Neither assertion can be defended, however—especially not in the 1980s, when more mothers of all classes work away from the home than ever before, and even more especially not in view of the empirical record for the children growing up under the current welfare system. Why should the mother be exempted by the system from the pressures that must affect everyone else's decision to work?

As we survey these prospects, important questions remain unresolved. The first of these is why, if federal social transfers are treacherous, should locally mandated transfers be less so? Why should a municipality be permitted to legislate its own AFDC or Food Stamp program if their results are so inherently bad?

Part of the answer lies in conceptions of freedom. I have deliberately avoided raising them—the discussion is about how to help the disadvantaged, not about how to help the advantaged cut their taxes, to which arguments for personal freedom somehow always get diverted. Nonetheless, the point is valid: Local or even state systems leave much more room than a federal system for everyone, donors and recipients alike, to exercise freedom of choice about the kind of system they live under. Laws are more easily made and changed, and people who find them unacceptable have much more latitude in going somewhere more to their liking.

But the freedom of choice argument, while legitimate, is not necessary. We may put the advantages of local systems in terms of the Law of Imperfect Selection. A federal system must inherently employ very crude, inaccurate rules for deciding who gets what kind of help, and the results are as I outlined them in chapter 16. At the opposite extreme—a neighbor helping a neighbor, a family member helping another family member—the law loses its validity nearly altogether. Very fine-grained judgments based on personal knowledge are being made about specific people and changing situations. In neighborhoods and small cities, the procedures can still bring much individualized information to bear on decisions. Even systems in large cities and states can do much better than a national system; a decaying industrial city in the Northeast and a booming sunbelt city of the same size can and probably should adopt much different rules about who gets what and how much.

A final and equally powerful argument for not impeding local systems is diversity. We know much more in the 1980s than we knew in the 1960s about what does not work. We have a lot to learn about what *does* work. Localities have been a rich source of experiments. Marva Collins in Chicago gives us an example of how a school can bring inner-city students up to national norms. Sister Falaka Fattah in Philadelphia shows us how homeless youths can be rescued from the streets. There are numberless such lessons waiting to be learned from the diversity of local efforts. By all means, let a hundred flowers bloom, and if the federal government can play a useful role in lending a hand and spreading the word of successes, so much the better.

The ultimate unresolved question about our proposal to abolish income maintenance for the working-aged is how many people will fall through the cracks. In whatever detail we try to foresee the consequences, the objection may always be raised: We cannot be *sure* that everyone will be taken care of in the degree to which we would wish. But this observation by no means settles the question. If one may point in objection to the child now fed by Food Stamps who would go hungry, one may also point with satisfaction to the child who would have an entirely different and better future. Hungry children should be fed; there is no argument about that. It is no less urgent that children be allowed to grow up in a system free of the forces that encourage them to remain poor and dependent. If a strategy reasonably promises to remove those forces, after so many attempts to "help the poor" have failed, it is worth thinking about.

But that rationale is too vague. Let me step outside the persona I have employed and put the issue in terms of one last intensely personal hypothetical example. Let us suppose that you, a parent, could know that tomorrow your own child would be made an orphan. You have a choice. You may put your child with an extremely poor family, so poor that your child will be badly clothed and will indeed sometimes be hungry. But you also know that the parents have worked hard all their lives, will make sure your child goes to school and studies, and will teach your child that independence is a primary value. Or you may put your child with a family with parents who have never worked, who will be incapable of overseeing your child's education—but who have plenty of food and good clothes, provided by others. If the choice about where one would put one's own child is as clear to you as it is to me, on what grounds does one justify support of a system that, indirectly but without doubt, makes the other choice for other children? The answer that "What we really want is a world where that choice is not forced upon us" is no answer. We have tried to have it that way. We failed. Everything we know about why we failed tells us that more of the same will not make the dilemma go away.

The Ideal of Opportunity

Billions for equal opportunity, not one cent for equal outcome—such is the slogan to inscribe on the banner of whatever cause my proposals constitute. Their common theme is to make it possible to get as far as one can go on one's merit, hardly a new ideal in American thought.

The ideal itself has never lapsed. What did lapse was the recognition that practical merit exists. Some people are better than others. They deserve more of society's rewards, of which money is only one small part. A principal function of social policy is to make sure they have the opportunity to reap those rewards. Government cannot identify the worthy, but it can protect a society in which the worthy can identify themselves.

I am proposing triage of a sort, triage by self-selection. In triage on the battlefield, the doctor makes the decision—this one gets treatment, that one waits, the other one is made comfortable while waiting to die. In our social triage, the decision is left up to the patient. The patient always has the right to say "I can do X" and get a chance to prove it. Society always has the right to hold him to that pledge. The patient always has the right to fail. Society always has the right to let him.

There is in this stance no lack of compassion but a presumption of respect. People—all people, black or white, rich or poor—may be unequally responsible for what has happened to them in the past, but all are equally responsible for what they do next. Just as in our idealized educational system a student can come back a third, fourth, or fifth time to a course, in our idealized society a person can fail repeatedly and always be qualified for another chance—to try again, to try something easier, to try something different. The options are always open. Opportunity is endless. There is no punishment for failure, only a total absence of rewards. Society —or our idealized society—should be preoccupied with making sure that achievement is rewarded.

There is no shortage of people to be rewarded. Go into any inner-city school and you will find students of extraordinary talent, kept from knowing how good they are by rules we imposed in the name of fairness. Go into any poor community, and you will find people of extraordinary imagination and perseverance, energy and pride, making tortured accommodations to the strange world we created in the name of generosity. The success stories of past generations of poor in this country are waiting to be repeated.

There is no shortage of institutions to provide the rewards. Our schools know how to educate students who want to be educated. Our industries know how to find productive people and reward them. Our police know how to protect people who are ready to cooperate in their own protection. Our system of justice knows how to protect the rights of individuals who know what their rights are. Our philanthropic institutions know how to multiply the effectiveness of people who are already trying to help themselves. In short, American society is very good at reinforcing the investment of an individual in himself. For the affluent and for the middle class, these mechanisms continue to work about as well as they ever have, and we enjoy their benefits. Not so for the poor. American government, in its recent social policy, has been ineffectual in trying to stage-manage their decision to invest, and it has been unintentionally punitive toward those who would make the decision on their own. It is time to get out of their way.

Escapism

It is entertaining to indulge in speculations about solutions, but they remain only speculations. Congress will not abolish income-maintenance for the working-aged. The public school system is not in jeopardy of replacement by vouchers. The federal government will not abandon legalized racial discrimination when it is thought to help the underdog. More generally, it is hard to imagine any significant reform of social policy in the near future. When one thinks of abolishing income maintenance, for example, one must recall that ours is a system that, faced with the bankruptcy of Social Security in the early 1980s, went into paroxysms of anxiety at the prospect of delaying the cost-of-living increase for six months.

But the cautiousness of the system is not in itself worrisome. Reforms should be undertaken carefully and slowly, and often not at all. What should worry us instead is a peculiar escapism that has gripped the consideration of social policy. It seems that those who legislate and administer and write about social policy can tolerate any increase in actual suffering as long as the system in place does not explicitly permit it. It is better, by the logic we have been living with, that we try to take care of 100 percent of the problem and make matters worse than that we solve 75 percent of the problem with a solution that does not try to do anything about the rest.

Escapism is a natural response. Most of us want to help. It makes us feel bad to think of neglected children and rat-infested slums, and we are happy to pay for the thought that people who are good at taking care of such things are out there. If the numbers of neglected children and numbers of rats seem to be going up instead of down, it is understandable that we choose to focus on how much we put into the effort instead of what comes out. The tax checks we write buy us, for relatively little money and no effort at all, a quieted conscience. The more we pay, the more certain we can be that we have done our part, and it is essential that we feel that way regardless of what we accomplish. A solution that would have us pay less *and* acknowledge that some would go unhelped is unacceptable.

To this extent, the barrier to radical reform of social policy is not the pain it would cause the intended beneficiaries of the present system, but the pain it would cause the donors. The real contest about the direction of social policy is not between people who want to cut budgets and people who want to help. When reforms finally do occur, they will happen not because stingy people have won, but because generous people have stopped kidding themselves.

Appendix: The Data

WITH the growing popularity of time-series analysis in the social sciences, it would seem natural to find compendia of long-term time-series data on the indicators discussed in the text. But they are scarce. The best-known ones—the *Statistical Abstract of the United States*, for example—seldom give year-by-year data, or data extending back more than the most recent five or ten years. Some of the best sources of data, such as the statistical appendix to the *Employment and Training Report of the President*, are relatively obscure government publications that many libraries do not possess. For some indicators, Washington, D.C., is one of the few places where a year-by-year record going back twenty or thirty years can be reconstructed. The Bureau of the Census and the libraries of the various government agencies protect nearly unique, complete archives of their respective publications.

Hence this appendix. It includes the data used to generate the figures in the text, plus the complete data sets for trends that are only summarized in the text. The variables are basic and applicable to a wide variety of investigations. I hope that the appendix will shorten the piecing-together time of others who are who are engaged in such research.

I have another motive in including the appendix—namely, to encourage others to do likewise. The problem with statistical accounts is not (usually) that people lie with statistics, but that there is more than one way to view a given data set, and the reader cannot determine whether the analysis is sound. The most exasperating examples are articles that interpret regression coefficients or canonical correlations at great length without telling enough about means, standard deviations, confidence intervals, sample sizes, and other useful items to let the reader determine whether the writer is drawing sensible conclusions. But the need for supplementary data is equally great for simple statistics such as the ones in this book. Arguments can go on *ad infinitum*, with one person stressing, for example, proportional changes and the other stressing the absolute changes, each drawing seemingly opposite conclusions, and the observer wondering whether numbers really mean anything except what advocates want them to mean. With the inclusion of the data, it is at least possible for readers to be quite specific about the nature of the difference in the use of the numbers, to work from the same data, and eventually, one hopes, to reach a consensus about the meaning of the data. Social scientists need to make their analyses more accessible to each other, and I hope the appendix contributes to that end.

A few comments about procedure:

The objective in each case was to develop a complete year-by-year data set for the period 1950–80. For many of the white/nonwhite breakdowns, however, annual racial data became available only in 1954 when the Current Population Survey (CPS) was amended to include racial identification of the respondent. For some of these variables, I could recover a 1950 figure for what was nominally the same variable, but one that was computed from decennial census data. Because of the substantial differences between the procedures used in the decennial census and the Current Population Survey, I do not include those figures.

In other cases, notably the data on natality, a consistent data base was available, but the published figures did not always include the variable I was working with. I reconstructed the needed figure whenever the data permitted. Such cases are specified in the notes.

Population figures used to calculate per capita, percent, or per-1,000 statistics are based on the civilian, resident, noninstitutional population. Readers who need such breakdowns by race and age are referred to the *Current Population Reports,* Series P-25, #310 (for 1950–60), #519 (for 1960–73), #721 (for 1970–75), and #870 (for 1976–79) (Washington, D.C.: Bureau of the Census).

Financial and access constraints generally limited the analysis to published data. One exception is the special computer runs for the UCR data from 1974–80, which permitted a consistent trendline for arrest data as discussed in note 1 to chapter 8.

Note that data for many populations not explicitly included in the following tables may be recovered by manipulating the information on both percentages and raw numbers. This is especially true of the data on poverty and labor market behavior. Sometimes inconsistencies persist. For example, the total population figures that can be interpolated from the poverty and labor force data will not agree exactly with the figures in the population table, even though, judging from the definitions in the sources, they "should" have been the same except for rounding error.

I put "NA," for "not available," in missing cells when, despite searching and inquiries, I was unable to obtain either the needed number or the name of a reference in which it might be found. I do so knowing, with anticipatory embarrassment, that there are references out there that will seem very obvious after I hear about them. "MD," for "missing data," is applied to a few years of budget data that remained stubbornly unobtainable even though the numbers surely exist somewhere.

Appendix: The Data

TABLE 1
The Resident Population of the United States
(In 1,000s)

Year	Persons Overall Total	Persons Overall 65 & Over	Persons Whites	Persons Blacks & Others	Families
1950	150790	12362	134611	16180	39303
1951	151599	12768	135207	16392	39929
1952	153892	13169	137148	16743	40578
1953	156595	13582	139493	17102	40832
1954	159695	14040	142141	17553	41202
1955	162967	14489	144915	18053	41951
1956	166055	14902	147540	18515	42889
1957	169110	15353	150107	19003	43497
1958	172226	15771	152735	19491	43696
1959	175277	16213	155289	19988	44232
1960	179979	16675	159381	20598	45111
1961	182992	17089	161891	21101	45539
1962	185771	17457	164185	21587	46418
1963	188483	17778	166413	22070	47059
1964	191141	18127	168577	22564	47540
1965	193526	18451	170499	23027	47956
1966	195576	18755	172111	23465	48509
1967	197457	19071	173562	23895	49214
1968	199399	19365	175096	24304	50111
1969	201385	19680	176641	24744	50823
1970	203810	20085	178551	25260	51586
1971	206212	20487	180408	25804	51948
1972	208230	20883	181899	26331	53296
1973	209851	21329	183049	26802	54373
1974	211390	21815	184109	27281	55053
1975	213137	22400	185198	27939	55712
1976	214680	22954	186241	28439	56245
1977	216400	23513	187409	28991	56710
1978	218228	24064	188657	29571	57215
1979	220099	24658	189968	30132	57804
1980	226505	25544	188341	38164	58426

Source for persons: Current Population Reports, Series P-25, as follows: for 1950-59, #310 (figures are for civilian population only); for 1960-73, #721; for 1976-79, #870. For 1974, 1975, and 1980, sources are SAUS-75, Table 35, SAUS-76, Table 28, and SAUS-81, Table 29 respectively. "65 and over" for 1950-59 taken from HSUS, A29-42. Note the warning in SAUS-81 that "[t]he 1980 totals for 'White' and 'Other' are not comparable with corresponding figures from the 1970 census and previous censuses." (p. 3). It is preferable to use the inter-censal estimate for 1980 (that is, the estimated racial breakdown in 1980 using the 1970 decenniel census data as the basis for the estimate) for purposes requiring a consistent time series. That estimate, provided from unpublished data by the Population Division of the Bureau of the Census, is as follows: Total resident population, 222,436,000; whites, 191,556,000; blacks and others, 30,880,000. It is not clear in the sources cited in the following tables whether inter-censal or census data were used for 1980 calculations. For that reason, conspicuous shifts in trends in 1979-80 should be interpreted cautiously.

Source for families: for 1950 and 1955-70, HSUS, A288-319; for 1951-54 and 1971-80, SAUS-81, Table 60, and comparable tables in earlier editions. A family is defined as two or more persons related by blood, marriage, or adoption, and residing together in a household. (SAUS-81, p. 3)

TABLE 2
Federal Social Welfare Expenditures Aggregated by the Standard Categories
(In Millions of 1980 Dollars)

Year	Social Insurance	Public Aid	Health & Medical Programs	Veterans' Programs	Education	Housing	Other Social Welfare	Total	Inflator (Based on CPI)
1950	7184	3768	2063	21816	536	51	594	36014	3.42
1951	8622	3785	3703	17917	570	70	548	35214	3.17
1952	10355	3752	4914	15843	954	77	449	36346	3.10
1953	12984	4184	4242	14204	1319	117	587	37637	3.07
1954	15583	4344	3702	13852	1282	165	817	39744	3.06
1955	19611	4619	3532	14657	1490	230	774	44914	3.07
1956	22806	4707	3802	15051	1441	278	990	49075	3.03
1957	26074	4937	4119	14840	1580	295	1113	52958	2.92
1958	30886	5220	4458	15092	1730	316	993	58694	2.84
1959	36815	5872	4842	15260	2163	361	1106	66418	2.82
1960	39714	5876	4822	14898	2409	400	1158	69277	2.78
1961	43887	6424	5357	15225	2752	437	1240	75322	2.75
1962	49734	7453	6096	15116	2964	470	1441	83276	2.72
1963	52177	8059	6559	15400	3555	519	1534	87804	2.69
1964	54717	8502	7286	15485	4293	562	1723	92568	2.65
1965	56827	9366	7247	15664	6437	620	2116	98277	2.61
1966	65042	11066	7973	16061	11608	636	2623	115010	2.53
1967	75234	12916	9067	16933	13002	697	3350	131200	2.46
1968	83681	15263	10009	17058	11823	768	4013	142614	2.36
1969	91654	17567	10194	17688	11046	954	4275	153378	2.24
1970	95841	20439	10115	18962	12447	1233	4785	163822	2.12
1971	109399	26364	10448	20967	13389	1770	5573	187911	2.03
1972	120535	32060	12442	22445	13227	2328	6209	209246	1.97
1973	133821	33453	12406	23899	13632	3241	6568	227021	1.85
1974	138325	34047	11932	23169	11760	3355	6516	229104	1.67
1975	152520	41612	13021	25345	13199	3887	6522	256104	1.53
1976	172919	47028	14327	27243	13046	4202	6648	285412	1.45
1977	182868	48041	13818	25597	13225	5437	7424	296411	1.36
1978	185697	50460	14586	24679	13726	6163	7502	302813	1.26
1979	185926	49520	13796	23087	13736	6588	7323	299976	1.14
1980	191107	49252	13348	21254	12990	6608	8786	303345	1.00

Source: SAUS-81, Table 518, and comparable tables in earlier editions. Consumer Price Index data taken from SAUS-81, Table 765.

Appendix: The Data

TABLE 3
Other Budgetary and Economic Data Cited in the Text
(In 1980 Dollars)

Year	Gross Nat'l Product (Billions)	Total Federal Income Transfers (1,000,000s) Cash	Noncash	Cash Public Assistance (1,000,000s)	Elementary & Secondary Education for the Deprived (1,000s)	Higher Education Loans (1,000s)	Educational Opportunity Grants (1,000s)	Law Enforcement Assistance Administration (1,000s)
1950	1052	17816	51	3744	0	0	0	0
1951	1140	18851	70	3760	0	0	0	0
1952	1182	20633	77	3752	0	0	0	0
1953	1227	24471	117	4184	0	0	0	0
1954	1212	27425	165	4301	0	0	0	0
1955	1294	32321	230	4426	0	0	0	0
1956	1322	35750	363	4429	0	0	0	0
1957	1346	39310	260	4703	0	0	0	0
1958	1340	44633	501	4791	0	0	0	0
1959	1420	51243	902	5144	0	0	0	0
1960	1451	54332	861	5158	131129	111939	0	0
1961	1489	59412	1143	5333	MD	MD	0	0
1962	1575	65636	1955	5645	144491	202940	0	0
1963	1638	68671	2335	5971	MD	MD	0	0
1964	1725	71594	2523	6236	178041	470138	0	0
1965	1829	74099	3247	6465	MD	MD	0	0
1966	1938	83172	4484	7107	2918211	597884	0	0
1967	1990	85611	14057	7663	MD	MD	0	0
1968	2082	90406	19992	8252	3985457	535101	243793	0
1969	2140	97194	23861	9218	MD	MD	MD	64982
1970	2136	101535	27107	9458	3690747	416958	302010	136787
1971	2209	116994	32469	11644	4545470	470260	MD	761751
1972	2334	127661	39482	12483	4107478	565131	329833	747337
1973	2470	140854	41897	12414	4221074	601139	MD	1092808
1974	2456	144209	42836	13577	3781453	605850	399472	1286577
1975	2428	157226	52383	15800	4229041	686578	931465	1304502
1976	2559	174364	61756	15274	3826935	607023	1658275	1330950
1977	2699	181952	66720	16101	3876221	513586	2288258	1147793
1978	2828	181548	72974	15525	4298274	942678	2425808	1018454
1979	2919	179219	74802	14528	4635578	1556681	2351348	734066
1980	2914	179068	79205	14260	4677394	1766312	2610924	640178

Sources: The figures for total federal cash transfers, total noncash transfers, and cash public assistance are rough estimates derived from the standard SAUS table, "Social Welfare Expenditures, By Source of Funds and Public Program" (Table 521 in SAUS-81). Using the wording of the categories in the table, the estimates were derived as follows:

Total Cash Transfers = (Social Insurance – Medicare – Workers' Compensation Hospital Benefits) + (Public Assistance – Medicaid – Social Services) + SSI + Veterans' Pensions.
Total Noncash Transfers = Social Insurance + Public Aid + Housing + Veterans' Pensions – Total Cash Transfers as computed above (in other words, the noncash elements of the Social Insurance and Public Aid categories, plus Housing).
Cash Public Assistance = Public Assistance – Medicaid – Social Services + SSI.

Figures on Veterans' pensions during the early 1950's (when they were not broken out as a separate category in the standard SAUS table) were obtained from HSUS Y984–997. Prior to the establishment of Medicaid, "Vendor Payments" under Public Aid was the equivalent noncash medical assistance category. Sources of other data: DES, Tables 161 and 163 (for educational budgets); EIRP-81, Table G-3 (for GNP); various editions of the Federal Budget Appendix (for LEAA outlays and, in 1979–80, for OJARS, which replaced LEAA).

TABLE 4
Data on Job Training Programs and Aid to Families with Dependent Children (AFDC)

Year	Work and Training Programs Administered by the Department of Labor		AFDC Recipients			
	Obligations in 1980 Dollars (Millions)	First-Time Enrollments (1,000s)	No. of Families (1,000s)	Total No. of Recipients (1,000s)	Number of Children (1,000s)	AFDC Families as a Percentage of All Families
1950	0	0	651	2233	1661	1.66
1951	0	0	592	2041	1523	1.48
1952	0	0	596	1991	1495	1.47
1953	0	0	547	1941	1464	1.34
1954	0	0	604	2173	1639	1.47
1955	0	0	602	2192	1661	1.44
1956	0	0	615	2270	1731	1.43
1957	0	0	667	2497	1912	1.53
1958	0	0	755	2486	2181	1.73
1959	0	0	776	2946	2265	1.75
1960	0	0	803	3073	2370	1.78
1961	0	0	916	3566	2753	2.01
1962	0	0	932	3789	2844	2.01
1963	151	34.1	954	3930	2951	2.03
1964	377	77.6	1012	4219	3170	2.13
1965	1079	156.9	1054	4396	3316	2.20
1966	1593	235.8	1127	4666	3526	2.32
1967	1960	833.3	1297	5309	3986	2.64
1968	1897	780.8	1522	6086	4555	3.04
1969	2311	1000.7	1875	7313	5413	3.69
1970	3005	1051.4	2552	9659	7033	4.95
1971	3015	1412.5	2918	10651	7707	5.62
1972	5308	1973.0	3122	11064	7983	5.86
1973	5100	1537.7	3156	10815	7813	5.80
1974	3579	1917.7	3323	11022	7901	6.04
1975	6285	2761.9	3566	11401	8105	6.40
1976	7354	3211.9	3585	11203	7909	6.37
1977	12928	3428.2	3547	10780	7572	6.25
1978	9293	3873.3	3488	10349	7226	6.10
1979	12060	4011.5	3560	10379	7207	6.16
1980	8778	3699.4	3841	11102	7600	6.57

Source for training data: EIRP-81, Table F-1, and comparable tables in earlier issues. This source (prepared by the Department of Labor) does not show any programs prior to 1963. It remains possible some very small programs existed during the period 1950-62 that could be classified as "work and training" programs.

Source for AFDC data: For 1950-70, HSUS H346-367; for 1971-80, SAUS-81, Table 559, and comparable tables in earlier issues. Percentage of all families is computed using data from appendix table 1.

Appendix: The Data

TABLE 5
Poverty Data by Race and Age
(Population Figures in 1,000s)

Year	Total Persons in Poverty						Persons 65 and Over			

Persons Beneath the Poverty Level

Year	All Races		Whites		Blacks & Others		Whites		Blacks & Others	
	n	%	n	%	n	%	n	%	n	%
1959	39490	22.4	28484	18.1	11006	58.2	4744	33.1	737	59.5
1960	39851	22.2	28309	17.8	11542	56.4	NA	NA	NA	NA
1961	39628	21.9	27890	17.4	11738	56.8	NA	NA	NA	NA
1962	38625	21.0	26672	16.4	11953	56.1	NA	NA	NA	NA
1963	36436	19.5	25238	15.3	11198	51.1	NA	NA	NA	NA
1964	36055	19.0	24957	14.9	11098	49.8	NA	NA	NA	NA
1965	33185	17.3	22496	13.3	10689	47.1	NA	NA	NA	NA
1966	30424	15.7	20751	12.2	9673	40.8	NA	NA	NA	NA
1966r	28510	14.7	19290	11.3	9220	39.7	4357	26.4	757	52.6
1967	27769	14.2	18983	11.0	8786	38.2	4646	27.7	742	49.7
1968	25389	12.8	17395	10.0	7994	32.8	3939	23.1	693	46.9
1969	24147	12.1	16659	9.5	7488	30.9	4052	23.3	735	48.0
1970	25420	12.6	17484	9.9	7936	31.6	3984	22.5	725	47.9
1971	25559	12.5	17780	9.9	7779	31.3	3605	19.9	668	40.1
1972	24460	11.9	16203	9.0	8257	32.4	3072	16.8	666	36.8
1973	22973	11.1	15142	8.4	7831	29.3	2698	14.4	656	35.6
1974	24260	11.6	16290	8.9	7970	30.5	2642	13.8	666	34.6
1974r	23370	11.2	15736	8.6	7634	29.7	2460	12.8	625	32.7
1975	25877	12.3	17770	9.7	8107	29.8	2634	13.4	683	33.8
1976	24975	11.8	16713	9.1	8262	29.5	2633	13.2	680	31.8
1977	24720	11.6	16416	8.9	8304	29.0	2426	11.9	751	35.0
1978	24497	11.4	16259	8.7	8238	29.4	2530	12.1	703	32.2
1979	25345	11.6	16823	8.9	8522	28.9	2840	13.2	746	33.4
1979r	26072	11.7	17214	9.0	8858	28.1	2911	13.3	771	33.0
1980	29272	13.0	19699	10.2	9573	29.9	3042	13.6	829	36.2

Figures for 1959 and thereafter are taken from the annual published poverty statistics from the March CPS of the Bureau of the Census, in recent years published under the title, Characteristics of the Population Below the Poverty Level. Figures in this table were taken from the advance report for 1981, Series P-60, No. 134 (which, unlike the full report, contains the data for 1961-65); the full report (P-60, No. 138); and, for "blacks and others" for the years 1960-65, from various editions of SAUS. The method for calculating the poverty statistic was revised in 1966, 1974, and 1979. The pre-revision and post-revision data are given for these years, with the revised figure indicated by "r." "Blacks and others" data after 1966 were computed from the numbers for "all races" less the numbers for whites only. This procedure enables consistent data to be presented for the entire 1959-80 period. For data from 1966-80 for blacks only, see P-60, No. 138, Table 1.

For 1950-58, retrospective estimates of the percentage of the population beneath the official poverty level were reported in "Economic Report to the President: Combating Poverty in a Prosperous Economy" (January, 1969), reprinted in Molly Orshansky, ed., The Measure of Poverty, Technical Paper I, vol. 1 (Washington, D.C.: Government Printing Office, n.d.), p. 349. Estimates recovered from the graphs in that report are: 1950, 30.2; 1951, 28.0; 1952, 27.9; 1953, 26.2; 1954, 27.9; 1955, 24.5; 1956, 22.9; 1957, 22.8; 1958, 23.1.

TABLE 6

Poverty Data for Households Headed by a Female, No Husband Present
(Population Figures in 1,000s)

Year	Female Head, All Ages				Female Head under 65			
	Whites		Blacks & Others		Whites		Blacks & Others	
	n	%	n	%	n	%	n	%
1959	7115	43.8	3275	73.5	5336	42.8	3023	73.8
1960	7207	42.3	3456	76.7	NA	NA	NA	NA
1961	7048	41.9	3750	75.1	NA	NA	NA	NA
1962	7015	41.8	4216	77.3	NA	NA	NA	NA
1963	6982	39.9	4115	75.8	NA	NA	NA	NA
1964	7046	38.3	3925	71.3	NA	NA	NA	NA
1965	7085	38.5	3973	70.5	NA	NA	NA	NA
1966	6914	36.5	3931	67.6	NA	NA	NA	NA
1966r	6511	33.9	3739	64.5	4412	31.0	3434	64.6
1967	6600	33.9	3991	60.3	4273	29.7	3689	60.3
1968	6400	32.3	3964	58.1	4334	29.8	3641	57.9
1969	6531	32.1	3881	57.3	4410	29.7	3520	56.7
1970	6832	31.4	4322	58.1	4668	28.8	3975	57.7
1971	7146	32.1	4263	54.9	5035	30.5	3929	55.1
1972	6682	29.4	4905	56.6	4835	28.8	4548	57.2
1973	6642	27.9	4715	54	5078	28.4	4386	54.7
1974	6852	27.2	4923	54.5	5344	28.0	4547	54.8
1974r	6673	26.5	4796	53.6	5238	27.4	4436	54.0
1975	7324	28.1	4944	52.6	5797	29.5	4566	53.0
1976	7356	27.3	5230	54.2	5784	28.5	4868	54.9
1977	7221	25.5	5403	53.1	5786	26.8	5011	53.7
1978	7262	24.9	5618	52.4	5767	26.0	5222	53.2
1979	7467	24.8	5663	51.2	5829	25.3	5247	51.5
1979r	7653	24.9	5850	51.0	5975	25.4	5419	51.1
1980	8569	27.1	6080	51.9	6724	27.7	5617	52.0

The figures for "blacks and others" were obtained by subtracting the "whites" figures from the "all races" figures in the Bureau of the Census publications cited previously.

TABLE 7
Male Unemployment Rates by Race and Age
(Percentage of Persons in Labor Force)

Year	Age Range							
	16–17		18–19		20–24		25–34	
	Whites	Blacks & Others	Whites	Blacks & Others	Whites	Blacks & Others	Whites	Blacks & Others
1951	9.5	8.7	6.7	9.6	3.6	6.7	2.0	5.5
1952	10.9	8.0	7.0	10.0	4.3	7.9	1.9	5.5
1953	8.9	8.3	7.1	8.1	4.5	8.1	2.0	4.3
1954	14.0	13.4	13.0	14.7	9.8	16.9	4.2	10.1
1955	12.2	14.8	10.4	12.9	7.0	12.4	2.7	8.6
1956	11.2	15.7	9.7	14.9	6.1	12.0	2.8	7.6
1957	11.9	16.3	11.2	20.0	7.1	12.7	2.7	8.5
1958	14.9	27.1	16.5	26.7	11.7	19.5	5.6	14.7
1959	15.0	22.3	13.0	27.2	7.5	16.3	3.8	12.3
1960	14.6	22.7	13.5	25.1	8.3	13.1	4.1	10.7
1961	16.5	31.0	15.1	23.9	10.0	15.3	4.9	12.9
1962	15.1	21.9	12.7	21.8	8.0	14.6	3.8	10.5
1963	17.8	27.0	14.2	27.4	7.8	15.5	3.9	9.5
1964	16.1	25.9	13.4	23.1	7.4	12.6	3.0	7.7
1965	14.7	27.1	11.4	20.2	5.9	9.3	2.6	6.2
1966	12.5	22.5	8.9	20.5	4.1	7.9	2.1	4.9
1967	12.7	28.9	9.0	20.1	4.2	8.0	1.9	4.4
1968	12.3	26.6	8.2	19.0	4.6	8.3	1.7	3.8
1969	12.5	24.7	7.9	19.0	4.6	8.4	1.7	3.4
1970	15.7	27.8	12.0	23.1	7.8	12.6	3.1	6.1
1971	17.1	33.4	13.5	26.0	9.4	16.2	4.0	7.4
1972	16.4	35.1	12.4	26.2	8.5	14.7	3.4	6.8
1973	15.1	34.4	10.0	22.1	6.5	12.6	3.0	5.8
1974	16.2	39.0	11.5	26.6	7.8	15.4	3.5	7.2
1975	19.7	39.4	17.2	32.9	13.2	22.9	6.3	11.9
1976	19.7	37.7	15.5	34.0	10.9	20.7	5.6	11.0
1977	17.6	38.7	13.0	36.1	9.3	21.7	5.0	10.6
1978	16.9	40.0	10.8	30.8	7.6	20.0	3.7	8.8
1979	16.1	34.4	12.3	29.6	7.4	17.0	3.6	8.6
1980	18.5	37.7	14.6	33.0	11.1	22.3	6.0	12.5

Year	Age Range							
	35–44		45–54		55–64		65 and Over	
	Whites	Blacks & Others	Whites	Blacks & Others	Whites	Blacks & Others	Whites	Blacks & Others
1951	1.8	3.4	2.2	3.6	2.7	4.1	3.4	4.7
1952	1.7	4.4	2.0	4.2	2.3	3.7	2.9	4.7
1953	1.8	3.6	2.0	5.1	2.7	3.6	2.3	3.1
1954	3.6	9.0	3.8	9.3	4.3	7.5	4.2	7.5
1955	2.6	8.2	2.9	6.4	3.9	9.0	3.8	7.1
1956	2.2	6.6	2.8	5.4	3.1	8.1	3.4	4.9
1957	2.5	6.4	3.0	6.2	3.4	5.5	3.2	5.9
1958	4.4	11.4	4.8	10.3	5.2	10.1	5.0	9.0
1959	3.2	8.9	3.7	7.9	4.2	8.7	4.5	8.4
1960	3.3	8.2	3.6	8.5	4.1	9.5	4.0	6.3
1961	4.0	10.7	4.4	10.2	5.3	10.5	5.2	9.4
1962	3.1	8.6	3.5	8.3	4.1	9.6	4.1	11.9
1963	2.9	8.0	3.3	7.1	4.0	7.4	4.1	10.1
1964	2.5	6.2	2.9	5.9	3.5	8.1	3.6	8.3
1965	2.3	5.1	2.3	5.1	3.1	5.4	3.4	5.2
1966	1.7	4.2	1.7	4.1	2.5	4.4	3.0	4.9
1967	1.6	3.1	1.8	3.4	2.2	4.1	2.7	5.1
1968	1.4	2.9	1.5	2.5	1.7	3.6	2.8	4.0
1969	1.4	2.4	1.4	2.4	1.7	3.2	2.1	3.2
1970	2.3	3.9	2.3	3.3	2.7	3.4	3.2	3.8
1971	2.9	4.9	2.8	4.5	3.2	4.7	3.4	3.4
1972	2.5	4.8	2.5	3.8	3.0	4.6	3.3	6.9
1973	1.8	4.0	2.0	3.2	2.4	3.1	2.9	3.6
1974	2.4	4.1	2.2	4.0	2.5	3.6	3.0	5.6
1975	4.5	8.3	4.4	9.0	4.1	6.1	5.0	9.5
1976	3.7	7.3	3.7	7.2	4.0	6.2	4.8	9.3
1977	3.1	6.1	3.0	5.2	3.3	6.4	4.9	8.3
1978	2.5	4.9	2.5	5.0	2.6	4.4	3.9	7.1
1979	2.5	5.8	2.5	5.2	2.5	4.8	3.1	6.3
1980	3.6	7.8	3.3	6.6	3.1	6.0	2.5	8.8

Source: EIRP-81, Table A-30. Data for 1951–53 from earlier editions of the EIRP.

TABLE 8
Male Labor Force Participation Rates by Race and Age
(Percentage of Civilian Noninstitutional Population)

Year	Total, 16 Years & Over		16–17		18–19		20–24		25–34	
	Whites	Blacks & Others	White	Blacks & Others	Whites	Blacks & Others	Whites	Blacks & Others	Whites	Blacks & Others
1954	85.6	85.2	47.1	46.7	70.4	78.4	86.4	91.1	97.5	96.2
1955	85.4	85.0	48.0	48.2	71.7	75.7	85.6	89.7	97.8	95.8
1956	85.6	85.1	51.3	49.6	71.9	76.4	87.6	88.9	97.4	96.2
1957	84.8	84.3	49.6	47.5	71.6	72.0	86.7	89.6	97.2	96.1
1958	84.3	84.0	46.8	45.1	69.4	71.7	86.7	88.7	97.2	96.3
1959	83.8	83.4	45.4	41.7	70.3	72.0	87.3	90.8	97.5	96.3
1960	83.4	83.0	46.0	45.6	69.0	71.2	87.8	90.4	97.7	96.2
1961	83.0	82.2	44.3	42.5	66.2	70.5	87.6	89.7	97.7	95.9
1962	82.1	80.8	42.9	40.2	66.4	68.8	86.5	89.3	97.4	95.3
1963	81.5	80.2	42.4	37.2	67.8	69.1	85.8	88.6	97.4	94.9
1964	81.1	80.0	43.5	37.3	66.6	67.2	85.7	89.4	97.5	95.9
1965	80.8	79.6	44.6	39.3	65.8	66.7	85.3	89.8	97.4	95.7
1966	80.6	79.0	47.1	41.1	65.4	63.7	84.4	89.9	97.5	95.5
1967	80.7	78.5	47.9	41.2	66.1	62.7	84.0	87.2	97.5	95.5
1968	80.4	77.6	47.7	37.9	65.7	63.3	82.4	85.0	97.2	95.0
1969	80.2	76.9	48.8	37.7	66.3	63.2	82.6	84.4	97.0	94.4
1970	80.0	76.5	48.9	34.8	67.4	61.8	83.3	83.5	96.7	93.7
1971	79.6	74.9	49.2	32.4	67.8	58.9	83.2	81.5	96.3	92.9
1972	79.6	73.7	50.2	34.1	71.1	60.1	84.3	81.5	96.0	92.7
1973	79.5	73.8	52.7	33.4	72.3	61.4	85.8	81.8	96.3	91.7
1974	79.4	73.3	53.3	34.6	73.6	62.4	86.5	82.1	96.3	92.3
1975	78.7	71.5	51.8	30.1	72.8	57.5	85.5	78.4	95.8	91.4
1976	78.4	70.7	51.8	30.2	73.5	55.6	86.2	78.4	95.9	90.6
1977	78.5	71.0	53.8	30.8	74.9	57.8	86.8	78.2	96.0	90.4
1978	78.6	72.1	55.3	33.2	75.3	59.5	87.2	78.0	96.0	90.9
1979	78.6	71.9	55.3	31.7	74.5	57.8	87.6	80.1	96.1	90.6
1980	78.3	70.8	53.6	31.9	74.1	56.3	87.1	78.9	95.9	90.4

Year	35–44		45–54		55–64		65 years & over	
	Whites	Blacks & Others	Whites	Blacks & Others	Whites	Blacks & Others	Whites	Blacks & Others
1954	98.2	96.6	96.8	93.2	89.2	83.0	40.4	41.2
1955	98.3	96.2	96.7	94.2	88.4	83.1	39.5	40.0
1956	98.1	96.2	96.8	94.4	88.9	83.9	40.0	39.8
1957	98.0	96.5	96.6	93.5	88.0	82.4	37.7	35.9
1958	98.0	96.4	96.6	93.9	88.2	83.3	35.7	34.5
1959	98.0	95.8	96.3	92.8	87.9	82.5	34.3	33.5
1960	97.9	95.5	96.1	92.3	87.2	82.5	33.3	31.2
1961	97.9	94.8	95.9	92.3	87.8	81.6	31.9	29.4
1962	97.9	94.5	96.0	92.2	86.7	81.5	30.6	27.2
1963	97.8	94.9	96.2	91.1	86.6	82.5	28.4	27.6
1964	97.6	94.4	96.1	91.6	86.1	80.6	27.9	29.6
1965	97.7	94.2	95.9	92.0	85.2	78.8	27.9	27.9
1966	97.6	91.1	95.8	90.7	84.9	81.1	27.2	25.6
1967	97.7	93.6	95.6	91.3	84.9	79.3	27.1	27.2
1968	97.6	93.4	95.4	90.1	84.7	79.6	27.3	26.6
1969	97.4	92.7	95.1	89.5	83.9	77.9	27.3	26.1
1970	97.3	92.2	94.9	88.2	83.3	79.2	26.7	27.4
1971	97.0	92.0	94.7	86.9	82.6	77.8	25.6	24.5
1972	97.0	91.4	94.0	86.1	81.2	73.6	24.4	23.6
1973	96.8	91.3	93.5	88.0	79.0	70.7	22.8	22.6
1974	96.7	90.9	93.0	84.7	78.1	70.2	22.5	21.7
1975	96.4	90.0	92.9	84.6	76.5	68.7	21.8	20.9
1976	96.0	90.6	92.5	83.4	75.4	65.7	20.3	19.7
1977	96.2	91.4	92.2	82.7	74.7	67.0	20.2	19.3
1978	96.3	91.0	92.1	84.5	73.9	69.1	20.4	21.3
1979	96.4	90.9	92.2	85.5	73.6	66.9	20.1	19.6
1980	96.2	89.7	92.2	83.9	73.3	63.5	19.3	17.5

Source: EIRP-81, Table A-5.

Appendix: The Data

TABLE 9
Number of Males in Civilian Labor Force by Race and Age
(Number of Persons in 1,000s)

Year	Total, 16 Years & Over		16-17		18-19		20-24		25-34	
	Whites	Blacks & Others	Whites	Blacks & Others	Whites	Blacks & Others	Whites	Blacks & Others	Whites	Blacks & Others
1954	39760	4203	895	127	1094	178	2656	396	9695	1074
1955	40196	4279	934	135	1121	178	2802	419	9720	1085
1956	40734	4359	1003	140	1111	181	3034	450	9594	1090
1957	40821	4376	992	135	1115	175	3153	473	9483	1088
1958	41080	4442	1001	133	1116	180	3278	493	9386	1089
1959	41397	4490	1077	130	1202	188	3408	532	9261	1085
1960	41742	4645	1140	150	1293	203	3559	564	9153	1099
1961	41986	4666	1067	142	1372	210	3681	575	9072	1103
1962	41931	4668	1041	136	1391	201	3726	553	8846	1074
1963	42404	4725	1183	138	1380	206	3955	558	8805	1070
1964	42893	4785	1345	154	1371	205	4166	588	8800	1074
1965	43400	4855	1359	172	1639	226	4279	614	8823	1079
1966	43572	4899	1423	187	1831	244	4200	620	8859	1089
1967	44042	4945	1464	194	1727	249	4416	628	9101	1106
1968	44554	4979	1504	183	1732	262	4432	639	9477	1133
1969	45185	5036	1583	187	1830	271	4615	667	9773	1167
1970	46013	5182	1628	180	1922	275	4983	725	10088	1223
1971	46801	5220	1675	175	2038	272	5422	772	10390	1263
1972	47930	5335	1749	195	2220	293	5890	804	10940	1267
1973	48648	5555	1862	196	2297	310	6206	874	11478	1370
1974	49486	5700	1905	213	2387	319	6382	871	11946	1447
1975	49881	5734	1851	189	2413	307	6531	867	12345	1509
1976	50506	5853	1844	193	2483	311	6758	908	12813	1570
1977	51421	6028	1920	198	2541	326	6944	934	13251	1635
1978	52258	6284	1969	216	2556	337	7100	963	13570	1714
1979	53074	6443	1937	208	2555	331	7225	1013	14001	1791
1980	53627	6518	1841	210	2534	327	7267	1020	14445	1881

Year	35-44		45-54		55-64		65 Years & Over	
	Whites	Blacks & Others	Whites	Blacks & Others	Whites	Blacks & Others	Whites	Blacks & Others
1954	9516	997	7914	790	5654	451	2338	187
1955	9598	998	8027	813	5653	468	2342	183
1956	9662	1002	8175	827	5736	484	2417	185
1957	9719	1012	8317	836	5735	487	2308	170
1958	9822	1021	8465	855	5800	505	2213	166
1959	9876	1023	8581	849	5833	512	2158	163
1960	9919	1049	8689	884	5861	538	2129	158
1961	9961	1050	8776	891	5988	542	2068	151
1962	10029	1087	8820	895	5995	564	2082	159
1963	10079	1109	8944	891	6090	584	1967	168
1964	10055	1101	9053	903	6160	580	1943	181
1965	10023	1098	9129	916	6188	575	1958	173
1966	9892	1090	9189	912	6250	597	1928	162
1967	9784	1076	9260	929	6349	590	1943	175
1968	9661	1064	9340	927	6427	598	1980	174
1969	9509	1048	9413	931	6467	592	1995	175
1970	9413	1052	9488	929	6515	609	1977	188
1971	9286	1037	9530	927	6542	604	1918	170
1972	9261	1063	9479	943	6548	590	1841	181
1973	9187	1083	9454	977	6432	571	1733	175
1974	9213	1099	9467	984	6437	592	1749	176
1975	9190	1098	9431	995	6390	592	1731	176
1976	9241	1128	9327	995	6396	575	1643	172
1977	9453	1167	9195	996	6445	598	1671	174
1978	9794	1192	9091	1031	6454	632	1725	198
1979	10111	1226	8994	1057	6511	628	1740	188
1980	10377	1249	8905	1047	6553	611	1704	173

Source: EIRP-81, Table A-4. The total does not always equal the sum of the age categories because of rounding.

TABLE 10
Women and the Labor Market, by Race and Age
(Number of Persons in 1,000s)

Labor Market Status	Year	Total, 16 Years & Over		16–17		18–19		20–24		25–34	
		Whites	Blacks & Others	Whites	Blacks & Others	Whites	Blacks & Others	Whites	Blacks & Others	Whites	Blacks & Others
In Labor Force (Employed or Not)											
	1955	17886	2663	576	65	966	117	2137	307	3546	706
	1960	20171	3069	731	74	1112	139	2228	352	3441	690
	1965	22736	3464	862	92	1405	154	2910	454	3568	761
	1970	27505	4015	1194	129	1695	222	4246	628	4790	907
	1975	32203	4795	1484	167	2110	277	5296	772	7176	1280
	1980	38544	6029	1568	171	2290	302	6134	959	10017	1825
Not in Labor Force											
	1955	33917	3109	1353	221	890	154	2534	350	7260	670
	1960	35044	3300	1702	261	1030	175	2645	370	6656	697
	1965	36865	3666	2137	356	1374	231	3008	369	6258	648
	1970	37119	4095	2066	404	1386	274	3118	461	6305	667
	1975	37912	4956	1994	465	1382	336	2802	601	6228	804
	1980	36618	5253	1749	485	1228	357	2549	639	5459	807
Employed											
	1955	17113	2438	509	55	892	92	2030	267	3394	634
	1960	19095	2779	625	55	984	105	2067	298	3244	627
	1965	21601	3147	733	57	1217	111	2727	392	3394	698
	1970	26025	3642	1011	82	1493	149	3955	534	4536	836
	1975	29429	4124	1200	102	1770	171	4701	598	6568	1115
	1980	36043	5239	1297	102	1991	196	5611	750	9389	1600

Labor Market Status	Year	35–44		45–54		55–64		65 Years & Over	
		Whites	Blacks & Others	Whites	Blacks & Others	Whites	Blacks & Others	Whites	Blacks & Others
In Labor Force (Employed or Not)									
	1955	4131	673	3654	499	2156	235	720	60
	1960	4531	771	4633	645	2661	324	835	73
	1965	4876	844	5032	680	3203	383	879	96
	1970	5112	855	5781	750	3734	419	952	104
	1975	5535	957	5884	781	3800	444	917	116
	1980	7381	1220	6065	908	4076	515	1014	130
Not in Labor Force									
	1955	6211	530	4912	414	4615	343	6142	427
	1960	6387	519	4903	419	4688	363	7030	497
	1965	6119	567	5056	449	4751	400	8163	645
	1970	5140	571	4979	496	5026	470	9100	751
	1975	4546	593	4946	595	5534	569	10482	992
	1980	3968	570	4104	565	5853	629	11708	1200
Employed									
	1955	3976	636	3530	473	2079	222	703	58
	1960	4341	705	4448	608	2574	310	812	70
	1965	4678	779	4880	649	3118	369	856	93
	1970	4891	814	5582	720	3637	405	921	102
	1975	5172	875	5543	729	3607	421	868	112
	1980	7016	1125	5805	851	3949	491	984	124

Source: EIRP-81, Tables A-4, A-13, and A-29. The total does not always equal the sum of the age categories because of rounding.

Appendix: The Data

TABLE 11
Occupational and Wage Data

Year	Percentage of Employed Persons in White Collar Jobs		Median Income of Year-Round, Full-Time Workers		
			In 1980 Dollars		Blacks & Others Median
			Whites	Blacks & Others	as Percentage of Whites Median
1955	*	*	13471	8200	60.9
1956	NA	NA	14032	8389	59.8
1957	NA	NA	14270	8733	61.2
1958	NA	NA	14540	9145	62.9
1959	45.9	14.4	15241	8905	58.4
1960	46.6	16.1	15504	10248	66.1
1961	47.1	16.3	16023	10169	63.5
1962	47.7	16.8	16328	9744	59.7
1963	47.3	17.8	16808	10817	64.4
1964	47.6	18.8	17154	11248	65.6
1965	47.9	19.5	17764	11157	62.8
1966	48.3	20.9	18228	11446	62.8
1967	48.8	22.9	18522	12365	66.8
1968	49.5	24.4	19059	13070	68.6
1969	49.8	26.2	20124	13720	68.2
1970	50.8	27.9	20047	14086	70.3
1971	50.6	29.1	20147	14255	70.8
1972	50.0	29.8	21505	14922	69.4
1973	49.9	31.1	21880	15387	70.3
1974	50.6	32.0	20718	15573	75.2
1975	51.7	34.2	20260	15541	76.7
1976	51.8	34.6	20659	15167	73.4
1977	51.7	35.3	20911	15008	71.8
1978	51.8	36.2	20664	16348	79.1
1979	52.5	37.9	20447	15464	75.6
1980	53.9	39.2	19720	14727	74.7

Source for white collar data: EIRP, Table A-21. Source for income data: Current Population Reports, Series P-60, no. 132, Table 44.

*SAUS-66, Table 322, gives the following percentages for 1950 and 1955 respectively: whites, 40.3 and 42.1; blacks and others, 10.2 and 12.0. The comparability of these data with the 1959-80 series could not be determined.

TABLE 12
Enrollment in Educational Institutions

Year	Percentage of Persons 14–17 Years Old		Percentage of Persons 20–24 Years Old	
	Whites	Blacks & Others	Whites	Blacks & Others
1950	84.5	75.5	10.0	7.0
1951	86.3	77.1	8.8	6.2
1952	NA	NA	NA	NA
1953	86.4	82.3	11.9	5.4
1954	88.3	78.8	12.0	5.8
1955	87.5	82.8	11.6	7.2
1956	89.2	81.2	13.4	8.7
1957	90.1	84.8	14.7	8.8
1958	90.0	82.8	14.1	8.7
1959	90.8	85.3	13.4	8.5
1960	90.8	86.8	13.9	7.5
1961	92.0	86.9	14.4	9.1
1962	92.8	86.6	16.5	9.9
1963	93.3	90.4	18.3	10.2
1964	93.5	90.7	17.9	9.1
1965	93.4	91.7	20.2	10.2
1966	94.0	91.6	21.3	10.2
1967	94.1	90.8	22.9	15.4
1968	94.5	92.2	22.4	14.0
1969	94.3	92.4	23.9	16.7
1970	94.5	92.1	22.5	15.2
1971	94.6	93.6	22.4	19.0
1972	93.3	93.4	22.1	17.8
1973	93.0	92.6	21.3	17.3
1974	93.0	92.3	21.6	19.7
1975	93.8	92.6	22.7	20.6
1976	93.6	94.1	23.4	22.9
1977	93.5	94.6	22.7	24.0
1978	93.5	95.1	21.7	22.4
1979	93.5	93.9	22.0	20.0
1980	93.2	94.3	22.7	19.9

Sources: Figures for 1953–70 are taken from HSUS, H442–476. Figures for 1971–80 are taken from Current Population Reports, Series P–20, Nos. 241, 260, 272, 286, 303, 319, 333, 346, 355, and 362. Figures for 1950 and 1951 are computed from population and enrollment data in SAUS–51 and SAUS–52. The figures for 1952 could not be recovered from the published data.

Appendix: The Data

TABLE 13
Mean General Academic Aptitude Scores for a Representative National Sample of 9th-Grade Pupils in 1960 (Project TALENT), by Race and Sex

Ethnic/Racial Group	Males		Females	
	Mean	Std. Error	Mean	Std. Error
Whites	444	3	469	3
Blacks	300	6	319	5
Orientals	504	29	465	28
Mexican-Americans	378	19	374	13
Total	432		455	

(n = 23042, std. dev. = 115)

Source: Lauress L. Wise, Donald H. McLaughlin, and Kevin J. Gilmartin, The American Citizen: Eleven Years After High School, vol. II. (Palo Alto, Calif.: American Institutes for Research, September, 1977), pp. A-v and A-51.

TABLE 14
Median Achievement Test Scores for a Representative National Sample of 1st- and 12th-Grade Pupils in 1965, by Race

Test	Racial/Ethnic Group Medians			
	Whites	Blacks	Orientals	Mexican-Americans
1st Grade				
Nonverbal	54.1	43.4	56.6	50.1
Verbal	53.2	45.4	51.6	46.5
12th Grade				
Nonverbal	52.0	40.9	51.6	45.0
Verbal	52.1	40.9	49.6	43.8
Reading	51.9	42.2	48.8	44.2
Mathematics	51.8	41.8	51.3	45.5
General Information	52.2	40.6	49.0	43.3
Average of the 5 Tests	52.0	41.1	50.1	44.4

Source: James S. Coleman et al., Equality of Educational Opportunity (Washington, D.C.: Department of Health, Education, and Welfare, 1966).

TABLE 15
Armed Forces Qualification Test (AFQT) Scores for a Representative National Sample of 1980 Youth, by Race and Selected Characteristics

Characteristic	Racial/Ethnic Group Means			Total	
	Whites	Blacks	Hispanics	Mean	Std. Dev.
Age					
18–19 Years	51.40	22.96	28.99	45.96	27.14
20–21 Years	55.81	23.58	30.11	49.84	28.17
22–23 Years	60.26	26.26	34.58	54.25	28.30
Sex					
Male	56.58	23.87	33.54	50.80	28.77
Female	55.33	24.70	29.39	49.49	27.23
Educational Level					
Non–High School Graduates	32.99	12.83	16.15	27.13	22.66
High School Graduates	61.92	30.02	43.05	57.32	25.85
Mother's Education					
Eighth Grade or Less	35.28	16.53	24.21	29.05	23.79
High School Graduate	57.12	27.33	42.77	53.84	25.74
College Graduate or More	73.83	43.85	61.98	71.42	22.02
Region (Chosen for Contrasting Levels of Educational Expenditure)					
Middle Atlantic ($2,793/pupil)	58.40	25.98	27.18	52.04	24.84
West North Central ($2,126/pupil)	61.02	20.78	37.41	57.70	24.11
East South Central ($1,378/pupil)	47.40	22.49	*	42.07	24.03
Overall Sample Size	5,533	2,298	1,342	9,173	
Overall Mean AFQT Score	55.97	24.29	31.48	50.15	
Overall Std. Dev.	26.17	20.81	24.77	28.03	

Source: Profile of American Youth: 1980 Nationwide Administration of the Armed Services Vocational Aptitude Battery (Washington, D.C.: Office of the Assistant Secretary of Defense for Manpower, Reserve Affairs, and Logistics, March, 1982), Tables C-1 to C-5. Whites include all racial/ethnic groups other than black or Hispanic. The geographic groupings are as follows. Middle Atlantic: New York, New Jersey, Pennsylvania; West North Central: Minnesota, Iowa, Missouri, Nebraska, North Dakota, Nebraska, Kansas; East South Central: Alabama, Kentucky, Mississippi, Tennessee. Public school expenditures per pupil taken from SAUS-81, Table 257.

*Sample size too small to permit reliable estimates.

254

Appendix: The Data

TABLE 16
Distribution of 1980 Scholastic Aptitude Test Scores by Race
(Percentage of Students Who Took the Test)

Score	Verbal Component				Mathematics Component			
	Whites	Blacks	Orientals	Mexican-Americans	Whites	Blacks	Orientals	Mexican-Americans
750-800	.21	.02	.26	.03	.83	.04	2.37	.16
700-749	.96	.08	1.07	.18	2.40	.15	5.26	.50
650-699	2.13	.24	1.75	.58	5.04	.48	8.05	1.65
600-649	4.89	.82	3.74	1.51	8.77	1.20	11.08	3.31
550-599	8.34	1.66	5.95	3.66	11.79	2.33	12.34	6.00
500-549	12.74	3.53	8.53	6.54	15.87	4.92	14.74	10.47
450-499	17.09	6.30	12.33	10.82	16.75	8.05	13.84	13.73
400-449	18.87	10.04	14.01	14.38	14.74	12.10	11.82	16.07
350-399	16.85	15.77	15.08	19.40	11.95	18.88	10.03	18.46
300-349	10.88	19.56	13.74	18.26	8.37	26.84	6.84	17.78
250-299	5.37	22.15	11.73	14.81	3.06	19.88	3.00	9.85
200-249	1.66	19.84	11.82	9.84	.43	5.13	.65	2.03
N	720,010	76,888	27,495	14,169	719,891	76,880	27,512	14,167
Mean	442	330	396	372	482	360	509	413
Std. Dev.	103	95	122	101	111	90	125	104

Source: Profiles, College-Bound Seniors, 1980, an unpublished report prepared by The College Board, 1983.

TABLE 17
Median 1980 Scholastic Aptitude Test Scores by Race and Selected Characteristics

Characteristic	Median Score, SAT-Verbal				Median Score, SAT-Math			
	Whites	Blacks	Orientals	Mexican-Americans	Whites	Blacks	Orientals	Mexican-Americans
Father's Highest Level of Education								
Grade School	398	292	341	332	432	327	495	376
High School Diploma	412	305	361	362	454	334	473	397
Graduate or Professional Degree	469	386	455	418	516	398	551	452
Mother's Highest Level of Education								
Grade School	391	286	332	333	429	323	505	377
High School Diploma	417	308	369	371	462	336	494	408
Graduate or Professional Degree	465	372	447	414	507	386	530	451
Annual Parental Income								
Under $6,000	407	284	294	322	438	318	466	360
$24,000 - $29,999	437	350	415	392	485	373	521	433
$50,000 or Over	455	403	435	409	501	424	552	441
Type of School								
Public School	433	312	389	357	480	339	508	399
Nonpublic School	440	356	391	386	471	367	517	406

Source: Profiles, College-Bound Seniors, 1980, an unpublished report prepared by the College Board, 1983.

TABLE 18
Overall Crime Rates, Homicide Data, and Clearance Rates

| Year | Overall Crime Rate per 100,000 Persons | | Homicides per 100,000 Persons | | | | Percentage of Known Offenses Cleared by Arrest | |
| | | | Arrests | | Male Victims | | | |
	Violent	Property	Whites	Blacks & Others	Whites	Blacks & Others	Robbery	Burglary
1950	153.6	1567.3	*	*	3.9	45.5	43.5	29.0
1951	149.7	1625.8	*	*	3.6	41.3	40.3	29.1
1952	161.5	1635.8	*	*	3.7	45.4	36.0	26.7
1953	168.7	1661.8	*	*	3.5	41.3	39.7	26.8
1954	168.9	1681.8	*	*	3.5	40.6	40.6	29.6
1955	160.5	1661.2	*	*	3.4	36.9	42.8	32.1
1956	160.7	1854.5	*	*	3.3	37.1	NA	NA
1957	164.3	1982.5	*	*	3.2	36.5	42.6	29.6
1958	*	*	*	*	3.4	34.9	42.7	29.7
1959	*	*	*	*	3.5	35.0	42.5	30.7
1960	160.9	1726.3	3.5	42.4	3.6	34.5	38.5	29.5
1961	158.1	1747.9	3.3	35.7	3.6	33.6	41.6	30.0
1962	162.3	1857.5	3.4	38.9	3.8	35.5	38.4	27.7
1963	168.2	2012.1	3.2	35.7	3.9	35.7	38.6	26.9
1964	190.6	2197.5	3.2	36.2	3.9	37.4	37.0	25.1
1965	200.2	2248.8	3.4	41.4	4.4	40.1	37.6	24.7
1966	220.0	2450.9	3.6	43.8	4.5	43.7	32.4	22.0
1967	253.2	2736.5	3.8	49.0	5.3	49.9	29.8	20.3
1968	298.4	3071.8	4.1	56.9	6.0	55.1	27.4	19.4
1969	328.7	3351.3	4.4	64.3	6.1	58.7	26.9	18.9
1970	363.5	3621.0	4.9	65.0	6.8	60.8	29.1	19.4
1971	396.0	3768.8	5.0	72.9	7.3	67.5	27.5	18.8
1972	401.0	3560.4	5.3	69.4	7.6	69.7	30.0	18.9
1973	417.4	3737.0	5.6	62.2	8.2	65.3	27.2	17.6
1974	461.1	4389.3	6.5	71.2	8.8	66.5	27.3	17.6
1975	481.5	4800.2	6.3	54.7	9.0	61.9	27.0	17.5
1976	459.6	4806.8	6.2	56.7	8.2	55.1	26.9	16.8
1977	466.6	4588.4	6.3	54.8	8.6	52.8	26.9	16.3
1978	486.9	4622.4	6.5	53.9	9.0	51.7	25.9	15.6
1979	535.5	4986.0	7.0	48.9	9.9	56.2	24.9	14.6
1980	580.8	5319.1	7.2	48.3	10.9	57.8	23.3	13.8

Sources: Crime rates from 1960–1980 were taken from Federal Bureau of Investigation, Crime in the United States (Washington, D.C.: Government Printing Office, issued annually), Table 2 in the 1975 and 1981 editions. Crime rates from 1950–957 were computed from data in HSUS, H962–970 and A57–72. See note 2, chapter 8, for discussion. Homicide arrest data were taken from UCR data and converted to rates per 100,000. See note 1, chapter 8 for procedure. Homicide victimization rates are from Robert D. Grove and Alice M. Hetzel, Vital Statistics Rates in the United States, 1940–1960 (New York: Arno Press, 1976); Facts of Life and Death (Washington, D.C.: National Center for Health Statistics, 1967), Table 19; and printouts provided to the author by the National Center for Health Statistics. All homicide victimization figures are based on the same data and procedural bases. Clearance rates are from FBI, Crime in the United States, annual editions from 1950–80, for urban reporting agencies.

*Data are available, but not comparable with subsequent data. See note 2, chapter 8.

Appendix: The Data

TABLE 19
Number of Arrests for Index Crimes by Race and Age

Year	Total Arrests for Index Crimes				Arrests of Persons 17 and Younger				Arrests of Persons 18 and Older			
	Violent Crime		Property Crime		Violent Crime		Property Crime		Violent Crime		Property Crime	
	Whites	Blacks & Others	Whites	Blacks & Others	Whites	Blacks & Others	Whites	Blacks & Others	Whites	Blacks & Others	Whites	Blacks & Others
1960	39369	51081	280041	126861	*	*	*	*	*	*	*	*
1961	55628	50806	319825	133030	*	*	*	*	*	*	*	*
1962	46994	59572	351574	155551	*	*	*	*	*	*	*	*
1963	46990	57345	370326	162183	*	*	*	*	*	*	*	*
1964	52531	61070	409103	183640	*	*	*	*	*	*	*	*
1965	56285	69691	429973	208636	8767	15711	241986	113253	47518	53980	187987	95383
1966	61725	71335	456887	211928	10138	16007	264454	116773	51587	55328	192433	95155
1967	70974	86622	509273	251228	11884	20382	290236	135051	59090	66240	219037	116177
1968	77092	97369	528375	278217	13197	23374	299554	150550	63895	73995	228821	127667
1969	80720	109337	541298	299087	13830	26828	298152	156181	66890	82509	243146	142906
1970	96100	118803	640968	340272	15292	28442	315173	158303	80808	90361	325795	181969
1971	103128	136251	700794	358547	17548	32338	343051	160856	85580	103913	357743	197691
1972	115021	144816	700144	348700	20515	36248	365298	163400	94506	108568	334846	185300
1973	118541	132930	699120	330714	22346	32567	371133	157745	96195	100363	327987	172969
1974	135371	145574	830487	396486	26560	35292	440461	186008	108811	110282	390026	210478
1975	154384	134444	936551	397577	30444	31962	473835	171924	123940	102482	462716	225653
1976	153747	145977	893459	456529	30298	31842	438830	189533	123449	114135	454629	266996
1977	174673	161879	922145	462217	34827	37679	447967	192742	139846	124200	474178	269475
1978	225157	211616	1060881	549952	39645	51319	504690	229174	185512	160297	556191	320778
1979	221422	191614	1079790	509274	40882	43195	489490	200009	180540	148419	590300	309265
1980	210207	179058	1017703	482607	36123	41056	429523	176501	174084	138002	588180	306106

Source: For 1960–1973, data from FBI, Crime in the United States, annual editions. For 1974–1980, UCR data on agencies reporting for full year. See note 1, chapter 8.

*Data are available but not comparable with subsequent data because of changes in reporting procedures. See note 2, Chapter 8.

TABLE 20
Arrest Rates By Race

Year	Total Arrests for Index Crimes Relative to Size of Male Population Aged 13–39 (Arrests per 100,000)				Total Arrests for Robbery and Burglary Relative to Size of Male Population Aged 13–39 (Arrests per 100,000)			
	Violent Crime		Property Crime		Robbery		Burglary	
	Whites	Blacks & Others	Whites	Blacks & Others	Whites	Blacks & Others	Whites	Blacks & Others
1960	250	2529	1776	6281	84	754	545	1969
1961	328	2329	1887	6098	87	715	594	1979
1962	259	2519	1936	6578	85	830	580	2054
1963	248	2295	1951	6490	79	713	566	1953
1964	274	2384	2131	7170	78	721	592	2161
1965	275	2526	2099	7561	81	843	577	2293
1966	287	2485	2125	7382	77	842	584	2164
1967	318	2807	2280	8142	87	1044	660	2503
1968	340	3091	2332	8833	95	1202	689	2707
1969	359	3443	2405	9418	94	1390	682	2750
1970	393	3392	2619	9716	101	1419	713	2741
1971	404	3694	2744	9722	104	1557	755	2829
1972	431	3713	2624	8941	106	1569	733	2579
1973	456	3472	2691	8638	114	1417	782	2460
1974	548	3950	3364	10758	143	1689	981	3091
1975	570	3281	3457	9702	147	1325	1039	2692
1976	534	3307	3103	10342	131	1300	898	2680
1977	577	3443	3045	9831	147	1382	886	2617
1978	640	3823	3017	9935	143	1532	873	2673
1979	641	3479	3127	9248	150	1343	876	2430
1980	661	3485	3200	9394	159	1441	905	2485

Source: For 1960–1973, data from FBI, Crime in the United States, annual editions. For 1974–1980, UCR data on agencies reporting for full year. See note 1, chapter 8, for discussion of data sources and use of age ranges as a basis for estimating arrest rates.

Appendix: The Data

TABLE 21
Arrest Rates By Race and Age

Year	Arrests of Persons 18 and Over Relative to Size of Male Population Aged 18-39 (Arrests per 100,000)				Arrests of Persons 17 and Younger Relative to Size of Male Population Aged 13-17 (Arrests per 100,000)			
	Violent Crime		Property Crime		Violent Crime		Property Crime	
	Whites	Blacks & Others	Whites	Blacks & Others	Whites	Blacks & Others	Whites	Blacks & Others
1965	310	2723	1225	4812	171	2021	4711	14572
1966	322	2698	1203	4641	184	1951	4806	14234
1967	354	3017	1314	5292	210	2289	5128	15170
1968	378	3319	1355	5726	229	2540	5189	16362
1969	398	3672	1449	6360	242	2889	5208	16817
1970	442	3649	1782	7349	247	2772	5093	15429
1971	447	3977	1867	7566	275	3008	5381	14962
1972	469	3912	1663	6676	313	3224	5578	14531
1973	488	3666	1664	6317	357	2986	5924	14464
1974	577	4152	2069	7924	455	3429	7545	18074
1975	595	3445	2222	7585	486	2847	7562	15311
1976	553	3538	2038	8276	467	2680	6762	15953
1977	592	3583	2006	7774	525	3050	6749	15601
1978	670	3895	2007	7794	531	3613	6766	16136
1979	656	3586	2144	7472	584	3157	6992	14620
1980	679	3538	2293	7848	587	3319	6976	14267

Source: For 1960–1973, data from FBI, Crime in the United States, annual editions. For 1974–1980, UCR data on agencies reporting for full year. See note 1, chapter 8, for discussion of data sources and use of age ranges as a basis for estimating arrest rates.

TABLE 22

Victimizations Per 100,000 Persons by Race and Income Level, 1965–66 and 1979

Year	Type of Victimization and Race of Victim	Family Income in 1980 Dollars			
		0–$7829	$7,830–15,659	$15,660–26,099*	$26,100+
1965–66					
	Forcible Rape**				
	White	58	46	10	17
	Black and Others	111	60	121	NA
	Robbery				
	White	116	91	42	34
	Black and Others	278	240	121	NA
	Aggravated Assault				
	White	146	289	147	220
	Black and Others	389	420	121	NA
	Burglary				
	White	1310	958	764	763
	Black and Others	1336	1261	2056	NA
	Larceny ($130+)***				
	White	378	700	565	916
	Black and Others	501	300	363	NA

Year		0–$3419	$3,420–8,549	$8,550–11399	$11,400–17,099	$17,100–28,499	$28,500+
1979							
	Rape and Attempted Rape						
	White	314	168	118	127	72	65
	Black and Others	467	99	342	120	30	0
	Robbery						
	White	758	807	744	586	401	439
	Black and Others	1632	1455	905	1474	455	894
	Aggravated Assault						
	White	2183	1173	1377	971	910	678
	Black and Others	1819	1320	2038	1364	766	738
	Burglary						
	White	NA	NA	NA	NA	NA	NA
	Black and Others	NA	NA	NA	NA	NA	NA
	Personal Larceny with Contact***						
	White	474	385	257	220	182	230
	Black and Others	786	511	456	730	469	204

Source for 1965–66 data: Philip H. Ennis, "Criminal Victimization in the United States. Field Surveys II. A Report of a National Survey," President's Commission on Law Enforcement and the Administration of Justice (Washington, D.C.: Government Printing Office, 1967), p. 31. Source for 1979 data: Timothy J. Flanagan, David J. van Alstyne, and Michael R. Gottfredson (eds.) Sourcebook of Criminal Justice Statistics—1981 (Washington, D.C.: Government Printing Office, 1982), Table 3.12.

*Black and other data are for all families with income greater than $15660 (there were too few nonwhite respondents with incomes above $26,100 to maintain as a separate category).

**Apparently uses the UCR definition, which includes attempted rape.

***Note differences in larceny definitions for 1965–66 and 1979.

Appendix: The Data

TABLE 23
Arrest and Imprisonment Data

Year	Estimated Total Arrests for Index Offenses	Prisoners in State and Federal Institutions	Prisoners per 1,000 Arrests	Percentage of Population Covered by Agencies Reporting UCR Arrest Data
1950	*	166123	*	*
1951	*	165640	*	*
1952	*	168200	*	*
1953	*	173547	*	*
1954	*	182848	*	*
1955	*	185780	*	*
1956	*	189421	*	*
1957	*	195256	*	*
1958	*	205493	*	*
1959	*	207446	*	*
1960	918001	212957	232	54
1961	978718	220149	225	57
1962	1018102	218830	215	60
1963	1026355	217283	212	62
1964	1145387	214336	187	62
1965	1182422	210395	178	65
1966	1223657	199654	163	66
1967	1340833	194896	145	68
1968	1443218	187914	130	68
1969	1559939	196007	126	66
1970	1711090	196429	115	70
1971	1827268	198061	108	71
1972	1805612	196183	109	72
1973	1854929	204349	110	69
1974	2345004	218205	93	64
1975	2344360	240593	103	69
1976	2280883	263291	115	72
1977	2298478	278141	121	75
1978	2384272	293546	123	86
1979	2396262	301470	126	84
1980	2527265	314272	124	75

Source for computation of estimated total arrests: For 1960–73, FBI, Uniform Crime Reports, annual editions. For 1974–80, UCR data on agencies reporting for full year. See note 1, chapter 8.

Source for prisoner data: For 1950–70, HSUS H1135–1143; for 1971–80, SAUS–81, Table 330, and comparable tables in earlier editions.

Computation of estimated arrests and prisoners per 1000 arrests was based on unrounded data. For procedure and discussion, see note 2, chapter 13.

*Data are available but not comparable with subsequent data because of changes in reporting procedures. See note 2, chapter 8.

TABLE 24
Illegitimate Births, Overall and to Women 15 to 19 Years Old, and Family Headship

| Year | Illegitimate Live Births, Overall | | | | Illegit. Births to Women Aged 15–19 | | | | Percentage of Families Headed by Married Couple | |
| | Total Number | | Rate per 1000 Live Births | | Total Number | | Rate per 1000 Live Births* | | | |
	Whites	Blacks & Others	Whites	Blacks & Others	Whites	Blacks & Others	Whites	Blacks & Others	Whites	Blacks & Others
1950	54000	88000	17.5	179.6	NA	NA	62	358	**	**
1951	52800	93900	16.3	182.8	19725	37720	58	366	NA	NA
1952	54700	104100	16.3	183.4	NA	NA	58	384	NA	NA
1953	57307	112400	16.9	191.1	NA	NA	59	389	NA	NA
1954	62700	113900	18.2	198.5	23209	44005	63	400	NA	NA
1955	64200	119200	18.6	202.4	23843	46790	64	407	NA	NA
1956	68000	126000	19.0	204.0	25217	47604	63	405	NA	NA
1957	71000	131000	19.6	206.7	26897	49598	63	409	88.4	74.7
1958	75000	134000	20.9	212.3	28515	50903	66	419	88.6	73.4
1959	80000	141000	22.1	218.0	31185	55756	69	427	88.8	72.0
1960	82500	141800	22.9	215.8	32928	54139	72	422	88.7	73.6
1961	91100	149100	25.3	223.4	36175	57132	77	439	88.6	74.4
1962	94700	150400	27.0	227.8	36556	58099	79	455	88.8	72.3
1963	104600	154900	30.4	235.5	41024	61528	93	471	88.7	71.6
1964	114300	161300	33.9	245.0	45476	66222	103	468	88.6	73.6
1965	123700	167500	39.6	263.2	50840	72390	115	492	88.6	73.1
1966	132900	169500	44.4	276.5	57521	78242	124	501	88.8	72.7
1967	142200	175800	48.7	293.8	60151	83999	138	521	88.6	72.3
1968	155200	183900	53.3	312.0	67078	90547	157	549	88.9	69.1
1969	163700	197200	54.7	325.1	70044	97751	161	574	88.8	68.7
1970	175100	223600	56.6	349.3	79152	111038	171	613	88.7	69.6
1971	163800	237500	56.1	373.3	76120	118081	170	652	88.3	67.4
1972	160500	242700	60.4	402.6	78786	123655	182	678	88.2	65.7
1973	163000	244300	63.9	416.9	81043	123792	191	691	87.8	63.2
1974	168500	249600	65.4	427.3	84762	125058	202	713	87.7	63.9
1975	186400	261600	73.0	441.7	93641	127924	228	743	86.9	63.9
1976	197100	271000	76.8	451.5	97445	127404	248	770	86.8	62.9
1977	220100	295500	81.8	464.9	106861	132754	272	795	86.7	61.9
1978	233600	310200	87.1	475.6	108946	131211	285	803	85.9	59.3
1979	263000	334800	93.6	488.1	116400	136700	303	825	85.7	58.8
1980	320063	345684	110.4	484.5	127984	134793	330	821	85.6	59.3

Source: Primary source is Vital Statistics of the United States (National Center for Health Statistics), various editions. Number of illegitimate births (overall) for 1950 and 1956–59 taken from HSUS, B28–35. Source for married couple data: SAUS-81, Table 61, and comparable tables in preceding editions. The ratio of illegitimate births to total births among 15–19 year-olds for 1950–60 was taken from Robert D. Grove and Alice M. Hetzel, Vital Statistics Rates in the United States 1940–1960 (New York: Arno Press, 1976), Table 28. For 1979 and 1980, they were computed directly from figures in the Monthly Vital Statistics Reports. For 1961–1977, the percentage was computed indirectly from the published figures in the annual Vital Statistics volume for birth rate of married 15–19–year-olds, birth rate for unmarried 15–19–year-olds, total number of births to 15–19 year-olds, and (from Bureau of the Census P-25 series) the population of 15–19–year-old women.

*Rate per 1000 live births to women aged 15–19.

**Data available but not directly comparable to subsequent years because of differences in the data base.

Appendix: The Data

TABLE 25
Persons Living in Families Headed by a Female, No Husband Present, by Race and Income Level

Year	Persons in Poor Families Headed by a Single Female						Persons in Low-Income Families Headed by a Single Female					
	Numbers of Persons (in 1,000s)			As a Percentage of All Persons Living in Poor Families			Numbers of Persons (in 1,000s)			As a Percentage of All Persons Living in Low-Income Families		
	Total	Whites	Blacks & Others	Total	Whites	Blacks & Others	Total	Whites	Blacks & Others	Total	Whites	Blacks & Others
1959	7014	4232	2782	20.29	17.31	27.49	962	751	211	6.53	5.89	10.63
1960	7247	4296	2951	20.75	17.71	27.68	1147	935	212	8.14	7.63	11.60
1961	7252	4062	3190	21.01	17.11	29.64	NA	NA	NA	NA	NA	NA
1962	7781	4089	3692	23.14	18.08	33.53	NA	NA	NA	NA	NA	NA
1963	7646	4051	3595	24.27	19.15	34.74	NA	NA	NA	NA	NA	NA
1964	7297	3911	3386	23.61	18.88	33.21	NA	NA	NA	NA	NA	NA
1965	7524	4092	3432	26.53	22.11	34.84	1372	1006	366	11.37	10.26	16.17
1966	6861	3646	3215	28.82	23.63	38.37	1469	1002	467	12.49	10.77	19.00
1967	6898	3453	3445	30.29	23.25	43.50	1435	938	497	13.75	11.52	21.68
1968	6990	3551	3439	33.78	26.21	48.10	1531	929	602	16.36	13.05	26.86
1969	6879	3577	3302	35.87	28.34	50.40	1760	1022	738	18.77	14.88	29.46
1970	7503	3761	3742	36.91	28.23	53.40	1622	1036	586	18.24	15.41	27.00
1971	7797	4099	3698	38.21	30.22	54.07	1964	1182	782	20.58	16.36	33.72
1972	8114	3770	4344	41.45	30.73	59.43	1923	1196	727	22.28	18.13	35.72
1973	8178	4003	4175	44.69	35.08	60.62	1870	1061	809	22.78	17.54	37.42
1974	8462	4278	4184	44.97	35.12	63.05	2075	1180	895	25.09	19.80	38.76
1975	8846	4577	4269	42.55	33.17	61.07	2082	1221	861	22.30	17.20	38.45
1976	9029	4463	4566	45.99	35.70	64.02	1912	1083	829	22.56	17.45	36.55
1977	9205	4474	4731	47.19	36.19	66.25	2222	1234	988	25.63	19.80	40.53
1978	9269	4371	4898	48.63	36.27	69.85	1902	1110	792	25.39	19.74	42.40
1979	9400	4375	5025	47.08	35.01	67.28	2226	1134	1092	27.25	19.24	48.00
1980	10120	4940	5180	44.78	33.87	64.64	2181	1275	906	24.53	18.73	43.47

Year	Persons in Mid-and-Upper-Income Families Headed by a Single Female					
	Numbers of persons (in 1,000's)			As a Percentage of All Persons Living in Mid-and-Upper-Income Families		
	Total	Whites	Blacks & Others	Total	Whites	Blacks & Others
1959	6216	5530	687	5.33	5.01	10.92
1960	6436	5805	632	5.39	5.13	10.09
1961	NA	NA	NA	NA	NA	NA
1962	NA	NA	NA	NA	NA	NA
1963	NA	NA	NA	NA	NA	NA
1964	NA	NA	NA	NA	NA	NA
1965	7487	6462	1025	5.41	4.98	11.93
1966	8916	7616	1301	6.11	5.65	11.74
1967	9473	7739	1734	6.35	5.62	15.15
1968	9532	7727	1805	6.22	5.49	14.53
1969	9359	7698	1661	5.97	5.39	11.96
1970	10541	8418	2123	6.72	5.84	16.79
1971	10406	8225	2181	6.57	5.70	15.37
1972	11228	8790	2438	6.97	6.00	16.81
1973	11795	9241	2554	7.24	6.28	16.39
1974	12621	9960	2661	7.71	6.72	17.31
1975	12675	9788	2887	7.89	6.75	18.51
1976	13265	10391	2874	8.13	7.08	17.68
1977	13966	11031	2935	8.61	7.48	19.89
1978	14869	11384	3485	9.04	7.72	20.52
1979	15286	11815	3471	9.14	7.86	20.52
1980	15280	11441	3838	9.24	7.78	21.01

Source: Characteristics of the Population Below the Poverty Level: 1980, computed from data in Tables 1 and 2. For purposes of the table, "poor" is defined as below the official poverty line; "low-income" is defined as all incomes from 100 to 125 percent of the poverty line; "mid-and-upper income" (next page) is defined as incomes greater than 125 percent of the poverty line.

NOTES

Prologue

1. "The Boom Goes On," *Life* 28 (24 April 1950): 38.
2. " 'Separate But Equal,' " *New York Times*, 6 June 1950.
3. "War Seen a Threat to Some Freedoms," *New York Times*, 15 December 1950.
4. F. Emerson Andrews, "We Are in a New Era of Giving," *New York Times Magazine*, 10 December 1950.
5. "The State of the Union," *The New Republic* 122 (16 January 1950): 14.
6. Robert L. Heilbroner, "Who Are the American Poor?" *Harper's* 200 (June 1950): 27.
7. "Will We Make It?" *The New Republic* 157 (6 January 1968): 10.
8. "Robin Hood in Reverse," *Commonweal* 108 (10 April 1981): 196.

Part I

1. Figures are taken from the *Statistical Abstract of the United States* 1981 (Washington, D.C.: Bureau of the Census, 1982), table 518, which uses the *Social Security Bulletin* as its source. The *Statistical Abstract* will subsequently be abbreviated as *SAUS*. Figures for 1980 were obtained directly from the Office of Research and Statistics, Social Security Administration. Adjustments for inflation are based on the Consumer Price Index prepared by the Bureau of Labor Statistics.

Chapter 1

1. "Text of President's Message to Congress Seeking Reforms in Welfare Programs," *New York Times*, 2 February 1962.
2. The Poor Law Commission for the Poor Law Reform of 1834, quoted in Mark Blaug, "The Myth of the Old Poor Law and the Making of the New," *Journal of Economic History* 23 (June 1963): 152.
3. Jacob Panken, "I Say Relief is Ruining Families," *Saturday Evening Post* 222 (30 September 1950): 25.
4. Society for the Prevention of Pauperism in New York, *First Annual Report of the Managers* (New York, 1818), quoted in Blanche D. Coll, *Perspectives in Public Welfare: A History* (Washington, D.C.: Government Printing Office, 1969), 34.
5. In 1960, the mean number of children in families with a female householder, no husband present, was .85 for whites and 1.57 for blacks. The percentage of such families with four or more children was 5.0 among whites, 16.5 among blacks. *SAUS–81*, tables 71, 48.
6. Ray Moseley, "Detroit's Welfare Empire," *Atlantic Monthly* 205 (April 1960): 46.
7. *SAUS–81*, tables 98, 65.
8. Michael Harrington, *Fragments of the Century* (New York: Simon and Schuster, 1972), 88–89.
9. Peter F. Drucker, "Three Unforeseen Jobs for the Coming Administration," *Harper's* 221 (July 1960): 46.
10. Arthur Krock, "In the Nation," *New York Times*, 12 February 1960.
11. Charles Frankel, "A Liberal is a Liberal is a Liberal——," *New York Times Magazine*, 28 February 1960, 21.
12. Ibid, 83.
13. "Relief is No Solution," *New York Times*, 2 February 1962.
14. Quoted in "Johnson Signs Bill to Fight Poverty; Pledges New Era," *New York Times*, 21 August 1964.

Chapter 2

1. U.S. Bureau of the Census, *Historical Statistics of the United States, Colonial Times to 1970* (Washington, D.C.: Government Printing Office, 1975), table F1–5. Hereafter, references to this source will be abbreviated as *HSUS*.
2. Quoted in *Time* 86 (31 December 1965): 64.
3. Ibid., 64, 67B.
4. In the card catalog of the Library of Congress, for example, under the heading of "poverty," these are the numbers of titles about American poverty by publication date:

1940–49	1
1950–59	1
1960–63	2
1964–69	89
1970–79	137

In all, one finds only four titles under "poverty" with a publication date during the twenty-four years from 1940 to 1963. Obviously, the holdings under the heading of "poverty" do not begin to exhaust the actual materials on the subject, but the proportions illustrate the relative interest in the topic over time.

266

5. Norman Podhoretz, *Breaking Ranks: A Political Memoir* (New York: Harper & Row, 1979), 75.

6. Arthur Schlesinger, *Kennedy or Nixon: Does It Make Any Difference?*, quoted in Podhoretz, *Breaking Ranks,* 101–102.

7. James T. Patterson, *America's Struggle Against Poverty 1900–1980* (Cambridge, Mass.: Harvard University Press, 1981), 94.

8. Michael Harrington, *The Other America* (New York: Macmillan, 1962).

9. Patterson, *America's Struggle,* 99.

10. John K. Galbraith, in *The Affluent Society* (Boston: Houghton Mifflin, 1958), had expressed a structuralist view of American poverty, but the message had been submerged in the attention given to his arguments about affluence and public goods. During the early 1960s officials within the Department of Health, Education, and Welfare, especially those around Wilbur Cohen, assistant secretary for legislation, were working on plans that foreshadowed the later reforms (Cohen himself became secretary of HEW under Johnson). See Patterson, *America's Struggle,* chapters 6–9, for an historical account of the rediscovery of poverty and the triumph of the structuralist approach during the 1960–65 period.

11. Podhoretz, who was in a transition from one end of the political spectrum to another, provides in *Breaking Ranks* an entertaining account of the period when *The Other America* was gaining attention.

12. See, for example, Stephen Thernstrom, "Is There Really a New Poor?" *Dissent* 15 (January/February 1968): 59–64.

13. Jeremy Larner and Irving Howe, eds., *Poverty: Views From the Left* (New York: William Morrow, 1968). The authors were writing these words in 1965, at the outset of the War on Poverty.

14. Quoted in "Idea Broker in the Race Crisis," *Life* 63 (3 November 1967): 75.

15. Published as *The Dark Ghetto: Dilemmas of Social Power* (New York: Harper & Row, 1965). The book also established the use of "ghetto" for the black inner city. Donald A. Cook, a psychologist who was associated with the War on Poverty from its inception, singles out the mimeographed version as being one of the key influences on planners as the War on Poverty first tackled the problems of urban blacks. (Donald A. Cook, personal communication, 1983).

16. The best-known exposition of this view is Frances Fox Piven and Richard A. Cloward, *Regulating the Poor: The Functions of Public Relief* (New York: Pantheon, 1971).

17. See, for example, Aaron Wildavsky, *Speaking Truth to Power: The Art and Craft of Policy Analysis* (Boston: Little, Brown, 1979), 103–105.

18. Martin Luther King, Jr., "The Role of the Behavioral Scientist in the Civil Rights Movement," *Journal of Social Issues* 24 (January 1968): 1–12.

19. *Newsweek* 66 (23 August 1965): 15.

20. The most ambitious of the assessments of white opinion at the time was undertaken as part of the staff work for the National Advisory Commission on Civil Disorders. The text draws from the findings in Angus Campbell and Howard Schuman, "Racial Attitudes in Fifteen American Cities" (Ann Arbor, Mich.: Survey Research Center, Institute for Social Research, 1968). See also data cited by King, "Behavioral Scientist," and H. Erskine, "Polls: Negro Employment," *Public Opinion Quarterly* 32 (Spring 1968): 132–53.

21. Nathan Wright, Jr., "The Economics of Race," *American Journal of Economics and Sociology* 26 (January 1967): 10.

22. "The Cry of the Ghetto," *The Saturday Evening Post* 239 (26 August 1967): 80.

23. Quoted in Daniel P. Moynihan, "The Professors and the Poor," in Moynihan, ed., *On Understanding Poverty* (New York: Basic Books, 1968), 33.

24. Ibid., 31. For a detailed and acerbic analysis of the ideology of the poverty issue, see Walter Miller, "The Elimination of the American Lower Class as a National Policy: A Critique of the Ideology of the Poverty Movement of the 1960s," in the same volume.

25. Amory Bradford, *Oakland's Not for Burning* (New York: McKay, 1968), 30.

26. This and subsequent figures on the HEW research and development budgets are computed from *HSUS,* W126–143, and *SAUS-80*, table 1065 (the total HEW research and development budget less the budget for the National Institute of Health).

27. Daniel P. Moynihan, *Maximum Feasible Misunderstanding: Community Action in the War Against Poverty* (New York: Free Press, 1969). It is revealing to read the other major histories and commentaries on community action in chronological order. Start with Robert J. Lampman, "Ends and Means in the War Against Poverty," in Leo Fishman, ed., *Poverty Amid Affluence* (New

Haven, Conn.: Yale University Press, 1966), then move on to Bradford, *Oakland's Not for Burning* (1968), Kenneth B. Clark and Jeannette Hopkins, *A Relevant War Against Poverty* (New York: Harper & Row, 1969), S.M. Miller and Martin Rein, "Participation, Poverty, and Administration," *Public Administration Review* 29 (January 1969): 15–25, Robert Levine, *The Poor Ye Need Not Have With You: Lessons from the War on Poverty* (Cambridge, Mass.: MIT Press, 1970), Louis A. Zurcher, Jr., *Poverty Warriors: The Human Experience of Planned Social Intervention* (Austin, Texas: University of Texas Press, 1970), and finish with Jeffrey L. Pressman and Aaron B. Wildavsky, *Implementation* (Berkeley, Calif.: University of California Press, 1973). The wonderful subtitle of the last is "How Great Expectations in Washington Are Dashed in Oakland; or, Why It's Amazing that Federal Programs Work at All, This Being a Saga of the Economic Development Administration as Told by Two Sympathetic Observers Who Seek to Build Morals on a Foundation of Ruined Hopes."

28. The account that follows is taken from Pressman and Wildavsky, *Implementation*, chapter 1.

29. "Urban Aid Kickoff," *The Wall Street Journal*, 25 April 1966.

30. Pressman and Wildavsky, *Implementation*, 2.

31. Bradford, *Oakland's Not for Burning*, 204–205.

32. "Urban Developer," *The New Yorker*, 44 (30 November 1968): 52.

33. *Los Angeles Times*, 16 March 1969.

34. Pressman and Wildavsky, *Implementation*, 5.

35. Orley Ashenfelter, "Estimating the Effects of Training Programs on Earnings," *Review of Economics and Statistics* 60 (February 1978): 47–57.

36. Nicholas M. Kiefer, "Population Heterogeneity and Inference from Panel Data on the Effects of Vocational Education," *Journal of Political Economy* 87 (October 1979): S213–S226.

37. See Joe N. Nay, John W. Scanlon, and Joseph S. Wholey, *Benefits and Costs of Manpower Training Programs: A Synthesis of Previous Studies with Reservations and Recommendations* (Washington, D.C.: The Urban Institute, 1971) for the early studies, and Charles Mallar et al., "The Short-Term Economic Impact of the Job Corps Program," in Ernst Stromsdorfer and G. Farkas, eds., *Evaluation Studies Review Annual, vol. 5* (Beverly Hills, Calif.: Sage Publications, 1980), 332–59, for the more recent ones.

38. I report the results in terms of the mean increase in earnings because that is the measure used, not because it is the best measure. A much more informative statistic would be a measure based on the job experience of individuals—for example, percentage of chronically unemployed persons who got and held jobs after completing the program. But almost all of the evaluations focus on the mean change in earnings. This does not make much difference, however, in reaching judgments about the effectiveness of the programs. As a few test calculations reveal, the small increases reported in the evaluations cannot be masking a major impact on job-acquiring and job-holding behavior. The changes in mean income are too small.

39. Only in the last few years have the technical evaluations started to take a close look at the interior of such programs—the individual human reactions that produced such meager results from the training programs. Even now the work is scattered and too often consists of a researcher administering a multiple-choice interview questionnaire to those program dropouts who can be located. By far the best look at the interior of a jobs program was written by a journalist, Ken Auletta, in *The Underclass* (New York: Random House, 1982).

40. Mallar et al., "Economic Impact," 334.

41. Tom Wicker, "The Right to Income," *New York Times*, 24 December 1967.

42. "U.S. Finds Only 1% on Welfare Lists Are Employable," *New York Times*, 20 April 1967.

Chapter 3

1. Thomas S. Kuhn, *The Structure of Scientific Revolutions*, 2nd ed. (Chicago: University of Chicago Press, 1962).

2. Daniel P. Moynihan, "The Professors and the Poor," in Moynihan, ed., *On Understanding Poverty* (New York: Basic Books, 1968), 20.

3. Theodore H. White, "Summing Up," *The New York Times Magazine*, 25 April 1982, 32 ff.

4. Quoted in Lewis D. Solomon and Judith S. Heeter, "Affirmative Action in Higher Education: Towards a Rationale for Preference," *Notre Dame Lawyer* 52 (October 1976): 45.

5. The key decision was *Gault* v. *Arizona*, 1967.

6. Quoted in Laurence E. Lynn, Jr., "A Decade of Policy Developments in the Income Maintenance System," in Robert H. Haveman, ed., *A Decade of Federal Antipoverty Programs: Achievements, Failures, and Lessons* (New York: Academic Press, 1977), 101.

7. The most entertaining account is Daniel P. Moynihan, *The Politics of a Guaranteed Income: The Nixon Administration and the Family Assistance Plan* (New York: Random House, 1973). See also Vincent J. Burke and Vee Burke, *Nixon's Good Deed: Welfare Reform* (New York: Columbia University Press, 1974), and Walter Williams, "The Continuing Struggle for a Negative Income Tax: A Review Article," *Journal of Human Resources* 10 (Fall 1975): 427–44.

8. Nathan Glazer, *Ethnic Dilemmas 1964–1982* (Cambridge, Mass.: Harvard University Press, 1983), 3.

9. The definition of a qualifying disability is "the inability to engage in any substantial gainful activity by reason of any medically determinable physical or mental impairment which can be expected to result in death or which has lasted or can be expected to last for a continuous period of not less than 12 months." Quoted in Donald O. Parsons, "Racial Trends in Male Labor Force Participation," *American Economic Review* 70 (December 1980), 913. See also Parsons, "The Decline in Male Labor Force Participation," *Journal of Political Economy* 88 (February 1980), 117–34.

10. *Social Security Bulletin* 44 (November 1981), table M–3. Figures include dependents.

11. *SAUS–81*, tables 3 and 528.

12. A variety of factors were at work—a greatly increased number of applications by persons potentially qualified for benefits, higher proportions of allowed applications, and reduced administrative review of disability determinations, to name just a few. For an analysis of the 1966–75 period, see Mordechai E. Lando and Aaron Krute, "Disability Insurance: Program Issues and Research," *Social Security Bulletin* 39 (October 1976): 3–17. For events in the last half of the 1970s, see Mordechai E. Lando, Alice V. Farley, and Mary A. Brown, "Recent Trends in the Social Security Disability Insurance Program," *Social Security Bulletin* 45 (August 1982): 3–14.

13. 1965 was the Food Stamp program's first full year of operation following its authorization in 1964. (Prior to 1964, it had existed as a pilot program.) Figures on participants are taken from *Social Security Bulletin* 45 (November 1982): table 24.

14. Figures are taken from the standard table on first-time enrollments in the statistical appendix of various issues of the annual *Employment and Training Report of the President* (Washington, D.C.: Government Printing Office). The report will henceforth be referred to as *ETRP*.

15. The increases in the post-Johnson era are even more spectacular if one includes Social Security, which underwent major growth in the 1970s because of increases in benefits and, especially, indexing of Social Security payments to the Consumer Price Index. Insofar as we are focusing on the working-age population, the change in the public aid budget is more appropriate.

16. In terms of percentages, which are less informative for our purposes than the real dollar increases, the assertion still holds. Johnson increased the Eisenhower/Kennedy (FY 1960–64) public aid expenditures by 82 percent, while Nixon (FY 1970–74) increased the Johnson expenditures by 121 percent.

Part II

1. The technical literature that uses racial breakdown is cited extensively in the subsequent chapters.

2. To take the other factors into account, it is necessary to have background information on the individuals in the sample. The Current Population Survey (CPS) conducted by the Bureau of the Census is the data base that comes closest to providing such a source over the last three decades—it began to identify the race of its respondents in 1954. But even the CPS has a number of limitations. Among others, we are limited to the published tabulations for the years before the data were put on public-use computer tapes. For topics in education and crime, we have no source at all that has collected socioeconomic information on the members of a large sample over the period 1950–80, or even a sizable chunk of that period.

3. *Money Income of Households, Families, and Persons in the United States: 1980*, Bureau of the Census, Current Population Reports, Series P–60, no. 132 (Washington, D.C.: Government Printing Office, 1982), table 3.

4. *Characteristics of the Population Below the Poverty Level: 1980*, Bureau of the Census, Current Population Reports, Series P–60, no. 133 (Washington, D.C.: Government Printing Office, 1982), table 1.

5. Why then use the term "black" in the text? Why not always specify "black and other" or perhaps "nonwhites"? The nomenclature is not a trivial issue. The question is, which term is more likely to mislead? "Black and other" or "nonwhite" entail two major types of misunderstanding. First, many people tend to think that such terms include the large Hispanic population. They do not. "Hispanic" (or Latino) is not a racial category and is not treated as such in government data. Hispanics are not included in "black and others." Second, the term "nonwhite" has a connotation of a mix of people of whom blacks are just one more group. But blacks constituted between 84 and 95 percent of the "nonwhite" population during the period 1950–1980, and the black data dominate the calculation of the mean. Deleting the "others" when it is possible to do so demonstrates that the statistic is changed by a small fraction of the "black and others" value. Thus my conclusion that, while "black" is imprecise, it conveys a more accurate impression than the terms "black and others" and "nonwhite." In the data tables and figures, the actual population ("black" or "black and other") is always specified, to avoid confusion in comparing those numbers with numbers in other sources.

6. Based on the CPS breakdown of the "others" in "blacks and others" for 1980; decenniel census data for 1950.

Chapter 4

1. Throughout the chapter, I use the device of posing common interpretations of the Great Society's effect on poverty. For a full-scale sympathetic presentation of some of these views, see John E. Schwarz, *America's Hidden Success: A Reassessment of Twenty Years of Public Policy* (New York: W.W. Norton, 1983).

2. To assess the trends in poverty, it will help to have some idea of the origins, definitions, and conundrums surrounding the measure of poverty.

Defining poverty was a prerequisite to waging war on it. A task force was assembled for this purpose within the Social Security Administration in 1963, and the result of its efforts was the definition that has been used since then, the one that is meant when politicians or newscasters or scholars cite the percentage of "people living in poverty."

Ideally, the task force wanted a definition of a minimal decent existence—adequate (but only barely) food, shelter, clothes, and amenities. But it ran up against a problem of subjectivity. No one knows what "adequate" means for housing or clothing or recreation. The single exception was diet. The task force reasoned that it could call on objective knowledge of basic nutritional requirements, integrate that knowledge with the realities of food preferences in the United States, and reach a dollar figure for the cost of a minimal-but-adequate diet.

The task force parlayed this one, relatively objective datum (which, predictably, has also been the subject of considerable controversy) into a definition of poverty by the elegantly simple assumption that the proportion of the typical family's budget spent on food is the "right" proportion. With this assumption, the task force would be able to determine a total budget for a poverty-level existence, even if it could not parse out the costs of each item within that budget.

The core calculation for the "poverty line" is simply $I = D/P$, where "I" is the number of dollars in income that equals the poverty line, "D" is the dollar cost of an adequate diet, and "P" is the "typical" proportion (from 0 to 1) of the family budget spent on food. Studies revealed that food costs accounted for approximately .33 of the typical American family's budget; therefore, an income at the poverty line consisted of an amount roughly three times $(1/.33 = 3)$ the cost of an adequate diet, adjusted for inflation and for a variety of family characteristics (mainly, size of the family and whether the family lives in a rural or nonrural setting). For a more detailed discussion of the history of the poverty line, see (among many choices) *The Measure of Poverty: A Report to Congress as Mandated by The Education Amendments of 1974*, U.S. Department of Health, Education, and Welfare (Washington, D.C.: Government Printing Office, April 1976). The dietary requirements were those established by the National Academy of Sciences–National Research Council in the Recommended Dietary Allowance. The cost was based on the Department of Agriculture's economy food plan originally developed in 1961. Mollie Orshansky, who was in charge of the development of the poverty measure, used a 1955 survey as the basis for the estimate that one-third of family (post-tax) income is spent on food. Note, however, that the one-third figure applied to the typical family, not to the typical low-income family. If, as seems extremely probable, low-income families spend a higher proportion of their income on food than do more affluent families, the effect is to inflate the estimate of a poverty-level income. That is, if low-income families typically spent 40 percent of their income on food, then the poverty level would be only $(1/.4 = 2.5)$ times the cost of an economy diet, rather than the $(1/.33 = 3)$ times the cost that was obtained by using the proportion associated with the average family.

The poverty definition has been attacked from all sides but continues to be used because, finally, it has a good deal of merit. The poverty line does not truly divide the "poverty-stricken" from the rest of us—the transition consists of a continuum, not a dividing line—but it gives us a common yardstick for talking about the issue. It is widely accepted, takes family size and inflation into account, and provides a consistent definition for examining income over time. Also, no one has proposed an alternative definition that has attracted widespread support.

Having noted its uses, we must remember some basic deficiencies of the poverty line measure. They continue to plague public debate about how many Americans are poor.

One of the easiest computational defects to fix is the definition's insensitivity to local differences in cost of living. Most things cost more in the South Bronx, for example, than they do in a small town in Iowa, even though both places are "nonrural."

A more important problem is almost impossible to fix: How does one capture the nonmonetary differences in quality of life between the South Bronx and that Iowa town? Even if we were to compensate for the differences in simple purchasing power, the environments are incomparably different, and lumping together two families, one from each place, because both are living "at the poverty level" is not necessarily a meaningful statement about their comparative well-being. Imagine, for example, how much money it would require to persuade the poor family in Iowa to move to the urban jungle—and vice versa, to persuade the family in the South Bronx to move to "the sticks."

Another charge leveled at the poverty line attacks the fundamentals: The poverty definition is based on *absolute* poverty rather than *relative* poverty. Commentators since Michael Harrington have acknowledged that the "poor" of the United States have been extraordinarily well-off compared with most of the rest of the world. Harlem in the 1940s, for example, had a per capita income that would have placed it fifth among the countries of the world. (See Edward C. Banfield, *The Unheavenly City Revisited* [Boston: Little, Brown, 1974, 127–47].) But, these critics argued, being better off than an Asian peasant is not much comfort when one lives in a society of the affluence of the United States. A distributional definition—the proportion of persons whose income was less than half the median income, for example—was said to be a superior way of assessing the number of people who are poor.

I do not analyze distributional data in the text. They are readily found in the standard income analyses of the Bureau of the Census. The Bureau of the Census annually publishes a volume on "Money Income of Households, Families, and Persons in the United States" as part of its Current Population Reports (series P–60). Longitudinal data for 1947–70 may be found in *HSUS*, G31–138. For a review of the quantitative literature on the relationship between federal policy and income distribution in recent years, see Sheldon Danziger, Robert Haveman, and Robert Plotnick, "How Income Transfer Programs Affect Work, Savings, and the Income Distribution: A Critical Review," *Journal of Economic Literature* 19 (September 1981), 1006–15. The results vary from study to study, but none points to a major shift in the income distribution profile of the nation.

Once poverty has been defined in terms of dollar income, it would seem simple enough to proceed with a head-count of who is poor and who is not. But a tricky question remains: What is to be included in the calculation of income that puts one above or below the poverty level? The answer to that question is shaped by cultural assumptions so embedded that they are not even recognized. We do not, for example, consider the possibility of combining the income of parents and their adult children in reaching a judgment about whether either parents or children should be considered impoverished. Other cultures would do so as a matter of course.

Apart from such culture-specific problems of deciding how to count income, we face the more prosaic one of finding out how much money people really have as opposed to what they say they have. We know from special studies of the problem that even legal income is underreported in interview surveys, including the Current Population Survey used by the Bureau of the Census to estimate poverty. The CPS data have shown steadily rising rates of nonresponse on income questions, from only 5.3 percent of the sample in 1948 to 11.2 percent in 1968 and to a whopping 27.9 percent in 1982. To cope with nonresponse, the Bureau of the Census uses an "imputation" procedure. A study by the Rand Corporation concluded that the imputation system understates non-reporters' income by 73 percent in 1980. Lee Lillard, James P. Smith, and Finis Welch, *What Do We Really Know About Wages: The Importance of Non-Reporting and Census Imputation* (Santa Monica, Calif.: Rand Corporation, 1982), 53. The Bureau of the Census has determined that the procedure imputes quite accurately (within a few percentage points) the amount of income that persons report to the IRS. (See Gordon Green and John Coder, "The March Current Population Survey Earnings Imputation System: An Explanation and Evaluation" [Paper presented at the meeting of the Census Advisory Committee on Population Statistics, Washington, D.C., 1 October 1982]). The problem, of course, is that earnings are known to be significantly underreported to the IRS as well. If the 73 percent figure obtained by the Rand Study is even close to accurate, the effects on estimates of persons living beneath the poverty line are substantial.

We also know that a huge underground economy exists, the income from which very seldom finds its way into admissions on an interview form. No one knows the size of the underground economy, although estimates of uncertain provenance are encountered in the daily press. For data and some sober interpretations, see Stanley L. Friedlander, *Unemployment in the Urban Core: An Analysis of Thirty Cities with Policy Recommendations* (New York: Praeger, 1972), 186–89. He estimates that in Harlem, about 20 percent of those not in the labor force and 18 percent of workers reported income that could not legally be accounted for. Even highly conservative assumptions about Friedlander's data indicate that more than 20 percent of total income in the Harlem area was illegal. Less conservative but still plausible assumptions drive the figure as high as 75 percent. See Banfield, *Unheavenly City Revisited,* 128–29, 319.

3. Figure 4.1 uses budget categories as reported in the *SAUS*'s annual table on Social Welfare Expenditures, By Source of Funds and Public Program. The total is calculated by summing the Public Assistance category (less Vendor Payments and Social Services, which were in kind) and Supplemental Security Income. These capture the cash programs that were most specifically intended for the poor, not total cash transfers (which include such general programs as government pensions and Social Security).

4. The contribution of the Johnson years is even more exactly a "fair share" than the text indicates. In 1966, the method for calculating the poverty line was changed. What would have been a large reduction of 1.6 percentage points from 1965–66 became a spectacular reduction of 2.6 percentage points, the largest single drop in the history of the poverty line. If the drop from 1964 to 1968 were based on a consistent measure, the Johnson years would have contributed about 4 percentage points out of a total drop of 15–16 percentage points from 1950 to 1968. Other revisions followed in 1974 and 1979. Data from *Characteristics of the Population Below the Poverty Level: 1980,* Bureau of the Census, Current Population Reports Series P–60, no. 133 (Washington, D.C.: Government Printing Office, 1982), table 1. The Current Population Survey (CPS) is conducted monthly by the Bureau of the Census. The augmented March survey is used to determine the poverty statistics.

5. Data in appendix, table 3.

6. It appears that the poverty-reduction power of economic growth diminished sharply at the turn of the 1970s. This finding is consistent across a variety of analyses, but a simple one will illustrate the general magnitude of the change. From 1950 to 1969, an increase in $100 (in constant 1980 dollars) in per capita GNP was associated with a reduction of .45 percentage points in the poverty level. From 1970 to 1980, the same increase in GNP was associated with a drop of .17 percentage points. For some reason, the poverty-reduction power of economic growth was about 2.6 times larger in 1950–69 than it was in 1970–80. These results are obtained from an ordinary least squares regression in which the independent variable is first difference in real GNP per capita and the dependent variable is first difference in percentage of population under the poverty line using the official measure of poverty.

7. This expectation would have been generally congenial to advocates of the "segmented labor market" or "dual labor market" theories that were in vogue in the early 1970s. For an excellent review, see Glen G. Cain, "The Challenge of Segmented Labor Market Theories to Orthodox Theory: A Survey," *Journal of Economic Literature* 14 (December 1976), 1215–57.

8. Timothy M. Smeeding, "The Antipoverty Effectiveness of In-Kind Transfers," *Journal of Human Resources* 12 (Summer 1977): 360–78, and Smeeding, "The Antipoverty Effect of In-Kind Transfers: A Good Idea Gone Too Far?" *Policy Studies Journal* 10 (1982): 499–522. For another analysis, see Morton Paglin, *Poverty and Transfers In Kind* (Stanford, Calif.: Hoover Institution Press, 1980). The generalizations I draw from Smeeding's analysis also apply to Paglin's.

9. The state of affairs represented by the percentage of net poor is ambiguous. It is by no means clear that a 1-percentage point reduction in official poverty and another one-point reduction when in-kind transfers are included mean the same thing. We must consider what it really means to survive on in-kind support; it is a style of life with uncomfortable parallels to being chattel of the company store. The economic point remains, however. As of 1980, the many overlapping and in-kind benefit programs had made it possible for almost anyone to place himself above the poverty threshold. If the ultimate criterion of social welfare policy is eliminating net poverty, the War on Poverty had very nearly been won. Martin Anderson made this point in *Welfare: The Political Economy of Welfare Reform in the United States* (Stanford, Calif.: Hoover Institution Press, 1978), chapter 1, as his "First Thesis." He argued that the time had come to worry about the efficiency of programs and how to eliminate dependency. Liberals pointed out with some relish that conservatives were now acknowledging the success of programs that would never have been passed if the conservatives had had their way.

10. The label "latent poverty" is my invention, but not the use of pretransfer income as a way of looking at poverty. Researchers at the Institute for Research on Poverty at the University of Wisconsin have calculated poverty levels before transfers (they call it poverty based on "pretransfer income" or sometimes "market" income) and I use their results. See for example Sheldon Danziger and Robert Plotnick, "The War on Income Poverty: Achievements and Failures," in *Welfare Reform in America* by Paul M. Sommers, ed. (Boston: Kluwer-Nijhoff, 1982), 31–52.

11. The number of latent poor is (by definition) larger than the number of official poor. The proportion of the population officially poor in 1950 was 30 percent. We know that the proportion of the population latently poor in 1965 (the first year for which we have figures) was 21 percent. Ergo, latent poverty declined from something in excess of 30 percent (probably between 32 and 35 percent) to 21 percent by 1965—a drop of at least a third. In figure 4.5, the numbers for latent and net poverty in 1950, 1955, and 1960 are estimated values. The procedure (more elaborate than necessary for our purposes, perhaps) is based on an ordinary least squares regression. For latent poverty, the calculation uses cash transfers (table 3, appendix) as the independent variable, and the gap between official poverty and latent poverty as the dependent variable. The Pearson correlation coefficient between the gap and cash transfers for the eight years in which the value of latent poverty is known is a nearly perfect .95. The estimated value of latent poverty in 1950, 1955, and 1960 is the sum of official poverty and the fitted value of the gap. A parallel procedure was used to compute net poverty for 1950–65, using noncash transfers (table 3, appendix) as the independent variable. The correlation was much lower, only .41, largely because the 1965 computation of net poverty shows a much larger gap with official poverty (5.2 percentage points) than the very small amount of in-kind benefits at that time (roughly $3.3 billion in 1980 dollars) would seem to warrant; in 1968, when in-kind benefits stood at $20 billion, the gap between official and net

poverty was only 2.9 percentage points. If the 1965 figure is deleted from the calculation, the relationship is reasonably strong ($r = .78$). The effect on the estimate of net poverty in the 1950s is probably to overestimate slightly the gap during that period.

12. Can the increase in latent poverty be attributed to an increase in the elderly? It seems more likely that the opposite is true. The evidence on this point is fragmentary but extremely provocative. In 1977, the Congressional Budget Office (CBO) conducted a study, *Poverty Status of Families Under Alternative Definitions of Income*, Background Paper no. 17, revised, June 1977) that included a pretransfer estimate of poverty—what I am calling latent poverty. The CBO study shows that, using 1976 CPS data, latent poverty stood at 27.0 percent of all families. If the families with a householder (formerly "head of household") of 65 or over were excluded, the percentage was 18.6. In other words, the overall figure for latent poverty was 45.2 percent greater than the figure for latent poverty among the working-aged population. In 1983, the Bureau of the Census conducted its own analysis of pretransfer poverty. This analysis revealed that in 1982 latent poverty overall stood at 21.8 percent of persons, whereas latent poverty among the working-aged population was 18.1 percent. In other words, the overall figure was only 20.4 percent greater than the working-aged figure. Because the 1976 analysis used families as the unit for reporting and the 1982 analysis used persons, the percentages of latent poor in 1976 and 1982 are not comparable, and it may be that the elderly and working-aged relationship within years is affected by the choice of unit (person or family). Dogmatic conclusions are not in order. A very conservative interpretation is that the slope of the rising trendline in latent poverty through 1980 was not inflated by the elderly population. More speculatively, the evidence suggests that the rise in latent poverty between 1976 and 1982 was steeper among the working-aged than among the elderly. The 1982 results are taken from unpublished data prepared by the Population Division of the Bureau of the Census.

13. *ETRP–81*, table A–1.

14. See, for example, Peter Gottschalk and Sheldon Danziger, "Macroeconomic Conditions, Income Transfers, and the Trend in Poverty," paper presented at the Urban Institute Conference "An Assessment of Reagan's Social Welfare Policy," Washington, D.C., 28–29 July 1983.

Chapter 5

1. *ETRP*, various editions, using the total figure for "work and training programs administered by the Department of Labor" (for example, in *ETRP–81*, table F–1).

2. The aggregate expenditures of the National Aeronautics and Space Administration from 1958 through FY 1969, in constant 1980 dollars, were $84.1 billion. The figure for the jobs programs from 1965 to 1980 was $85.5 billion. When one compares the technological and industrial spinoffs created by the space program with the gloomy evaluations of the jobs programs, one is inclined to conclude that NASA, in addition to its other accomplishments, was much more effective at creating jobs than the jobs programs were.

3. *ETRP–81*, table 2, 27.

4. Throughout the discussion in the text, the terms "unemployment" and "labor force participation" are used as defined by the federal government.

The unemployment rate is estimated monthly through the Current Population Survey of the Bureau of the Census. An "unemployed person" is defined as one who did not work during the survey week, who made specific efforts to find a job within the past four weeks, and who was available for work during the survey week; alternatively, one could be considered "unemployed" if he were waiting to be called back to an old job or to report to a new one within thirty days.

The monthly rate is computed as the percentage of unemployed persons in the the the labor force. The annual unemployment rate which we shall be using is the average of the monthly rates. Full and consistent data (by race and age group) are available for the 1951–80 period and are drawn here from the statistical appendix of *ETRP–81*.

Participation in the labor force means that a person is at least sixteen years old and available for work in a job outside the home: either employed or "unemployed" as just defined. The total labor force includes members of the armed forces. The most commonly used statistic of labor force participation and the one used here is based on the civilian noninstitutional population. Comments about the unemployment data apply to LFP as well: data are collected through the CPS, and *ETRP* is the data source used here. The population age limit was changed from fourteen to sixteen in 1966; all data presented here consistently apply the sixteen-year-old limit to the 1950–65 data. Full data are available from 1954; data on black LFP from 1950 to 1953 were obtained from the 1964 edition of the *ETRP* (then called *Manpower Report of the President*).

5. In a five-year moving average as plotted, the point for 1960 represents the average unemployment rate for 1960 and the two adjacent years on each side (1958–62).

6. John F. Cogan, "The Decline in Black Teenage Employment, 1950–70," *American Economic Review* 72 (September 1982): 621–38.

7. Among older workers, the story is happier—with qualifications. Beginning in the late 1950s, black males from the ages of 25 to 44 experienced marked, sometimes dramatically rapid progress in achieving employment parity with whites. From the late 1950s to the turn of the 1970s, the average ratios dropped by about a third for black males in the 25–34 and 35–44 age groups. The reductions are based on the mean ratios for the 1955–59 and 1968–72 periods. The changes were from 3.0 to 2.0 for the 25–34-year-olds, and from 2.8 to 1.8 for the 35–44-year-olds. The older age groups experienced large improvements as well, beginning somewhat later. But all the age groups, like the job entrants, lost ground during the 1970s.

8. *SAUS–67*, table 316. The projected rates are shown as a percentage of the entire population, whereas actual rates (as reported in the text) are a percentage of the population sixteen years and older. The actual and projected trendlines may be compared, but not the actual and projected rates.

9. *The Social and Economic Status of the Black Population in the United States: An Historical View, 1790–1978*, Bureau of the Census, Current Population Reports: Special Studies, Series P–23, no. 80 (Washington, D.C.: Government Printing Office, n.d.), tables 41 and 42.

10. Joseph D. Mooney, "Urban Poverty and Labor Force Participation," *American Economic Review* 57 (March 1967), 104–19.

11. A number of other hypotheses are available to explain why young black males participated at lower rates, and they are the center of attention in part III. I am concerned at this point with hypotheses that, in effect, explain why the lower participation rates are a mirage —that suggest the LFP statistic is misleading.

12. *SAUS–80*, table 229.

13. For males of all races in 1970, student LFP was 39 percent, 41 percent, and 51 percent for the 16–17, 18–19, and 20–24 age groups, respectively. For persons not in school, LFP for the same three groups was 76 percent, 87 percent, and 95 percent. *ETRP–81*, table B–9. A racial breakdown is not available.

14. Martin Feldstein, "The Retreat from Keynesian Economics," *The Public Interest* no. 64 (Summer 1981): 94. See also Feldstein's "The Economics of the New Unemployment," *The Public Interest* no. 33 (Fall 1973): 3–42.

Chapter 6

1. Employment in a white-collar job means that the job was classified as "professional and technical," "managers and administrators, except farm," "salesworkers," or "clerical workers" in the federal government's occupational classification system. An annual racial breakdown did not begin until 1959. Data are from table A–21 in the *ETRP*. Median income of year-round full-time workers refers to total money income ("the algebraic sum of money wages and salaries, net income from self-employment, and income other than earnings") of

persons who "worked primarily at full-time civilian jobs for 50 weeks or more" during the year in question. Definitions are from *Money Income of Households, Families, and Persons in the United States: 1980*, Bureau of the Census, Current Population Reports, series P–60, no. 132 (Washington, D.C.: Government Printing Office, 1982), 222 and 225. Data are taken from table 44 of the same publication.

2. Diane N. Westcott, "Blacks in the 1970s: Did They Scale the Job Ladder?" *Monthly Labor Review* 104 (June 1982): 31. For those who use the March Current Population Survey for such analyses, be it noted that the data Westcott presents (the data used by the Bureau of Labor Statistics) are taken from the Basic Survey Form (CPS–1) of the Current Population Survey and show higher ratios than the data from the March CPS, because the monthly survey captures earnings-while-working with less confounding with unemployment than does the March CPS. Because black unemployment is so much higher than white unemployment, the BLS figures are a more accurate representation of the remaining wage discrimination problem, as distinct from the combination of wage and employment discrimination.

3. Michael K. Brown and Stephen P. Erie, "Blacks and the Legacy of the Great Society: The Economic and Political Impact of Federal Social Policy," *Public Policy* 12 (Summer 1981): 308.

4. Before we leave the occupational indicators, a final important reminder needs to be added. The discussion has referred solely to employed persons, not to all persons in the labor force or all persons in the population. The temptation is to trace a chain that goes something like this: White-collar workers have much lower unemployment rates than blue-collar and service workers (true), and many more blacks have moved into white-collar jobs (true), therefore black employment must be improving (false). The trick in interpreting the generally positive results lies in remembering that they have nothing to do with the unemployment problem or the nonparticipation problem. Restricting our inquiry to "employed persons" helps to answer one quite specific, pertinent question: Among black persons who find employment, what kinds of jobs do they find? The situation for such persons was far different, and better, in 1980 than in 1950.

5. Westcott, "Blacks in the 1970s," 36.

6. Richard B. Freeman, "Black Economic Progress Since 1964," *The Public Interest* no. 52 (Summer 1978): 54. See also Freeman, *Black Elite: The New Market for Highly Educated Black Americans* (New York: McGraw Hill, 1977).

7. For an account of the Dunbar story, which may well provide some hints for retrieving inner-city education, see Thomas Sowell, "Black Excellence: The Case of Dunbar High School," *The Public Interest* no. 35 (Spring 1974): 1–21.

8. Otis Dudley Duncan, "Inheritance of Poverty or Inheritance of Race," in Daniel P. Moynihan, ed., *On Understanding Poverty* (New York: Basic Books, 1968). See also Robert M. Hauser and David L. Featherman, "Racial Inequalities and Socioeconomic Achievement in the United States, 1962–1973," Institute for Research on Poverty Discussion Paper no. 275–75 (Madison, Wis.: University of Wisconsin, 1975).

9. Christopher Jencks et al., *Inequality: A Reassessment of the Effect of Family and Schooling in America* (New York: Basic Books, 1972; Harper Colophon edition, 1973), 218.

10. Ibid., 218.

11. Finis Welch, "Black-White Differences in Returns to Schooling," *American Economic Review* 63 (December 1973): 893–907. The data are taken from Table 1, 897, and report the direct increment to 1966 income as estimated from the Survey of Economic Opportunity.

12. See Saul D. Hoffman, "Black-White Life-Cycle Earnings Differences and the Vintage Hypothesis: A Longitudinal Analysis," *American Economic Review* 69 (December 1979): 855–67, and James P. Smith and Finis Welch, "Race Differences in Earnings: A Survey and New Evidence," R–2295–NSF (Santa Monica, Calif.: Rand Corporation, March 1978). For earlier bouts in the dispute, see G. Hanoch, "An Economic Analysis of Earnings and Schooling," *Journal of Human Resources* 2 (Summer 1967): 319–29; Charles Link and Edward Ratledge, "Social Returns to Quality and Quantity of Education: A Further Statement," *Journal of Human Resources* 10 (Winter 1975): 78–89; Link, Ratledge, and K. Lewis, "Black-White Differences in Returns to Schooling: Some New Evidence," *American Economic Review* 66 (March 1976): 221–23; and T. Kniesner, A. Padilla, and S. Polachek, "The Rate of Return to Schooling and the Business Cycle," *Journal of Human Resources* 13 (Spring 1978): 264–77. One of the more vocal criticisms of the optimism is Robert B. Hill, *The Widening Economic Gap* (Washington, D.C.: National Urban League Research Department, 1979). Hill's conclusion was based, however, on a

recessionary period in the early 1970s. For a Marxist interpretation of returns to education as a function of class rather than race, see Erik Olin Wright, "Race, Class, and Income Inequality," *American Journal of Sociology* 83 (May 1978): 1368–97.

13. Westcott, "Blacks in the 1970s," 36.

14. Edward Lazear, "The Narrowing of Black-White Wage Differentials is Illusory," *American Economic Review* 69 (September 1979): 553–64. Lazear seems generally more alarmist about the problem than the data would seem to warrant. See, for example, Greg J. Duncan and Saul Hoffman, "On-the-Job Training and Earnings Differentials by Race and Sex," *Review of Economics and Statistics* 61 (November 1979): 594–603, in which they find, as did Lazear, that whites get more on-the-job training than blacks, but that the returns to OJT were as great for blacks as for whites. The lower levels of black OJT are not easily explained as reflecting an intent to discriminate on the part of the employer; one would have to develop a theory in which employers discriminate in the decision to provide OJT, but not in the salary increases that follow from OJT.

15. In Larry Lyon and Troy Abell, "Male Entry into the Labor Force: Estimates of Occupational Rewards and Labor Market Discrimination," *Sociological Quarterly* 21 (Winter 1980): 81–92, Lyon and Abell compare findings from an analysis of NLS data with earlier studies to demonstrate a pattern of decline in the role played by racial discrimination when controls for labor market experience are introduced. See also the earlier studies they cite, Michael D. Ornstein, *Entry into the American Labor Force* (New York: Academic Press, 1976) and William T. Bielby, Robert Hauser, and David Featherman, "Response Errors of Black and Nonblack Males in Models of Intergenerational Transmission of Socioeconomic Status," *American Journal of Sociology* 82 (May 1977): 1242–88. They conclude that returns to education for blacks are better than even data like Welch's indicate, because of response error: "by ignoring measurement error we have been systematically *under*estimating the degree to which schooling is converted into occupational successes, by about 15 percent for nonblacks and probably by much more than that for blacks" (p. 1277; emphasis in the original). This is not to say that the racism hypothesis is dead. See, for example, William A. Darity, Jr.'s critique of the human capital approach, "The Human Capital Approach to Black-White Earnings Inequality: Some Unsettled Questions," *Journal of Human Resources* 17 (Winter 1982): 72–93, in which he argues that the accepted theoretic schemes do not give adequate play for "a dominant role for outright racial discrimination" in explaining income inequalities (p. 90).

16. Martin Kilson, "Black Social Classes and Intergenerational Poverty," *The Public Interest* no. 64 (Summer 1981): 64–68.

Chapter 7

1. The National Commission on Excellence in Education, *A Nation at Risk: The Imperative for Educational Reform* (Washington, D.C.: Government Printing Office, 1983), 5.

2. *DES–81*, tables 161 and 163. The figure for elementary and secondary education refers to the budget under the line item "Educationally deprived/economic opportunity programs" under "Elementary and secondary education." The loans and grants are totals from the student loan program of the NDEA and the Educational Opportunity Grants.

3. The measure of the percentage of an age cohort in school, based on the Current Population Survey of the Bureau of the Census, provides the most consistent indicator over the entire period 1950–80. Other commonly used indicators, such as percentage of persons with a high-school degree and mean years of schooling, are based on the entire population, including those who were in school decades earlier—another form of the "vintage effect" observed in the analysis of black earnings. The numbers in the CPS data relating to 14–17-year-olds probably include a number of part-time students, or those who were in school and were the right age to be in high school but were in some other grade. Such is the implication of a comparison with Department of Education statistics gathered from the state school systems (*DES–81*, table 38, 49), which indicate that in 1949–50 only 77 percent of the

14–17-year-old population was enrolled, compared with the CPS figure of 82 percent for October 1949. It was not until 1965 that the two figures finally converged. The figures for 18–19-year-olds show a similar story—one of the reasons that I chose to represent college enrollment by 20–24-year-olds rather than 18–19-year-olds. In general, the 20–24-year-old age group shows a cleaner estimate of students in college (as opposed to vocational training), and likely to complete college, than the 18–19-year-olds.

4. Finis Welch, "Black-White Differences in Return to Schooling," *American Economic Review* 63 (December 1973), 900.

5. From 1977 to 1980, I directed the evaluation of the "Cities in Schools" program, a federal demonstration program to provide intensive social and educational services to students in inner-city schools. The schools studied most intensively as part of the evaluation served predominantly black, low-income students in Harlem, the South Bronx, Atlanta, and Indianapolis. The statements about absences and cuts are based on our findings when we compared actual time in-school with the official records. For further information about the program, see Charles A. Murray et al., *National Evaluation of the Cities in Schools Program: Final Report* (Washington, D.C.: National Institute of Education, 1981).

6. National Commission on Excellence in Education, *A Nation at Risk,* 8–23 passim.

7. Paul Copperman, quoted in *A Nation at Risk,* 11.

8. Welch, "Black-White Differences," 904.

9. Ibid., 905.

10. Ibid., Table 4, 902. Test performance improved very slightly for the third-graders through 1969. For the sixth-graders, the improvement stopped and reversed between the 1965 and 1969 testing periods. Students from predominantly white schools followed a similar pattern, except that reading scores for the third-graders as well as the sixth-graders declined in 1969 compared with 1965. Welch emphasizes that the black-white gap narrowed through the 1969 data—which is true, but only because white sixth-grade scores fell even more than black sixth-grade scores, hardly the way that we intended to diminish the white-black achievement discrepancy.

11. The seven tests were English usage, reading comprehension, mathematical achievement (the three most heavily weighted components), vocabulary, mathematical knowledge, abstract reasoning, and creativity. There has been a veritable library of volumes produced from the TALENT data. The data on black-white GAA scores are taken from Lauress L. Wise, Donald H. McLaughlin, and Kevin J. Gilmartin, *The American Citizen: Eleven Years after High School* (Palo Alto, Calif.: American Institutes for Research, 1977), A–v, A–51. The source includes a description of the technical characteristics of the sample and corrections for nonresponse bias (pp. 4–13). The data reported in the text are from a representative subsample of persons for whom racial identification was obtained. Sample size: 23,042. See appendix, table 13, for additional data.

12. James S. Coleman et al., *Equality of Educational Opportunity,* (Washington, D.C.: U.S. Department of Health, Education, and Welfare, Office of Education, 1966). See appendix, table 14, for additional data.

13. Put very briefly, the standard deviation is a measure of the variability of the scores. For example, if 100 students all score between 40 and 60 points on a test, the standard deviation is much smaller than that for a test in which the students' scores range between 10 and 90. If the difference between the black mean score and the white mean score was 25 points and the standard deviation for that test was 75 points, then we may express the black-white difference as being .33 standard deviations. To determine the standard deviation, compute the square of the difference between each score and the mean score, sum the squared differences, divide the sum by the number of scores, and take the square root of the result.

14. A noted psychologist in the early 1920s imputed to innate stupidity the low scores of recent immigrants on a multiple-choice test that consisted of questions like: "Crisco is a: patent medicine, disinfectant, toothpaste, food product." (Quoted in Stephen Jay Gould, *The Mismeasure of Man* [New York: W.W. Norton, 1981], 200.) When black test scores became an educational hot potato in the late sixties, this kind of history gave mental tests a bad name and put a cloud of "cultural bias" over every report of differences between white and black test scores.

The question raised by cultural bias may be stated colloquially as follows: Do items (or entire tests) give false readings of the "thing they are intended to measure" because of extraneous material set to a cultural norm? Suppose, for example, that a test intending to measure verbal aptitude uses vocabulary which the test-taker would not ordinarily have encountered in his cultural milieu. The score will be misleading—the test-taker did not have a fair chance to demonstrate his verbal aptitude. Cultural bias may be demonstrated.

Now consider a more complicated case. In this example, the item uses vocabulary common to all, but it is an "analogy" item—the student is asked to fill in the blank in a sentence such as, "Small is to large as a minute is to ———," given multiple-choice answers. Cultural bias can easily contaminate such questions. For example, an analogy item in an early test intended to measure innate intelligence was "Washington is to Adams as first is to ———"—easy if one knows a little American history, ambiguous if one knows a little more American history, and pure guesswork if one knows no American history (quoted in Gould, *Mismeasure*, 199). But once such items have been changed to rid them of the obvious forms of bias, suppose that critics of the test are able to prove that even the improved analogy items reward a form of ratiocination that is common in the dominant culture but not in a minority culture. What do we make of this more subtle form of cultural bias?

It depends on the "thing that the test is intended to measure." If the "thing" is raw intellectual potential, the cultural bias in the test will understate the test scores of the cultural minority. Its children will be inaccurately labeled as less intelligent than the children of the dominant culture. If, on the other hand, the "thing" is ability to comprehend the novels of Henry James, there is no cultural bias. People who score high on analogy items will tend to get more out of *The Portrait of a Lady* than people who score low. The test score is not a moral judgment on causes or character, but a measure of a state-of-affairs—in the case of analogy items and their ilk, the state of intellectual preparation for the kind of work that goes on in a challenging college curriculum.

The "thing to be measured" can be defined however one wishes. Thus, for example, it is easy to develop tests on which blacks will score higher than whites, and for a time such tests were in vogue as proof of the foolishness of test scores. One, named BITCH (Black Intelligence Test of Cultural Homogeneity), was developed under a grant from the National Institute of Mental Health. The problem is that the tests did not respond to the bias issue. All of them used the same tactic: a series of questions that were a vocabulary test of ghetto slang. They proved that blacks know more ghetto slang than whites do. But, whatever else their faults, the standardized tests being attacked were not so simply vocabulary tests in disguise, nor had any serious critics accused them of being such. The question was not whether black English contains words that whites fail to understand and vice versa, but whether the items on widely used aptitude and achievement tests were falsely masking black mental aptitudes or black achievement on the "thing to be measured."

Such a question is susceptible to falsifiable hypotheses and to statistical analysis. The major tests were subjected to such analysis, in painstaking detail. Items were discarded and revised. But when it came to the overall scores on the major tests, the feared cultural bias failed to explain the discrepancies in test scores. The existence of cultural bias continues to be assumed in public discussion of education. It continues to be the subject of rhetorical controversy in educational circles. Among specialists in educational testing, however, it has fallen to the status of a minor issue for which a great many of the interesting questions have been answered.

Arthur R. Jensen, *Bias in Mental Testing* (New York: Free Press, 1980), is the monumental work on the subject. Jensen, who was attacked as a racist for his earlier publications, responded by pulling together, in full technical detail, the huge body of work that had been done on bias and applying it to all the known hypotheses relating to cultural bias. By the time his book was published, however, most of the technical brouhaha had already died down. Even in the early 1970s, liberal scholars were not seriously questioning the reality of a racial difference in tests of cognitive skills. See for example the discussion of test scores in Christopher Jencks et al., *Inequality: A Reassessment of the Effect of Family and Schooling in America* (New York: Basic Books, 1972), chapter 3 and appendix A; and Luciano L'Abate, Yvonne Oslin, and Vernon W. Stone, "Educational Achievement," in Kent S. Miller and Ralph Mason Dreger, eds., *Comparative Studies of Blacks and Whites in the United States* (New York: Seminar Press, 1973), 325–56.

15. These and the following AFQT scores are taken from *Profile of American Youth* (Washington, D.C.: Office of the Assistant Secretary of Defense, Manpower, Reserve Affairs and Logistics, April 1982), table C–2. The scores are for a sample of 9,173. Standard deviation for the test was 28.03.

16. Ibid., table C–9.

17. Admissions Testing Program of the College Board, *Profiles, College-Bound Seniors, 1981* (New York: College Entrance Examination Board, 1982), iii. It is a most remarkable way for the College Board to describe the contending logics. One would expect at least some substantial faction arguing for release of the scores on grounds that not releasing them would show disregard of the board's scholarly obligations.

18. The College Board, *Profiles, College-Bound Seniors, 1980* (unpublished), table 10 (each table is repeated for each racial group). An examination of the breakdowns by race combined with other variables—parents' education, income, high-school rank, for example—reveals that the racial differences persist even when these factors are taken into account. (Ibid., tables 1–9.) To date, the College Board has released test scores by race only for the years since 1976, which leaves as *terra incognita* the entire reform period. For the years we do have, 1976–80, black test scores showed small changes (SAT–Verbal dropped from 332 to 330, SAT–Math rose from 354 to 360). Whether this means that black educational achievement among the college-bound turned around earlier than white educational achievement or had been on the rise for many years cannot be determined from the available data.

19. If one considers the entire spectrum of scores, the correlation between college performance and test scores leaves much room for the student with scores in the 500s to outperform one in the 600s or even 700s. I am making the more restrictive statement that below a certain point, a valid score (that is, a score that reflects the student's best efforts, not the fact that he had the flu the day he took the test) means that the student is very unlikely to be able to handle difficult college material.

Chapter 8

1. The FBI computes the rate-per-hundred-thousand for these crimes, using offenses reported to the police as the data base, and adds these rates. The violent crime index consists of a simple addition of the rates for murder and nonnegligent homicide, forcible rape, robbery, and aggravated assault (meaning with "assault with intent to kill or for the purpose of inflicting severe bodily injury by shooting, cutting, stabbing, maiming, poisoning, scalding, or by the use of acids, explosives, or other means"). The property crime index consists of the added rates for burglary, larceny, and auto theft. For the rates by race, I use the raw numbers of arrests by race as reported in the UCR and weight them by the proportion of the population covered by the reporting agencies. The arrest rates by race in the text are calculated as $\hat{R}_t = (a_t/p_t)/n_t$,

where $\hat{R}$ is the rate, t is the year, a is the number of UCR arrests for the arrestee population in question, p is the proportion (from 0 to 1) of the U.S. population represented in the UCR data, and n is the number of persons (in hundred thousands) in the reference population.

One recent characteristic of the published UCR data should be noted. Beginning in 1974, the annual UCR volume includes raw data provided by jurisdictions that reported for less than the complete 12-month period, introducing significant distortions if an attempt is made to analyze annual rates using the raw data. The FBI will prepare tables for the "12-month-complete" sample of reporting agencies on request, making the data consistent with the pre-1974 volumes. All post-1973 crime statistics in this volume use consistent data, and can therefore *not* be reproduced using the published figures in the UCR volumes from 1974 to 1980.

2. The FBI has been publishing its crime statistics since 1932. But the procedures for reporting national crime statistics changed significantly in 1958 (reporting procedures), 1960 (proportion of agencies represented), and 1964–65 (for juvenile crime). The FBI does not recommend using UCR data for time series comparisons prior to those break points. We may, however, recover a general picture of crime during the 1950s against which to compare the general picture of crime during the 1960s and 1970s. The data consist of crime reports from 353 cities of populations of 25,000 persons or more. The same 353 departments were included

each year and were limited to those which had not made major changes in their reporting procedures during the period covered. Description of the data and procedures is taken from *HSUS*, 408 and H962–70. To reach an estimated rate per 100,000, the known population of the 353 cities as of 1950 was assumed to have grown at a rate of 2.55 percent per year, the 1950–60 growth rate for cities of 25,000+ population (see *HSUS*, A57–72).

The estimates of crime in the 1950s produced by this procedure are more likely to be exaggerated than underestimated. The differences between the data for 1950–57 and 1960–80 (which are the reason for not linking 1957 and 1960 in the graph) all tend to inflate the 1950s rates compared with the post-1960 rates. The figures for 1950–57 include statutory rapes, whereas the post-1960 data do not, and they include small larcenies that were excluded after 1960. Also, the 1950–57 data are limited to 353 cities with a population of at least 25,000, whereas the 1960–80 data include small towns and rural areas, with their lower crime rates. Comparisons with the published UCR data in the 1950s suggest that the overall effect of these factors on the estimated index rates is small. This inference is reinforced by the apparent continuity of the data in the early 1960s.

3. *HSUS*, H971–86, 414.

4. For an example of the 1960s skepticism, see Albert D. Biderman and Albert J. Reiss, Jr., "On Exploring the 'Dark Figure' of Crime," *The Annals of the American Academy of Political and Social Science* 374 (1967): 1–15.

5. For a synthesis of recent findings, see Jan M. Chaiken and Marcia R. Chaiken, "Crime Rates and the Active Criminal," in James Q. Wilson, ed., *Crime and Public Policy* (San Francisco: ICS Press, 1983), especially p. 15.

6. Ibid., table 1, 16. For varying assessments of the National Crime Survey and UCR data, see John Ernest Eck and Lucius J. Riccio, "Relationship Between Reported Crime Rates and Victimization Survey Results: An Empirical and Analytical Study," *Journal of Criminal Justice* 7 (Winter 1979): 293–308; James P. Levine, "The Potential for Crime Overreporting in Criminal Victimization Surveys," *Criminology* 14 (December 1976): 307–30; Michael D. Maltz, "Crime Statistics: A Historical Perspective," *Crime and Delinquency* 23 (January 1977): 32–40; Robert M. O'Brien, David Shichor, and David L. Decker, "An Empirical Comparison of the Validity of UCR and NCS Crime Rates," *The Sociological Quarterly* 21 (Summer 1980): 391–401; and Wesley G. Skogan, "Crime and Crime Rates," in Wesley G. Skogan, ed., *Sample Surveys of the Victims of Crime* (Cambridge, Mass.: Ballinger, 1976), 105–19.

7. We see in these statistics and the ones that follow a classic source of confusion in the interpretation of trend lines. Black arrests did not increase as a proportion of total arrests. Black arrest rates rose by roughly the same proportion as white arrest rates. Black arrest rates increased by much larger amounts (arrests per 1,000 persons) than white arrest rates. All three statements are true. Each is pertinent to certain issues about the crime problem and not to others, as suggested in the text. The reason for the apparent differences among them (and a common source of difficulty in many comparisons of proportions and rates of change across two populations) are: (1) The black baseline rate was many times higher than the white baseline rate, decisively affecting the nature of the proportional change represented per unit change in the arrest rate; and (2) blacks constitute a small proportion of the total population, meaning that a very large increase in any behavior may have no effect on the black proportion of the whole. Thus, for example, if in a town of 10,000 people the 100 Hatfields and McCoys increase their crimes per year from 10 to 20, and the other 9,900 people increase their annual crimes from 1 to 2, the proportionate increases of the Hatfield/McCoys and the rest of the town will be identical (100 percent for each group). The proportion of total arrests accounted for by the Hatfield/McCoys will remain absolutely unchanged (9.2 percent). And it will also be true that the behavior of the Hatfield/McCoys changed in a much different way than did the behavior of everybody else, and something really ought to be done about it.

8. Robert D. Grove and Alice M. Hetzel, *Vital Statistics Rates in the United States 1940–1960*, National Center for Health Statistics (Washington, D.C.: Government Printing Office, 1968), table 63.

9. *SAUS-81*, table 15, p. 14.

10. Arnold Barnett, Daniel J. Kleitman, and Richard C. Larson, "On Urban Homicide," Working Paper WP–04–74 (Operations Research Center, Massachusetts Institute of Technology, March, 1974), cited in James Q. Wilson, *Thinking About Crime*, rev. ed. (New York: Basic Books, 1983), 24.

11. Can we equate arrests of blacks with the commission of crimes by blacks? Historically,

blacks have been convenient scapegoats for any number of white complaints, and presumably such racism has entered into police decisions to make arrests. In dealing with this issue, the crime of murder provides our best leverage in the official data. It has a number of advantages. Murder is almost always reported. A high proportion of murders are solved—not just "cleared" in the way that unsolved burglaries might be casually attributed to a known offender, but truly solved through witnesses or incontrovertible evidence. And we have two separate data sources to compare: UCR arrest data and the statistics on the *victims* collected from death certificates by the National Center for Health Statistics.

With these considerations in mind, we may reexamine figure 8.2, in which the trendline for male victims of criminal homicides per 100,000, using data collected from death certificates by the National Center for Health Statistics, was superimposed on the homicide arrest rate per 100,000 as reported by the UCR data.

The match was nearly perfect. Knowing only the black murder arrest rate per 100,000, one could quite accurately have predicted the black male homicide victimization rate throughout the entire period. Examined in closer detail, the match is even better than it appears: We know from a study by the National Commission on the Causes and Prevention of Violence the racial and sex characteristics of the offender/victim dyad for the year 1967. Applying these data, using the "naive" assumption that the police always arrest the right person, we can predict both black and white victimization rates for 1967 within a few percentage points. (See Donald J. Mulvihill and Melvin Tumin, *Crimes of Violence,* vol. 11, A Staff Report Submitted to the National Commission on the Causes and Prevention of Violence, December 1969, 267.)

These numbers apparently reflect with reasonable accuracy real changes in the commission of crime by each group. The individual is innocent until proven guilty but, looking at large numbers of cases, the trends in arrests accurately parallel changes in criminal behavior among the people who are being arrested.

Still, it could be argued that murder is a special case. In other, lesser crimes, were blacks really behaving differently? Or was something else at work—distortions in the arrest data such as differential arrest procedures for whites and blacks or improved police reporting on inner-city crimes? Researchers have conducted numerous studies of the extent to which such deformations affect arrest data at any given time, and a consensus has been forming that the racial differences in real rates of crime are just about as large as the official data would have us believe. (See citations at end of this note.)

But we are less concerned about the actual crime rate in any particular year than the trend over the period 1960–80. And in any case, when it comes to trends there is a more difficult logical argument to surmount. If one is to appeal to differential treatment of blacks and whites to explain the explosion in black arrests for violent crimes, it is not sufficient to assert that differential treatment exists. One must also assert that the differential treatment suddenly changed—increased in pernicious ways—during the late 1960s. If it happened, it did so in the face of expanded laws to prevent discrimination in general, increased participation of blacks on police forces, increased measures for civilian oversight of police activities, a high level of public advocacy by black and white groups alike specifically intended to forestall or detect such discrimination, and several major judicial rulings that had broadened the practical protections afforded to poor and minority defendants. I am unaware of any empirical work that tries to make such a case; on the face of it, it seems unlikely that blacks in the late 1960s were being discriminated against in ways that blacks in the 1950s were not. The more plausible assumption is that fewer blacks were being unjustly arrested in the 1960s than before, and that the increases we observe reflect other forces at work.

In reality, the surge in criminal activity among young black males in the 1960s is probably considerably *under*stated by the official data. The reason: Fewer and fewer reported offenses were resulting in an arrest. In police terminology, fewer crimes were being "cleared by arrest."

A "cleared" offense is one that is followed by an arrest of the perpetrator—perpetrator in the estimation of the police. This does not necessarily result in a conviction. Whether the person is eventually charged, let alone convicted, depends on a variety of circumstances, only a few of which have to do with the likelihood of guilt. Nor does a clearance necessarily mean that the crime has been solved. Police may arrest someone just to get a crime off the books; they may do all sorts of things which make any particular "clearance" open to dispute about its meaning. But using the huge numbers of cases in a national sample and focusing on trends, clearance rates are a useful index of the extent to which reported crimes result in the apprehension of an offender. The reductions in such rates between 1960 and 1980 were

Note to page 117

substantial, especially if one looks at them in terms of change in the odds that any given offense results in an arrest. The change from 1960 to 1980 was as follows:

Crime	Percentage Change in Clearance Rate
Murder	−22
Forcible Rape	−34
Robbery	−40
Aggravated Assualt	−24
Burglary	−53
Larceny	−8
Auto Theft	−49

Only the rate for larceny, which even in 1960 resulted in an arrest for only one in five reported offenses, stayed about the same. The clearance rates for everything else dropped by more than a fifth to a half. Furthermore, the lowest clearance rates are recorded in the largest cities, where the "urban crime" problem that dominates the concern about crime is concentrated.

These changes in clearance rates affect the interpretation of the arrest trendlines. Let us turn again to robbery as an example. The figure below presents the arrest rate for robbery and the implied rate of actual offenses, using a straightforward interpolation: if the clearance rate for robbery is 33 percent, then the total number of offenses committed by population X is three times the number of persons arrested. The ratio is not exact, of course: sometimes there are multiple offenders in a single offense; sometimes many offenses "on the books" will be cleared by the arrest of a single offender. But to get an idea of how much actual crime is

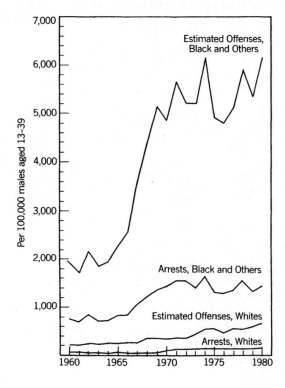

represented by arrest rates, this straightforward weighting approach may be applied to the breakdown of arrests by race.

The black-white gap in estimated offenses is so large that one looks for an artifact at work. But it must be remembered that the gap in robbery offenses begins to take on the same dimensions as the increase in the homicide gap for which the data are much more complete. The upper line is not necessarily the "true" rate—but the true rate could be higher as well as lower, depending on a variety of unanswered questions about the variables involved. I present the figure as an illustration of the general effect, other things being equal, of the falling clearance rates: They lead to an underestimate of the disparity in criminal behavior that opened up between the races in the 1960s. If, as I argue throughout the book, a racial discrepancy is a proxy for a discrepancy in the behavior of poor males and not-poor males, the change in the criminal behavior of poor males (mostly in their teens and twenties) is plausibly much larger, and the magnitude of the *change* in behavior in the late 1960s is much more radical, than the large differences that are already acknowledged.

The literature on the general topic of racial differences in offense rates is extensive. See Michael J. Hindelang, "Race and Involvement in Common Law Personal Crimes," *American Sociological Review* 43 (February 1978): 93–109, and Hindelang, Travis Hirschi, and Joseph G. Weis, "Correlates of Delinquency: The Illusion of Discrepancy Between Self-Report and Official Measures," *American Sociological Review* 44 (December 1979): 995–1014, for a review and analysis of the official versus self-report issue. The latter paper responds to one of the most exhaustive presentations of the opposing view, Charles R. Tittle, Wayne J. Villemez, and Douglas A. Smith, "The Myth of Social Class and Criminality: An Empirical Assessment of the Empirical Evidence," *American Sociological Review* 43 (October 1978): 643–56. Tittle et al. are subjected to yet another critical appraisal in John Braithwaite, " 'The Myth of Social Class and Criminality' Reconsidered," *American Sociological Review* 46 (February 1981): 36–57. For additional discussions of the effect of seriousness of the crime on self-report data, see Martin Gold, *Delinquent Behavior in an American City* (Belmont, Calif.: Brooks/Cole, 1970); and John P. Clark and Eugene P. Wenninger, "Socio-Economic Class and Area as Correlates of Illegal Behavior Among Juveniles," *American Sociological Review* 27 (December 1962): 826–34. For a discussion of the underrepresentation of the plausible "most delinquent" in self-report samples, see Travis Hirschi, *Causes of Delinquency* (Berkeley, Calif.: University of California Press, 1969), 70–75.

12. Overall arrest rates by race are presented as the number of arrests relative to the size (in 100,000s) of the male population aged 13–39. For example, the black robbery arrest rate is the total number of arrests of blacks for robbery per 100,000 black males aged 13–39.

The reason for choosing males aged 13 to 39 rather than the entire population is that the great bulk of crimes are committed by that subgroup. Using it as the denominator in figuring a rate therefore provides a much more realistic compensation for population change than using the entire population. Ideally, the rate would be presented in terms of the numbers of arrests of white or black males, aged 13 to 39 not total arrests; but such breakdowns by race and sex and age have not been published, nor could I recover them from the original UCR data files for the period 1960–80.

The text discusses violent crime because of its central importance as an indicator. The data for violent and property crime, and for juveniles and adults, are presented in the appendix. Briefly, the changes in property crime arrests—for burglary, larceny, auto theft—were of the same order of magnitude as the increases in arrests for violent crime. As of 1960, the black arrest rate for property crime was 6,281 per 100,000, compared with 1,776 for whites. From 1960 to 1963, black arrests for property crime were inconsistent, increasing substantially once (1961–62), decreasing the other two years. A sustained increase began in 1963–64, continuing with only a single interruption (1965–66) through 1971. After bouncing up and down in the 1970s, black arrests for property crime in 1980 were at essentially the level they had reached in 1970. Like arrests for violent crime, the precipitous increase in black arrests for property crime were concentrated in the last half of the 1960s. The overall increase in property crime rate from 1960 to 1980 was from 6,281 to 9,394, with 69 percent of the increase occurring between 1965 and 1970.

13. Philip H. Ennis, "Criminal Victimization in the United States, Field Surveys II, A Report of a National Survey," President's Commission on Law Enforcement and the Administration of Justice (Washington, D.C.: Government Printing Office, 1967), 31.

14. Ibid., and Timothy J. Flanagan, David J. van Alstyne, and Michael R. Gottfredson, eds., *Sourcebook of Criminal Justice Statistics—1981* (Washington, D.C.: Government Printing Office, 1982), table 3.12. The figures per 100,000 for the middle income group in 1965 and 1979 are as follows: Rape: from 10 to 72; robbery: from 42 to 401; aggravated assault: from 147 to 910.

15. The comparison of the 1965 and 1979 numbers cannot be treated as exact. Even though the definitions of the crimes were quite similar, and even though the samples were large and representative, the 1979 survey is by no means a replication of the 1965 study. I also have a number of reservations about victimization surveys in general (which, however, would not necessarily influence a comparison between two such surveys). I present the data because, even after we factor a good deal of conservatism into an interpretation of the numbers, the main point seems incontrovertible: the poor and the black have suffered extraordinarily from the rise in crime.

Chapter 9

1. "Text of President's Message to Congress Seeking Reforms in Welfare Programs," *New York Times*, 2 February, 1962. See chapter 1.

2. "Illegitimate" means any birth to an unmarried woman, based on the response on the birth certificate. No correction is made for underreporting. Data for illegitimate births and low birth weight are taken from *Vital Statistics of the United States*, Public Health Service, Center for Health Statistics (Washington, D.C.: Government Printing Office, various editions). Data on the size of the white and black teenaged populations are computed from the age breakdowns in the *ETRP-80* for women in and not in the labor force, 1954–80.

Two indicators are used with regard to families headed by a single female. One is percentage of all families headed by a married couple, with data taken from *SAUS-81*, table 61, and earlier issues. The other is percentage of persons living in families who are living in a family with a female householder, no husband present, calculated from material presented in *Money Income and Poverty Status of Families and Persons in the United States: 1981 (Advance Data from the March 1982 Current Population Survey)*, Bureau of the Census, Current Population Reports, Series P–60, no. 134 (Washington, D.C.: Government Printing Office, 1982), table 15 (for persons beneath the poverty level); and *Characteristics of the Population Below the Poverty Level: 1980*, same series, no. 133 (Washington, D.C.: Government Printing Office, 1982), table 2 (for persons below 125 percent of the poverty level).

As a supplement to the analysis in the text, it may be helpful to clear away some statistical underbrush in the form of an important distinction between family breakup and marital breakup. The indicator most often cited in the popular press as evidence of the breakdown of the family is divorce rate. The divorce rate had decreased during the 1950s and held steady through 1963. Then came a slow climb until 1967–68, when the rate jumped. The figures speak for themselves: from 1950 through 1967, the divorce rate increased by 9 percent. From 1968 to 1976, it doubled.

Curiously, however, the increasing divorce rate had very little effect on the prevalence of the married couple as the basis for the family. The number of divorces increased, but in any given year they represented a small proportion of marriages. Adding in the remarriages, the net effect on the composition of the family was small. The percentage of married couples in the general population dropped by only 2.4 percentage points from 1950 to 1978—the same period when the divorce rate increased by 113 percent. Divorce rate means annual number of divorces per 1,000 married women fifteen years old and older. The source for 1950–70 is *HSUS*, series B216–220. For 1971–80, the source is *SAUS-81*, table 124, and earlier issues. Marital status is represented by percentage of women, fourteen years and over, who are married. The source is *Social Indicators III*, Bureau of the Census (Washington, D.C.: Government Printing Office, 1980), table 1/15. Those who use the *SAUS* for such analysis should note that the age range changed after 1960 from "fourteen and over" to "eighteen and over." Thus, for example, the table on marital status in *SAUS–81* (table 46) shows a spurious increase in percent-married during the late 1960s. The reduction of 2.4 percentage points cited above is based on the "standardized scores" computed by the Bureau of the Census on the basis of the age distribution in 1960, and recommended by the Bureau for comparisons over time.

3. In interpreting these data, we confront a problem similar to the one we faced with arrest data: To what extent are the racial differences real? To what extent do they represent artifacts in reporting? William Ryan has written an emphatic defense of the proposition that the white-black gap is far narrower than the statistics indicate (William Ryan, *Blaming the Victim,* rev. ed. [New York: Vintage Books: 1976], chapter 4). Three of his points are plausible: (1) White illegitimate births have been underreported; (2) many more whites than blacks terminated unmarried pregnancies through an abortion (at least prior to the legalization of abortion); and (3) "forced" marriages legitimized a higher proportion of unmarried pregnancies among whites than among blacks.

The issue is not the relative premarital sexual activity of whites and blacks, however, but the number of illegitimate births, and on this score the gaps in the trendlines cannot significantly be narrowed. The underreporting of white illegitimate births was likely to have been greater in the 1950s than in the 1960s and 1970s. (As Ryan himself points out, acceptance of births to single women has historically been greater among blacks than among whites.) Insofar as this is the case, the effect on the trendlines since 1950 would be to artifically narrow, not artificially inflate, the growth of the real black-white gap.

4. Charles F. Westoff, Gerard Calot, and Andrew D. Foster, "Teenage Fertility in Developed Nations: 1971–1980," *Family Planning Perspectives* 15 (May/June 1983): 108.

5. The roles of the specific components of the familial situation—parents' IQ and education, income, presence of two parents, and a host of other factors—on the child's development are the subject of a large and inconclusive literature. Everything interacts. Parents with high incomes tend to have more successful children than parents with low incomes, partly because they tend to have higher IQs, partly because they tend to ensure that their children get a good education, partly because they provide a different home environment, partly because they pass on a financial or professional inheritance, and so on. See for example Christopher Jencks et al., *Inequality: A Reassessment of the Effect of Family and Schooling in America* (New York: Basic Books, 1972), and Zena Smith Blau, *Black Children/White Children* (New York: The Free Press, 1981). For discussions of the methods of childrearing as they relate to socioeconomic characteristics of the parent, see Basil A. Bernstein, "Social Class and Linguistic Development: A Theory of Social Learning," in A.H. Halsey, J. Floud, and C.A. Anderson, eds., *Education, Economy and Society* (Glencoe, Ill.: The Free Press, 1961), 288–314; Blau, *Black Children;* Frank Furstenberg, "The Transmission of Mobility Orientation in the Family," *Social Forces* 49 (1971): 595–603; Elizabeth Herzog and Cecelia E. Sudia, "Children in Fatherless Families," in B.M. Caldwell and H.N. Ricciuti, eds., *Review of Child Development Research,* vol. 3 (Chicago: University of Chicago Press, 1973), 141–232; C. Kamii and N. Radin, "Class Differences in the Socialization Practices of Negro Mothers," in Robert F. Winch and G. Spanier, eds., *Selected Studies in Marriage and the Family* (New York: Holt, Rinehart and Winston, 1974), 235–47; and Arleen Leibowitz, "Home Investments in Children," *Journal of Political Economy* 82 (March/April 1974), S111–31. In addition to such sources, one may also ask elementary school teachers in the inner city to describe the range of cognitive development they observe among children arriving in kindergarten.

6. Daniel P. Moynihan, *The Negro Family: The Case for National Action* (Washington, D.C.: Department of Labor, March 1965).

7. Slope of the trendline for percentage of blacks and others living in two-parent families from 1950–65 was −.31; slope of the trendline 1966–80 was −1.00. The strength of the time relationship also increased. Correlation of rate with year, 1950–65, was −.78; for 1966–80, it was −.98. Data and source information are given in the appendix, table 24.

8. The statistics that follow are based on all families in which the householder is a single female, no husband present. It is possible to compute parallel statistics for the subset of such families which have dependent children under the age of eighteen. The trendlines have generally the same shape, most of them in more exaggerated form.

9. Gordon Green and Edward Welniak, *Changing Family Composition and Income Differentials,* Special Demographic Analyses CDS–80–7 (Washington, D.C.: Government Printing Office, 1982), 13.

Chapter 10

1. I (the 1966 policy analyst) consider the possibility that my 1954–61 and 1961–65 trendlines will overproject progress because of very low baselines. For many processes, early progress slows as the "easy" part is completed—witness the experience of most of us when learning a new skill. Thus a linear projection of a trendline that begins from a low baseline is likely to exaggerate future attainments. Fortunately, I do not have this problem with most of my indicators, which in the pessimistic projection are *heading in a negative direction.* To fall within the projected range of outcomes by 1980, it is not necessary that things get better; only that they get worse less rapidly than they did during the "pessimistic" period. Only three indicators—income ratio for full-time year-round workers, persons employed in white-collar jobs, and persons of college age enrolled in school—are headed in a positive direction under both the optimistic and pessimistic projections. As we will see, in two of these three instances, actual progress exceeded the prediction of progress. In other words, the baseline problem is worrisome in the interpretation of only one out of the nine indicators used in the exercise.

2. See, for example, Michael J. Flax, *Blacks and Whites: An Experiment in Social Indicators* (Washington, D.C.: The Urban Institute, 1971), in which data from 1960–68 are used to project the year in which blacks could be expected to reach the 1968 level of whites on a number of indicators.

3. I used ordinary least squares to project a linear trendline. Various more elaborate models could be constructed, but none accurately predicts the real trendline from 1966 to 1980—not, at any rate, using assumptions that anyone would have accepted in 1966.

4. The exception to this may—and I stress *may*—consist of certain health indicators. For example, black infant mortality dropped most rapidly in the 1960s and 1970s; but maternal mortality dropped in the 1950s and relatively little thereafter, and the percentage of low-birth-weight newborns actually increased from 1950 to 1980. I will leave the health question to others. The generalization in the text seems to apply quite consistently to the social and economic indicators that are available—including, by the way, voting through 1980, despite the 1965 Voting Rights Act.

Chapter 11

1. The most famous example is the regression analysis in the "Coleman Report" (James S. Coleman et al., *Equality of Educational Opportunity* [Washington, D.C.: U.S. Department of Health, Education and Welfare, Office of Education, 1966]), which was the basis for concluding that black children would benefit from busing and was cited to that effect by the courts. Within a few years of its publication, the analysis in the report was being used in university courses (at least, at MIT and Harvard) as a textbook example of technical errors in causal inference from regression analysis. For an example of criticism by persons sympathetic to the conclusions, see Glen G. Cain and Harold W. Watts, "Problems in Making Policy Inferences from the Coleman Report" (Discussion paper, Madison, Wis.: Institute for Research on Poverty, 1968).

2. For accounts of the origins of the NIT experiment, see Hugh Heclo and Martin Rein, "Social Science and Negative Income Taxation," in Suzanne Berger, ed., *The Utilisation of the Social Sciences in Policy-Making in the United States* (Paris: Organization for Economic Cooperation and Development, 1980); Robert A. Levine, "How and Why the New Jersey Negative Income Tax Experiment Came About" (Paper delivered at the Brookings Conference on Income Maintenance Experiments, Washington, D.C., 29–30 April 1974); Martin Anderson, *Welfare: The Political Economy of Welfare Reform in the United States* (Stanford, Calif.: Hoover Institution Press,

1978); and Daniel P. Moynihan, *The Politics of a Guaranteed Income: The Nixon Administration and the Family Assistance Plan* (New York: Random House, 1973).

3. The Fall 1980 issue of *Journal of Human Resources* was devoted entirely to the final analyses of the NIT data and contained an integrated bibliography. The estimate of the number of sources is drawn from that bibliography; the total number could be much larger. It is worthwhile to read some of the earlier accounts of the results of the NIT (or recent accounts that use earlier research findings as their basis), to get a flavor for the early optimism. The first reports suggested that the work disincentives were small or even nonexistent. Heclo and Rein, for example, who published their account of the experiment in 1980, were still writing under the impression that the experiment had, by and large, confirmed the sponsors' expectations. In this context, the publication of the later analyses came as something of a shock.

4. The Negative Income Tax has a long intellectual lineage, stretching back to the Speenhamland system of eighteenth-century England. In the United States, the NIT was first mentioned in an article by George Stigler, "The Economics of Minimum Wage Legislation," *American Economic Review* 36 (June 1946): 358–65. Milton Friedman was another early proponent of an NIT. The NIT actually implemented in the NIT experiment bore only a family resemblance to the original conceptions.

5. Milton Friedman, *Capitalism and Freedom* (Chicago: Chicago University Press, 1962), 191–92.

6. Heclo and Rein, "Social Science," 34.

7. David Kershaw and Jerilyn Fair, *The New Jersey Income-Maintenance Experiment*, Institute for Research on Poverty Monograph Series, vol. 1 (New York: Academic Press, 1976), quoted in Anderson, *Welfare*, 103.

8. Heclo and Rein, "Social Science," 35.

9. Some subpopulations were given a five-year guarantee, to test the sensitivity of the results to the length of the experiment. A few families were guaranteed twenty years of support.

10. The best one-volume source on SIME/DIME is the Fall 1980 issue of the *Journal of Human Resources* mentioned above. A good nontechnical summary of the NIT experiments is Robert A. Moffit, "The Negative Income Tax: Would It Discourage Work?" *Monthly Labor Review* 104 (April 1981): 23–27.

11. Philip K. Robins and Richard W. West, "Labor Supply Response Over Time," *Journal of Human Resources* 15. (Fall 1980): 524.

12. Ibid., 566.

13. Robins and West, "Labor Supply Response," 524.

14. Joseph D. Mooney, "Urban Poverty and Labor Force Participation," *American Economic Review* 57 (March 1967): 104–119.

15. Richard W. West, "The Effects on the Labor Supply of Young Nonheads," *Journal of Human Resources* 15 (Fall 1980): 587.

16. Ibid., 588.

17. Philip K. Robins, Nancy Brandon Tuma, and K.E. Yeager, "Effects of SIME/DIME on Changes in Employment Status," *Journal of Human Resources* 15 (Fall 1980): 566.

18. John H. Bishop, "Jobs, Cash Transfers, and Marital Instability: A Review and Synthesis of the Evidence," *Journal of Human Resources* 15 (Summer 1980): 312.

19. The descriptions of the Gary experiment vary slightly. Bishop reports this impression was the result of a mistake in the instructions. He also considers the influence of the fact that only the husband filed, and the NIT check was made out to him, whereas in the other sites the check required the endorsement of both husband and wife ("Jobs," p. 320). Another description (Lyle P. Groeneveld, Nancy Brandon Tuma, and Michael T. Hannan, "The Effects of Negative Income Tax Programs on Marital Dissolution," *Journal of Human Resources* 15 [Fall 1980]: 654–74) says flatly, "In the Gary experiment, families on an NIT plan were told that any one-person unit formed as a result of a marital dissolution would not be eligible for the NIT" (p. 671).

20. See Groeneveld et al., "Marital Dissolution."

21. Anderson, *Welfare*, 105–117. In each case, the bias is systematic—that is, the error tends to be in one direction. See also Henry J. Aaron, "Cautionary Notes on the Experiment," in Joseph A. Pechman and P. Michael Timpane, eds., *Work Incentives and Income Guarantees: The New Jersey Negative Income Tax Experiment* (Washington, D.C.: The Brookings Institution, 1975). That the NIT experiment understated the actual effects is generally agreed in the literature. For

the only dissent I have encountered, see Charles E. Metcalf, "Making Inferences from Controlled Income Maintenance Experiments," *The American Economic Review* 63 (June 1973): 478–83.

22. In *Welfare,* which was written before the final results were available, Anderson carries out an exercise in which he estimates minimal and maximal effects for each of the nine types of bias, then computes a range of projected work reduction outcomes if the NIT program had been extended to the national population. He generates a best-case estimate of a 29 percent work reduction, an average-case estimate of 51 percent, and a worst-case estimate of 72 percent (pp. 117–27). He concludes, "I would urge anyone who is concerned about the accuracy of the estimates in the example to go through the exercise of reconstructing Table 1—bias by bias—using estimates they feel are more reasonable" (p. 127). His point, ingeniously made, is that it is very difficult to make remotely plausible estimates that show anything but a severe work reduction.

23. See West, "Young Nonheads," and Robins and West, "Labor Supply Response."

24. See Heclo and Rein, "Social Science."

Chapter 12

1. The short time frame that poor people use for making decisions has been a central feature of the "culture of poverty" discussions beginning with Oscar Lewis's *The Children of Sanchez* (New York: Random House, 1961). In such discussions, however, the source of the foreshortened time horizon has generally been seen in cultural or mental attributes. It is hard to understand why the logical reason for shortsightedness—that the poor person hasn't the luxury of thinking about far-distant events—has received so little attention.

2. Not all the experts will take this line. See, for example, Samuel Popkin, *The Rational Peasant* (Berkeley, Calif.: University of California Press, 1979).

3. The figures for AFDC payments are based on the "highest monthly amount for payment standard" (that is, the amount guaranteed a woman with one child and no other income, as in Phyllis's hypothesized case), using data obtained from the Office of Family Assistance, Department of Health and Human Services. The specific figures for AFDC and unemployment benefits are based on those obtainable in Pennsylvania—neither the most liberal nor most conservative of states on social welfare payments, but typical of the industrial states in which most of the welfare population lives. AFDC eligibility and benefit rules vary widely from state to state, and arriving at an "average" package after Food Stamps and subsidized housing, Women, Infant, and Children (WIC) food supplements, and Medicaid came into effect is impossible. Rather than focus on the large sums which can be obtained legally in many of the northern states, I use estimates that are arguably too low to represent fairly the true seductions of putting together a welfare package. But even these make the point about comparative attractions of work and welfare, and too much has been made elsewhere of the problem of the "professional welfare mothers" who bring in middle-class-level incomes. Welfare cheats are not the problem. Other data sources include Elizabeth H. Chief, ed., *Characteristics of State Plans for Aid to Families with Dependent Children* (Washington, D.C.: Government Printing Office, 1981); *Alternative Methods for Valuing Selected In-Kind Transfer Benefits and Measuring Their Effect on Poverty,* Bureau of the Census, Technical Paper no. 50, (Washington, D.C.: Government Printing Office, 1982); personal communication with staff of the Office of Family Assistance, Social Security Administration, Department of Health and Human Services; and the annual summaries of state-by-state unemployment insurance plans in the library of the Employment and Training Administration, Department of Labor.

4. Of the alternative ways of valuing Medicaid, this yields the most conservative (smallest) estimate. See Bureau of the Census, *Alternative Methods.*

5. It may be argued that the picture is not so bleak. Given a minimum-wage job, Harold also would be eligible for Food Stamps and perhaps, depending on his specific circumstances, subsidized housing and Medicaid. Therefore the total package if he is working will be greater

than Phyllis's package if he is not working. But note: Insofar as these programs are means-tested, he will get these benefits whether he is employed or not; indeed, in some instances their value will increase if he is unemployed. For practical purposes, Harold's benefits are a constant added to all the cells in the table I present.

6. In addition to the evidence from the NIT, a variety of other analyses point to the specific effects of Unemployment Insurance on search effort, duration of unemployment, and other aspects of labor market behavior. Unemployment benefits do in fact tend to prolong unemployment, and this seems to hold true when the problem is approached from a variety of analytic perspectives. One may examine the "exhaustion" rate—the probability that an unemployed person will remain unemployed until the benefits run out. A study that did so found that: (1) the higher the unemployment benefits relative to the average weekly wage, the more likely that people remained unemployed until benefits were exhausted; (2) the stricter the enforcement of eligibility rules, the less likely that people remained unemployed until benefits were exhausted; (3) the stricter the enforcement of "acceptance of suitable work," the less likely that people remained unemployed until benefits were exhausted; and (4) if "extended benefits" were made available, people were more likely to remain unemployed until the regular benefit period was exhausted. See Walter Nicholson, "A Statistical Model of Exhaustion of Unemployment Insurance Benefits," *Journal of Human Resources* 16 (Winter 1981): 117–28.

Taking another slant, Barron and Mellow (who have conducted a number of investigations of this issue) documented a "duration of unemployment approximately 25 percent higher for individuals receiving UI [Unemployment Insurance] benefits," then went on to describe the several reasons for believing that this was a "lower-bound estimate" (that is, to the extent that the 25 percent figure was wrong, it was probably too low). See John M. Barron and Wesley Mellow, "Search Effort in the Labor Market," *Journal of Human Resources* 14 (Summer 1979): 389–404. Other sources on this topic include Stephen W. Salant, "Search Theory and Duration Data: A Theory of Sorts," *Quarterly Journal of Economics* 91 (February 1977): 45–63; Stanley P. Stephenson, Jr., "The Economics of Youth Job Search Behavior," *Review of Economics and Statistics* 58 (February 1976): 104–11; and Stephen T. Marston, "The Impact of Unemployment Insurance on Job Search," *Brookings Papers on Economic Activity* 1 (Washington, D.C.: The Brookings Institution, 1975): 13–60.

The tendency to move in and out of the labor force seems to share the age-related patterns exhibited by blacks and whites in unemployment and labor force participation. Among older blacks, a longitudinal analysis using CPS data has shown that the probability of experiencing unemployment (among members of the labor force) in two successive years was roughly the same for blacks and whites above the age of twenty-five. But below the age of twenty-five, black youth were much more likely than whites of the same age to experience unemployment in two successive years. These results obtained for both two-year periods examined, 1974–75 and 1977–78. Similarly, older blacks and whites showed roughly equivalent duration of employment, whereas young blacks had markedly shorter durations of employment than young whites. See Norman Bowers, "Tracking Youth Joblessness: Persistent or Fleeting?" *Monthly Labor Review* 104 (February 1982): 3–13. I interpret these data as being consistent not only with the usually cited problems of black youths in getting jobs (no skills, bad job market), but also with the availability of other options which make minimum-wage-level jobs unattractive. White teenagers and black older workers are more likely to be weighing employment options that pay more money, and therefore to be less susceptible to the economic attractions I sketched for Harold. Provocative evidence consistent with this hypothesis is found in Ronald G. Ehrenberg and Alan J. Marcus, "Minimum Wages and Teenagers' Enrollment and Employment Outcomes: A Multinomial Logit Model," *Journal of Human Resources* 17 (Winter 1982): 39–58, suggesting that black teenagers have a higher reservation wage (lower than which the job seeker will not accept employment) than white teenagers, one exceeding the minimum wage. The data on the likelihood of quits in Robert J. Flanagan, "Discrimination Theory, Labor Turnover, and Racial Unemployment Differentials," *Journal of Human Resources* 13 (Spring 1978): 187–207, reinforce this interpretation. Flanagan discusses his findings in terms of reaction to wage discrimination, but his data suggest that something else may be at work. Note his finding for young blacks that "a 1 percent reduction in the wage relative to the average wage received by individuals with similar schooling, training, experience, and industry raises the probability that an individual will quit his job within the ensuing two years by over 10 percent" (p. 200). It is not easily argued that such large effects on behavior are caused by such imperceptible differences in wages. Differences in incentives to accept very low-wage jobs are at least as plausible as a line of inquiry.

7. With regard to the basic question of whether people really "get on welfare" through anything resembling a deliberate decision-making process, two points need to be emphasized. The first is that such decisions need not be the product of a discrete moment in time when someone sits down and says, "I think that rather than pursue my luck in the job market I will put together a package of welfare benefits and episodic or underground work." They can be formed in a much more diffuse fashion and still qualify as decisions. The second point is that the NIT data are devastating on this issue. But we need not extrapolate from the NIT approach. C.T. Brehm and T.R. Saving, in "Demand for General Assistance Payments," *American Economic Review* 54 (December 1964): 1002–18, investigated the question with regard to General Assistance Payments. They theorized that "in addition to the 'hard-core' of unemployables and low-income earners the set of GAP recipients should contain consumers who deliberately have chosen to bring their earned income below the minimum set by society" (p. 1017). They proceeded to support their hypothesis with statewide data. The authors were noticeably apologetic about their findings (they were writing as early as 1964, when such topics were especially sensitive). They opened and closed the article by emphasizing that the results did not imply a need to cut back on General Assistance Payments; they "only indicate that GAP recipients are like the remainder of consumers in that they react to economic incentives" (p. 1018)—which is, of course, precisely my point.

8. For a compilation of legislation and court decisions relating to AFDC, see Frank S. Bloch, "Cooperative Federalism and the Role of Litigation in the Development of Federal AFDC Eligibility Policy," *Wisconsin Law Review* 1 (1979): 1–53. For a discussion of the IV-D provision, see Judith B. Stauder, "Child Support Enforcement and Establishment of Paternity as Tools of Welfare Reform—Social Services Amendments of 1974, pt. B, 42 U.S.C. Paragraphs 651–60 (Supp. V, 1975)," *Washington Law Review* 52 (1976): 169–192. The list of important events does not include a theoretical disincentive of the 1967 amendments: the provision of WIN (Work INcentive program) that provided for "workfare," allowing states to drop persons who could work but refused to. In practice, the HEW interpretation of the rule effectively gutted it: only AFDC-UP (Unemployed Parent) fathers, WIN dropouts over sixteen years of age, and mothers of school-aged children who had access to free day care were required to register for work. The WIN program in general never approached the hoped-for level of implementation. See James T. Patterson, *America's Struggle Against Poverty 1900–1980* (Cambridge, Mass.: Harvard University Press, 1981), 174–75.

9. Do people really marry or divorce because of welfare considerations? The clear-cut results from the NIT experiment are echoed in a variety of studies of the existing welfare system. One of the first scholarly attempts to derive quantitative estimates of the effects of the AFDC program was Marjorie Honig's 1974 study, which took advantage of the wide variation in AFDC grants from state to state and used 1960 and 1970 census data to analyze the relationship between the size of AFDC payments and marital dissolution. She translated the results of the regression analyses with an example: "Thus, a 10 percent increase in the AFDC stipend would result in an increase in the AFDC recipient rate of approximately 14 percent for the nonwhite population, slightly less than half of which would be due to desertions of supporting males. The estimated impact on the white recipient rate is 19 percent, with more than three-quarters due to desertion" (pp. 315–16). See Marjorie Honig, "AFDC Income, Recipient Rates, and Family Dissolution," *Journal of Human Resources* 9 (Summer 1974): 303–22.

Robert M. Hutchens, in "Welfare, Remarriage, and Marital Search," *American Economic Review* 69 (June 1979): 369–79, tackled the same general question with other data and another econometric model. He too used an illustration: "The results can be illustrated with a simple example. For a family of four (a woman and three children) the 1971 [AFDC] guarantee in New York was $305 while the guarantee in Mississippi was $60. If a Mississippi woman with three children had a .50 probability of remarriage, what effect would Mississippi's adoption of the New York guarantee have on her probability of remarriage?" The answer: it would drop from .50 to .14—from one chance in two to one chance in seven (p. 375).

Steven Bahr sought to overcome the disadvantages of cross-sectional analyses by using the National Longitudinal Survey to track the same families from 1967 to 1974. For persons receiving welfare in 1967, the rate of marital dissolution by 1975 was 2.4 times the rate for persons not receiving welfare. When he controlled for income, the effect remained. For example, among the families in which the husband earned less than $4,000, the rate of dissolution among those who also received welfare benefits was 67 percent higher than among those who did not. This is an especially striking result when one contemplates the situation of a family in which the husband earned less than $4,000 a year and the family was not receiving any welfare at all. Although Bahr does not comment on this issue, it may be that a self-selection bias was at work: If in the late 1960s a family that poor did not avail itself of any welfare, odds are that it was a conscious decision not to accept help—the "poor but proud" family that, by the same token, might have an unusually strong commitment to staying together despite it all. Bahr also found large differences in family dissolution (on the order of two and three times the non–welfare family rate) when he controlled for age, age at marriage, duration of current marriage, education, and whether it was a first marriage. When he examined remarriage, he found that "[a]mong both blacks and whites, the remarriage rate was about three times more frequent among non–AFDC recipients than among those who were receiving AFDC" (p. 557). See Steven J. Bahr, "The Effects of Welfare on Marital Stability and Remarriage," *Journal of Marriage and the Family* 41 (August 1979): 553–60. Figures are aggregated from data in table 2, 556.

For a one-source review of the literature, see John H. Bishop, "Jobs, Cash Transfers, and Marital Instability: A Review and Synthesis of the Evidence," *Journal of Human Resources* 15 (Summer 1980): 301–34.

10. Frank Levy, "The Labor Supply of Female Household Heads, or AFDC Work Incentives Don't Work Too Well," *Journal of Human Resources* 14 (Winter 1979): 79. See also Martin Anderson, *Welfare: The Political Economy of Welfare Reform in the United States* (Stanford, Calif.: Hoover Institution, 1978), chapter 2, where he calculates the effects of marginal tax rates on net income. The results take the form of a "poverty wall"—so named because it actually looks like a wall when graphed. See also Henry J. Aaron, "Alternative Ways to Increase Work Effort Under Income Maintenance Systems," in Irene Lurie, ed., *Integrating Income Maintenance Programs* (New York: Academic Press, 1975), 161–62.

11. Statistics on average AFDC payments per person are taken from *Social Security Bulletin* 44 (November 1981), table M–28.

12. See Frances Fox Piven and Richard A. Cloward, *Regulating the Poor: The Functions of Public Welfare* (New York: Pantheon, 1971), chapter 10, for a variety of data—quantitative, case histories, anecdotes—about the increase in the AFDC rolls. For technical analyses of the AFDC caseload trends, see Barbara Boland, "Participation in the Aid to Families with Dependent Children Program (AFDC)," in *The Family, Poverty, and Welfare Programs: Factors Influencing Family Instability,* Studies in Public Welfare Paper no. 12 (part 1), U.S. Congress, Joint Economic Committee, Subcommittee on Fiscal Policy (Washington, D.C.: Government Printing Office, 1973); David M. Gordon, "Income and Welfare in New York City," *The Public Interest* no. 16 (Summer 1969): 64–88; and Cynthia Rence and Michael Wiseman, "The California Welfare Reform Act and Participation in AFDC," *Journal of Human Resources* 13 (Winter 1978): 37–59.

13. Patterson, *America's Struggle,* 179.

Chapter 13

1. Estimated odds against going without an arrest for five crimes are based on clearance rates. As note 11 for chapter 8 discusses, clearance rates declined substantially in the 1960s and, to a lesser extent, in the 1970s. In the 1950s, more than 40 percent of robberies were cleared. By 1970, that figure had dropped to 23 percent. In the 1950s, approximately 30 percent of burglaries were cleared. In 1954, the clearance rate for burglary was 30 percent; by 1970, it had dropped to 14 percent. The change in the odds for robbery is the more dramatic, but the drop in the odds of getting caught for several burglaries was also large: from more than six to one in 1954 to only two to one by 1970. Data are taken from Federal Bureau of Investigation, *Uniform Crime Reports,* described in chapter 8.

2. Most reports in the press about the prison population stress the overcrowded conditions

and (in the last half of the 1970s) the growing number of prisoners. The fall in the prison population during the 1960s is less well known.

Note that the persons in prison in a given year are not the perpetrators of the crimes during that year, and that I ignore the large number of persons in local jails. Thus the numbers considerably underestimate the probability that some form of incarceration would follow arrest. They are used to indicate the proportional relationship of arrests to imprisonment over the period. (See appendix, table 23, for data and sources.) The estimate of total arrests used in the calculation of prisoners per 1,000 arrests is $\hat{A} = a/p$, where $\hat{A}$ is the estimate of total arrests, a is the number of index arrests in the UCR data, and p is the proportion of the U.S. population (between 0 and 1) covered by the UCR data. Data for calculating the proportion are taken from appendix table 1 and the UCR population coverage as reported annually in the table for total arrests by race. Because crime rates are higher in cities, and cities tended participate in the UCR program earlier, the rising UCR coverage in the 1960–80 period may be expected to have produced relatively overestimated arrests in the earlier years and, therefore, underestimated rates of imprisonment in those years. If so, the real drop in risk of imprisonment was greater during the 1960s than shown in figure 13.2.

3. Data collected by the author from the records of the Illinois Department of Corrections, Juvenile Division, for all Cook County commitments from 1 October 1974 to 31 July 1976.

4. Charles A. Murray and Louis A. Cox, Jr., *Beyond Probation: Juvenile Corrections and the Chronic Delinquent* (Beverly Hills, Calif.: Sage Publications, 1979), 35.

5. The generalization is based on interpolations from arrest rates for juveniles by city and from statewide commitment to institutions. A detailed, precise comparison with a second major city, Philadelphia, will be possible as the results of the major study of the 1958 birth cohort (members of which were at risk of being delinquent during roughly the years 1971–75) become available. The study is being conducted by Marvin Wolfgang, Robert Figlio, and Paul E. Tracy, all of the University of Pennsylvania. When paired with an earlier study of the 1945 Philadelphia birth cohort, members of which were at risk of being delinquent during roughly the years 1958–62, the possibilities for direct analyses of change in delinquent behavior and system response from 1960 to the mid-1970s will expand enormously. For the analysis of the earlier birth cohort, see Marvin E. Wolfgang, Robert M. Figlio, and Thorsten Sellin, *Delinquency in a Birth Cohort* (Chicago: University of Chicago Press, 1972).

6. The best recent summary of the evidence on the effects of changing the costs and benefits of crime is in James Q. Wilson, *Thinking About Crime*, rev. ed. (New York: Basic Books, 1983), chapters 7–10. Some of the points that he draws from the literature are:

- When the probability of imprisonment goes up, it appears that robbery goes down. See Isaac Ehrlich, "Participation in Illegitimate Activities: A Theoretical and Empirical Investigation," *Journal of Political Economy* 81 (January 1973): 521–65; and Alfred Blumstein, Jacqueline Cohen, and Daniel Nagin, eds., *Deterrence and Incapacitation: Estimating the Effects of Criminal Sanctions on Crime Rates* (Washington, D.C.: National Academy of Sciences, 1978). For a summary of the criticisms of Ehrlich's work and his response to them, see Isaac Ehrlich and Mark Randall, "Fear of Deterrence," *Journal of Legal Studies* 6 (January 1977): 293–316.

- Studies based on victim surveys (thereby avoiding problems associated with studies based on reported crime) have also found that as sanctions become more likely, crime becomes less common. See Itzhak Goldberg, "A Note on Using Victimization Rates to Test Deterrence," Technical Report CERDCR–5–78, Center for Econometric Studies of the Justice System (Palo Alto, Calif.: Stanford University, 1978); and James Q. Wilson and Barbara Boland, "Crime," in William Gorham and Nathan Glazer, eds., *The Urban Predicament* (Washington, D.C.: Urban Institute, 1976).

- Studies that are able to avoid problems of the "swamping" effect (in which clearance rates go down because the system is overburdened) have found evidence of a deterrent effect. See Alfred Blumstein and Daniel Nagin, "The Deterrent Effect of Legal Sanctions on Draft Evasion," *Stanford Law Review* 29 (January 1977): 241–75.

- Studies of the deterrent effect on individuals (as opposed to aggregate data about cities, states, and countries) support a deterrence hypothesis. See Ann Dryden Witte, "Estimating the Economic Model of Crime with Individual Data," *Quarterly Journal of Economics* 94 (February 1980): 57–84; and Murray and Cox, *Beyond Probation.*

The indispensable treatise on the use of punishment to control crime is Ernest van den Haag, *Punishing Criminals: Concerning a Very Old and Painful Question* (New York: Basic Books, 1975).

7. Wilson, *Thinking About Crime*, 121.

8. Robert J. Rubel, *The Unruly School: Disorders, Disruptions, and Crimes* (Lexington, Mass.: Lexington Books, 1977), 60–66. His book includes a comprehensive bibliography. The federal government's data on the school crime problem is detailed in *Violent Schools–Safe Schools: The Safe School Study Report to the Congress*, Department of Health, Education and Welfare (Washington, D.C.: Government Printing Office, 1978).

9. Jonathan Kozol, *Death at an Early Age* (Boston: Houghton Mifflin, 1967). For the best account of the ferment in ideology during the late 1960s, see Diane Ravitch, *The Troubled Crusade: American Education 1945–1980* (New York: Basic Books, 1983), chapter 7.

10. For variations on the theme that black culture is unique and mostly superior to white middle-class culture, see Joyce A. Ladner, ed., *The Death of White Sociology* (New York: Random House, 1973). The theme, while less common in the 1980s, has not disappeared altogether. See H. Morgan, "How Schools Fail Black Children," *Social Policy* 10 (January 1980): 49–54, which applies an elaborate psychological rationale for arguing that schools should adjust their behavior to lower-class black norms of behavior, rather than the other way around.

11. See, for example, the influential booklet *Academic Freedom in the Secondary Schools* (New York: American Civil Liberties Union, 1968). For a discussion of the role of the courts and children in general (with emphasis on education), see Edward A. Wynne, "What Are the Courts Doing to Our Children?" *The Public Interest* no. 64 (Summer 1981): 3–18; the reply to Wynne by Julius Menacker, "The Courts Are Not Killing Our Children," *The Public Interest* no. 67 (Spring 1982): 131–36; and Wynne's rejoinder in the same issue, pp. 136–39.

12. The abolishment of penalties and neglect of scholastic achievement was most extreme in the early and mid-1970s. By 1980, the pendulum had started to swing back, and some large school systems were already reinstituting stricter codes. The description in the text was still accurate in 1980, however, if for no other reason than that court decisions following from *Gault* v. *Arizona* still sharply limited a local school district's discretion in many of the practices taken for granted in the 1950s. For a discussion of current practice, see Gerald Grant, "Children's Rights and Adult Confusions," *The Public Interest* no. 69 (Fall 1982): 83–99.

13. Jackson Toby, "Crime in the Schools," in James Q. Wilson, ed., *Crime and Public Policy* (San Francisco: ICS Press, 1983), 73–74.

14. Ibid., 74.

15. For the role of the learning environment—discipline, demands on the student, and so forth—in contrast to teaching technology and facilities as an explanation for educational outcomes, the material is just beginning to burgeon, as of 1983. The most ambitious data base was accumulated by James S. Coleman, of "Coleman Report" fame in the mid-1960s. This time, he and his colleagues surveyed 58,000 students in 893 public and 122 private high schools. They found that the typical private school, with larger classrooms, lower-paid teachers, and fewer resources, was producing substantially better academic achievement than its public counterpart. The reason was not much more complicated than the ones I included under the heading of incentives. The most thorough discussion of the findings, along with replies to the fierce criticism of their first publications on this topic, can be found in James S. Coleman, Thomas Hoffer, and Sally Kilgore, *High School Achievement: Public, Catholic, and Private Schools Compared* (New York: Basic Books, 1982). The most provocative and hopeful of Coleman's findings was put in italics when he first published it in "Private Schools, Public Schools, and the Public Interest," *The Public Interest* no. 64 (Summer 1981): "When we examined, wholly within the public sector, the performance of students similar to the average public school sophomore, but with the levels of homework and attendance attributable to school policy in the Catholic or other private schools, and those levels of disciplinary climate and student behavior attributable to school policy in the Catholic or other private schools, the levels of achievement are approximately the same as those found in the Catholic and other private sectors" (p. 25).

Although the Coleman study has received the most attention, others have been reaching compatible conclusions since the early 1970s. The first was a study of four inner-city schools that were producing students at or near the national reading norms. The report—G. Weber,

294

Inner-City Children Can Be Taught to Read: Four Successful Schools (Washington, D.C.: Council for Basic Education, 1974)—identified four characteristics as essential: strong leadership by the principal, high expectations of the students, an orderly environment, and close, continuing evaluation of the students' progress. Ronald Edmonds, in "Effective Schools for the Urban Poor," *Educational Leadership* 37 (October 1979): 15–24, summarizes a number of subsequent studies, arguing that in one fashion or another all the effective schools reinforced these fundamental characteristics. The principal studies that he discusses are: "School Factors Influencing Reading Achievement: A Case Study of Two Inner City Schools," State of New York, Office of Education Performance Review (March 1974); W.B. Brookover and L.W. Lezotte, *Changes in School Characteristics Coincident with Changes in Student Achievement* (East Lansing, Mich.: Michigan State University, College of Urban Development, 1977); and Ronald R. Edmonds and and J.R. Fredericksen, *Search for Effective Schools: The Identification and Analysis of City Schools That Are Instructionally Effective for Poor Children* (Cambridge, Mass.: Harvard Center for Urban Studies, 1978). I find one of Edmonds's statements particularly compelling: "There has never been a time in the life of the American public school when we have not known all we needed to in order to teach all those whom we chose to teach" (p. 16). At least with regard to the last twenty years, his statement could be amended to read "when we have not known all we needed to and have not had all the money we needed. . . ." While a number of points remain unresolved about the nature of the decline of education since 1965, the literature seems amply to document that lack of resources and lack of pedagogical knowledge have not been important explanatory variables. Further, the extensive investigations into the outcomes of compensatory education programs strongly support the proposition that the way out of our problem does not lie in innovations in educational technique (innovations, that is, construed as something we do not presently know how to do if we choose to do so). For a good one-source review of the evaluation literature on compensatory education, see Laurence R. Marcus and Benjamin D. Stickney, *Race and Education: The Unending Controversy* (Springfield, Ill.: Charles C Thomas, 1981), 171–223.

Chapter 14

1. I do not exclude the importance of values. Values operate independently (at least for a time) of money and status rewards, and for many persons they determine behavior almost to the exclusion of other considerations. But while social policy can erode or reinforce existing values, it is questionable whether social policy in a free society can create values that broadly affect behavior. Even totalitarian societies find it a daunting task. In contrast, status rewards are easily manipulated by governments, companies, and communities of all sorts.

2. Most farmers were cash poor until this century. As many as 40 percent of wage earners were poor by the standards of the day in 1900, using the figures of John Ryan, *A Living Wage* (New York: Arno, 1971, copyright 1906). Robert Hunter, *Poverty* (New York: Macmillan, 1907) uses a rock-bottom poverty level based on a standard of living "that a man would demand for his horses or slaves" and arrives at an estimate of 20 percent poor in the northern industrial states. By the contemporary standard (the official poverty line), it seems likely that a large majority of the population was living in poverty. See the discussion in James T. Patterson, *America's Struggle Against Poverty 1900–1980* (Cambridge, Mass.: Harvard University Press, 1981), 6–13.

3. Figures cited in Patterson, *America's Struggle,* 172.

4. Frances Fox Piven and Richard A. Cloward, *Regulating the Poor: The Functions of Public Welfare* (New York: Vintage Books, 1971) is an excellent source of data on this issue.

5. Ibid., 287–305.

6. I am indebted for information on the magnet school experience to Dr. Norman Gold, Senior Research Associate at the National Institute of Education, who was a leading partici-

pant in the development and evaluation of the early magnet school experiments. For the published record, see Eugene C. Royster, D. Catherine Baltzell, and Fran Cheryl Simmons, *Study of the Emergency School Aid Act Magnet School Program: Final Report* (Washington, D.C.: National Institute of Education, 1979); and Robert A. Dentler, D. Catherine Baltzell, and Kent J. Chabotar, *Quality Integrated Magnet Schools and Their Cost* (Washington, D.C.: National Institute of Education, 1983).

7. Piven and Cloward, in *Regulating the Poor*, make a similar point: "When large numbers of people come to subsist on the dole, many of them spurning what little low-wage work may exist, those of the poor and near-poor who continue to work are inevitably affected. From their perspective, the ready availability of relief payments (often at levels only slightly below prevailing wages) undermines their chief claim to social status: namely, that although poor they nevertheless earn their livelihood. If most of them react with anger, others react by asking, 'Why work?' " (p. 343). Parenthetically, it is interesting how many of Piven's and Cloward's points, made in support of a left-radical critique of social policy, coincide with those in critiques from the other end of the political spectrum.

8. Other examples are the untouchables of India and, more generally, peasants in highly structured social systems that attach permanent stigma to being from a certain social stratum. These may be contrasted with the very different attitudes (comparable to the feisty "I'm as good as anybody" attitude of traditional America) in peasant cultures that differentiate among classes but permit mobility. Thailand is an example.

9. Among the nonfiction accounts are John Langston Gwaltney, *Drylongso: A Self-Portrait of Black America* (New York: Vintage Books, 1981); Douglas G. Glasgow, *The Black Underclass: Poverty, Unemployment, and Entrapment of Ghetto Youth* (New York: Vintage Books, 1981); Elliot Liebow, *Tally's Corner* (Boston: Little, Brown, and Co., 1967). For accounts of the pre-1960 period, see Claude Brown, *Manchild in the Promised Land* (New York: Macmillan, 1965) and the classic work of Franklin E. Frazier, *The Negro Family in the United States* (Chicago: University of Chicago Press, 1939).

10. The pendulum began to shift in the late 1970s. From the mid-1960s until that time, programs for the gifted in inner-city schools were scarce, and in some jurisdictions (for example, Washington, D.C.), they were virtually proscribed by laws designed to prevent tracking by ability.

11. See Glasgow, *Black Underclass*, 91.

12. See James Bovard, "Busy Doing Nothing: Government Job Creation," *Policy Review* no. 24 (Spring 1983): 87–102.

13. I am not aware of studies that compare the progress of black poor who live in inner-city ghettos with those who live in communities with a high degree of socioeconomic diversity. If we take the simpler issue of whether poverty and/or welfare are intergenerational, the answer seems to be, "sort of." A recent major study of intergenerational poverty and welfare using data from the Panel Study of Income Dynamics is available: Martha S. Hill et al., *Final Report of the Project: "Motivation and Economic Mobility of the Poor," Part 1: Intergenerational and Short-Run Dynamic Analyses* (Ann Arbor, Mich.: Survey Research Center, Institute for Social Research, University of Michigan, 3 August 1983). With regard to poverty, it reveals that the majority of young adults whose parents were in the lowest quintile on a poverty measure (income relative to needs) moved up to a higher quintile (a third of them to the top three quintiles); on the other hand, 42 percent did not move up at all. In all, young adults whose parents were in the lowest quintile were 3.3 times as likely other young adults to be in the lowest quintile when they became adults (p. 44). With regard to welfare dependency, only half of those whose parents received welfare had yet received welfare themselves (when the survey was taken); on the other hand, those reared in welfare-receiving homes were twice as likely to have received welfare by the time of the survey as those whose parents had not been on welfare (p. 46). Without time series data, it is not possible to determine whether intergenerational poverty and dependency are increasing, diminishing, or remaining the same.

The point in the text, however, is a more limited one. In any ghetto school there are dozens of students who should, by virtue of their abilities, be not only escaping poverty (or welfare) but also becoming doctors, lawyers, and business executives. Unsystematic evidence from the inner-city schools that I have observed and the testimony of teachers and counselors in such schools suggest that this form of mobility is nearly nonexistent. Was it any better twenty years ago? We do not know. It could hardly have been any worse. We do know that in many cities with a large black population, there was at least one fine public high school in the ghetto, a claim that is much harder to make today.

14. Glasgow, *Black Underclass*, 58–59.

Chapter 15

1. Robert Nozick, *Anarchy, State, and Utopia* (New York: Basic Books, 1974), 232.

Chapter 16

1. Other types of rewards (a trip to Jamaica, or a full college scholarship for one's first-born, for example) do not seem to change the nature of the calculation, nor does the payment schedule associated with the reward.

2. *SAUS–81*, table 202.

3. Even a one-time program would not work unless the government could convince people that it meant what it said. Some people, aware of the inertial tendencies of government programs, are sure to assume that the reward will be available again in the future and behave accordingly.

4. Herbert Costner, "Theory, Deduction, and Rules of Correspondence," in Hubert M. Blalock, Jr., ed., *Causal Models in the Social Sciences* (Chicago: Aldine Atherton, 1971), 299–319.

5. Probably the most extreme available example is the $82 million "Supported Work" program conducted by the Manpower Demonstration Research Corporation. Its findings are summarized in Board of Directors, Manpower Demonstration Research Corporation, *Summary and Findings of the National Supported Work Demonstration* (Cambridge, Mass.: Ballinger, 1980). The hardcore unemployed who volunteered for the program were provided with intensive orientation *and* nonjob supports *and* a subsidized job (generally for twelve months). The evaluation claimed modest success (in terms of the cost-benefit ratio over the long term) for two of the groups, AFDC mothers and ex-addicts; it did not claim success for the other two groups (ex-offenders and youth). The salient point is that, even taking the conclusions at face value, the program, providing an unprecedented level of support, did not make a substantial dent in the behavior of the hardcore unemployed. We do not yet know what level of intervention would do the job. Even at the levels of support provided by the Supported Work program, the unintended reward is quite tangible and large. See Ken Auletta, *The Underclass* (New York: Random House, 1982), for an absorbing narrative account of the people and the program.

Glossary of Source
Abbreviations

CPR   *Current Population Reports.* Periodic publications in several series. Series P-25 (population characteristics) and series P-60 (consumer income) were used for this book. The reports are prepared by the Bureau of the Census.

CPS   Current Population Survey. The monthly survey conducted by the Bureau of the Census and used as the basis for the *Current Population Reports.* "March CPS" refers to the March survey, in which the questionnaire is augmented with income questions used to compute (among other things) the poverty statistic.

DES   *Digest of Education Statistics,* issued annually by the Department of Education.

ETRP   *Employment and Training Report of the President,* prepared annually by the Department of Labor. In the 1960s, it was called the *Manpower Report of the President.*

HSUS   *Historical Statistics of the United States, Colonial Times to 1970* (two volumes), prepared by the Bureau of the Census and published in 1975.

Glossary of Source Abbreviations

SAUS *Statistical Abstract of the United States,* prepared annually by the Bureau of the Census.

UCR Uniform Crime Reports, the data received by the FBI and used in the preparation of its annual report, *Crime in the United States.*

All the above documents are published by the Government Printing Office, Washington, D.C.

Bibliography

Aaron, Henry J. "Alternative Ways to Increase Work Effort Under Income Maintenance Systems." In *Integrating Income Maintenance Programs,* edited by Irene Lurie. New York: Academic Press, 1975.

Aaron, Henry J. "Cautionary Notes on the Experiment." In *Work Incentives and Income Guarantees: The New Jersey Negative Income Tax Experiment,* edited by Joseph A. Pechman and P. Michael Timpane. Washington, D.C.: The Brookings Institution, 1975.

Adelman, Clifford. *Devaluation, Diffusion and the College Connection: A Study of High School Transcripts, 1964–81.* Washington: National Institute of Education, 1983.

Adler, Seymour. "Self-Esteem and Causal Attributions for Job Satisfaction and Dissatisfaction." *Journal of Applied Psychology* 65 (June 1980): 327–32.

Allen, Walter R. "Preludes to Attainment: Race, Sex, and Student Achievement Orientations." *The Sociological Quarterly* 21 (Winter 1980): 65–79.

Allison, Paul D. "Measures of Inequality." *American Sociological Review* 43 (December 1978): 865–80.

American Civil Liberties Union. *Academic Freedom in Secondary Schools.* New York: American Civil Liberties Union, 1968.

American Statistical Association. Ad Hoc Committee on Affirmative Action Statistics. "Summary Notes on the Statistics of Federal Affirmative Action Programs." *American Journal of Economics and Sociology* 41 (October 1982): 32–322.

Anderson, J.E. "Poverty, Unemployment, and Economic Development." *Journal of Politics* 29 (February 1967): 70–93.

Anderson, Martin. *Welfare: The Political Economy of Welfare Reform in the United States.* Stanford, Calif.: Hoover Institution Press, 1978.

Anderson, W.H. Locke. "Trickling Down: The Relationship Between Economic Growth and the Extent of Poverty Among American Families." *Quarterly Review of Economics* 78 (November 1964): 511–24.

Andrisani, Paul J. "Internal-External Attitudes, Personal Initiative, and the Labor Market Experience of Black and White Men." *Journal of Human Resources* 13 (Summer 1977): 308–28.

Ashenfelter, Orley. "Estimating the Effects of Training Programs on Earnings." *Review of Economics and Statistics* 60 (February 1978): 47–57.

Auletta, Ken. *The Underclass.* New York: Random House, 1982.

Azrin, N.H., R.A. Philip, P. Thienes-Hontos, and V.A. Besalel. "Comparative Evaluation of the Job Club Program with Welfare Recipients." *Journal of Vocational Behavior* 16 (April 1980): 133–45.

Bibliography

Bahr, Stephen J. "The Effects of Welfare on Marital Stability and Remarriage." *Journal of Marriage and the Family* 41 (August 1979): 553–60.

Baker, Keith, and Robert J. Rubel, eds. *Violence and Crime in the Schools*. Lexington, Mass.: D.C. Heath, 1980.

Banfield, Edward C. *The Unheavenly City Revisited*. Boston: Little, Brown, 1974.

Baratz, Joan C. "Policy Implications of Minimum Competency Testing." In *Minimum Competency Achievement Testing*, edited by Richard M. Jaeger and Carol Kehr Tittle. Berkeley: McCutchan Publishing Corp., 1980.

Barnett, Arnold, Daniel J. Kleitman, and Richard C. Larson. "On Urban Homicide." Working Paper WP-04-74. Operations Research Center, Massachusetts Institute of Technology, March 1974.

Barnow, Burt S., and Glen G. Cain. "A Reanalysis of the Effects of Head Start on Cognitive Development: Methodology and Empirical Findings." *Journal of Human Resources* 12 (Spring 1977): 177–97.

Barron, John M., and Wesley Mellow. "Changes in Labor Force Status Among the Unemployed." *Journal of Human Resources* 16 (Summer 1981): 427–44.

Barron, John M., and Wesley Mellow. "Search Effort in the Labor Market." *Journal of Human Resources* 14 (Summer 1979): 389–404.

Bartel, Ann P. "Race Differences in Job Satisfaction: A Reappraisal." *Journal of Human Resources* 16 (Spring 1981): 294–303.

Beck, E.M., Patrick M. Horan, and Charles M. Tolbert II. "Stratification in a Dual Economy: A Sectoral Model of Earnings Determination." *American Sociological Review* 43 (October 1978): 704–20.

Becker, Gary S. "A Theory of Marriage: Part II." *Journal of Political Economy* 82 (March/April 1974): S11–S26.

Bergland, Bruce W., and Gerald W. Lundquist. "The Vocational Exploration Group and Minority Youth: An Experimental Outcome Study." *Journal of Vocational Behavior* 7 (December 1975): 289–96.

Bernstein, Basil A. "Social Class and Linguistic Development: A Theory of Social Learning." In *Education, Economy, and Society*, edited by A.H. Halsey, J. Floud, and C.A. Anderson, Glencoe, Ill.: The Free Press, 1961, 288–314.

Bernstein, Blanche. *The Politics of Welfare: The New York City Experience*. Boston: Abt Books, 1982.

Bernstein, Morty, and Faye Crosby. "An Empirical Examination of Relative Deprivation Theory." *Journal of Experimental Social Psychology* 16 (September 1980): 442–56.

Bianchi, Suzanne M. "Racial Differences in Per Capita Income, 1960–76: The Importance of Household Size, Headship, and Labor Force Participation." *Demography* 17 (May 1980): 129–43.

Bianchi, Suzanne M., and R. Failey. "Racial Differences in Family Living Arrangements and Economic Well-Being: An Analysis of Recent Trends." *Journal of Marriage and the Family* 41 (August 1979): 537–51.

Biderman, Albert D. and Albert J. Reiss, Jr. "On Exploring the 'Dark Figure' of Crime." *The Annals of the American Academy of Political and Social Science* 374 (1967): 1–15.

Bielby, William T., Robert Hauser, and David Featherman. "Response Errors of Black and Nonblack Males in Models of Intergenerational Transmission of Socioeconomic Status." *American Journal of Sociology* 82 (May 1977): 1242–88.

Bishop, John H. "Jobs, Cash Transfers, and Marital Instability: A Review and Synthesis of the Evidence." *Journal of Human Resources* 15 (Summer 1980): 301–34.

Black, Donald J. "Production of Crime Rates." *American Sociological Review* 35 (August 1970): 733–47.

"Black Education: 25 Years After the Brown Decision." *Black Scholar* 11 (September 1979): 2–28.

Black, Matthew. "An Empirical Test of the Theory of On-the-Job Search." *Journal of Human Resources* 16 (Winter 1981): 129–40.

Blau, Francine D., and Lawrence M. Kahn. "Race and Sex Differences in Quits by Young Workers." *Industrial and Labor Review* 34 (July 1981): 563–77.

Blau, Zena Smith. *Black Children/White Children*. New York: The Free Press, 1981.

Blaug, Mark. "The Myth of the Old Poor Law and the Making of the New." *Journal of Economic History* 23 (June 1963): 151–84.

Bibliography

Bloch, Frank S. "Cooperative Federalism and the Role of Litigation in the Development of Federal AFDC Eligibility Policy." *Wisconsin Law Review* 1 (1979): 1–53.

Block, Herman D. "Some Economic Effects of Discrimination on Employment." *American Journal of Economics and Sociology* 25 (January 1966): 1–18.

Blumstein, Alfred, Jacqueline Cohen, and Daniel Nagin, eds. *Deterrence and Incapacitation: Estimating the Effects of Criminal Sanctions on Crime Rates*. Washington, D.C.: National Academy of Sciences, 1978.

Blumstein, Alfred, and Daniel Nagin. "The Deterrent Effect of Legal Sanctions on Draft Evasion." *Stanford Law Review* 29 (January 1977): 241–75.

Boland, Barbara. "Participation in the Aid to Families with Dependent Children Program (AFDC)." In *The Family, Poverty, and Welfare Programs: Factors Influencing Family Instability*. Studies in Public Welfare Paper no. 12 (Part 1), U.S. Congress, Joint Economic Committee, Subcommittee on Fiscal Policy. Washington, D.C.: Government Printing Office, 1973.

Boland, Barbara, and James Q. Wilson. "Age, Crime, and Punishment." *The Public Interest* no. 51 (Spring 1978): 22–34.

Bonacich, Edna. "Advanced Capitalism and Black/White Race Relations in the United States: A Split Labor Market Interpretation." *American Sociological Review* 41 (February 1976): 34–51. Comment and rejoinder: Kay Oehler. "Another Look at the Black/White Trend in Unemployment Rate." *American Sociological Review* 44 (April 1979): 339–42.

Bovard, James. "Busy Doing Nothing: Government Job Creation." *Policy Review* no. 24 (Spring 1983): 87–102.

Bowers, Norman. "Tracking Youth Joblessness: Persistent or Fleeting?" *Monthly Labor Review* 104 (February 1982): 3–13.

Bowles, Samuel, and Henry Levin. "The Determinants of Scholastic Achievement—An Appraisal of Some Recent Evidence." *Journal of Human Resources* 3 (Winter 1968): 3–24.

Bradbury, Katharine, Sheldon Danziger, Eugene Smolensky, and Paul Smolensky. "Public Assistance, Female Headship, and Economic Well-Being." *Journal of Marriage and the Family* 41 (August 1979): 519–35

Bradford, Amory. *Oakland's Not for Burning*. New York: McKay, 1968.

Braithwaite, John. " 'The Myth of Social Class and Criminality' Reconsidered." *American Sociological Review* 46 (February 1981): 36–57.

Brehm, C.T., and T.R. Saving. "Demand for General Assistance Payments." *American Economic Review* 54 (December 1964): 1002–18.

Brown, Claude. *Manchild in the Promised Land*. New York: Macmillan, 1965.

Brown, Frank. "Equal Educational Opportunity, the Law, and the Courts." *Urban Education* 11 (July 1976): 135–50.

Brown, Frank, and Elsie Smith. "The Allocation of Educational Environment, Ability Grouping, and the Law." *Urban Education* 11 (July 1976): 201–16.

Brown, Michael K., and Stephen P. Erie. "Blacks and the Legacy of the Great Society: The Economic and Political Impact of Federal Social Policy." *Public Policy* 12 (Summer 1981): 299–330.

Burke, Vincent J., and Vee Burke. *Nixon's Good Deed: Welfare Reform*. New York: Columbia University Press, 1974.

Burstein, Paul. "Equal Employment Opportunity Legislation and the Income of Women and Nonwhites." *American Sociological Review* 44 (June 1979): 367–91.

"Business Leaders and Economists Back Income Guaranty Plans." *Social Service Review* 42 (September 1968): 365–66.

Bybee, Rodger W., and E. Gordon Gee. *Violence, Values, and Justice in the Schools*. Boston: Allyn and Bacon, 1982.

Cain, Glen G. "The Challenge of Segmented Labor Market Theories to Orthodox Theory: A Survey." *Journal of Economic Literature* 14 (December 1976): 1215–57.

Cain, Glen G., and Harold W, Watts. "Problems in Making Policy Inferences from the Coleman Report." Discussion Paper. Madison, Wisc.: Institute for Research on Poverty, 1968.

Campbell, Angus, and Howard Schuman. *Racial Attitudes in Fifteen American Cities*. Ann Arbor, Mich.: Survey Research Center, Institute for Social Research, 1968.

Carter, David G. "Children and Student Rights: A Legal Analysis." *Urban Education* 11 (July 1976): 185–200.

Centra, John A. "Graduate Degree Aspirations of Ethnic Student Groups." *American Educational Research Journal* 17 (Winter 1980): 459–78.

Chaiken, Jan M., and Marcia R. Chaiken. "Crime Rates and the Active Criminal." In *Crime and Public Policy*, edited by James Q. Wilson. San Francisco: ICS Press, 1983.

Chall, Jeanne S. *An Analysis of Textbooks in Relation to Declining SAT Scores*. Princeton, N.J.: College Entrance Examination Board, 1977.

Chief, Elizabeth H., ed. *Characteristics of State Plans for Aid to Families With Dependent Children*. Washington, D.C.: Government Printing Office, 1981.

Ciscel, David H., and Barbara B. Tuckman. "Peripheral Worker: CETA Training As Imperfect Job Socialization." *Journal of Economic Issues* 15 (June 1981): 489–500.

Clark, John P., and Eugene P. Wenninger. "Socio-Economic Class and Area as Correlates of Illegal Behavior Among Juveniles." *American Sociological Review* 27 (December 1962): 826–34.

Clark, Kenneth B. *The Dark Ghetto: Dilemmas of Social Power*. New York: Harper & Row, 1965.

Clark, Kenneth B., and Jeannette Hopkins. *A Relevant War Against Poverty*. New York: Harper & Row, 1969.

Clark, Ramsay. *Crime in America: Observations on Its Nature, Causes, Prevention, and Control*. New York: Simon and Schuster, 1970.

Cleary, T. Anne, Lloyd G. Humphreys, S.A. Kendrick, and Alexander Wesman. "Educational Use of Tests With Disadvantaged Students." *American Psychologist* 30 (January 1975): 15–41.

Cogan, John F. "The Decline in Black Teenage Employment: 1950–70." *American Economic Review* 72 (September 1982): 621–38.

Cohen, Lawrence E., and James R. Kleugel. "Determinants of Juvenile Court Dispositions: Ascriptive and Achieved Factors in Two Metropolitan Courts." *American Sociological Review* 43 (April 1978): 162–76.

Coleman, James S. "Private Schools, Public Schools, and the Public Interest." *The Public Interest* no. 64 (Summer 1981): 19–30.

Coleman, James S., Ernest Q. Campbell, Carol J. Hobson, James McPartland, Alexander M. Mood, Frederic D. Weinfeld, and Robert L. Yonk. *Equality of Educational Opportunity*. Washington, D.C.: U.S. Department of Health, Education, and Welfare, Office of Education, 1966.

Coleman, James S., Thomas Hoffer, and Sally Kilgore. *High School Achievement: Public, Catholic, and Private Schools Compared*. New York: Basic Books, 1982.

Coll, Blanche D. *Perspectives in Public Welfare: A History*. Washington, D.C.: Government Printing Office, 1969.

College Entrance Examination Board. Admissions Testing Program. *Profiles, College-Bound Seniors, 1981*. New York: CEEB, 1982.

College Entrance Examination Board, *On Further Examination: Report of the Advisory Panel on the Scholastic Aptitude Test Score Decline*. Princeton, N.J.: CEEB, 1977.

Congran, J.G. "Changes in White Attitudes Toward Blacks: 1963–77." *Public Opinion Quarterly* 43 (Winter 1979): 463–76.

Congressional Budget Office. *The Food Stamp Program: Income or Food Supplementation?* Washington, D.C.: Government Printing Office, January 1977.

Copperman, Paul. *The Literacy Hoax: The Decline of Reading, Writing, and Learning in the Public Schools and What We Can Do About It*. New York: William Morrow and Co., 1978.

Corcoran, Mary, and Greg J. Duncan. "Work History, Labor Force Attachment, and Earnings Differences Between the Races and Sexes." *Journal of Human Resources* 14 (Winter 1979): 3–19.

Coser, Lewis A. "Presidential Address: Two Methods in Search of a Substance." *American Sociological Review* 40 (December 1975): 691–700.

Crain, Robert L., and Rita E. Maynard. "Desegregation and Black Achievement: A Review of the Research." *Law and Contemporary Problems* 42 (Summer 1978): 17–56.

Cunliffe, M. "Black Culture and White America." *Encounter* 34 (January 1970): 22–35.

Danigelis, Nicholas L. "Black Political Participation in the United States: Some Recent Evidence." *American Sociological Review* 43 (October 1978): 756–71.

Danziger, Sandra K. "Postprogram Changes in the Lives of AFDC Supported Work Participants: A Qualitative Assessment." *Journal of Human Resources* 16 (Fall 1981): 637–48.

Danziger, Sheldon. "Children in Poverty: The Truly Needy Who Fall Through the Safety Net." Institute for Research on Poverty Discussion Paper. Madison, Wisc.: Univ. of Wisconsin, 1981.

Danziger, Sheldon. "The Distribution of Income: An Account of Past Trends and a Projection

Bibliography

of the Impacts of the Reagan Economic Program." Institute for Research on Poverty Discussion Paper. Madison, Wisc.: Univ. of Wisconsin, 1982.

Danziger, Sheldon, Robert Haveman, and Robert Plotnick. "How Income Transfer Programs Affect Work, Savings, and the Income Distribution: A Critical Review." *Journal of Economic Literature* 19 (September 1981): 975–1028.

Danziger, Sheldon, and Robert Plotnick. "The War on Income Poverty: Achievements and Failures." In *Welfare Reform in America*, 31–52, edited by Paul M. Sommers, Boston: Kluwer-Nijhoff, 1982.

Darity, William A., Jr. "The Human Capital Approach to Black-White Earnings Inequality: Some Unsettled Questions." *Journal of Human Resources* 17 (Winter 1982): 72–93.

Davis, James A. "Achievement Variables and Class Cultures: Family, Schooling, Job, and Forty-Nine Dependent Variables in the Cumulative GSS." *American Sociological Review* 47 (October 1982): 569–86.

Dawkins, Marvin P., and Graham C. Kinloch. "Black Students and the Labor Market: An Analysis of Occupational Expectations." *Journal of Black Studies* 12 (September 1981): 107–16.

Dellaportas, G. "Effectiveness of Public Assistance Payments in Reducing Poverty." *American Journal of Economics and Sociology* 39 (April 1980): 113–21.

Dentler, Robert A., D. Catherine Baltzell, and Kent J. Chabotar. Quality Integrated Magnet Schools and Their Cost. Washington, D.C.: National Institute of Education, 1983.

Department of Health, Education, and Welfare. *Violent Schools–Safe Schools: The Safe School Study Report to the Congress.* Washington, D.C.: Government Printing Office, 1978.

Dibble, U. "Socially Shared Deprivation and the Approval of Violence: Another Look at the Experience of American Blacks During the 1960s." *Ethnicity* 8 (June 1981): 149–68.

Dillard, John M. "Relationship between Career Maturity and Self-Concepts of Suburban and Urban Middle- and Urban-Lower Class Preadolescent Black Males." *Journal of Vocational Behavior* 9 (December 1976): 311–20.

Dillingham, G.L. "Emerging Black Middle Class: Class Consciousness or Race Consciousness?" *Ethnic and Racial Studies* 4 (October 1981): 432–51.

Downs, Anthony. "Alternative Futures for the American Ghetto." *Daedalus* 97 (Fall 1968): 1331–78.

DuBois, Philip H., and Wimburn L. Wallace, Technical Reviews of the SAT. In *The Seventh Mental Measurements Yearbook*, edited by Oscar K. Buros, 640, 646–50. New Jersey: The Gryphon Press, 1972.

Duncan, Greg J., and Saul Hoffman. "On-the-Job Training and Earnings Differentials by Race and Sex." *Review of Economics and Statistics* 61 (November 1979): 594–603.

Duncan, Otis Dudley. "Inheritance of Poverty or Inheritance of Race." In *On Understanding Poverty*, edited by Daniel P. Moynihan. New York: Basic Books, 1968.

Dutton, Diana B. "Explaining the Low Use of Health Services by the Poor: Costs, Attitudes, or Delivery Systems?" *American Sociological Review* 43 (June 1978): 348–68.

Eck, John Ernest, and Lucius J. Riccio. "Relationship Between Reported Crime Rates and Victimization Survey Results: An Empirical and Analytical Study." *Journal of Criminal Justice* 7 (Winter 1979): 293–308.

Edmonds, Ronald R. "Effective Schools for the Urban Poor." *Educational Leadership* 37 (October 1979): 15–24.

Edmonds, Ronald R. "Some Schools Work and More Can." *Social Policy* 9 (March/April 1979): 28–32.

Edmonds, Ronald R., and J.R. Fredericksen. *Search for Effective Schools: The Identification and Analysis of City Schools That Are Instructionally Effective for Poor Children.* Cambridge, Mass.: Harvard Center for Urban Studies, 1978.

Ehrenberg, Ronald G., and Alan J. Marcus. "Minimum Wages and Teenagers' Enrollment and Employment Outcomes: A Multinomial Logit Model." *Journal of Human Resources* 17 (Winter 1982): 39–58.

Ehrlich, Isaac. "Participation in Illegitimate Activities: A Theoretical and Empirical Investigation." *Journal of Political Economy* 81 (January 1973): 521–65.

Ehrlich, Isaac, and Mark Randall. "Fear of Deterrence." *Journal of Legal Studies* 6 (January 1977): 293–316.

Elman, Richard M. *The Poorhouse State: The American Way of Life on Public Assistance.* New York: Pantheon, 1967.

Ennis, Philip H. "Criminal Victimization in the United States. Field Surveys II. A Report of a National Survey." President's Commission on Law Enforcement and the Administration of Justice. Washington, D.C.: Government Printing Office, 1967.

Eron, Leonard D. "Parent-Child Interaction, Television Violence, and Aggression of Children." *American Psychologist* 37 (February 1982): 197–211.

Erskine, H. "Polls: Negro Employment." *Public Opinion Quarterly* 32 (Spring 1968): 132–53.

Fainstein, Norman I., and Susan S. Fainstein. "The Future of Community Control." *American Political Science Review* 70 (September 1976): 921–22.

Farley, Reynolds. "Trends in Racial Inequalities: Have the Gains of the 1960s Disappeared in the 1970s?" *American Sociological Review* 42 (April 1977): 189–208.

Feldstein, Martin. "The Retreat From Keynesian Economics." *The Public Interest* no. 64 (Summer 1981): 92–105.

Feldstein, Martin, and Anthony Pellechio. "Social Security and Household Wealth Accumulation: New Microeconometric Evidence." *Review of Economics and Statistics* 61 (August 1979): 361–68.

Ferguson, Richard L. "The Decline in ACT Test Scores: What Does It Mean?" In *The Test Score Decline: Meaning and Issues,* edited by Lawrence Lipsitz. Englewood Cliffs, N.J.: Educational Technology Publications, 1977.

Ferriss, Abbott L. *Indicators of Trends in American Education.* New York: Russell Sage Foundation, 1969.

Firebaugh, Glenn. "A Rule for Inferring Individual-Level Relationships from Aggregate Data." *American Sociological Review* 43 (August 1978): 557–72.

Fisher, Robert M. *Twenty Years of Public Housing: Economic Aspects of the Federal Program.* New York: Harper, 1959.

Flanagan, Robert J. "Discrimination Theory, Labor Turnover, and Racial Unemployment Differentials." *Journal of Human Resources* 13 (Spring 1978): 187–207.

Flax, Michael J. *Blacks and Whites: An Experiment in Social Indicators.* Washington, D.C.: The Urban Institute, 1971.

Frazier, Franklin E. *The Negro Family in the United States.* Chicago: University of Chicago Press, 1939.

Freeman, Richard B. "Black Economic Progress Since 1964." *The Public Interest* no. 52 (Summer 1978): 52–68.

Freeman, Richard B. *Black Elite: The New Market for Highly Educated Black Americans.* New York: McGraw Hill, 1977.

Freeman, Richard B. "Crime and Unemployment." In *Crime and Public Policy,* edited by James Q. Wilson, 89–106. San Francisco: ICPS Press, 1983.

Freiden, Alan. "The United States Marriage Market." *Journal of Political Economy* 82 (March/April 1974): S34–S53.

Friedlander, Stanley L. *Unemployment in the Urban Core: An Analysis of Thirty Cities With Policy Recommendations.* New York: Praeger, 1972.

Friedman, Milton. *Capitalism and Freedom.* Chicago: University of Chicago Press, 1962.

Friedman, Rose D. *Poverty—Definition and Perspective.* Washington, D.C.: American Enterprise Institute, 1965.

Furstenberg, Frank. "The Transmission of Mobility Orientation in the Family." *Social Forces* 49 (1971): 595–603.

Galbraith, John K. *The Affluent Society.* Boston: Houghton Mifflin, 1958.

General Accounting Office. *Public Assistance Benefits Vary Widely from State to State, But Generally Exceed the Poverty Line.* Washington, D.C.: Government Printing Office, 1980.

Gilbert, Neil, and Joseph W. Eaton. "Favoritism as a Strategy in Race Relations." *Social Problems* 18 (Summer 1970): 38–52.

Gilder, George. *Visible Man: A True Story of Post-Racist America.* New York: Basic Books, 1978.

Gilder, George. *Wealth and Poverty.* New York: Basic Books, 1980.

Gilman, S.C. "Black Rebellion in the 1960's: Between Nonviolence and Black Power." *Ethnicity* 8 (December 1981): 452–75.

Glasgow, Douglas G. *The Black Underclass: Poverty, Unemployment, and Entrapment of Ghetto Youth.* New York: Vintage Books, 1981.

Glazer, Nathan. *Affirmative Discrimination: Ethnic Inequality and Public Policy.* New York: Basic Books, 1975.

306

Bibliography

Glazer, Nathan. "America's Race Paradox." *Encounter* 31 (October 1968): 9–18.
Glazer, Nathan. *Ethnic Dilemmas 1964–1982.* Cambridge, Mass.: Harvard University Press, 1983.
Goedhart, Theo, Victor Halberstadt, Arnie Kapteyn, and Bernard Van Praag. "The Poverty Line: Concept and Measurement." *Journal of Human Resources* 12 (Fall 1977): 503–20.
Gold, Martin. *Delinquent Behavior in an American City.* Belmont, Calif.: Brooks/Cole, 1970.
Goldberg, Itzhak. "A Note on Using Victimization Rates to Test Deterrence." Technical Report CERDCR–5–78, Center for Econometric Studies of the Justice System. Palo Alto, Calif.: Stanford University, 1978.
Goldman, Roy D., and Regina Richards. "The SAT Prediction of Grades for Mexican-American Versus Anglo-American Students at the University of California, Riverside." *Journal of Educational Measurement* 11 (Summer 1974): 129–35.
Gordon, David M. "Income and Welfare in New York City." *The Public Interest* no. 16 (Summer 1969): 64–88.
Gordon, David M. *Theories of Poverty and Underemployment.* Lexington, Mass.: Lexington Books, 1972.
Gortmaker, Steven L. "Poverty and Infant Mortality in the United States." *American Sociological Review* 44 (April 1979): 280–97.
Gottfredson, Denise C. "Black-White Differences in the Educational Attainment Process: What Have We Learned?" *American Sociological Review* 46 (October 1981): 542–57.
Gottschalk, Peter T. "Earnings, Transfers, and Poverty Reduction." *Research in Labor Economics* 2 (1978): 237–72.
Gottschalk, Peter, and Sheldon Danziger. "Macroeconomic Conditions, Income Transfers, and the Trend in Poverty." Paper presented at the Urban Institute Conference, An Assessment of Reagan's Social Welfare Policy, Washington, D.C., 28–29 July 1983.
Gould, Stephen Jay. *The Mismeasure of Man.* New York: W.W. Norton, 1981.
Grant, Gerald. "Children's Rights and Adult Confusions." *The Public Interest* no. 69 (Fall, 1982): 83–99.
Green, Gordon, and John Coder. "The March Current Population Survey Earnings Imputation System: An Explanation and Evaluation." Paper presented at the meeting of the Census Advisory Committee on Population Statistics, Washington, D.C., 1 October, 1982.
Green, Gordon, and Edward Welniak. *Changing Family Composition and Income Differentials.* Special Demographic Analyses CDS–80–7. Washington, D.C.: Government Printing Office, 1982.
Groeneveld, Lyle P., Nancy Brandon Tuma, and Michael T. Hannan. "The Effects of Negative Income Tax Programs on Marital Dissolution." *Journal of Human Resources* 15 (Fall 1980): 654–74.
Gwaltney, John Langston. *Drylongso: A Self-Portrait of Black America.* New York: Vintage Books, 1981.
Hanoch, G. "An Economic Analysis of Earnings and Schooling." *Journal of Human Resources* 2 (Summer 1967): 319–29.
Harnishchfeger, Annagret, and David E. Wiley. "The Marrow of Achievement Test Score Declines." In *The Test Score Decline: Meaning and Issues,* edited by Lawrence Lipsitz. Englewood Cliffs, N.J.: Educational Technology Publications, 1976.
Harrington, Michael. *Fragments of the Century.* New York: Saturday Review Press, 1973.
Harrington, Michael. *The Other America.* New York: Macmillan, 1962.
Harris, Marvin. *Cows, Pigs, Wars, and Witches.* New York: Vintage Books, 1974.
Harris, William U. "The SAT Score Decline: Facts, Figures, and Emotions." In *The Test Score Decline: Meaning and Issues,* edited by Lawrence Lipsitz. Englewood Cliffs, N.J.: Educational Technology Publications, 1976.
Harrison, Bennett. "Human Capital, Black Poverty, and 'Radical' Economics." *Industrial Relations* 10 (October 1971): 277–86.
Hauser, Robert M., and David L. Featherman. "Racial Inequalities and Socioeconomic Achievement in the United States, 1962–1973." Institute for Research on Poverty Discussion Paper no. 275–75. Madison, Wis.: University of Wisconsin, 1975.
Hausman, J.A., and D.A. Wise. "Attrition Bias in Experimental and Panel Data." *Econometrica* 47 (March 1979): 455–73.
Haveman, Robert H., ed., *A Decade of Federal Antipoverty Programs: Achievements, Failures and Lessons.* New York: Academic Press, 1977.

Bibliography

Heckman, James J. "Effects of Child-Care Programs on Women's Work Effort." *Journal of Political Economy* 82 (March/April 1974): S136–S163.

Heclo, Hugh, and Martin Rein. "Social Science and Negative Income Taxation." In *The Utilisation of the Social Sciences in Policy-Making in the United States,* edited by Suzanne Berger. Paris: Organization for Economic Cooperation and Development, 1980.

Herzog, Elizabeth, and Cecelia E. Sudia. "Children in Fatherless Families." In *Review of Child Development Research,* vol. 3, edited by B.M. Caldwell and H.N. Ricciuti, 141–232. Chicago: University of Chicago Press, 1973.

Hill, C. Russell. "The Determinants of Labor Supply for Working Urban Poor." In *Income Maintenance and Labor Supply,* edited by Glen Cain and Harold Watts, 182–204. Chicago: Rand McNally College Publishing Company, 1973.

Hill, C. Russell, and Frank P. Stafford. "Intergenerational Wealth Transfers and the Educational Decisions of Male Youth: An Alternative Interpretation." *Quarterly Journal of Economics* 58 (March 1978): 515–24.

Hill, Martha S., Sue Augustyniak, Greg J. Duncan, Gerald Gurin, Jeffrey K. Liker, James N. Morgan, and Michael Ponza. *Final Report of the Project: "Motivation and Economic Mobility of the Poor." Part 1: Intergenerational and Short-Run Dynamic Analyses.* Ann Arbor, Mich.: Survey Research Center, Institute for Social Research, University of Michigan, 3 August 1983.

Hill, Robert B. *The Widening Economic Gap.* Washington, D.C.: National Urban League Research Department, 1979.

Hinckley, Robert. "Black Teenage Unemployment." *Journal of Economic Issues* 15 (June 1981): 501–12.

Hindelang, Michael J. "Race and Involvement in Common Law Personal Crimes." *American Sociological Review* 43 (February 1978): 93–109.

Hindelang, Michael J. "Variations in the Sex-Race-Age-Specific Incidence Rates of Offending." *American Sociological Review* 46 (August 1981): 461–74.

Hindelang, Michael J., Travis Hirschi, and Joseph G. Weis. "Correlates of Delinquency: The Illusion of Discrepancy Between Self-Report and Official Measures." *American Sociological Review* 44 (December 1979): 995–1014.

Hirschi, Travis. *Causes of Delinquency.* Berkeley, Calif.: University of California Press, 1969.

Hobbs, Charles D. *The Welfare Industry.* Washington, D.C.: The Heritage Foundation, 1978.

Hobbs, Nicholas, and Sally Robinson. "Adolescent Development and Public Policy," *American Psychologist* 37 (Feb 1982): 212–23.

Hoffman, Saul D. "Black-White Life Cycle Earnings Differences and the Vintage Hypothesis: A Longitudinal Analysis." *American Economic Review* 69 (December 1979): 855–67.

Hoffman, Saul D. "On-the-Job Training: Differences by Age and Sex." *Monthly Labor Review* 104 (July 1981): 34–36.

Honig, Marjorie. "AFDC Income, Recipient Rates, and Family Dissolution." *Journal of Human Resources* 9 (Summer 1974): 303–22.

Horan, Patrick M. "Is Status Attainment Research Atheoretical?" *American Sociological Review* 43 (August 1978): 534–41.

Humphries, Lloyd G. "Race and Intelligence Reexamined." *The Humanist* 40 (July/August 1980): 52–55.

Hunter, Robert. *Poverty.* New York: Macmillan, 1907.

Hutchens, Robert M. "Welfare, Remarriage, and Marital Search." *American Economic Review* 69 (June 1979): 369–79.

Institute for Research on Poverty. "Poverty in the United States: Where Do We Stand?" *IRP Focus* 5 (Winter 1981–82): 11.

Ito, Henry H. "The Effective Wage Rate, Labor Force Participation and the Rate of Return to Investment in Human Capital." *Southern Journal of Economics* 45 (April 1979): 1059–71.

Jencks, Christopher, Marshall Smith, Henry Acland, Mary Jo Bane, David Cohen, Herbert Gintis, Barbara Heyns, and Stephan Michelson. *Inequality: A Reassessment of the Effect of Family and Schooling in America.* New York: Basic Books, 1972.

Jensen, Arthur R. *Bias in Mental Testing.* New York: The Free Press, 1980.

Jensen, Arthur R. *Straight Talk About Mental Tests.* New York: The Free Press, 1981.

Johoda, Marie. "Work, Employment, and Unemployment: Values, Theories, and Approaches in Social Research." *American Psychologist* 36 (February 1981): 184–91.

Bibliography

Kamii, C., and N. Radin. "Class Differences in the Socialization Practices of Negro Mothers." In *Selected Studies in Marriage and the Family*, edited by Robert Winch and G. Spanier, 235–47. New York: Holt, Rinehart and Winston, 1974.

Kapsalis, Constantine. "Poverty Lines: An Alternative Method of Estimation." *Journal of Human Resources* 16 (Summer 1981): 477–80.

Keeley, Michael C. "The Economics of Family Formation." *Economic Inquiry* 15 (April 1977): 238–50.

Keeley, Michael C. *Labor Supply and Public Policy: A Critical Review.* New York: Academic Press, 1981.

Kelly, William R., and David Snyder. "Racial Violence and Socioeconomic Changes Among Blacks in the United States." *Social Forces* 58 (March 1980): 739–60.

Kelso, Geoffrey I. "The Influence of Stage of Leaving School on Vocational Maturity and Realism of Vocational Choice." *Journal of Vocational Behavior* 7 (August 1975): 29–39.

Kershaw, David, and Jerilyn Fair. *The New Jersey Income Maintenance Experiment.* Institute for Research on Poverty Monograph Series, vol. 1. New York: Academic Press, 1976.

Kesselman, J. "The Labor-Supply Effects of Income, Income, Work, and Wage Subsidies." *Journal of Human Resources* 4 (Summer 1969): 275–92.

Kiefer, Nicholas M. "Population Heterogeneity and Inference from Panel Data on the Effects of Vocational Education." *Journal of Political Economy* 87 (October 1979): S213–S226.

Kiker, B.F, and C.M. Condon. "The Influence of Socioeconomic Background on the Earnings of Young Men." *Journal of Human Resources* 16 (Winter 1981): 94–105.

Kilson, Martin. "Black Social Classes and Intergenerational Poverty." *The Public Interest* no. 64 (Summer 1981): 58–78.

King, Martin Luther, Jr. "The Role of the Behavioral Scientist in the Civil Rights Movement." *Journal of Social Issues* 24 (January 1968): 1–12.

Kleck, Gary. "Racial Discrimination in Criminal Sentencing: A Critical Evaluation of the Evidence with Additional Evidence on the Death Sentence." *American Sociological Review* 46 (December 1981): 783–805.

Kleugel, James R., and Eliot R. Smith. "Whites' Beliefs About Blacks' Opportunity." *American Sociological Review* 47 (August 1982): 518–32.

Knieser, T., A. Padilla, and S. Polachek. "The Rate of Return to Schooling and the Business Cycle." *Journal of Human Resources* 13 (Spring 1978): 264–77.

Kohl, H. *36 Children.* New York: New American Library, 1967.

Konar, Ellen. "Explaining Racial Differences in Job Satisfaction." *Journal of Applied Psychology* 66 (August 1981): 522–24.

Kozol, Jonathan. *Death at an Early Age.* Boston: Houghton Mifflin, 1967.

Kuhn, Thomas S. *The Structure of Scientific Revolutions,* 2nd ed. Chicago: University of Chicago Press, 1962.

L'Abate, Luciano, Yvonne Oslin, and Vernon W. Stone. "Educational Achievement." In *Comparative Studies of Blacks and Whites in the United States,* edited by Kent S. Miller and Ralph Mason Dreger, 325–56. New York: Seminar Press, 1973.

Ladner, Joyce. *Tomorrow's Tomorrow: The Black Woman.* Garden City, N.Y.: Doubleday, 1971.

Ladner, Joyce A., ed. *The Death of White Sociology.* New York: Random House, 1973.

Lampman, Robert J. *Ends and Means of Reducing Income Poverty.* New York: Academic Press, 1971.

Lando, Mordechai E., Alice V. Farley, and Mary A. Brown. "Recent Trends in the Social Security Disability Insurance Program." *Social Security Bulletin* 45 (August 1982): 3–14.

Lando, Mordechai E., and Aaron Krute. "Disability Insurance: Program Issues and Research." *Social Security Bulletin* 39 (October 1976): 3–17.

Larner, Jeremy, and Irving Howe, eds. *Poverty: Views from the Left.* New York: William Morrow, 1968.

Lawrence, William J., and Stephen Leeds. *An Inventory of State and Local Income Transfer Programs.* White Plains, N.Y.: Institute for Sociological Studies, 1980.

Lazarus, Mitchell. *Goodbye to Excellence: A Critical Look at Minimum Competency Testing.* Boulder, Colo.: Westview Press, 1981.

Lazear, Edward. "The Narrowing of Black-White Wage Differentials Is Illusory." *American Economic Review* 69 (September 1979): 553–64.

Lefkowitz, Joel, and Alan W. Fraser. "Assessment of Achievement and Power Motivation of

Blacks and Whites, Using a Black and White TAT, with Black and White Administrators." *Journal of Applied Psychology* 65 (December 1980): 685–96.

Leibowitz, Arleen. "Home Investments in Children." *Journal of Political Economy* 82 (March/April 1974): S111–31.

Lerner, Barbara. "American Education: How Are We Doing?" *The Public Interest* no. 69 (Fall, 1982): 59–82.

Lerner, Barbara. "War on Testing: David, Goliath, and Gallup." *The Public Interest* no. 60 (Summer 1980): 119–47.

Levin, Henry M. "A Decade of Policy Developments in Improving Education and Training for Low-Income Populations." In *A Decade of Federal Antipoverty Programs,* edited by Robert H. Haveman. New York: Academic Press, 1977.

Levine, James P. "The Potential for Crime Overreporting in Criminal Victimization Surveys." *Criminology* 14 (December 1976): 307–30.

Levine, Robert A. "How and Why the New Jersey Negative Income Tax Experiment Came About." Paper delivered at the Brookings Conference on Income Maintenance Experiments. Washington, D.C.: April 29–30, 1974.

Levine, Robert A. *The Poor Ye Need Not Have With You: Lessons from the War on Poverty.* Cambridge, Mass.: M.I.T. Press, 1970.

Levitan, Sar A., William B. Johnston, and Robert Taggart. *Still a Dream: The Changing Status of Blacks Since 1960.* Cambridge, Mass.: Harvard University Press, 1975.

Levy, Frank. "The Labor Supply of Female Household Heads, or AFDC Work Incentives Don't Work Too Well." *Journal of Human Resources* 14 (Winter 1979): 76–97.

Lewis, Oscar. *The Children of Sanchez.* New York: Random House, 1961.

Lewis, Oscar. "The Culture of Poverty." *Scientific American* 215 (October 1966): 19–25.

Lieberson, Stanley. "A Reconsideration of the Income Differences Found Between Migrants and Northern-born Blacks." *American Journal of Sociology* 83 (January 1978): 940–66.

Lieberson, Stanley, and Arnold R. Silverman. "The Precipitants and Underlying Conditions of Race Riots." *American Sociological Review* 30 (December 1965): 887–98.

Liebow, Elliot. *Tally's Corner: A Study of Negro Streetcorner Men.* Boston: Little, Brown, 1967.

Liker, Jeffrey K. "Wage and Status Effects of Employment on Affective Well-Being Among Ex-Felons." *American Sociological Review* 47 (April 1982): 264–83.

Lillard, Lee, James P. Smith, and Finis Welch. *What Do We Really Know About Wages: The Importance of Non-Reporting and Census Imputation.* Santa Monica, Calif.: Rand Corporation, 1982.

Link, Charles, and Edward C. Ratledge. "Social Returns to Quality and Quantity of Education: A Further Statement." *Journal of Human Resources* 10 (Winter 1975): 78–89.

Link, Charles, Edward C. Ratledge, and K. Lewis. "Black-White Differences in Returns to Schooling: Some New Evidence." *American Economic Review* 66 (March 1976): 221–23.

Linn, Robert L. "Admissions Testing on Trial." *American Psychologist* 37 (March 1982): 279–91.

Linneman, Peter. "The Economic Impacts of Minimum Wage Laws: A New Look at an Old Question." *Journal of Political Economy* 90 (May 1982): 443–69.

Lynn, Laurence E., Jr. "A Decade of Policy Developments in the Income Maintenance System." In *A Decade of Federal Antipoverty Programs: Achievements, Failures, and Lessons,* edited by Robert H. Haveman. New York: Academic Press, 1977.

Lyon, Larry, and Troy Abell. "Male Entry into the Labor Force: Estimates of Occupational Rewards and Labor Market Discrimination." *Sociological Quarterly* 21 (Winter 1980): 81–92.

Mallar, Charles D., Stuart H. Kerachsky, and Craig V.D. Thornton. "The Short-Term Economic Impact of the Job Corps Program." In *Evaluation Studies Review Annual,* vol. 5, edited by Ernst Stromsdorfer and G. Farkas, 332–59. Beverly Hills, Calif.: Sage Publications, 1980.

Maltz, Michael D. "Crime Statistics: A Historical Perspective." *Crime and Delinquency* 23 (January 1977): 32–40.

Manpower Demonstration Research Corporation. *Summary and Findings of the National Supported Work Demonstration.* Cambridge, Mass.: Ballinger Publishing Co., 1980.

Marcus, Laurence R., and Benjamin D. Stickney. *Race and Education: The Unending Controversy.* Springfield, Ill.: Charles C. Thomas, 1981.

Mare, Robert D. "Change and Stability in Educational Stratification." *American Sociological Review* 46 (February 1981): 72–87.

Marston, Stephen T. "The Impact of Unemployment Insurance on Job Search." *Brookings Papers on Economic Activity* 1. Washington, D.C.: The Brookings Institution, 1975: 13–60.

Matarazzo, J.D., and A.N. Wiens. "Black Intelligence Test of Cultural Homogeneity and

Bibliography

Wechsler Adult Intelligence Scale Scores of Black and White Police Applicants." *Journal of Applied Psychology* 62 (February 1977): 57–63.

McConahay, J.B. "Has Racism Declined in America: It Depends on Who is Asking and What is Asked." *Journal of Conflict Resolution* 25 (December 1981): 563–79.

McDonald, John F., and Stanley P. Stephenson, Jr. "Effects of Income Maintenance on the School Enrollment and Labor Supply Decisions of Teenagers." *Journal of Human Resources* 14 (Fall 1979): 488–95.

Melican, Gerald J., and Leonard S. Feldt. "An Empirical Study of the Zajonc-Markus Hypothesis for Achievement Test Score Declines." *American Educational Research Journal* 17 (Spring 1980): 5–19.

Menacker, Julius, "The Courts Are Not Killing Our Children." *The Public Interest* no. 67 (Spring 1982): 131–36.

Menninger, Karl. *The Crime of Punishment.* New York: Viking, 1968.

Mercy, James A., and Lala Carr Steelman. "Familial Influence on the Intellectual Attainment of Children." *American Sociological Review* 47 (August 1982): 532–42.

Merton, Robert K. *Social Theory and Social Structure.* Glencoe, Ill.: The Free Press, 1957.

Metcalf, Charles E. "Making Inferences from Controlled Income Maintenance Experiments." *The American Economic Review* 63 (June 1973): 478–83.

Meuller, Andre L. "Economic Growth and Minorities." *American Journal of Economics* 26 (July 1967): 225–30.

Miller, S.M., and Martin Rein. "Participation, Poverty, and Administration." *Public Administration Review* 29 (January 1969): 15–25.

Miller, Kent S., and Ralph Mason Dreger, eds. *Comparative Studies of Blacks and Whites in the United States.* New York: Seminar Press, 1973.

Miller, Walter. "The Elimination of the American Lower Class as a National Policy: A Critique of the Ideology of the Poverty Movement of the 1960s." In *On Understanding Poverty*, edited by Daniel P. Moynihan. New York: Basic Books, 1968.

Mills, D. Quinn, and Shirley Frobes. "Impact of Increases in the Federal Minimum Wage on Target Groups in Urban Areas." *Public Policy* 29 (Summer 1981): 277–97.

Mincer, Jacob. "Labor Force Participation and Unemployment: A Review of Recent Evidence." In *Prosperity and Unemployment,* edited by Robert Aaron Gordon and Margaret S. Gordon, 73–112. New York: John Wiley, 1966.

Mincer, Jacob. "Unemployment Effects on Minimum Wages." *Journal of Political Economy* 84 (August 1976): 887–S104.

Mirengoff, William, and Lester Rindler. "Overview." In *The Comprehensive Employment and Training Act—Impact on People, Places, and Programs: An Interim Report,* 1–19. Washington, D.C.: National Academy of Sciences, 1976.

Moch, Michael K. "Racial Differences in Job Satisfaction: Testing Four Common Explanations." *Journal of Applied Psychology* 65 (June 1980): 299–306.

Modu, Christopher, and June Stern. "The Stability of the SAT Score Scale." Princeton, N.J.: Educational Testing Service, 1975.

Moffitt, Robert A. "The Negative Income Tax: Would It Discourage Work?" *Monthly Labor Review* 104 (April 1981): 23–37.

Moon, Marilyn. "The Incidence of Poverty Among the Aged." *Journal of Human Resources* 14 (Spring 1979): 211–21.

Mooney, Joseph D. "Urban Poverty and Labor Force Participation." *American Economic Review* 57 (March 1967): 104–19.

Morgan, H. "How Schools Fail Black Children." *Social Policy* 10 (January 1980): 49–54.

Morgan, William R., Duane F. Alwin, and Larry J. Griffin. "Social Origins, Parental Values, and the Transmission of Inequality." *American Journal of Sociology* 85 (July 1979): 156–66.

Mortensen, D.T. "Job Search, the Duration of Unemployment and the Phillips Curve." *American Economic Review* 60 (December 1970): 847–62.

Moynihan, Daniel P. "Employment, Income, and the Ordeal of the Negro Family." In *The Negro American,* edited by Talcott Parsons and Kenneth B. Clark, 134–59. Boston: Beacon Press, 1966.

Moynihan, Daniel P. *Maximum Feasible Misunderstanding: Community Action in the War Against Poverty.* New York: Free Press, 1969.

Moynihan, Daniel P. *The Negro Family: The Case for National Action.* Washington, D.C.: Department of Labor, March 1965.

Moynihan, Daniel P. *The Politics of a Guaranteed Income: The Nixon Administration and the Family Assistance Plan.* New York: Random House, 1973.

Moynihan, Daniel P. "The Professors and the Poor." In *On Understanding Poverty,* edited by Daniel P. Moynihan. New York: Basic Books, 1968.

Muchinsky, Paul M. "Employee Absenteeism: A Review of the Literature." *Journal of Vocational Behavior* 10 (June 1977): 316–40.

Mulvihill, Donald J., and Melvin Tumin. "Crimes of Violence, vol. II, A Staff Report Submitted to the National Commission on the Causes and Prevention of Violence." Washington, D.C.: Government Printing Office, December 1969.

Murray, Charles A., and Blair B. Bourque. *Budget Priorities and Trends in the Federal Effort to Combat Juvenile Delinquency.* Washington, D.C.: Government Printing Office, 1976.

Murray, Charles A., Blair B. Bourque, and Susan Mileff. *National Evaluation of the Cities in Schools Program: Final Report.* Washington, D.C.: National Institute of Education, 1981.

Murray, Charles A., and Louis A. Cox, Jr. *Beyond Probation: Juvenile Corrections and the Chronic Delinquent.* Beverly Hills, Calif.: Sage Publications, 1979.

National Commission on Excellence in Education. *A Nation at Risk: The Imperative for Educational Reform.* Washington, D.C.: Government Printing Office, 1983.

Nay, Joe N., John W. Scanlon, and Joseph S. Wholey. *Benefits and Costs of Manpower Training Programs: A Synthesis of Previous Studies with Reservations and Recommendations.* Washington, D.C.: The Urban Institute, 1971.

Nelson, H.A. "Charity, Poverty, and Race." *Phylon* 29 (Fall 1968): 303–16.

Newman, Katherine K. "Internal Value Conflict in Inner City Students." *Urban Education* 12 (January 1978): 463–75.

Nicholson, Walter. "A Statistical Model of Exhaustion of Unemployment Insurance Benefits." *Journal of Human Resources* 16 (Winter 1981): 117–28.

Nock, S.L., and Peter H. Rossi. "Ascription Versus Achievement in the Attribution of Family Social Status." *American Journal of Sociology* 84 (November 1978): 565–90. (Discussion, 86 (November 1980): 641–45.)

Nozick, Robert. *Anarchy, State, and Utopia.* New York: Basic Books, 1974.

O'Brien, Robert M., David Shichor, and David L. Decker. "An Empirical Comparison of the Validity of UCR and NCS Crime Rates." *The Sociological Quarterly* 21 (Summer 1980): 391–401.

O'Connor, J. Frank, and J. Patrick Madden. "The Negative Income Tax and the Quality of Dietary Intake." *Journal of Human Resources* 14 (Fall 1979): 507–17.

Oehler, Kay. "Another Look at the Black/White Trend in Unemployment Rates." *American Sociological Review* 44 (April 1979): 339–44.

Offner, Paul. "Labor Force Participation in the Ghetto." *Journal of Human Resources* 7 (Fall 1972): 460–81.

Olsen, Marvin E. "Social and Political Participation of Blacks." *American Sociological Review* 35 (August 1970): 682–97.

Ornstein, Michael D. *Entry into the American Labor Force.* New York: Academic Press, 1976.

Paglin, Morton. *Poverty and Transfers In Kind.* Stanford, Calif.: Hoover Institution Press, 1980.

Parsons, Donald O. "The Decline in Male Labor Force Participation." *Journal of Political Economy* 88 (February 1980): 117–34.

Parsons, Donald O. "Intergenerational Wealth Transfers and the Educational Decisions of Male Youth." *Quarterly Journal of Economics* 89 (November 1975): 603–17.

Parsons, Donald O. "Racial Trends in Male Labor Force Participation." *American Economic Review* 70 (December 1980): 911–20.

Patterson, James T. *America's Struggle Against Poverty 1900–1980.* Cambridge, Mass.: Harvard University Press, 1981.

Peng, Samuel S., and William B. Fetters. "Variables Involved in Withdrawal During the First Two Years of College." *American Educational Research Journal* 15 (Summer 1978): 361–72.

Piven, Frances Fox, and Richard A. Cloward. *Regulating the Poor: The Functions of Public Welfare.* New York: Pantheon, 1971.

Podhoretz, Norman. *Breaking Ranks: A Political Memoir.* New York: Harper & Row, 1979.

Pope, H. "Negro-White Differences in Decisions Regarding Illegitimate Children." *Journal of Marriage and the Family* 31 (November 1969): 756–64.

Popkin, Samuel. *The Rational Peasant.* Berkeley: University of California Press, 1979.

Prescott, James R. *Economic Aspects of Public Housing.* Beverly Hills, Calif.: Sage Publications, 1974.

Bibliography

President's Commission on Income Maintenance Programs. *Poverty Amid Plenty: The American Paradox.* Washington, D.C.: Government Printing Office, 1969.

Pressman, Jeffrey L., and Aaron B. Wildavsky. *Implementation.* Berkeley, Calif.: University of California Press, 1973.

Profile of American Youth. Washington, D.C.: Department of Defense, Office of the Assistant Secretary of Defense, Manpower, Reserve Affairs and Logistics, 1982.

Ragan, James F., Jr. "Minimum Wages and the Youth Labor Market." *Review of Economics and Statistics* 59 (May 1977): 129–36.

Rainwater, Lee. "The Problem of Lower-Class Culture and Poverty-War Strategy." In *On Understanding Poverty,* edited by Daniel P. Moynihan. New York: Basic Books, 1968.

Ravitch, Diane. *The Troubled Crusade: American Education 1945–1980.* New York: Basic Books, 1983.

Rea, Samuel A., Jr. "The Impact of Taxes and Transfers on Labour Supply: A Review of the Evidence." Report to the Ontario Economic Council, 1982.

Read, Frank T. "Judicial Evolution of the Law of School Integration Since *Brown* v. *Board of Education.*" *Law and Contemporary Problems* 39 (Winter, 1975): 7–49.

Redfering, David L. "Relationships Among Vocational Training, Income, and Job Complexity of High School Dropouts and High School Graduates." *Journal of Vocational Behavior* 16 (April 1980): 158–62.

Reich, Michael. "Changes in the Distribution of Benefits from Racism in the 1960's." *Journal of Human Resources* 16 (Spring 1981): 314–32.

Rence, Cynthia, and Michael Wiseman. "The California Welfare Reform Act and Participation in AFDC." *Journal of Human Resources* 13 (Winter 1978): 37–59.

Research Triangle Institute. *Evaluation of the 1981 AFDC Amendments: Final Report.* Washington: Office of Family Assistance, Department of Health and Human Services, 1983.

Robins, Philip K., Nancy Brandon Tuma, and K.E. Yeager. "Effects of SIME/DIME on Changes in Employment Status." *Journal of Human Resources* 15 (Fall 1980): 545–74.

Robins, Philip K., and Richard W. West. "Labor-Supply Response Over Time," *Journal of Human Resources* 15 (Fall 1980): 524–44.

Rosen, Lawrence. "Matriarchy and Lower Class Negro Male Delinquency." *Social Problems* 17 (Fall 1969): 175–89.

Rossi, Peter H., and Zahava D. Blum. "Class, Status, and Poverty." In *On Understanding Poverty,* edited by Daniel P. Moynihan, 36–63, New York: Basic Books, 1968.

Royster, Eugene C., D. Catherine Baltzell, and Fran Cheryl Simmons. *Study of the Emergency School Aid Act Magnet School Program: Final Report.* Washington, D.C.: National Institute of Education, 1979.

Rubel, Robert J. *The Unruly School: Disorders, Disruptions, and Crimes.* Lexington, Mass.: Lexington Books, 1977.

Ryan, John. *A Living Wage.* New York: Arno, 1971, copyright 1906.

Ryan, William. *Blaming the Victim,* rev. ed. New York: Vintage Books, 1976.

Rymer, Marilyn P. *Medicaid Eligibility: Problems and Solutions.* Boulder, Colo.: Westview Press, 1979.

Salins, Peter D. *The Ecology of Housing Destruction: Economic Effects of Public Intervention in the Housing Market.* New York: New York University Press, 1980.

Savas, E.S. *Privatizing the Public Sector.* Chatham, N.J.: Chatham House, 1982.

Scarr, Sandra, and Richard A. Weinberg. "The Influence of 'Family Background' on Intellectual Attainment." *American Sociological Review* 43 (October 1978): 674–92.

Schiller, Bradley R. "Lessons from WIN: A Manpower Evaluation." *Journal of Human Resources* 13 (Fall 1978): 502–23.

Schmitt, Neal, and Martha Lappin. "Race and Sex as Determinants of the Mean and Variance of Performance Ratings." *Journal of Applied Psychology* 65 (August 1980): 428–35.

Schwarz, John E. *America's Hidden Success: A Reassessment of Twenty Years of Public Policy.* New York: W. W. Norton, 1983.

Sewell, Trevor E., and Robert H. Walker. "Effects of Material and Symbolic Incentives on the Learning Ability of Low SES Black Children." *Journal of General Psychology* 106 (January 1982): 93–100.

Silberman, Charles. *Crisis in the Classroom: The Remaking of American Education.* New York: Random House, 1970.

Singleton, Royce Jr., and Eliot R. Smith. "Does Grade Inflation Decrease the Reliability of Grades?" *Journal of Educational Measurement* 15 (Spring 1978): 37–41.

Skogan, Wesley G. "Crime and Crime Rates." In *Sample Surveys of the Victims of Crimes,* edited by Wesley G. Skogan. Cambridge, Mass.: Ballinger, 1976.

Skogan, Wesley G. "The Validity of Official Crime Statistics: An Empirical Investigation." *Social Science Quarterly* 55 (June 1974): 25–38.

Smeeding, Timothy M. *Alternative Methods for Valuing Selected In-Kind Transfer Benefits and Measuring Their Effect on Poverty.* Technical Paper No. 50, Bureau of the Census. Washington, D.C.: Government Printing Office, 1982.

Smeeding, Timothy M. "The Antipoverty Effectiveness of In-Kind Transfers." *Journal of Human Resources* 12 (Summer 1977): 360–78.

Smeeding, Timothy M. "The Antipoverty Effect of In-Kind Transfers: A Good Idea Gone Too Far?" *Policy Studies Journal* 10 (1982): 499–522.

Smith, James P., and Finis Welch. "Race Differences in Earnings: A Survey and New Evidence." R–2295–NSF. Santa Monica, Calif.: Rand Corporation, March 1978.

Solomon, Lewis D., and Judith S. Heeter. "Affirmative Action in Higher Education: Towards a Rationale for Preference." *Notre Dame Lawyer* 52 (October 1976): 41–76.

Sowell, Thomas. *Ethnic America: A History.* New York: Basic Books, 1981.

Sowell, Thomas. "Race and IQ Reconsidered." In *Essays and Data on American Ethnic Groups,* edited by Thomas Sowell. Washington, D.C.: The Urban Institute, 1978.

Spilerman, Seymour. "Careers, Labor Market Structure, and Socioeconomic Achievement." *American Journal of Sociology* 83 (November 1977): 551–93.

Spilerman, Seymour. "Causes of Racial Disturbances: A Comparison of Alternative Explanations." *American Sociological Review* 35 (August 1970): 627–49.

Staples, Robert. "Race and Marital Status." In *Black Families,* edited by Harriette Pipes McAdoo, 173–75. Beverly Hills, Calif.: Sage Publications, 1981.

Staples, Robert, and Alfredo Mirande. "Racial and Cultural Variations among American Families: A Decennial Review of the Literature on Minority Families." *Journal of Marriage and the Family* 42 (November 1980): 887–904.

Stauder, Judith B. "Child Support Enforcement and Establishment of Paternity as Tools of Welfare Reform—Social Services Amendments of 1974, pt. B, 42 U.S.C. Paragraphs 651–60 (Supp. V, 1975)." *Washington Law Review* 52 (1976): 169–92.

Stephenson, Stanley P., Jr., and John F. McDonald. "Disaggregation of Income Maintenance Impacts on Family Earnings." *Review of Economics and Statistics* 16 (August 1979): 354–60.

Stickney, Benjamin D. "The Fading Out of Gains in 'Successful' Compensatory Education Programs." *Urban Education* 12 (October 1977): 271–82.

Stigler, George. "The Economics of Minimum Wage Legislation." *American Economic Review* 36 (June 1946): 358–65.

Tharenou, Phyllis. "Employee Self-Esteem: A Review of the Literature." *Journal of Vocational Behavior* 15 (December 1979): 316–46.

Theobald, Robert, ed. *The Guaranteed Income: Next Step in Income Evolution?* Garden City, N.Y.: Doubleday, 1966.

Thernstrom, Abigail M. "Odd Evolution of the Voting Rights Act." *The Public Interest* no. 55 (Spring 1979): 49–76.

Thernstrom, Stephen. "Is There Really a New Poor?" *Dissent* 15 (January/February 1968): 59–64.

Thompson, Kenrick S. "Comparison of Black and White Adolescent Beliefs About Having Children." *Journal of Marriage and the Family* 42 (February 1980): 133–39.

Thornberry, Terence P., and Margaret Farnworth. "Social Correlates of Criminal Involvement: Further Evidence on the Relationship Between Social Status and Criminal Behavior." *American Sociological Review* 47 (August 1982): 505–18.

Thurow, Lester C. *Poverty and Discrimination.* Washington, D.C.: Brookings Institution, 1969.

Tittle, Charles R., Wayne J. Villemez, and Douglas A. Smith. "The Myth of Social Class and Criminality: An Empirical Assessment of the Empirical Evidence." *American Sociological Review* 43 (October 1978): 643–56.

Tobin, James. "On Improving the Economic Status of the Negro." *Daedalus* 94 (Fall 1965): 878–98.

Toby, Jackson. "Crime in the Schools." In *Crime and Public Policy,* edited by James Q. Wilson. San Francisco: ICS Press, 1983.

Tracy, Paul E., and Robert M. Figlio. *Chronic Recidivism in the 1958 Birth Cohort.* Washington, D.C.: Office of Juvenile Justice and Delinquency Prevention, 1983.

Bibliography

Uguroglu, Margaret E., and Herbert H. Walberg. "Motivation and Achievement: A Quantitative Synthesis." *American Educational Research Journal* 16 (Fall 1979): 375–89.

van den Haag, Ernest. *Punishing Criminals: Concerning a Very Old and Painful Question.* New York: Basic Books, 1975.

Wachter, Michael. "Primary and Secondary Labor Markets: A Critique of the Dual Approach." *Brookings Papers on Economic Activities* 3 (1974): 637–80.

Wallace, Phyllis A. "A Decade of Policy Developments in Equal Opportunities in Employment and Housing." In *A Decade of Federal Antipoverty Programs,* edited by Robert H. Haveman. New York: Academic Press, 1977.

Waters, Brian K. *The Test Score Decline: A Review and Annotated Bibliography.* Technical Memorandum 81–2, Directorate for Accession Policy, Office of the Secretary of Defense, August 1981.

Weber, G. *Inner-City Children Can Be Taught to Read: Four Successful Schools.* Washington, D.C.: Council for Basic Education, 1974.

Webster, Murray, Jr., and James E. Driskell, Jr. "Status Generalization: A Review and Some New Data." *American Sociological Review* 43 (April 1978): 220–36.

Weissberg, Norman C. "Intergenerational Welfare Dependency: A Critical Review." *Social Problems* 18 (Fall 1970): 257–74.

Welch, Finis. "Affirmative Action and Its Enforcement." *American Economic Review* 71 (May 1981): 127–33.

Welch, Finis. "Black-White Differences in Returns to Schooling." *American Economic Review* 63 (December 1973): 893–907.

West, Richard W. "The Effects on the Labor Supply of Young Nonheads." *Journal of Human Resources* 15 (Fall 1980): 574–90.

Westcott, Diane N. "Blacks in the 1970s: Did They Scale the Job Ladder?" *Monthly Labor Review* 104 (June 1982): 29–38.

Westoff, Charles F., Gerard Calot, and Andrew D. Foster. "Teenage Fertility in Developed Nations: 1971–1980." *Family Planning Perspectives* 15 (May/June 1983): 105–110.

White, Lynn K. "Note on Racial Differences in the Effect of Female Economic Opportunities on Marriage Rates." *Demography* 18 (August 1981): 349–54.

Wiatrowski, Michael D., David B. Griswold, and Mary K. Roberts. "Social Control Theory and Delinquency." *American Sociological Review* 46 (October 81): 525–41.

Wiatrowski, Michael D., Stephen Hansell, Charles R. Massey, and David L. Wilson. "Curriculum Tracking and Delinquency." *American Sociological Review* 47 (February 1982): 151–60.

Wildavsky, Aaron. *Speaking Truth to Power: The Art and Craft of Policy Analysis.* Boston: Little, Brown, 1979.

Williams, Walter. "The Continuing Struggle for a Negative Income Tax: A Review Article." *Journal of Human Resources* 10 (Fall 1975): 427–44.

Williams, Walter. *The State Against Blacks.* New York: McGraw Hill, 1982.

Wilson, James Q. *Thinking About Crime,* rev. ed. New York: Basic Books, 1983.

Wilson, James Q., and Barbara Boland. "Crime." In *The Urban Predicament,* edited by William Gorham and Nathan Glazer. Washington: Urban Institute, 1976.

Wilson, Kenneth L. "Effects of Integration and Class on Black Educational Attainment." *Sociology of Education* 52 (April 1979): 84–98.

Wilson, Stephanie, Danny Steinberg, and Jane C. Kulik. "Guaranteed Employment, Work Incentives, and Welfare Reform: Insights from the Work Equity Project." *American Economic Review Papers and Proceedings* 70 (May 1980): 132–37.

Wilson, William J. "Black Community in the 1980's: Questions of Race, Class, and Public Policy." *American Academy of Political and Social Science Annals* 454 (March 1981): 26–41.

Wilson, William J. *The Declining Significance of Race: Blacks and Changing American Institutions.* Chicago: University of Chicago Press, 1978.

Wise, Lauress L., Donald H. McLaughlin, and Kevin J. Gilmartin. *The American Citizen: Eleven Years After High School.* Palo Alto, Calif.: American Institutes for Research, 1977.

Witte, Anne Dryden. "Estimating the Economic Model of Crime with Individual Data." *Quarterly Journal of Economics* 94 (February 1980): 57–84.

Wolf, Alison. "The State of Urban Schools: New Data on an Old Problem." *Urban Education* 13 (July 1978): 179–94.

Wolfe, John R. "The Impact of Family Resources on Childhood IQ." *Journal of Human Resources* 17 (Spring 1982): 213–36.

Wolfgang, Marvin E. and Simon I. Singer. "Victim Categories of Crime." *The Journal of Criminal Law and Criminology* 69 (1978): 379–94.

Wolfgang, Marvin E., Robert M. Figlio, and Thorsten Sellin. *Delinquency in a Birth Cohort.* Chicago: University of Chicago Press, 1972.

Wright, Erik Olin. "Race, Class, and Income Inequality." *American Journal of Sociology* 83 (May 1978): 1368–97.

Wright, Nathan, Jr. "The Economics of Race." *American Journal of Economics and Sociology* 26 (January 1967): 1–12.

Wright, Robert J. and Andrew G. Bean. "The Influence of Socioeconomic Status on the Predictability of College Performance." *Journal of Educational Measurement* 11 (Winter 1974): 277–83.

Wynne, Edward A. "Courts, Schools, and Family Choice." *The Public Interest* no. 67 (Spring 1982): 136–39.

Wynne, Edward A. "What Are the Courts Doing to Our Children?" *The Public Interest* no. 64 (Summer 1981): 3–18.

Zaharia, E.S., and A.A. Baumeister. "Job Preview Effects During the Critical Initial Employment Period." *Journal of Applied Psychology* 66 (February 1981): 19–22.

Zeckhauser, Richard J. "Optimal Mechanisms for Income Transfer." *American Economic Review* 61 (June 1971): 324–34.

Zurcher, Louis A. *Poverty Warriors: The Human Experience of Planned Social Intervention.* Austin, Tex.: University of Texas Press, 1970.

Index

Aaron, Henry J., 288, 292
Abell, Troy, 277
AFDC, *see* Aid to Families with Dependent Children
Affirmative Action, 13, 43, 85, 91, 93–94, 106, 221, 223
Aid to Families with Dependent Children, 5, 13, 17–19, 45, 48, 67, 124–25, 157–66, 181, 185, 210–11, 215, 231–32, 289, 291–92; eligibility rules for, 19, 48, 67, 162–64, 166, 289, 291
American Civil Liberties Union, 4, 173
Anderson, C. A., 286
Anderson, Martin, 153, 273, 287, 289, 292
Andrews, F. Emerson, 265
Anti-poverty bills, 23–24, 28, 33–35, 83, 122
Area Redevelopment Act, 83
Aschenfelter, Orley, 268
Auletta, Ken, 268, 297

Bahr, Steven, 290–91
Bakke case, 20
Baltzell, D. Catherine, 295–96
Banfield, Edward C., 271
Barnett, Arnold, 117, 281
Barron, John M., 290
Berger, Suzanne, 287

Bernstein, Basil A., 286
Biderman, Albert D., 281
Bielby, William T., 277
Bishop, John H., 288, 292
Blacks: composition of families of, 129–32, 222; and crime, 113, 115–19, 136, 138, 222, 281–82, 284; education of, 29, 54, 97–105, 173, 183–84, 189, 222, 226, 277; ghettos and, 187–91, 267, 296; illegitimate births among, 125–28, 136, 138–39, 222; in the labor force, 76–82, 85–92, 136, 138, 140–42, 190, 222, 275, 277, 290; poverty among, 54–55, 61–63, 69, 71, 141, 221–22; unemployment and, 71–75, 85, 92, 142, 276
Blalock, Hubert M., Jr., 197
Blau, Zena Smith, 286
Blaug, Mark, 266
Bloch, Frank S., 291
Blumstein, Alfred, 293
Boland, Barbara, 292–93
Bowers, Norman, 290
Bradford, Amory, 267–68
Braithwaite, John, 285
Brehm, C. T., 291
Brookover, W. B., 295
Brown, Claude, 296
Brown, Michael, 87, 276
Brown, Rap, 31
Brown v. *Board of Education*, 98, 102, 108–9, 137
Bureau of Labor Statistics, 76

Index

Index